Jon E. Lewis has written about Western and popular fiction for numerous publications, including *Time Out*. He was born in Hereford, England, in 1961 and now lives in South Wales, where he works as a freelance writer and critic. His previous books include the crime anthology *Red Handed*.

THE WEST

THE WEST

Edited by Jon E. Lewis

This is a Parragon Book
This edition published 2001

Parragon
Queen Street House
4 Queen Street
Bath BA1 1HE, UK

First published in the UK in 1991 as *The Mammoth Book of The Western,* by Robinson Publishing
(of Constable & Robinson Ltd, London)

Front cover photograph Lazy Boy, Blackfoot,
by Roland Reed, 1915, courtesy Paul Harbaugh

A copy of the British Library Cataloguing-in-Publication Data is available from the British Library

ISBN 0-75255-870-6

Printed and bound in the EC

10 9 8 7 6 5 4 3 2 1

Contents

ACKNOWLEDGEMENTS

I would like to thank the following people for their help with this book, and on the trail which led up to it: Tony Williams, Phil Lucas, Maria Lexton, Edward Buscombe, Nick Robinson, Stephanie Maury, Alex Stitt and, as ever, Penny Stempel.

Introduction

THE WESTERN IS ONE OF the truly great genres of world literature. For over a century and half, ever since James Fenimore Cooper published *The Pioneers* in 1823, stories set in the American West have entertained generations and millions of readers. Even in the 1980s, when the Western was supposedly heading off towards the sunset (not for the first time in the Western's life the reports of its death were much exaggerated), Western author Louis L'Amour sold more books than nearly anybody else on earth.

Yet, although the Western has an international readership, it also has a special relationship to America: it is America's only truly original art form. No other country has a Western literature. But then, of course, no other country has a West: that vast spectacular landscape—and even bigger sky—that lies between the Mississippi and the Pacific Ocean. Moreover, no other country has such an heroic history of pioneering settlement (forgetting, for the moment, the annihilation of the Native Americans on the frontier).

The Western is the American Myth. What the epics of Homer are to Greece, the plays of Shakespeare to England, the Western is to America. America finds its national identity in the Western story.

The importance of the Western to America has meant that the Western story has always attracted writers of rare calibre, including such giants of American literature as Mark Twain, Stephen Crane, Jack London, and Willa Cather.

At the same time, in reverse, the Western has had a decisive influence on the course of American literature.

The present-day excellence of the American short story, for instance, is partly traceable to the 'pulp' magazines which proliferated between the 1920s and 1960s, and which served as a training school for several generations of US writers (among them Sinclair Lewis and Tennessee Williams). And of the pulp magazines, the biggest number by far were Westerns.

All this notwithstanding, the Western has a bad literary reputation. A common view of the Western is that it is for pre-pubescent boys and men who never grew up, where the good characters always wear white hats and the bad characters wear black ones, and where the only good 'injun' is one whose moccasins are pointing skywards.

Of course, such Western fiction does exist. But it is not representative of the best of the genre. And never has been.

Although stories set in the Wild West existed before the acknowledged father of the Western, James Fenimore Cooper (1789–1851), began writing, it was Cooper who turned these frontier stories into a fictional form with definite shape, characters and theme. In the Leatherstocking Tales, the most famous of which is *The Last of the Mohicans* (1826), Fenimore Cooper created the figure of Natty Bumppo, frontiersman and hero. Cooper also gave the Western its lasting focus: the tension between the Wild West and the encroaching Civilised East (a tension later played out in such conflicts as outlaws v. deputies, ranchers v. homesteaders).

To a large extent Bumppo was based on the real frontier scout, Daniel Boone. The Western has, since its earliest days, drawn on the historical reality of the West (albeit in somewhat varying degrees). Behind every Western fictional hero—or heroine—stands some actually existing frontier figure such as Buffalo Bill or Calamity Jane.

After Fenimore Cooper the Western story took two paths: one popular, the other self-consciously literary. In its popular form—beginning with the dime novels printed in their thousands in the late 1800s by such publishers as Beadle & Adams—the elements of Cooper's Western tales became formalised, with standard characters and plot situations (usually resolved by violent action). The popular Western still works to this basic formula: hence it is often termed the 'formulary' Western.

Two names stand out above all others in the early history of the formulary Western: Owen Wister and Zane Grey. It was Wister who made the cowboy the Western character par excellence (so replacing the frontiersman). The eponymous hero of Wister's *The Virginian*, published in 1902, was a romantic figure, a knight wearing a six-gun (the novel featured the first Western shoot-out) and with a code of honour etched on his heart. Under a thousand different names, the Virginian still rides the range of Western fiction to this day.

The Virginian was a best-seller the month it was published, and became the book for other Western authors to imitate. Prime among those who did so was Zane Grey, the most famous Western writer of all time. Grey deepened the romanticism of Wister, and introduced a large dose of melodrama into the Western—a recipe which was spectacularly successful. Even before the advent of softback publishing, Grey's books had sold several million copies, with *Riders of the Purple Sage* (1910) leading the way.

After Wister and Grey, the next major phase in the history of the formulary Western was the advent of the 'pulp' magazines (so-called because of the cheapness of the paper they used). In 1919 the publishers Street & Smith revamped one of their dime novel periodicals into a new format (7 × 10 inches), and *Western Story Magazine*, the first pulp Western, was born. The spectacular success of *Western Story Magazine* spawned a host of imitations: *Dime Western*, *.44 Western*, *New Western*, among a hundred others.

The pulps paid a cent a word. And the king of the Western pulps was Max Brand (one of twenty pseudonyms used by Frederick Faust). In the 1920s and 1930s Brand was a prolific author of escapist Western stories with supermen heroes, where the Western settings were reduced to the most minimal mentions of deserts and britches. What set Brand's stories apart from those of his numerous competitors was a remarkable ability to pen an exciting suspense storyline.

For three decades *Western Story Magazine* was the leading pulp Western, just as the pulps themselves were the leading purveyors of fiction to the masses in America, Britain and elsewhere. (There were other important outlets for popular fiction at the time: the digest magazine—which really only differed from the pulps in size—and the more quality journals, or 'slicks'). The pulps took a dent during World War Two—paper shortages killed off a large number—but came back in the late 1940s and early 1950s for what was, in retrospect, the Golden Age of the popular Western.

The War changed the mainstream Western, both in terms of its quality and its view of the world. Although the good guy still tended to win, he was less likely to be a clean-cut cowboy hero like the old Virginian. Moreover, the moral, social, and psychological issues broached in Western stories were handled with greater complexity. (Although the stories of Ernest Haycox had anticipated this in the 1930s). The attitude to the American Indian was a case in point. Up to the 1950s, the American Indian in popular Western fiction had been variously a noble savage or a savage savage, but a savage nonetheless. The problem had been amplified by the decision of the Curtis magazine group that the Indian point-of-view must not be shown in its journals, a decision which stemmed from the audience outrage which greeted Zane Grey's fictional attempt in 1922 to depict a love affair between a white woman and Amerindian man in *Ladies' Home Journal*). From the 1950s, however, the American Indian began to be more sympathetically—and realistically—portrayed in the popular Western, with one of the milestones being Dorothy M. Johnson's 'A Man Called Horse' in 1953. Similarly, the attitude of the genre to Mexicans and blacks became more positive after the war, a change heralded in the latter case by James Warner Bellah's series of stories featuring Sergeant Rutledge.

Dorothy Johnson herself is a good reminder that the Western is not an exclusively male form. Among the other women writers who have achieved prominence in the Western field are: B.M. Bower, Mari Sandoz, Willa Cather, Peggy Simpson Curry, Mary Austen, and Laura Wilder (*Little House on the Prairie*). Not surprisingly, perhaps, women authors have often foregrounded women characters in their Western fiction, while 'ranch romances' of the type written by Janet Dailey have developed a large following.

While some formulary Westerns continued to make only the most minimal references to the real West in the post-War period, the popular Western as a whole began to make a fuller use of Western history (a big factor in its improved quality). Historical reconstructions of actual events like the Battle of Little Big Horn or the siege of the Alamo became popular amongst both readers and authors, and it was a brave Western author who did not know his Sharps from his Navy Colt. Increasingly, the popular Western began to leave its reader with the feeling: Yes, that's how it was on the frontier.

By the 1960s television had become the main form of cheap entertainment for ordinary people; the pulps had come to the end of the trail. Their legacy was enormous. The pulp short story demanded special skills of compression and economy (not to mention a fertile imagination, if the author was to keep pumping out storylines week after week) which have worked their way into contemporary American short story writing; for instance, the Dirty Realists.

This is not to suggest that all pulp Westerns were somehow superb pieces of fiction. Pulp authors were entertainers. They wrote quickly for money. But within the demands of their profession, some authors produced exceptional writing. The tragic thing is that many of the best Western stories from the pulp era lie neglected, their authors forgotten.

Also forgotten is that some of America's leading contemporary crime writers came up writing pulp Westerns, including Elmore Leonard. Indeed, the case of Leonard serves to underline the point that there has always been a close relationship between the popular Western and the crime story. What else is the big city's private eye or policeman but the cowboy/sheriff gone East? Loren D.

Estleman is another popular American writer who has slipped with ease between tales of the naked city and of the frontier.

It was not only from television that the popular Western came under attack in the 1960s and 1970s. There was the arrival in town of the porno or 'wicked' Western, as made made infamous by the British writer, George G. Gilman (*Edge: The Loner* etc). Also, the sheer amount of formulary Western stories and novels—not to mention films and TV series—in the 1950s had produced a sense of overkill.

And in a sense the popular Western no longer fitted the times. By the 1970s and 1980s a certain urban cynicism ruled. The formulary Western can be many things, but it's not urban and it's not cynical.

Time magazine once famously called the Western the 'American Morality Play', and suggested that it is a form of fictional reassurance (things will be alright: the good guys will win); one which simultaneously stresses a code of individual morality and offers an escapist experience.

There is, undoubtedly, some truth in this (although much the same can be said of the detective story, among other popular genres). However, the moralism of the Western can be overplayed, so too the notion that it always stands for the same political point of view—usually interpreted as right-wing. The truth of the matter is that the Western can be made to fit any political philosophy from red (Jack London) to redneck (J.T. Edson). Recently, the lesbian Western has arrived on the scene, courtesy of Penny Hayes. If the Western has a natural political centre of gravity it is Populism, the politics of distrust of big industrial capitalism (typified by the banker and the rail magnate), reinforced by an attachment to the misfit—a sentiment which first entered the genre in the Californian mining stories of Bret Harte.

Times, of course, change. The good news for aficionados of the popular Western is that there are definite signs on the ground of a revival. In America, for example, a new outlet for the Western short story has emerged with the aptly named *New Frontiers* volumes, while the return of the screen

Western can only aid matters. In the age after Wall Street, the formulary Western looks as though it might ride again.

Meanwhile, what of the literary Western? Like the popular Western, the literary Western owes its origins to Fenimore Cooper, but has tended to be more realistic, less formulaic than its mainstream counterpart in the ensuing years. In the literary Western the frontier environment is usually of central importance (the Nebraska stories of Willa Cather, for example), and not just a useful backcloth as it sometimes is in the sage-brush saga. One of the prime tasks, moreover, of the literary Western has been the debunking of some of the more preposterous illusions fostered about the Wild West by the popular Western itself. Among the first to do so in the literary Western tradition were Mark Twain and Stephen Crane.

In *Roughing It*, published in 1872, Twain recorded a personal journey through the Far West—but one which also burlesques, in a series of 'tall tales', some of the wilder fantasies about the frontier. (The result was one of the best American books ever written, one which is unfortunately hardly known today). Stephen Crane's approach, in stories such as *Blue Hotel* (1898), was more subtle and ironic than Twain's, but designed for a similarly subversive end. The tradition is carried on today (via Wallace Stegner, the author of *The Big Rock Candy Mountain*, 1943) by such writers as Larry McMurtry.

The desire of the literary Western to set the record straight, also meant that positive, realistic portraits of American Indians appeared much earlier in this branch of the Western, a landmark being John G. Neihardt's stories in the first decades of this century.

Of course, classifying Western fiction into 'popular' and 'literary' is an enterprise full of buffalo-sized problems. What about Jack London, one of the most popular authors of all time, but whose stories are often strongly literary and realistic? Popular or literary? In truth, a good many Western authors fall between the two camps, and the division between them anyway narrowed considerably after the Second World War.

Still, some sort of division is useful to separate out the different types of Western writing because at times their style and emphasis have been radically different. I have included both types of Western story in this anthology (although the emphasis is on the popular Western), because I believe, ultimately, that they compliment each other, and together demonstrate the breadth of fiction available under that signpost 'Western'.

I said at the outset that the Western has a world readership. But, if it is an American art form and myth, why does it have an international readership? To begin with, the Western myth is a saloon open to people of all nationalities from China to Switzerland—since the real West was settled by immigrants from the world over. Moreover, many of the moral issues at the heart of the formulary Western are of universal significance. Nor is it necessary to have a first-hand knowledge of the West to enjoy frontier stories (or even write them: the German author, Karl May, did not visit the USA until after he had written his hugely successful Western novels) since the success of the Western genre has made trans-Mississippi America as familiar to most people as their own country's topography. Perhaps even more so.

This knowledge of what the West looks like (and the West's looks are a big part of the Western's attraction) has been most successfully communicated by the Western film. The success of the written Western—especially the stories of Wister and Zane Grey—made it hugely attractive to the nascent American film industry. The first Western movie, *The Great Train Robbery*, was made in 1903 and in the years which immediately followed, Westerns became the staple part of the American film industry's output. In fact, Hollywood became the film centre of the USA only because of its proximity to a real Western setting. (In the early days of Hollywood, the cowboy extras were drawn from the saloons of Los Angeles, then still a frontier town). And as the American film industry came to dominate the world, Western films were shown on every big screen in every village and town the world over.

There has always been a close relationship between Western literature and Western film, and they have shared much the same history throughout the twentieth century. At the core of this relationship is the fact that most great Western films have been based on great Western short stories or novels. (Conversely, a good many B-Movies have come from some dreadful, lowdown Western stories). Most of the films which made John Ford unsurpassed as a Hollywood Western director in the 1930s to 1950s came from short stories by Ernest Haycox (*Stagecoach*) and James Warner Bellah (*Fort Apache*, *Rio Grande* etc). To underline the connection between the written Western and the screen Western, I have deliberately chosen, in this anthology, several stories which have proved the basis for important Western films, 'A Man Called Horse' by Dorothy Johnson among them.

But overall my aim in compiling the anthology has been to show the best of the West, from its earliest days to today, as well as the diversity of Western fiction: from the sheer entertainment of Max Brand's formulary 'Wine on the Desert', to Loren D. Estleman's end-of-the-West 'The Bandit', by way of John G. Neihardt's poetic 'The Last Thunder Song' and Jack London's atmospheric 'All Gold Canyon'. The stories in the book are arranged roughly according to date of publication, so that the reader who wants to understand the general changing shape of the Western story can begin at the beginning and read through. So too can the reader who wants a good read, because I have not selected stories to illustrate arguments, but because they seem to me the greatest offerings of the genre. (Unfortunately, due to copyright restrictions it has not been possible to include a story by Louis L'Armour in this volume).

The Western was primarily a short form of fiction, so there has been a wealth of stories and short novels to chose from. However, in three cases I have taken extracts from full-length works: Mark Twain's *Roughing It* ('The Way West'), T.V. Olsen's *Arrow in the Sun* ('Soldier Blue') and Elmer Kelton's *The Wolf and the Buffalo* ('Desert Command') because these are the finest things these three authors have written.

Some of the authors in this collection will be familiar to just about anybody. But there are authors here—most of them from the heydays of the pulps—who will probably be unknown to all but the most devoted Western fan, even though they deserve to have a front position in the great posse of popular authors. Hopefully, this anthology will play a part in rescuing them from neglect. I have prefaced each story with biographical notes about the author, for the information of interested readers. In the same vein, the book closes with my personal choices for the hundred best Western novels and short stories of all time.

The Western is the American literary form. It is also fiction at its best. I hope you enjoy this anthology.

And now, as they say, dear reader, 'Once Upon A Time in the West . . .'

BRET HARTE
The Outcasts of Poker Flat

Francis Bret Harte (1836–1902) was born in New York, but later moved to California, where he worked as a schoolteacher, journalist and typesetter. His literary career took off in 1868, when he became the editor of *Overland Monthly*. It was in this journal that the tales of the California mining camps which made him famous were first published: 'The Luck of Roaring Camp', 'The Outcasts of Poker Flat' and 'Tennessee's Partner'. Few people have been so influential in determining the course of the Western as Harte, since the characters he established in these, and other, stories have since become stock figures in the genre, among them the noble gambler and prostitute with a heart of gold, both of which, for instance, appear in the classic 1939 movie, *Stagecoach*, directed by John Ford. Harte was also responsible for introducing a certain "upside-down" morality into the Western, since his outcast figures are often morally superior to the supposedly respectable people around them. In mid-career as writer, Harte took a job as an US diplomat in Germany, later moving to London, where he died.

'The Outcasts of Poker Flat' is from 1868. The story has been filmed several times, including by John Ford in 1919.

AS MR JOHN OAKHURST, Gambler, stepped into the main street of Poker Flat on the morning of the twenty-third of November, 1850, he was conscious of a change in its moral atmosphere since the preceding night. Two or three men, conversing earnestly together, ceased as he approached, and exchanged significant glances. There was a Sabbath lull in the air, which, in a settlement unused to Sabbath influences, looked ominous.

Mr Oakhurst's calm, handsome face betrayed small concern in these indications. Whether he was conscious of any predisposing cause was another question. "I reckon they're after somebody," he reflected; "likely it's me." He returned to his pocket the handkerchief with which he had been whipping away the red dust of Poker Flat from his neat boots, and quietly discharged his mind of any further conjecture.

In point of fact, Poker Flat was "after somebody". It had lately suffered the loss of several thousand dollars, two valuable horses, and a prominent citizen. It was experiencing a spasm of virtuous reaction, quite as lawless and ungovernable as any of the acts that had provoked it. A secret committee had determined to rid the town of all improper persons. This was done permanently in regard of two men who were then hanging from the boughs of a sycamore in the gulch, and temporarily in the banishment of certain other objectionable characters. I regret to say that some of these were ladies. It is but due to the sex, however, to state that their impropriety was professional, and it was only in such easily established standards of evil that Poker Flat ventured to sit in judgement.

Mr Oakhurst was right in supposing that he was included in this category. A few of the committee had urged hanging him as a possible example, and a sure method of reimbursing themselves from his pockets of the sums he had won from them. "It's agin justice," said Jim Wheeler, "to let this yer young man from Roaring Camp—an entire stranger—carry away our money." But a crude sentiment of equity residing in the breasts of those who had been fortunate enough to win from Mr Oakhurst overruled this narrower local prejudice.

Mr Oakhurst received his sentence with philosophic calmness, none the less coolly that he was aware of the hesitation of his judges. He was too much of a gambler not to accept Fate. With him life was at best an uncertain game, and he recognized the usual percentage in favour of the dealer.

A body of armed men accompanied the deported wickedness of Poker Flat to the outskirts of the settlement. Besides Mr Oakhurst, who was known to be a coolly desperate man, and for whose intimidation the armed escort was intended, the expatriated party consisted of a young woman familiarly known as "The Duchess"; another, who had won the title of "Mother Shipton"; and "Uncle Billy", a suspected sluice-robber and confirmed drunkard. The cavalcade provoked no comments from the spectators, nor was any word uttered by the escort. Only when the gulch which marked the uttermost limit of Poker Flat was reached, the leader spoke briefly and to the point. The exiles were forbidden to return at the peril of their lives.

As the escort disappeared, their pent-up feelings found vent in a few hysterical tears from the Duchess, some bad language from Mother Shipton, and a Parthian volley of expletives from Uncle Billy. The philosophic Oakhurst alone remained silent. He listened calmly to Mother Shipton's desire to cut somebody's heart out, to the repeated statements of the Duchess that she would die in the road, and to the alarming oaths that seemed to be bumped out of Uncle Billy as he rode forward. With the easy good-humour characteristic of his class, he insisted upon exchanging his own riding-horse, "Five Spot", for the sorry mule which the Duchess rode. But even this act did not draw the party into any closer sympathy. The young woman readjusted her somewhat draggled plumes with a feeble, faded coquetry; Mother Shipton eyed the possessor of "Five Spot" with malevolence; and Uncle Billy included the whole party in one sweeping anathema.

The road to Sandy Bar—a camp that, not having as yet experienced the regenerating influences of Poker Flat, consequently seemed to offer some invitation to the emigrants—lay over a steep mountain range. It was distant a day's severe travel. In that advanced season, the party soon passed out of the moist, temperate regions of the foot-hills into the dry, cold, bracing air of the Sierras. The trail was narrow and difficult. At noon the Duchess, rolling out of her saddle upon the ground, declared her intention of going no farther, and the party halted.

The spot was singularly wild and impressive. A wooded amphi-theatre, surrounded on three sides by precipitous cliffs of naked granite, sloped gently toward the crest of another precipice that overlooked the valley. It was, undoubtedly, the most suitable spot for a camp, had camping been advisable. But Mr Oakhurst knew that scarcely half the journey to Sandy Bar was accomplished, and the party were not equipped or provisioned for delay. This fact he pointed out to his companions curtly, with a philosophic commentary on the folly of "throwing up their hand before the game was played out". But they were furnished with liquor, which in this emergency stood them in place of food, fuel, rest, and prescience. In spite of his remonstrances, it was not long before they were more or less under its influence. Uncle Billy passed rapidly from a bellicose state into one of stupor, the Duchess became maudlin, and Mother Shipton snored. Mr Oakhurst alone remained erect, leaning against a rock, calmly surveying them.

Mr Oakhurst did not drink. It interfered with a profession which required coolness, impassiveness, and presence of mind, and, in his own language, he "couldn't afford it". As he gazed at his recumbent fellow-exiles, the loneliness begotten of his pariah-trade, his habits of life, his very vices, for the first time seriously oppressed him. He bestirred himself in dusting his black clothes, washing his hands and face, and other acts characteristic of his studiously neat habits, and for a moment forgot his annoyance. The thought of deserting his weaker and more pitiable companions never perhaps occurred to him. Yet he could not help feeling the want of that excitement which, singularly enough, was most conducive to that calm equanimity for which he was notorious. He looked at the gloomy walls that rose a thousand feet sheer above the circling pines around him: at the sky, ominously clouded; at the valley below, already deepening into shadow. And, doing so, suddenly he heard his own name called.

A horseman slowly ascended the trail. In the fresh, open face of the newcomer Mr Oakhurst recognized Tom Simson, otherwise known as "The Innocent" of Sandy Bar. He had met him some months before over a "little game", and had, with perfect equanimity, won the entire fortune—amounting to some forty dollars—of that guileless youth. After the game was finished, Mr Oakhurst drew the youthful speculator behind the door, and thus addressed him: "Tommy, you're a good little man, but you can't gamble worth a cent. Don't try it over again." He then handed him his money back, pushed him gently from the room, and so made a devoted slave of Tom Simson.

There was a remembrance of this in his boyish and enthusiastic greeting of Mr Oakhurst. He had started, he said, to go to Poker Flat to seek his fortune. "Alone?" No, not exactly alone; in fact (a giggle), he had run away with Piney Woods. Didn't Mr Oakhurst remember Piney? She had used to wait on the table at the Temperance House? They had been engaged a long time, but old Jake Woods had objected, and so they had run away, and were going to Poker Flat to be married, and here they were. And they were tired out, and how lucky it was they had found a place to camp and company. All this the Innocent delivered rapidly, while Piney, a stout, comely damsel of fifteen, emerged from behind the pine-tree, where she had been blushing unseen, and rode to the side of her lover.

Mr Oakhurst seldom troubled himself with sentiment, still less with propriety; but he had a vague idea that the situation was not fortunate. He retained, however, his presence of mind sufficiently to kick Uncle Billy, who was about to say something, and Uncle Billy was sober enough to recognize in Mr Oakhurst's kick a superior power that would not bear trifling. He then endeavoured to dissuade Tom Simson from delaying further, but in vain. He even pointed out the fact that there was no provision, nor means of making a camp. But, unluckily, the Innocent met this objection by assuring the party that he was provided with an extra mule loaded with provisions, and by the discovery of a rude attempt at a log-house near the trail. “Piney can stay with Mrs Oakhurst,” said the Innocent, pointing to the Duchess, “and I can shift for myself.”

Nothing but Mr Oakhurst’s admonishing foot saved Uncle Billy from bursting into a roar of laughter. As it was, he felt compelled to retire up the cañon until he could recover his gravity. There he confided the joke to the tall pine-trees, with many slaps of his leg, contortions of his face, and the usual profanity. But when he returned to the party, he found them seated by a fire—for the air had grown strangely chill and the sky overcast—in apparently amicable conversation. Piney was actually talking in an impulsive, girlish fashion to the Duchess, who was listening with an interest and animation she had not shown for many days. The Innocent was holding forth, apparently with equal effect, to Mr Oakhurst and Mother Shipton, who was actually relaxing into amiability. “Is this yer a d—d picnic?” said Uncle Billy, with inward scorn, as he surveyed the sylvan group, the glancing firelight, and the tethered animals in the foreground. Suddenly an idea mingled with the alcoholic fumes that disturbed his brain. It was apparently of a jocular nature, for he felt impelled to slap his leg again and cram his fist into his mouth.

As the shadows crept slowly up the mountain, a slight breeze rocked the tops of the pine-trees, and moaned through their long and gloomy aisles. The ruined cabin, patched and covered with pine-boughs, was set apart for the ladies. As the lovers parted, they unaffectedly exchanged a kiss, so honest and sincere that it might have been heard above the swaying pines. The frail Duchess and the malevolent Mother Shipton were probably too stunned to remark upon this last evidence of simplicity, and so turned without a word to the hut. The fire was replenished, the men lay down before the door, and in a few minutes were asleep.

Mr Oakhurst was a light sleeper. Toward morning he awoke benumbed and cold. As he stirred the dying fire, the wind, which was now blowing strongly, brought to his cheek that which caused the blood to leave it—snow!

He started to his feet with the intention of awakening the sleepers, for there was no time to lose. But turning to where Uncle Billy had been lying, he found him gone. A suspicion leaped to his brain and a curse to his lips. He ran to the spot where the mules had been tethered; they were no longer there. The tracks were already rapidly disappearing in the snow.

The momentary excitement brought Mr Oakhurst back to the fire with his usual calm. He did not waken the sleepers. The Innocent slumbered peacefully, with a smile on his good-humoured, freckled face; the virgin Piney slept beside her frailer sisters as sweetly as though attended by celestial guardians, and Mr Oakhurst, drawing his blanket over his shoulders, stroked his moustaches and waited for the dawn. It came slowly in a whirling mist of snow-flakes, that dazzled and confused the eye. What could be seen of the landscape appeared magically changed. He looked over the valley, and summed up the present and future in two words—"snowed in!"

A careful inventory of the provisions, which, fortunately for the party, had been stored within the hut, and so escaped the felonious fingers of Uncle Billy, disclosed the fact that with care and prudence they might last ten days longer. "That is," said Mr Oakhurst, *sotto voce* to the Innocent, "if you're willing to board us. If you ain't—and perhaps you'd better not—you can wait till Uncle Billy gets back with provisions." For some occult reason, Mr Oakhurst could not bring himself to disclose Uncle Billy's rascality, and so offered the hypothesis that he had wandered from the camp and had accidentally stampeded the animals. He dropped a warning to the Duchess and Mother Shipton, who of course knew the facts of their associate's defection. "They'll find out the truth about us *all* when they find out anything," he added, significantly, "and there's no good frightening them now."

Tom Simson not only put all his worldly store at the disposal of Mr Oakhurst, but seemed to enjoy the prospect of their enforced seclusion. "We'll have a good camp for a week, and then the snow'll melt, and we'll all go back together." The cheerful gaiety of the young man and Mr Oakhurst's calm infected the others. The Innocent, with the aid of pine-boughs, extemporized a thatch for the roofless cabin, and the Duchess directed Piney in the rearrangement of the interior with a taste and tact that opened the blue eyes of that provincial maiden to their fullest extent. "I reckon now you're used to fine things at Poker Flat," said Piney. The Duchess turned away sharply to conceal something that reddened her cheeks through its professional tint, and Mother Shipton requested Piney not to "chatter". But when Mr Oakhurst returned from a weary search for the trail, he heard the sound of happy laughter echoed from the rocks. He stopped in some alarm, and his thoughts first naturally reverted to the whisky, which he had prudently cachéd. "And yet it don't somehow sound like whisky," said the gambler. It was not until he caught sight of the blazing fire through the still blinding storm and the group around it, that he settled to the conviction that it was "square fun".

Whether Mr Oakhurst had cachéd his cards with the whisky as something debarred the free access of the community, I cannot say. It was certain that, in Mother Shipton's words, he "didn't say cards once" during that evening. Haply the time was beguiled by an accordion, produced somewhat ostentatiously by Tom Simson from his pack. Notwithstanding some difficulties attending the manipulation of this instrument, Piney Woods managed to pluck several reluctant melodies from its keys, to an accompaniment by the Innocent on a pair of bone castinets. But the crowning festivity of the evening was reached in a rude camp-meeting hymn, which the lovers, joining hands, sang with great earnestness and vociferation. I fear that a certain defiant tone and Covenanter's swing to its chorus, rather than any devotional quality, caused it speedily to infect the others, who at last joined in the refrain:

"I'm proud to live in the service of the Lord,
And I'm bound to die in His army."

The pines rocked, the storm eddied and whirled above the miserable group, and the flames of their altar leaped heavenward, as if in token of the vow.

At midnight the storm abated, the rolling clouds parted, and the stars glittered keenly above the sleeping camp. Mr Oakhurst, whose professional habits had enabled him to live on the smallest possible amount of sleep, in dividing the watch with Tom Simson, somehow managed to take upon himself the greater part of that duty. He excused himself to the Innocent by saying that he had "often been a week without sleep". "Doing what?" asked Tom. "Poker!" replied Oakhurst, sententiously; "when a man gets a streak of luck—nigger-luck—he don't get tired. The luck gives in first. Luck," continued the gambler, reflectively, "is a mighty queer thing. All you know about it for certain is that it's bound to change. And it's finding out when it's going to change that makes you. We've had a streak of bad luck since we left Poker Flat—you come along, and slap you get into it, too. If you can hold your cards right along you're all right. For," added the gambler, with cheerful irrelevance

"I'm proud to live in the service of the Lord,
And I'm bound to die in His army."

The third day came, and the sun, looking through the white-curtained valley, saw the outcasts divide their slowly decreasing store of provisions for the morning meal. It was one of the peculiarities of that mountain climate that its rays diffused a kindly warmth over the wintry landscape, as if in regretful commiseration of the past. But it revealed drift on drift of snow piled high around the hut—a hopeless, unchartered, trackless sea of white lying below the rocky shores to which the castaways still clung. Through the marvellously clear air the smoke of the pastoral village of Poker Flat rose miles away. Mother Shipton saw it, and from a remote pinnacle of her rocky fastness, hurled in that direction a final malediction. It was her last vituperative attempt, and perhaps for that reason was invested with a certain degree of sublimity. It did her good, she privately informed the Duchess. "Just you go out there and cuss, and see." She then set herself to the task of amusing "the child", as she and the Duchess were pleased to call Piney. Piney was no chicken, but it was a soothing and original theory of the pair thus to account for the fact that she didn't swear and wasn't improper.

When night crept up again through the gorges, the reedy notes of the accordion rose and fell in fitful spasms and long-drawn gasps by the flickering camp-fire. But music failed to fill entirely the aching void left by insufficient food, and a new diversion was proposed by Piney—story-telling. Neither Mr Oakhurst nor his female companions caring to relate their personal experiences, this plan would have failed, too, but for the Innocent. Some months before he had chanced upon a stray copy of Mr Pope's ingenious translation of the *Iliad*. He now proposed to narrate the principal incidents of that poem—having thoroughly mastered the argument and fairly forgotten the words—in the current vernacular of Sandy Bar. And so for the rest of that night the Homeric demigods again walked the earth. Trojan bully and wily Greek wrestled in the winds, and the great pines in the cañon seemed to bow to the wrath of the son of Peleus. Mr Oakhurst listened with quiet satisfaction. Most especially was he interested in the fate of "Ash-heels", as the Innocent persisted in denominating the "swift-footed Achilles".

So with small food and much of Homer and the accordion, a week passed over the heads of the outcasts. The sun again forsook them, and again from leaden skies the snowflakes were sifted over the land. Day by day closer around them drew the snowy circle, until at last they looked from their prison over drifted walls of dazzling white, that towered twenty feet above their heads. It became more and more difficult to replenish their fires, even from the fallen trees beside them, now half hidden in the drifts. And yet no one complained. The lovers turned from the dreary prospect and looked into each other's eyes, and were happy. Mr Oakhurst settled himself coolly to the losing game before him. The Duchess, more cheerful than she had been, assumed the care of Piney. Only Mother Shipton—once the strongest of the party—seemed to sicken and fade. At midnight on the tenth day she called Oakhurst to her side. "I'm going," she said, in a voice of querulous weakness, "but don't say anything about it. Don't waken the kids. Take the bundle from under my head and open it." Mr Oakhurst did so. It contained Mother Shipton's rations for the last week, untouched. "Give 'em to the child," she said, pointing to the sleeping Piney. "You've starved yourself," said the gambler. "That's what they call it," said the woman, querulously, and she lay down again, and, turning her face to the wall, passed quietly away.

The accordion and the bones were put aside that day, and Homer was forgotten. When the body of Mother Shipton had been committed to the snow, Mr Oakhurst took the Innocent aside, and showed him a pair of snow-shoes, which he had fashioned from the old pack-saddle. "There's one chance in a hundred to save her yet," he said, pointing to Piney, "but it's there," he added, pointing toward Poker Flat. "If you can reach there in two days she's safe." "And you?" asked Tom Simson. "I'll stay here," was the curt reply.

The lovers parted with a long embrace. "You are not going, too?" said the Duchess, as she saw Mr Oakhurst apparently waiting to accompany him. "As far as the canyon," he replied. He turned suddenly, and kissed the Duchess, leaving her pallid face aflame, and her trembling limbs rigid with amazement.

Night came, but not Mr Oakhurst. It brought the storm again and the whirling snow. Then the Duchess, feeding the fire, found that some one had quietly piled beside the hut enough fuel to last a few days longer. The tears rose to her eyes, but she hid them from Piney.

The woman slept but little. In the morning, looking into each other's faces, they read their fate. Neither spoke; but Piney, accepting the position of the stronger, drew near and placed her arm around the Duchess's waist. They kept this attitude for the rest of the day. That night the storm reached its greatest fury, and, rending asunder the protecting pines, invaded the very hut.

Toward morning they found themselves unable to feed the fire, which gradually died away. As the embers slowly blackened, the Duchess crept closer to Piney, and broke the silence of many hours: "Piney, can you pray?" "No, dear," said Piney, simply. The Duchess, without knowing exactly why, felt relieved, and, putting her head upon Piney's shoulder, spoke no more. And so reclining, the younger and purer pillowing the head of her soiled sister upon her virgin breast, they fell asleep.

The wind lulled as if it feared to waken them. Feathery drifts of snow, shaken from the long pine-boughs, flew like white-winged birds, and settled about them as they slept. The moon through the rifted clouds looked down upon what had been the camp. But all human stain, all trace of earthly travail, was hidden beneath the spotless mantle mercifully flung from above.

They slept all that day and the next, nor did they waken when voices and footsteps broke the silence of the camp. And when pitying fingers brushed the snow from their wan faces, you could scarcely have told, from the equal peace that dwelt upon them, which was she that had sinned. Even the law of Poker Flat recognized this, and turned away, leaving them still locked in each other's arms.

But at the head of the gulch, on one of the largest pine-trees, they found the deuce of clubs pinned to the bark with a bowie-knife. It bore the following, written in pencil, in a firm hand:

BENEATH THIS TREE LIES THE BODY OF
JOHN OAKHURST
WHO STRUCK A STREAK OF BAD LUCK
ON THE 23RD OF NOVEMBER, 1850,
AND HANDED IN HIS CHECKS
ON THE 7TH DECEMBER, 1850.

And pulseless and cold, with a Derringer by his side and a bullet in his heart, though still calm as in life, beneath the snow lay he who was at once the strongest and yet the weakest of the outcasts of Poker Flat.

MARK TWAIN
The Way West

Mark Twain (1835–1910) was born Samuel Langhorne Clemens in Florida. Missouri. Although Twain was not primarily a Western writer—his most famous books, *The Adventures of Tom Sawyer* (1876) and *The Adventures of Huckleberry Finn* (1894) are both set in the Missisippi valley of his childhood—he did produce one of the very best books about the West, *Roughing It* (1872), as well as a number of Western short stories. Among these are 'The Celebrated Jumping Frog of Calaveras County' (1865), one of the first Western 'tall tales', and the story which launched Twain to fame as a writer and humorist.

'The Way West', as I have titled the following, is a series of linked extracts from the early pages of *Roughing It*. The book tells of Twain's journey West with his brother—who had secured an appointment as Secretary to the Governor of Nevada—and of Twain's subsequent sojourn in the state. As a firsthand account of the Wild West, *Roughing It* is unrivalled. But more than that, the book is also a classic of American humorous literature, since Twain often considerably embellished and fictionalised what he saw and heard. 'The Way West' commences with the brothers Clemens at St. Joseph, Missouri, about to begin their great Westwards journey.

THE FIRST THING WE DID ON that glad evening that landed us at St. Joseph was to hunt up the stage-office, and pay a hundred and fifty dollars apiece for tickets per overland coach to Carson City, Nevada.

The next morning, bright and early, we took a hasty breakfast, and hurried to the starting-place. Then an inconvenience presented itself which we had not properly appreciated before, namely, that one cannot make a heavy traveling trunk stand for twenty-five pounds of baggage—because it weighs a good deal more. But that was all we could take—twenty-five pounds each. So we had to snatch our trunks open, and make a selection in a good deal of a hurry. We put our lawful twenty-five pounds apiece all in one valise, and shipped the trunks back to St. Louis again. It was a sad parting, for now we had no swallow-tail coats and white kid gloves to wear at Pawnee receptions in the Rocky Mountains, and no stove-pipe hats nor patent-leather boots, nor anything else necessary to make life calm and peaceful. We were reduced to a war-footing. Each of us put on a rough, heavy suit of clothing, woolen army shirt and "stogy" boots included; and into the valise we crowded a few white shirts, some underclothing and such things. My brother, the Secretary, took along about four pounds of United States statutes and six pounds of Unabridged Dictionary; for we did not know—poor innocents—that such things could be bought in San Francisco on one day and received in Carson City the next. I was armed to the teeth with a pitiful little Smith & Wesson's seven-shooter, which carried a ball like a homeopathic pill, and it took the whole seven to make a dose for an adult. But I thought it was grand. It appeared to me to be a dangerous weapon. It only had one fault—you could not hit anything with it. One of our "conductors" practised awhile on a cow with it, and as long as she stood still and behaved herself she was safe; but as soon as she went to moving about, and he got to shooting at other things, she came to grief. The Secretary had a small-sized Colt's revolver strapped around him for protection against the Indians, and to guard against accidents he carried it uncapped. Mr George Bemis was dismally formidable. George Bemis was our fellow-traveler. We had never seen him before. He wore in his belt an old original "Allen" revolver, such as irreverent people called a "pepper-box." Simply drawing the trigger back, cocked and fired the pistol. As the trigger came back, the hammer would begin to rise and the barrel to turn over, and presently down would drop the hammer, and away would speed the ball. To aim along the turning barrel and hit the thing aimed at was a feat which was probably never done with an "Allen" in the world. But George's was a reliable weapon, nevertheless, because, as one of the stage-drivers afterward said, "If she didn't get what she went after, she would fetch something else." And so she did. She went after a deuce of spades nailed against a tree, once, and fetched a mule standing about thirty yards to the left of it. Bemis did not want the mule; but the owner came out with a double-barreled shotgun and persuaded him to buy it, anyhow. It was a cheerful weapon—the "Allen." Sometimes all its six barrels would go off at once, and then there was no safe place in all the region round about, but behind it.

We took two or three blankets for protection against frosty weather in the mountains. In the matter of luxuries we were modest—we took none along but some pipes and five pounds of smoking-tobacco. We had two large canteens to carry water in, between stations on the Plains, and we also took with us a little shot-bag of silver coin for daily expenses in the way of breakfasts and dinners.

By eight o'clock everything was ready, and we were on the other side of the river. We jumped into the stage, the driver cracked his whip, and we bowled away and left "the States" behind us. It was a superb summer morning, and all the landscape was brilliant with sunshine. There was a freshness and breeziness, too, and an exhilarating sense of emancipation from all sorts of cares and responsibilities, that almost made us feel that the years we had spent in the close, hot city, toiling and slaving, had been wasted and thrown away. We were spinning along through Kansas, and in the course of an hour and a half we were fairly abroad on the great Plains. Just here the land was rolling—a grand sweep of regular elevations and depressions as far as the eye could reach—like the stately heave and swell of the ocean's bosom after a storm. And everywhere were cornfields, accenting with squares of deeper green this limitless expanse of grassy land. But presently this sea upon dry ground was to lose its "rolling" character and stretch away for seven hundred miles as level as a floor!

Our coach was a great swinging and swaying stage, of the most sumptuous description—an imposing cradle on wheels. It was drawn by six handsome horses, and by the side of the driver sat the "conductor," the legitimate captain of the craft; for it was his business to take charge and care of the mails, baggage, express matter, and passengers. We three were the only passengers, this trip. We sat on the back seat, inside. About all the rest of the coach was full of mail-bags—for we had three days' delayed mails with us. Almost touching our knees, a perpendicular wall of mail matter rose up to the roof. There was a great pile of it strapped on top of the stage, and both the fore and hind boots were full. We had twenty-seven hundred pounds of it aboard, the driver said—"a little for Brigham, and Carson, and 'Frisco, but the heft of it for the Injuns, which is powerful troublesome 'thout they get plenty of truck to read." But as he just then got up a fearful convulsion of his countenance which was suggestive of a wink being swallowed by an earthquake, we guessed that his remark was intended to be facetious, and to mean that we would unload the most of our mail matter somewhere on the Plains and leave it to the Indians, or whosoever wanted it.

We changed horses every ten miles, all day long, and fairly flew over the hard, level road. We jumped out and stretched our legs every time the coach stopped, and so the night found us still vivacious and unfatigued.

After supper a woman got in, who lived about fifty miles further on, and we three had to take turns at sitting outside with the driver and conductor. Apparently she was not a talkative woman. She would sit there in the gathering twilight and fasten her steadfast eyes on a mosquito rooting into her arm, and slowly she would raise her other hand till she had got his range, and then she would launch a slap at him that would have jolted a cow; and after that she would sit and contemplate the corpse with tranquil satisfaction—for she never missed her mosquito; she was a dead shot at short range. She never removed a carcass, but left them there for bait. I sat by this grim Sphinx and watched her kill thirty or forty mosquitoes—watched her, and waited for her to say something, but she never did. So I finally opened the conversation myself. I said:

"The mosquitoes are pretty bad, about here, madam."

"You bet!"

"What did I understand you to say, madam?"

"YOU BET!"

Then she cheered up, and faced around and said:

"Danged if I didn't begin to think you fellers was deef and dumb. I did, b' gosh. Here I've sot, and sot, and sot, a-bust'n' muskeeters and wonderin' what was ailin' ye. Fust I thot you was deef and dumb, then I thot you was sick or crazy, or suthin', and then by and by I begin to reckon you was a passel of sickly fools that couldn't think of nothing to say. Where'd ye come from?"

The Sphinx was a Sphinx no more! The fountains of her great deep were broken up, and she rained the nine parts of speech forty days and forty nights, metaphorically speaking, and buried us under a desolating deluge of trivial gossip that left not a crag or pinnacle of rejoinder projecting above the tossing waste of dislocated grammar and decomposed pronunciation!

How we suffered, suffered, suffered! She went on, hour after hour, till I was sorry I ever opened the mosquito question and gave her a start. She never did stop again until she got to her journey's end toward daylight; and then she stirred us up as she was leaving the stage (for we were nodding, by that time), and said:

"Now you git out at Cottonwood, you fellers, and lay over a couple o' days, and I'll be along some time to-night, and if I can do ye any good by edgin' in a word now and then, I'm right thar. Folks 'll tell you 't I've always ben kind o' offish and partic'lar for a gal that's raised in the woods, and I *am*, with the ragtag and bobtail, and a gal *has* to be, if she wants to *be* anything, but when people comes along which is my equals, I reckon I'm a pretty sociable heifer after all."

We resolved not to "lay by at Cottonwood."

It was now just dawn; and as we stretched our cramped legs full length on the mail-sacks, and gazed out through the windows across the wide wastes of greensward clad in cool, powdery mist, to where there was an expectant look in the eastern horizon, our perfect enjoyment took the form of a tranquil and contented ecstasy. The stage whirled along at a spanking gait, the breeze flapping curtains and suspended coats in a most exhilarating way; the cradle swayed and swung luxuriously, the pattering of the horses' hoofs, the cracking of the driver's whip, and his "Hi-yi! g'lang!" were music; the spinning ground and the waltzing trees appeared to give us a mute hurrah as we went by, and then slack up and look after us with interest, or envy, or something; and as we lay and smoked the pipe of peace and compared all this luxury with the years of tiresome city life that had gone before it, we felt that there was only one complete and satisfying happiness in the world, and we had found it.

After breakfast, at some station whose name I have forgotten, we three climbed up on the seat behind the driver, and let the conductor have our bed for a nap. And by and by, when the sun made me drowsy, I lay down on my face on top of the coach, grasping the slender iron railing, and slept for an hour more. That will give one an appreciable idea of those matchless roads. Instinct will make a sleeping man grip a fast hold of the railing when the stage jolts, but when it only swings and sways, no grip is necessary. Overland drivers and conductors used to sit in their places and sleep thirty or forty minutes at a time, on good roads, while spinning along at the rate of eight or ten miles an hour. I saw them do it, often. There was no danger about it; a sleeping man *will* seize the irons in time when the coach jolts. These men were hard worked, and it was not possible for them to stay awake all the time.

By and by we passed through Marysville, and over the Big Blue and Little Sandy; thence about a mile, and entered Nebraska. About a mile further on, we came to the Big Sandy—one hundred and eighty miles from St. Joseph.

As the sun was going down, we saw the first specimen of an animal known familiarly over two thousand miles of mountain and desert—from Kansas clear to the Pacific Ocean—as the "jackass rabbit." He is well named. He is just like any other rabbit, except that he is from one-third to twice as large, has longer legs in proportion to his size, and has the most preposterous ears that ever were mounted on any creature *but* a jackass. When he is sitting quiet, thinking about his sins, or is absent-minded or unapprehensive of danger, his majestic ears project above him conspicuously; but the breaking of a twig will scare him nearly to death, and then he tilts his ears back gently and starts for home. All you can see, then, for the next minute, is his long gray form stretched out straight and "streaking it" through the low sage-brush, head erect, eyes right, and ears just canted a little to the rear, but showing you where the animal is, all the time, the same as if he carried a jib. Now and then he makes a marvelous spring with his long legs, high over the stunted sage-brush, and scores a leap that would make a horse envious. Presently, he comes down to a long, graceful "lope," and shortly he mysteriously disappears. He has crouched behind a sage-bush, and will sit there and listen and tremble until you get within six feet of him, when he will get under way again. But one must shoot at this creature once, if he wishes to see him throw his heart into his heels, and do the best he knows how. He is frightened clear through, now, and he lays his long ears down on his back, straightens himself out like a yardstick every spring he makes, and scatters miles behind him with an easy indifference that is enchanting.

Our party made this specimen "hump himself," as the conductor said. The Secretary started him with a shot from the Colt; I commenced spitting at him with my weapon; and all in the same instant the old "Allen's" whole broadside let go with a rattling crash, and it is not putting it too strong to say that the rabbit was frantic! He dropped his ears, set up his tail, and left for San Francisco at a speed which can only be described as a flash and a vanish! Long after he was out of sight we could hear him whiz.

I do not remember where we first came across "sage-brush," but as I have been speaking of it I may as well describe it. This is easily done, for if the reader can imagine a gnarled and venerable live-oak tree reduced to a little shrub two feet high, with its rough bark, its foliage, its twisted boughs, all complete, he can picture the "sage-brush" exactly. Often, on lazy afternoons in the mountains I have lain on the ground with my face under a sage-bush, and entertained myself with fancying that the gnats among its foliage were lilliputian birds, and that the ants marching and countermarching about its base were lilliputian flocks and herds, and myself some vast loafer from Brobdingnag waiting to catch a little citizen and eat him.

It is an imposing monarch of the forest in exquisite miniature, is the "sage-brush." Its foliage is a grayish green, and gives that tint to desert and mountain. It smells like our domestic sage, and "sage-tea" made from it tastes like the sage-tea which all boys are so well acquainted with. The sage-brush is a singularly hardy plant, and grows right in the midst of deep sand, and among barren rocks where nothing else in the vegetable world would try to grow, except "bunch-grass." The sage-bushes grow from three to six or seven feet apart, all over the mountains and deserts of the Far West, clear to the borders of California. There is not a tree of any kind in the deserts, for hundreds of miles—there is no vegetation at all in a regular desert, except the sage-brush and its cousin the "greasewood," which is so much like the sage-brush that the difference amounts to little. Camp-fires and hot suppers in the deserts would be impossible but for the friendly sage-brush. Its trunk is as large as a boy's wrist (and from that up to a man's arm), and its crooked branches are half as large as its trunk—all good, sound, hard wood, very like oak.

When a party camps, the first thing to be done is to cut sage-brush; and in a few minutes there is an opulent pile of it ready for use. A hole a foot wide, two feet deep, and two feet long, is dug, and sage-brush chopped up and burned in it till it is full to the brim with glowing coals; then the cooking begins, and there is no smoke, and consequently no swearing. Such a fire will keep all night, with very little replenishing; and it makes a very sociable camp-fire, and one around which the most impossible reminiscences sound plausible, instructive, and profoundly entertaining.

Sage-brush is very fair fuel, but as a vegetable it is a distinguished failure. Nothing can abide the taste of it but the jackass and his illegitimate child, the mule. But their testimony to its nutritiousness is worth nothing, for they will eat pine-knots, or anthracite coal, or brass filings, or lead pipe, or old bottles, or anything that comes handy, and then go off looking as grateful as if they had had oysters for dinner. Mules and donkeys and camels have appetites that anything will relieve temporarily, but nothing satisfy. In Syria, once, at the headwaters of the Jordan, a camel took charge of my overcoat while the tents were being pitched, and examined it with a critical eye, all over, with as much interest as if he had an idea of getting one made like it; and then, after he was done figuring on it as an article of apparel, he began to contemplate it as an article of diet. He put his foot on it, and lifted one of the sleeves out with his teeth, and chewed and chewed at it, gradually taking it in, and all the while opening and closing his eyes in a kind of religious ecstasy, as if he had never tasted anything as good as an overcoat before in his life. Then he smacked his lips once or twice, and reached after the other sleeve. Next he tried the velvet collar, and smiled a smile of such contentment that it was plain to see that he regarded that as the daintiest thing about an overcoat. The tails went next, along with some percussion-caps and cough-candy, and some fig-paste from Constantinople. And then my newspaper correspondence dropped out, and he took a chance in that—manuscript letters written for the home papers. But he was treading on dangerous ground, now.

He began to come across solid wisdom in those documents that was rather weighty on his stomach; and occasionally he would take a joke that would shake him up till it loosened his teeth; it was getting to be perilous times with him, but he held his grip with good courage and hopefully, till at last he began to stumble on statements that not even a camel could swallow with impunity. He began to gag and gasp, and his eyes to stand out, and his forelegs to spread, and in about a quarter of a minute he fell over as stiff as a carpenter's work-bench, and died a death of indescribable agony. I went and pulled the manuscript out of his mouth, and found that the sensitive creature had choked to death on one of the mildest and gentlest statements of fact that I ever laid before a trusting public.

I was about to say, when diverted from my subject, that occasionally one finds sage-bushes five or six feet high, and with a spread of branch and foliage in proportion, but two or two and a half feet is the usual height.

As the sun went down and the evening chill came on, we made preparation for bed. We stirred up the hard leather letter-sacks, and the knotty canvas bags of printed matter (knotty and uneven because of projecting ends and corners of magazines, boxes and books). We stirred them up and redisposed them in such a way as to make our bed as level as possible. And we *did* improve it, too, though after all our work it had an upheaved and billowy look about it, like a little piece of a stormy sea. Next we hunted up our boots from odd nooks among the mail-bags where they had settled, and put them on. Then we got down our coats, vests, pantaloons and heavy woolen shirts, from the arm-loops where they had been swinging all day, and clothed ourselves in them—for, there being no ladies either at the stations or in the coach, and the weather being hot, we had looked to our comfort by stripping to our underclothing, at nine o'clock in the morning. All things being now ready, we stowed the uneasy Dictionary where it would lie as quiet as possible, and placed the water-canteen and pistols where we could find them in the dark. Then we smoked a final pipe, and swapped a final yarn; after which, we put the pipes, tobacco, and bag of coin in snug holes and caves among the mail-bags, and then fastened down the coach curtains all around and made the place as "dark as the inside of a cow," as the conductor phrased it in his picturesque way. It was certainly as dark as any place could be—nothing was even dimly visible in it. And finally, we rolled ourselves up like silkworms, each person in his own blanket, and sank peacefully to sleep.

Whenever the stage stopped to change horses, we would wake up, and try to recollect where we were—and succeed—and in a minute or two the stage would be off again, and we likewise. We began to get into country, now, threaded here and there with little streams. These had high, steep banks on each side, and every time we flew down one bank and scrambled up the other, our party inside got mixed somewhat. First we would all be down in a pile at the forward end of the stage, nearly in a sitting posture, and in a second we would shoot to the other end, and stand on our heads. And we would sprawl and kick, too, and ward off ends and corners of mail-bags that came lumbering over us and about us; and as the dust rose from the tumult, we would all sneeze in chorus, and the majority of us would grumble, and probably say some hasty thing, like: "Take your elbow out of my ribs!—can't you quit crowding?"

Every time we avalanched from one end of the stage to the other, the Unabridged Dictionary would come too; and every time it came it damaged somebody. One trip it "barked" the Secretary's elbow; the next trip it hurt me in the stomach, and the third it tilted Bemis's nose up till he could look down his nostrils—he said. The pistols and coin soon settled to the bottom, but the pipes, pipe-stems, tobacco, and canteens clattered and floundered after the Dictionary every time it made an assault on us, and aided and abetted the book by spilling tobacco in our eyes, and water down our backs.

Still, all things considered, it was a very comfortable night. It wore gradually away, and when at last a cold gray light was visible through the puckers and chinks in the curtains, we yawned and stretched with satisfaction, shed our cocoons, and felt that we had slept as much as was necessary. By and by, as the sun rose up and warmed the world, we pulled off our clothes and got ready for breakfast. We were just pleasantly in time, for five minutes afterward the driver sent the weird music of his bugle winding over the grassy solitudes, and presently we detected a low hut or two in the distance. Then the rattling of the coach, the clatter of our six horses' hoofs, and the driver's crisp commands, awoke to a louder and stronger emphasis, and we went sweeping down on the station at our smartest speed. It was fascinating—that old Overland stage-coaching.

We jumped out in undress uniform. The driver tossed his gathered reins out on the ground, gaped and stretched complacently, drew off his heavy buckskin gloves with great deliberation and insufferable dignity—taking not the slightest notice of a dozen solicitous inquiries after his health, and humbly facetious and flattering accostings, and obsequious tenders of service, from five or six hairy and half-civilized station-keepers and hostlers who were nimbly unhitching our steeds and bringing the fresh team out of the stables—for, in the eyes of the stage-driver of that day, station-keepers and hostlers were a sort of good enough low creatures, useful in their place, and helping to make up a world, but not the kind of beings which a person of distinction could afford to concern himself with; while, on the contrary, in the eyes of the station-keeper and the hostler, the stage-driver was a hero—a great and shining dignitary, the world's favorite son, the envy of the people, the observed of the nations. When they spoke to him they received his insolent silence meekly, and as being the natural and proper conduct of so great a man; when he opened his lips they all hung on his words with admiration (he never honored a particular individual with a remark, but addressed it with a broad generality to the horses, the stables, the surrounding country *and* the human underlings); when he discharged a facetious insulting personality at a hostler, that hostler was happy for the day; when he uttered his one jest—old as the hills, coarse, profane, witless, and inflicted on the same audience, in the same language, every time his coach drove up there—the varlets roared, and slapped their thighs, and swore it was the best thing they'd ever heard in all their lives. And how they would fly around when he wanted a basin of water, a gourd of the same, or a light for his pipe!—but they would instantly insult a passenger if he so far forgot himself as to crave a favor at their hands. They could do that sort of insolence as well as the driver they copied it from—for, let it be borne in mind, the Overland driver had but little less contempt for his passengers than he had for his hostlers.

The hostlers and station-keepers treated the really powerful *conductor* of the coach merely with the best of what was their idea of civility, but the *driver* was the only being they bowed down to and worshipped. How admiringly they would gaze up at him in his high seat as he gloved himself with lingering deliberation, while some happy hostler held the bunch of reins aloft, and waited patiently for him to take it! And how they would bombard him with glorifying ejaculations as he cracked his long whip and went careering away.

The station buildings were long, low huts, made of sun-dried, mud-colored bricks, laid up without mortar (*adobes*, the Spaniards call these bricks, and Americans shorten it to '*dobies*). The roofs, which had no slant to them worth speaking of, were thatched and then sodded or covered with a thick layer of earth, and from this sprung a pretty rank growth of weeds and grass. It was the first time we had ever seen a man's front yard on top of his house. The buildings consisted of barns, stable-room for twelve or fifteen horses, and a hut for an eating-room for passengers. This latter had bunks in it for the station-keeper and a hostler or two. You could rest your elbow on its eaves, and you had to bend in order to get in at the door. In place of a window there was a square hole about large enough for a man to crawl through, but this had no glass in it. There was no flooring, but the ground was packed hard. There was no stove, but the fireplace served all needful purposes. There were no shelves, no cupboards, no closets. In a corner stood an open sack of flour, and nestling against its base were a couple of black and venerable tin coffee-pots, a tin teapot, a little bag of salt, and a side of bacon.

By the door of the station-keeper's den, outside, was a tin wash-basin, on the ground. Near it was a pail of water and a piece of yellow bar-soap, and from the eaves hung a hoary blue woolen shirt, significantly—but this latter was the station-keeper's private towel, and only two persons in all the party might venture to use it—the stage-driver and the conductor. The latter would not, from a sense of decency; the former would not, because he did not choose to encourage the advances of a station-keeper. We had towels—in the valise; they might as well have been in Sodom and Gomorrah. We (and the conductor) used our handkerchiefs, and the driver his pantaloons and sleeves. By the door, inside, was fastened a small old-fashioned looking-glass frame, with two little fragments of the original mirror lodged down in one corner of it. This arrangement afforded a pleasant double-barreled portrait of you when you looked into it, with one half of your head set up a couple of inches above the other half. From the glass frame hung the half of a comb by a string—but if I had to describe that patriarch or die, I believe I would order some sample coffins. It had come down from Esau and Samson, and had been accumulating hair ever since—along with certain impurities. In one corner of the room stood three or four rifles and muskets, together with horns and pouches of ammunition. The station-men wore pantaloons of coarse, country-woven stuff, and into the seat and the inside of the legs were sewed ample additions of buckskin, to do duty in place of leggings, when the man rode horseback—so the pants were half dull blue and half yellow, and unspeakably picturesque. The pants were stuffed into the tops of high boots, the heels whereof were armed with great Spanish spurs, whose little iron clogs and chains jingled with every step. The man wore a huge beard and mustachios, an old slouch hat, a blue woolen shirt, no suspenders, no vest, no coat—in a leathern sheath in his belt, a great long "navy" revolver (slung on right side, hammer to the front), and projecting from his boot a horn-handled bowie-knife. The furniture of the hut was neither gorgeous nor much in the way. The rocking-chairs and sofas were not present, and never had been, but they were represented by two three-legged stools, a pine-board bench four feet long, and two empty candle-boxes. The table was a greasy board on stilts, and the table-cloth and napkins had not come—and they were not looking for them, either. A battered tin platter, a knife and fork, and a tin pint cup, were at each man's place, and the driver had a queens-ware saucer that had seen better days. Of course, this duke sat at the head of the table. There was one isolated piece of table furniture that bore about it a touching air of grandeur in misfortune. This was the caster. It was German silver, and crippled and rusty, but it was so preposterously out of place there that it was suggestive of a tattered exiled king among barbarians, and the majesty of its native position compelled respect even in its degradation. There was only one cruet left, and that was a stopperless, fly-specked, broken-necked thing, with two inches of vinegar in it, and a dozen preserved flies with their heels up and looking sorry they had invested there.

The station-keeper up-ended a disk of last week's bread, of the shape and size of an old-time cheese, and carved some slabs from it which were as good as Nicholson pavement, and tenderer.

He sliced off a piece of bacon for each man, but only the experienced old hands made out to eat it, for it was condemned army bacon which the United States would not feed to its soldiers in the forts, and the stage company had bought it cheap for the sustenance of their passengers and employees. We may have found this condemned army bacon further out on the Plains than the section I am locating it in, but we *found* it—there is no gainsaying that.

Then he poured for us a beverage which he called "*Slumgullion*," and it is hard to think he was not inspired when he named it. It really pretended to be tea, but there was too much dish-rag, and sand, and old bacon-rind in it to deceive the intelligent traveler. He had no sugar and no milk—not even a spoon to stir the ingredients with.

We could not eat the bread or the meat, nor drink the "Slumgullion." And when I looked at that melancholy vinegar-cruet, I thought of the anecdote (a very, very old one, even at that day) of the traveler who sat down to a table which had nothing on it but a mackerel and a pot of mustard. He asked the landlord if this was all. The landlord said:

"*All!* Why, thunder and lightning, I should think there was mackerel enough there for six."

"But I don't like mackerel."

"Oh—then help yourself to the mustard."

In other days I had considered it a good, a very good, anecdote, but there was a dismal plausibility about it, here, that took all the humor out of it.

Our breakfast was before us, but our teeth were idle.

I tasted and smelt, and said I would take coffee, I believed. The station-boss stopped dead still, and glared at me speechless. At last, when he came to, he turned away and said, as one who communes with himself upon a matter too vast to grasp:

"*Coffee!* Well, if that don't go clean ahead of me, I'm d—d!"

We could not eat, and there was no conversation among the hostlers and herdsmen—we all sat at the same board. At least there was no conversation further than a single hurried request, now and then, from one employee to another. It was always in the same form, and always gruffly friendly. Its Western freshness and novelty startled me, at first, and interested me; but it presently grew monotonous, and lost its charm. It was:

"Pass the bread, you son of a skunk!" No, I forget—skunk was not the word; it seems to me it was still stronger than that; I know it was, in fact, but it is gone from my memory, apparently. However, it is no matter—probably it was too strong for print, anyway. It is the landmark in my memory which tells me where I first encountered the vigorous new vernacular of the occidental plains and mountains.

We gave up the breakfast, and paid our dollar apiece and went back to our mail-bag bed in the coach, and found comfort in our pipes. Right here we suffered the first diminution of our princely state. We left our six fine horses and took six mules in their place. But they were wild Mexican fellows, and a man had to stand at the head of each of them and hold him fast while the driver gloved and got himself ready. And when at last he grasped the reins and gave the word, the men sprung suddenly away from the mules' heads and the coach shot from the station as if it had issued from a cannon. How the frantic animals did scamper! It was a fierce and furious gallop—and the gait never altered for a moment till we reeled off ten or twelve miles and swept up to the next collection of little station huts and stables.

So we flew along all day. At 2 P.M. the belt of timber that fringes the North Platte and marks its windings through the vast level floor of the Plains came in sight. At 4 P.M. we crossed a branch of the river, and at 5 P.M. we crossed the Platte itself, and landed at Fort Kearney, *fifty-six hours out from St. Joe*—THREE HUNDRED MILES!

Next morning just before dawn, our mud-wagon broke down. We were to be delayed five or six hours, and therefore we took horses, by invitation, and joined a party who were just starting on a buffalo-hunt. It was noble sport galloping over the plain in the dewy freshness of the morning, but our part of the hunt ended in disaster and disgrace, for a wounded buffalo bull chased the passenger Bemis nearly two miles, and then he forsook his horse and took to a lone tree. He was very sullen about the matter for some twenty-four hours, but at last he began to soften little by little, and finally he said:

"Well, it was not funny, and there was no sense in those gawks making themselves so facetious over it. I tell you I was angry in earnest for a while. I should have shot that long gangly lubber they called Hank, if I could have done it without crippling six or seven other people—but of course I couldn't, the old 'Allen' 's so confounded comprehensive. I wish those loafers had been up in the tree; they wouldn't have wanted to laugh so. If I had had a horse worth a cent—but no, the minute he saw that buffalo bull wheel on him and give a bellow, he raised straight up in the air and stood on his heels. The saddle began to slip, and I took him round the neck and laid close to him, and began to pray. Then he came down and stood up on the other end awhile, and the bull actually stopped pawing sand and bellowing to contemplate the inhuman spectacle. Then the bull made a pass at him and uttered a bellow that sounded perfectly frightful, it was so close to me, and that seemed to literally prostrate my horse's reason, and make a raving distracted maniac of him, and I wish I may die if he didn't stand on his head for a quarter of a minute and shed tears. He was absolutely out of his mind—he was, as sure as truth itself, and he really didn't know what he was doing. Then the bull came charging at us, and my horse dropped down on all fours and took a fresh start—and then for the next ten minutes he would actually throw one handspring after another so fast that the bull began to get unsettled, too, and didn't know where to start in—and so he stood there sneezing, and shoveling dust over his back, and bellowing every now and then, and thinking he had got a fifteen-hundred-dollar circus horse for breakfast, certain. Well, I was first out on his neck—the horse's, not the bull's—and then underneath, and next on his rump, and sometimes head up, and sometimes heels—but I tell you it seemed solemn and awful to be ripping and tearing and carrying on so in the presence of death, as you might say. Pretty soon the bull made a snatch for us and brought away some of my horse's tail (I suppose, but do not know, being pretty busy at the time), but *something* made him hungry for solitude and suggested to him to get up and hunt for it. And then you ought to have seen that spider-legged old skeleton go! and you ought to have seen the bull cut out after him, too—head down, tongue out, tail up, bellowing like everything, and actually mowing down the weeds, and tearing up the earth, and boosting up the sand like a whirlwind! By George, it was a hot race! I and the saddle were back on the rump, and I had the bridle in my teeth and holding on to the pommel with both hands. First we left the dogs behind; then we passed a jackass-rabbit; then we overtook a coyote, and were gaining on an antelope when the rotten girths let go and threw me about thirty yards off to the left, and as the saddle went down over the horse's rump he gave it a lift with his heels that sent it more than four hundred yards up in the air, I wish I may die in a minute if he didn't. I fell at the plot of the only solitary tree there was in nine counties adjacent (as any creature could see with the naked eye), and the next second I had hold of the bark with four sets of nails and my teeth, and the next second after that I was astraddle of the main limb and blaspheming my luck in a way that made my breath smell of brimstone. I *had* the bull, now, if he did not think of *one* thing. But that one thing I dreaded. I dreaded it very seriously. There was a possibility that the bull might not think of it, but there were greater chances that he would. I made up my mind what I would do in case he did. It was a little over forty feet to the ground from where I sat. I cautiously unwound the lariat from the pommel of my saddle—"

"Your *saddle?* Did you take your saddle up in the tree with you?"

"Take it up in the tree with me? Why, how you talk! Of course I didn't. No man could do that. It *fell* in the tree when it came down."

"Oh—exactly."

"Certainly. I unwound the lariat, and fastened one end of it to the limb. It was the very best green rawhide, and capable of sustaining tons. I made a slip-noose in the other end, and then hung it down to see the length. It reached down twenty-two feet—half-way to the ground. I then loaded every barrel of the Allen with a double charge. I felt satisfied. I said to myself, if he never thinks of that one thing that I dread, all right—but if he does, all right anyhow—I am fixed for him. But don't you know that the very thing a man dreads is the thing that always happens? Indeed it is so. I watched the bull, now, with anxiety—anxiety which no one can conceive of who has not been in such a situation and felt that at any moment death might come. Presently a thought came into the bull's eye. I knew it! said I—if my nerve fails now, I am lost. Sure enough, it was just as I had dreaded, he started in to climb the tree—"

"What, the bull?"

"Of course—who else?"

"But a bull can't climb a tree."

"He can't, can't he? Since you know so much about it, did you ever see a bull try?"

"No! I never dreamt of such a thing."

"Well, then, what is the use of your talking that way, then? Because you never saw a thing done, is that any reason why it can't be done?"

"Well, all right—go on. What did you do?"

"The bull started up, and got along well for about ten feet, then slipped and slid back. I breathed easier. He tried it again—got up a little higher—slipped again. But he came at it once more, and this time he was careful. He got gradually higher and higher, and my spirits went down more and more. Up he came—an inch at a time—with his eyes hot, and his tongue hanging out. Higher and higher—hitched his foot over the stump of a limb, and looked up, as much as to say, 'You are my meat, friend.' Up again—higher and higher, and getting more excited the closer he got. He was within ten feet of me! I took a long breath—and then said I, 'It is now or never.' I had the coil of the lariat all ready; I paid it out slowly, till it hung right over his head; all of a sudden I let go of the slack and the slip-noose fell fairly round his neck! Quicker than lightning I out with the Allen and let him have it in the face. It was an awful roar, and must have scared the bull out of his senses. When the smoke cleared away, there he was, dangling in the air, twenty foot from the ground, and going out of one convulsion into another faster than you could count! I didn't stop to count, anyhow—I shinned down the tree and shot for home."

"Bemis, is all that true, just as you have stated it?"

"I wish I may rot in my tracks and die the death of a dog if it isn't."

"Well, we can't refuse to believe it, and we don't. But if there were some proofs—"

"Proofs! Did I bring back my lariat?"

"No."

"Did I bring back my horse?"

"No."

"Did you ever see the bull again?"

"No."

"Well, then, what more do you want? I never saw anybody as particular as you are about a little thing like that."

I made up my mind that if this man was not a liar he only missed it by the skin of his teeth.

O. HENRY
The Caballero's Way

O. Henry (1862–1910) was born William Sydney Porter in Greensboro, North Carolina, and was educated at Harvard, where he founded *The Iconoclast* (the forerunner of *Rolling Stone* magazine). Later he was accused of embezzling funds from the First National Bank in Austin, and fled to South America, where he became an acquintance of the bank robber, Al Jennings. Eventually Porter returned to the USA, and served a five year prison sentence. It was in prison that he adopted the O. Henry pseudonym and started writing the sharply plotted short stories which made him one of the leading authors of his day.

As a young man Porter had spent two years living in southern Texas, and this was the setting for most of his Western fiction, including 'The Caballero's Way' (1904). The story introduces O. Henry's most famous creation, the Cisco Kid, later to become the central character (somewhat modified) in over twenty Western films, among them the first talkie Western, *In Old Arizona* (1929).

THE CISCO KID HAD KILLED six men in more or less fair scrimmages, had murdered twice as many (mostly Mexicans), and had winged a larger number whom he modestly forbore to count. Therefore a woman loved him.

The Kid was twenty-five, looked twenty; and a careful insurance company would have estimated the probable time of his demise at, say, twenty-six. His habitat was anywhere between the Frio and the Rio Grande. He killed for the love of it—because he was quick-tempered—to avoid arrest—for his own amusement—any reason that came to his mind would suffice. He had escaped capture because he could shoot five-sixths of a second sooner than any sheriff or ranger in the service, and because he rode a speckled roan horse that knew every cow-path in the mesquite and pear thickets from San Antonio to Matamoras.

Tonia Perez, the girl who loved the Cisco Kid, was half Carmen, half Madonna, and the rest—oh, yes, a woman who is half Carmen and half Madonna can always be something more—the rest, let us say, was humming-bird. She lived in a grass-roofed *jacal* near a little Mexican settlement at the Lone Wolf Crossing of the Frio. With her lived a father or grandfather, a lineal Aztec, somewhat less than a thousand years old, who herded a hundred goats and lived in a continuous drunken dream from drinking *mescal*. Back of the *jacal* a tremendous forest of bristling pear, twenty feet high at its worst, crowded almost to its door. It was along the bewildering maze of this spinous thicket that the speckled roan would bring the Kid to see his girl. And once, clinging like a lizard to the ridge-pole, high up under the peaked grass roof, he had heard Tonia, with her Madonna face and Carmen beauty and humming-bird soul, parley with the sheriff's posse, denying knowledge of her man in her soft *mélange* of Spanish and English.

One day the adjutant-general of the State, who is, *ex officio*, commander of the ranger forces, wrote some sarcastic lines to Captain Duval of Company X, stationed at Laredo, relative to the serene and undisturbed existence led by murderers and desperadoes in the said captain's territory.

The captain turned the colour of brick dust under his

tan, and forwarded the letter, after adding a few comments, per ranger Private Bill Adamson, to ranger Lieutenant Sandridge, camped at a water hole on the Nueces with a squad of five men in preservation of law and order.

Lieutenant Sandridge turned a beautiful *couleur de rose* through his ordinary strawberry complexion, tucked the letter in his hip pocket, and chewed off the ends of his gamboge moustache.

The next morning he saddled his horse and rode alone to the Mexican settlement at the Lone Wolf Crossing of the Frio, twenty miles away.

Six feet two, blond as a Viking, quiet as a deacon, dangerous as a machine gun, Sandridge moved among the *Jacales*, patiently seeking news of the Cisco Kid.

Far more than the law, the Mexicans dreaded the cold and certain vengeance of the lone rider that the ranger sought. It had been one of the Kid's pastimes to shoot Mexicans "to see them kick": if he demanded from them moribund Terpsichorean feats, simply that he might be entertained, what terrible and extreme penalties would be certain to follow should they anger him! One and all they lounged with upturned palms and shrugging shoulders, filling the air with "*quien sabes*" and denials of the Kid's acquaintance.

But there was a man named Fink who kept a store at the Crossing—a man of many nationalities, tongues, interests, and ways of thinking.

"No use to ask them Mexicans," he said to Sandridge. "They're afraid to tell. This *hombre* they call the Kid—Goodall is his name, ain't it?—he's been in my store once or twice. I have an idea you might run across him at—but I guess I don't keer to say, myself. I'm two seconds later in pulling a gun than I used to be, and the difference is worth thinking about. But this Kid's got a half-Mexican girl at the Crossing that he comes to see. She lives in that *jacal* a hundred yards down the arroyo at the edge of the pear. Maybe she—no, I don't suppose she would, but that *jacal* would be a good place to watch, anyway."

Sandridge rode down to the *jacal* of Perez. The sun was

low, and the broad shade of the great pear thicket already covered the grass-thatched hut. The goats were enclosed for the night in a brush corral near by. A few kids walked the top of it, nibbling the chaparral leaves. The old Mexican lay upon a blanket on the grass, already in a stupor from his mescal, and dreaming, perhaps, of the nights when he and Pizarro touched glasses to their New World fortunes—so old his wrinkled face seemed to proclaim him to be. And in the door of the *jacal* stood Tonia. And Lieutenant Sandridge sat in his saddle staring at her like a gannet agape at a sailorman.

The Cisco Kid was a vain person, as all eminent and successful assassins are, and his bosom would have been ruffled had he known that at a simple exchange of glances two persons, in whose minds he had been looming large, suddenly abandoned (at least for the time) all thought of him.

Never before had Tonia seen such a man as this. He seemed to be made of sunshine and blood-red tissue and clear weather. He seemed to illuminate the shadow of the pear when he smiled, as though the sun were rising again. The men she had known had been small and dark. Even the Kid, in spite of his achievements, was a stripling no larger than herself, with black, straight hair and a cold, marble face that chilled the noonday.

As for Tonia, though she sends description to the poorhouse, let her make a millionaire of your fancy. Her blue-black hair, smoothly divided in the middle and bound close to her head, and her large eyes full of the Latin melancholy, gave her the Madonna touch. Her motions and air spoke of the concealed fire and the desire to charm that she had inherited from the *gitanas* of the Basque province. As for the humming-bird part of her, that dwelt in her heart; you could not perceive it unless her bright red skirt and dark blue blouse gave you a symbolic hint of the vagarious bird.

The newly lighted sun-god asked for a drink of water. Tonia brought it from the red jar hanging under the brush shelter. Sandridge considered it necessary to dismount so as to lessen the trouble of her ministrations.

I play no spy; nor do I assume to master the thoughts of any human heart; but I assert, by the chronicler's right, that before a quarter of an hour had sped, Sandridge was teaching her how to plait a six-strand rawhide stake-rope, and Tonia had explained to him that were it not for her little English book that the peripatetic *padre* had given her and the little crippled *chivo*, that she fed from a bottle, she would be very, very lonely indeed.

Which leads to a suspicion that the Kid's fences needed repairing, and that the adjutant-general's sarcasm had fallen upon unproductive soil.

In his camp by the water hole Lieutenant Sandridge announced and reiterated his intention of either causing the Cisco Kid to nibble the black loam of the Frio country prairies or of hauling him before a judge and jury. That sounded business-like. Twice a week he rode over to the Lone Wolf Crossing of the Frio, and directed Tonia's slim, slightly lemon-tinted fingers among the intricacies of the slowly growing lariata. A six-strand plait is hard to learn and easy to teach.

The ranger knew that he might find the Kid there at any visit. He kept his armament ready, and had a frequent eye for the pear thicket at the rear of the *jacal*. Thus he might bring down the kite and the humming-bird with one stone.

While the sunny-haired ornithologist was pursuing his studies the Cisco Kid was also attending to his professional duties. He moodily shot up a saloon in a small cow village on Quintana Creek, killed the town marshal (plugging him neatly in the centre of his tin badge), and then rode away, morose and unsatisfied. No true artist is uplifted by shooting an aged man carrying an old-style .38 bulldog.

On his way the Kid suddenly experienced the yearning that all men feel when wrong-doing loses its keen edge of delight. He yearned for the woman he loved to reassure him that she was his in spite of it. He wanted her to call his bloodthirstiness bravery and his cruelty devotion. He wanted Tonia to bring him water from the red jar under the brush shelter, and tell him how the *chivo* was thriving on the bottle.

The Kid turned the speckled roan's head up the ten-mile pear flat that stretches along the Arroyo Hondo until it ends at the Lone Wolf Crossing of the Frio. The roan whickered; for he had a sense of locality and direction equal to that of a belt-line street-car horse; and he knew he would soon be nibbling the rich mesquite grass at the end of a forty-foot stake-rope while Ulysses rested his head in Circe's straw-roofed hut.

More weird and lonesome than the journey of an Amazonian explorer is the ride of one through a Texas pear flat. With dismal monotony and startling variety the uncanny and multiform shapes of the cacti lift their twisted trunks, and fat, bristly hands to encumber the way. The demon plant, appearing to live without soil or rain, seems to taunt the parched traveller with its lush grey greenness. It warps itself a thousand times about what look to be open and inviting paths, only to lure the rider into blind and impassable spine-defended "bottoms of the bag", leaving him to retreat, if he can, with the points of the compass whirling in his head.

To be lost in the pear is to die almost the death of the thief on the cross, pierced by nails and with grotesque shapes of all the fiends hovering about.

But it was not so with the Kid and his mount. Winding, twisting, circling, tracing the most fantastic and bewildering trail ever picked out, the good roan lessened the distance to the Lone Wolf Crossing with every coil and turn that he made.

While they fared the Kid sang. He knew but one tune and sang it, as he knew but one code and lived it, and but one girl and loved her. He was a single-minded man of conventional ideas. He had a voice like a coyote with bronchitis, but whenever he chose to sing his song he sang it. It was a conventional song of the camps and trail, running at its beginning as near as may be to these words:

Don't you monkey with my Lulu girl
Or I'll tell you what I'll do

and so on. The roan was inured to it, and did not mind.

But even the poorest singer will, after a certain time, gain his own consent to refrain from contributing to the world's noises. So the Kid, by the time he was within a mile or two of Tonia's *jacal*, had reluctantly allowed his song to die away—not because his vocal performance had become less charming to his own ears, but because his laryngeal muscles were aweary.

As though he were in a circus ring the speckled roan wheeled and danced through the labyrinth of pear until at length his rider knew by certain landmarks that the Lone Wolf Crossing was close at hand. Then, where the pear was thinner, he caught sight of the grass roof of the *jacal* and the hackberry tree on the edge of the arroyo. A few yards farther the Kid stopped the roan and gazed intently through the prickly openings. Then he dismounted, dropped the roan's reins, and proceeded on foot, stooping and silent, like an Indian. The roan, knowing his part, stood still, making no sound.

The Kid crept noiselessly to the very edge of the pear thicket and reconnoitred between the leaves of a clump of cactus.

Ten yards from his hiding-place, in the shade of the *jacal*, sat his Tonia calmly plaiting a rawhide lariat. So far she might surely escape condemnation; women have been known, from time to time, to engage in more mischievous occupations. But if all must be told, there is to be added that her head reposed against the broad and comfortable chest of a tall red-and-yellow man, and that his arm was about her, guiding her nimble small fingers that required so many lessons at the intricate six-strand plait.

Sandridge glanced quickly at the dark mass of pear when he heard a slight squeaking sound that was not altogether unfamiliar. A gunscabbard will make that sound when one grasps the handle of a six-shooter suddenly. But the sound was not repeated; and Tonia's fingers needed close attention.

And then, in the shadow of death, they began to talk of their love; and in the still July afternoon every word they uttered reached the ears of the Kid.

"Remember, then," said Tonia, "you must not come again until I send for you. Soon he will be here. A *vaquero* at the *tienda* said to-day he saw him on the Guadalupe three days ago. When he is that near he always comes. If he comes and finds you here he will kill you. So, for my sake, you must come no more until I send you the word."

"All right," said the ranger. "And then what?"

"And then," said the girl, "you must bring your men here and kill him. If not, he will kill you."

"He ain't a man to surrender, that's sure," said Sandridge. "It's kill or be killed for the officer that goes up against Mr Cisco Kid."

"He must die," said the girl. "Otherwise there will not be any peace in the world for thee and me. He has killed many. Let him so die. Bring your men, and give him no chance to escape."

"You used to think right much of him," said Sandridge.

Tonia dropped the lariat, twisted herself around, and curved a lemon-tinted arm over the ranger's shoulder.

"But then," she murmured in liquid Spanish, "I had not beheld thee, thou great, red mountain of a man! And thou art kind and good, as well as strong. Could one choose him, knowing thee? Let him die; for then I will not be filled with fear by day and night lest he hurt thee or me."

"How can I know when he comes?" asked Sandridge.

"When he comes," said Tonia, "he remains two days, sometimes three. Gregorio, the small son of old Luisa, the *lavandera*, has a swift pony. I will write a letter to thee and send it by him, saying how it will be best to come upon him. By Gregorio will the letter come. And bring many men with thee, and have much care, oh, dear red one, for the rattlesnake is not quicker to strike than is *El Chivato*, as they call him, to send a ball from his *pistola*."

"The Kid's handy with his gun, sure enough," admitted Sandridge, "but when I come for him I shall come alone. I'll get him by myself or not at all. The Cap wrote one or two things to me that make me want to do the trick without any help. You let me know when Mr Kid arrives, and I'll do the rest."

"I will send you the message by the boy Gregorio," said the girl. "I knew you were braver than that small slayer of men who never smiles. How could I ever have thought I cared for him?"

It was time for the ranger to ride back to his camp on the water hole. Before he mounted his horse he raised the slight form of Tonia with one arm high from the earth for a parting salute. The drowsy stillness of the torpid summer air still lay thick upon the dreaming afternoon. The smoke from the fire in the *jacal*, where the *frijoles* blubbered in the iron pot, rose straight as a plumb-line above the clay-daubed chimney. No sound or movement disturbed the serenity of the dense pear thicket ten yards away.

When the form of Sandridge had disappeared, loping his big dun down the steep banks of the Frio crossing, the Kid crept back to his own horse, mounted him, and rode back along the tortuous trail he had come.

But not far. He stopped and waited in the silent depths of the pear until half an hour had passed. And then Tonia heard the high, untrue notes of his unmusical singing coming nearer and nearer; and she ran to the edge of the pear to meet him.

The Kid seldom smiled; but he smiled and waved his hat when he saw her. He dismounted, and his girl sprang into his arms. The Kid looked at her fondly. His thick, black hair clung to his head like a wrinkled mat. The meeting brought a slight ripple of some undercurrent of feeling to his smooth, dark face that was usually as motionless as a clay mask.

"How's my girl?" he asked, holding her close.

"Sick of waiting so long for you, dear one," she answered. "My eyes are dim with always gazing into that devil's pincushion through which you come. And I can see into it such a little way, too. But you are here, beloved one, and I will not scold. *Que mal muchacho!* not to come to see your *alma* more often. Go in and rest, and let me water your horse and stake him with the long rope. There is cool water in the jar for you."

The Kid kissed her affectionately.

"Not if the court knows itself do I let a lady stake my horse for me," said he. "But if you'll run in, *chica*, and throw a pot of coffee together while I attend to the *caballo*, I'll be a good deal obliged."

Besides his marksmanship the Kid had another attribute for which he admired himself greatly. He was *muy caballero*, as the Mexicans express it, where the ladies were concerned. For them he had always gentle words and consideration. He could not have spoken a harsh word to a woman. He might ruthlessly slay their husbands and brothers, but he could not have laid the weight of a finger in anger upon a woman. Wherefore many of that interesting division of humanity who had come under the spell of his politeness declared their disbelief in the stories circulated about Mr Kid. One shouldn't believe everything one heard, they said. When confronted by their indignant men folk with proof of the *caballero's* deeds of infamy, they said maybe he had been driven to it, and that he knew how to treat a lady, anyhow.

Considering this extremely courteous idiosyncrasy of the Kid and the pride that he took in it, one can perceive that the solution of the problem that was presented to him by what he saw and heard from his hiding-place in the pear that afternoon (at least as to one of the actors) must have been obscured by difficulties. And yet one could not think of the Kid overlooking little matters of that kind.

At the end of the short twilight they gathered around a supper of *frijoles*, goat steaks, canned peaches, and coffee, by the light of a lantern in the *jacal*. Afterward, the ancestor, his flock corralled, smoked a cigarette and became a mummy in a grey blanket. Tonia washed the few dishes while the Kid dried them with the flour-sacking towel. Her eyes shone; she chatted volubly of the inconsequent happenings of her small world since the Kid's last visit; it was as all his other homecomings had been.

Then outside Tonia swung in a grass hammock with her guitar and sang sad *canciones de amor*.

"Do you love me just the same, old girl?" asked the Kid, hunting for his cigarette papers.

"Always the same, little one," said Tonia, her dark eyes lingering upon him.

"I must go over to Fink's," said the Kid, rising, "for some tobacco. I thought I had another sack in my coat. I'll be back in a quarter of an hour."

"Hasten," said Tonia, "and tell me—how long shall I call you my own this time? Will you be gone again tomorrow, leaving me to grieve, or will you be longer with your Tonia?"

"Oh, I might stay two or three days this trip," said the Kid, yawning. "I've been on the dodge for a month, and I'd like to rest up."

He was gone half an hour for his tobacco. When he returned Tonia was still lying in the hammock.

"It's funny," said the Kid, "how I feel. I feel like there was somebody lying behind every bush and tree waiting to shoot me. I never had mullygrubs like them before. Maybe it's one of them presumptions. I've got half a notion to light out in the morning before day. The Guadalupe country is burning up about that old Dutchman I plugged down there."

"You are not afraid—no one could make my brave little one fear."

"Well, I haven't been usually regarded as a jackrabbit when it comes to scrapping; but I don't want a posse smoking me out when I'm in your *jacal*. Somebody might get hurt that oughtn't to."

"Remain with your Tonia; no one will find you here."

The Kid looked keenly into the shadows up and down the arroyo and toward the dim lights of the Mexican village.

"I'll see how it looks later on," was his decision.

At midnight a horseman rode into the rangers' camp, blazing his way by noisy "halloes" to indicate a pacific mission. Sandridge and one or two others turned out to investigate the row. The rider announced himself to be Domingo Sales, from the Lone Wold Crossing. He bore a letter for Señor Sandridge. Old Luisa, the *lavendero*, had persuaded him to bring it, he said, her son Gregorio being too ill of a fever to ride.

Sandridge lighted the camp lantern and read the letter. These were its words:

> *Dear One*: He has come. Hardly had you ridden away when he came out of the pear. When he first talked he said he would stay three days or more. Then as it grew later he was like a wolf or a fox, and walked about without rest, looking and listening. Soon he said he must leave before daylight when it is dark and stillest. And then he seemed to suspect that I be not true to him. He looked at me so strange that I am frightened. I swear to him that I love him, his own Tonia. Last of all he said I must prove to him I am true. He thinks that even now men are waiting to kill him as he rides from my house. To escape he says he will dress in my clothes, my red skirt and the blue waist I wear and the brown mantilla over the head, and thus ride away. But before that he says that I must put on his clothes, his *pantalones* and *camisa* and hat, and ride away on his horse from the *jacal* as far as the big road beyond the crossing and back again. This before he goes, so he can tell if I am true and if men are hidden to shoot him. It is a terrible thing. An hour before daybreak this is to be. Come, my dear one, and kill this man and take me for your Tonia. Do not try to take hold of him alive, but kill him quickly. Knowing all, you should do that. You must come long before the time and hide yourself in the little shed near the *jacal* where the wagon and saddles are kept. It is dark in there. He will wear my red skirt and blue waist and brown mantilla. I send you a hundred kisses. Come surely and shoot quickly and straight.
>
> THINE OWN TONIA.

Sandridge quickly explained to his men the official part of the missive. The rangers protested against his going alone.

"I'll get him easy enough," said the lieutenant. "The girl's got him trapped. And don't even think he'll get the drop on me."

Sandridge saddled his horse and rode to the Lone Wolf Crossing. He tied his big dun in a clump of brush on the arroyo, took his Winchester from its scabbard, and carefully approached the Perez *jacal*. There was only the half of a high moon drifted over by ragged, milk-white gulf clouds.

The wagon-shed was an excellent place for ambush; and the ranger got inside it safely. In the black shadow of the brush shelter in front of the *jacal* he could see a horse tied and hear him impatiently pawing the hard-trodden earth.

He waited almost an hour before two figures came out of the *jacal*. One, in man's clothes, quickly mounted the horse and galloped past the wagon-shed toward the crossing and village. And then the other figure, in skirt, waist, and mantilla over its head, stepped out into the faint moonlight, gazing after the rider. Sandridge thought he would take his chance then before Tonia rode back. He fancied she might not care to see it.

"Throw up your hands," he ordered loudly, stepping out of the wagon-shed with his Winchester at his shoulder.

There was a quick turn of the figure, but no movement to obey, so the ranger pumped in the bullets—one—two—three—and then twice more; for you never could be too sure of bringing down the Cisco Kid. There was no danger of missing at ten paces, even in that half moonlight.

The old ancestor, asleep on his blanket, was awakened by the shots. Listening further, he heard a great cry from some man in mortal distress or anguish, and rose up grumbling at the disturbing ways of moderns.

The tall, red ghost of a man burst into the *jacal*, reaching one hand, shaking like a *tule* reed, for the lantern hanging on its nail. The other spread a letter on the table.

"Look at this letter, Perez," cried the man. "Who wrote it?"

"*Ah Dios!* it is Señor Sandridge," mumbled the old man, approaching. "*Pues, señor*, that letter was written by *El Chivato*, as he is called—by the man of Tonia. They say he is a bad man; I do not know. While Tonia slept he wrote the letter and sent it by this old hand of mine to Domingo Sales to be brought to you. Is there anything wrong in the letter? I am very old; and I did not know. *Valgame Dios!* it is a very foolish world; and there is nothing in the house to drink—nothing to drink."

Just then all that Sandridge could think of to do was to go outside and throw himself face downward in the dust by the side of his humming-bird, of whom not a feather fluttered. He was not a *caballero* by instinct, and he could not understand the niceties of revenge.

A mile away the rider who had ridden past the wagon-shed struck up a harsh, untuneful song, the words of which began:

Don't you monkey with my Lulu girl
Or I'll tell you what I'll do—

STEPHEN CRANE
The Blue Hotel

Stephen Crane (1871–1900) was born in Newark, New Jersey. While Crane is best-known today for his novel about the American Civil War, *Red Badge of Courage* (1895), his Western writings constitute —arguably— an even greater achievement. The success of *Red Badge of Courage* enabled Crane to persuade the Bacheller publishing group to finance him on a long trip through the Far West (a journey Crane had wanted to undertake for a number of years). On his return Crane wrote a series of Western masterpieces, including 'The Bride Comes to Yellow Sky', 'A Man and Some Others', 'Twelve O'clock', 'The Five White Mice', and the remarkable short novel *The Blue Hotel*. These stories introduced realism and irony into the Western form and in some ways Crane has been the most influential Western stylist. He died of tuberculosis at the age of twenty-eight, after reporting the Spanish–American War.

The Blue Hotel is from 1898.

THE PALACE HOTEL AT FORT ROMPER was painted a light blue, a shade that is on the legs of a kind of heron, causing the bird to declare its position against any background. The Palace Hotel, then, was always screaming and howling in a way that made the dazzling winter landscape of Nebraska seem only a grey swampish hush. It stood alone on the prairie, and when the snow was falling the town two hundred yards away was not visible. But when the traveller alighted at the railway station he was obliged to pass the Palace Hotel before he could come upon the company of low clapboard houses which composed Fort Romper, and it was not to be thought that any traveller could pass the Palace Hotel without looking at it. Pat Scully, the proprietor, had proved himself a master of strategy when he chose his paints. It is true that on clear days, when the great transcontinental expresses, long lines of swaying Pullmans, swept through Fort Romper, passengers were overcome at the sight, and the cult that knows the brown-reds and the subdivisions of the dark greens of the East expressed shame, pity, horror, in a laugh. But to the citizens of this prairie town and to the people who would naturally stop there, Pat Scully had performed a feat. With this opulence and splendour, these creeds, classes, egotisms, that streamed through Romper on the rails day after day, they had no colour in common.

As if the displayed delights of such a blue hotel were not sufficiently enticing, it was Scully's habit to go every morning and evening to meet the leisurely trains that stopped at Romper and work his seductions upon any man that he might see wavering, gripsack in hand.

One morning, when a snow-crusted engine dragged its long string of freight cars and its one passenger coach to the station, Scully performed the marvel of catching three men. One was a shaky and quick-eyed Swede, with a great shining cheap valise; one was a tall bronzed cowboy, who was on his way to a ranch near the Dakota line; one was a little silent man from the East, who didn't look it, and didn't announce it. Scully practically made them prisoners. He was so nimble and merry and kindly that each probably felt it would be the height of brutality to try to escape. They trudged off over the creaking board sidewalks in the wake of the eager little Irishman. He wore a heavy fur cap squeezed tightly down on his head. It caused his two red ears to stick out stiffly, as if they were made of tin.

At last, Scully, elaborately, with boisterous hospitality, conducted them through the portals of the blue hotel. The room which they entered was small. It seemed to be merely a proper temple for an enormous stove, which, in the centre, was humming with godlike violence. At various points on its surface the iron had become luminous and glowed yellow from the heat. Besides the stove Scully's son Johnnie was playing High-Five with an old farmer who had whiskers both grey and sandy. They were quarrelling. Frequently the old farmer turned his face toward a box of sawdust—coloured brown from tobacco juice—that was behind the stove, and spat with an air of great impatience and irritation. With a loud flourish of words Scully destroyed the game of cards, and bustled his son upstairs with part of the baggage of the new guests. He himself conducted them to three basins of the coldest water in the world. The cowboy and the Easterner burnished themselves fiery red with this water, until it seemed to be some kind of metal-polish. The Swede, however, merely dipped his fingers gingerly and with trepidation. It was notable that throughout this series of small ceremonies the three travellers were made to feel that Scully was very benevolent. He was conferring great favours upon them. He handed the towel from one to another with an air of philanthropic impulse.

Afterward they went to the first room, and, sitting about the stove, listened to Scully's officious clamour at his daughters, who were preparing the midday meal. They reflected in the silence of experienced men who tread carefully amid new people. Nevertheless, the old farmer, stationary, invincible in his chair near the warmest part of the stove, turned his face from the sawdust-box frequently and addressed a glowing commonplace to the strangers. Usually he was answered in short but adequate sentences by either the cowboy or the Easterner. The Swede said nothing. He seemed to be occupied in making furtive estimates of each man in the room. One might have thought that he had the sense of silly suspicion which comes to guilt. He resembled a badly frightened man.

Later, at dinner, he spoke a little, addressing his conversation entirely to Scully. He volunteered that he had come from New York, where for ten years he had worked as a tailor. These facts seemed to strike Scully as fascinating, and afterward he volunteered that he had lived at Romper for fourteen years. The Swede asked about the crops and the price of labour. He seemed barely to listen to Scully's extended replies. His eyes continued to rove from man to man.

Finally, with a laugh and a wink, he said that some of these Western communities were very dangerous; and after his statement he straightened his legs under the table, tilted his head, and laughed again, loudly. It was plain that the demonstration had no meaning to the others. They looked at him wondering and in silence.

II

As the men trooped heavily back into the front room, the two little windows presented views of a turmoiling sea of snow. The huge arms of the wind were making attempts—mighty, circular, futile—to embrace the flakes as they sped. A gatepost like a still man with a blanched face stood aghast amid this profligate fury. In a hearty voice Scully announced the presence of a blizzard. The guests of the blue hotel, lighting their pipes, assented with grunts of lazy masculine contentment. No island of the sea could be exempt in the degree of this little room with its humming stove. Johnnie, son of Scully, in a tone which defined his opinion of his ability as a card-player, challenged the old farmer of both grey and sandy whiskers to a game of High-Five. The farmer agreed with a contemptuous and bitter scoff. They sat close to the stove, and squared their knees under a wide board. The cowboy and the Easterner watched the game with interest. The Swede remained near the window, aloof, but with a countenance that showed signs of an inexplicable excitement.

The play of Johnnie and the grey-beard was suddenly ended by another quarrel. The old man arose while casting a look of heated scorn at his adversary. He slowly buttoned his coat, and then stalked with fabulous dignity from the room. In the discreet silence of all the other men the Swede laughed. His laughter rang somehow childish. Men by this time had begun to look at him askance, as if they wished to inquire what ailed him.

A new game was formed jocosely. The cowboy volunteered to become the partner of Johnnie, and they all then turned to ask the Swede to throw in his lot with the little Easterner. He asked some questions about the game, and, learning that it wore many names, and that he had played it when it was under an alias, he accepted the invitation. He strode toward the men nervously, as if he expected to be assaulted. Finally, seated, he gazed from face to face and laughed shrilly. This laugh was so strange that the Easterner looked up quickly, the cowboy sat intent and with his mouth open, and Johnnie paused, holding the cards with still fingers.

Afterward there was a short silence. Then Johnnie said, "Well, let's get at it. Come on now!" They pulled their chairs forward until their knees were bunched under the board. They began to play, and their interest in the game caused the others to forget the manner of the Swede.

The cowboy was a board-whacker. Each time that he held superior cards he whanged them, one by one, with exceeding force, down upon the improvised table, and took the tricks with a glowing air of prowess and pride that sent thrills of indignation into the hearts of his opponents. A game with a board-whacker in it is sure to become intense. The countenances of the Easterner and the Swede were miserable whenever the cowboy thundered down his aces and kings, while Johnnie, his eyes gleaming with joy, chuckled and chuckled.

Because of the absorbing play none considered the strange ways of the Swede. They paid strict heed to the game. Finally, during a lull caused by a new deal, the Swede suddenly addressed Johnnie: "I suppose there have been a good many men killed in this room." The jaws of the others dropped and they looked at him.

"What in hell are you talking about?" said Johnnie.

The Swede laughed again his blatant laugh, full of a kind of false courage and defiance. "Oh, you know what I mean all right," he answered.

"I'm a liar if I do!" Johnnie protested. The card was halted, and the men stared at the Swede. Johnnie evidently felt that as the son of the proprietor he should make a direct inquiry. "Now, what might you be drivin' at, mister?" he asked. The Swede winked at him. It was a wink full of cunning. His fingers shook on the edge of the board. "Oh, maybe you think I have been to nowheres. Maybe you think I'm a tenderfoot?"

"I don't know nothin' about you," answered Johnnie, "and I don't give a damn where you've been. All I got to say is that I don't know what you're driving at. There hain't never been nobody killed in this room."

The cowboy, who had been steadily gazing at the Swede, then spoke: "What's wrong with you, mister?"

Apparently it seemed to the Swede that he was formidably menaced. He shivered and turned white near the corners of his mouth. He sent an appealing glance in the direction of the little Easterner. During these moments he did not forget to wear his air of advanced pot-valour. "They say they don't know what I mean," he remarked mockingly to the Easterner.

The latter answered after prolonged and cautious reflection. "I don't understand you," he said, impassively.

The Swede made a movement then which announced that he thought he had encountered treachery from the only quarter where he had expected sympathy, if not help. "Oh, I see you are all against me. I see—"

The cowboy was in a state of deep stupefaction. "Say," he cried, as he tumbled the deck violently down upon the board, "say, what are you gittin' at, hey?"

The Swede sprang up with the celerity of a man escaping from a snake on the floor. "I don't want to fight!" he shouted. "I don't want to fight!"

The cowboy stretched his long legs indolently and deliberately. His hands were in his pockets. He spat into the sawdust-box. "Well, who the hell thought you did?" he inquired.

The Swede backed rapidly toward a corner of the room. His hands were out protectingly in front of his chest, but he was making an obvious struggle to control his fright. "Gentlemen," he quavered, "I suppose I am going to be killed before I can leave this house! I suppose I am going to be killed before I can leave this house!" In his eyes was the dying-swan look. Through the windows could be seen the snow turning blue in the shadow of dusk. The wind tore at the house, and some loose thing beat regularly against the clapboards like a spirit tapping.

A door opened, and Scully himself entered. He paused in surprise as he noted the tragic attitude of the Swede. Then he said, "What's the matter here?"

The Swede answered him swiftly and eagerly: "These men are going to kill me."

"Kill you!" ejaculated Scully. "Kill you! What are you talkin'?"

The Swede made the gesture of a martyr.

Scully wheeled sternly upon his son. "What is this, Johnnie?"

The lad had grown sullen. "Damned if I know," he answered. "I can't make no sense to it." He began to shuffle the cards, fluttering them together with an angry snap. "He says a good many men have been killed in this room, or something like that. And he says he's going to be killed here too. I don't know what ails him. He's crazy, I shouldn't wonder."

Scully then looked for explanation to the cowboy, but the cowboy simply shrugged his shoulders.

"Kill you?" said Scully again to the Swede. "Kill you? Man, you're off your nut."

"Oh, I know," burst out the Swede. "I know what will happen. Yes, I'm crazy—yes. Yes, of course, I'm crazy—yes. But I know one thing—" There was a sort of sweat of misery and terror upon his face. "I know I won't get out of here alive."

The cowboy drew a deep breath, as if his mind was passing into the last stages of dissolution. "Well, I'm doggoned," he whispered to himself.

Scully wheeled suddenly and faced his son. "You've been troublin' this man!"

Johnnie's voice was loud with its burden of grievance. "Why, good Gawd, I ain't done nothin' to 'im."

The Swede broke in. "Gentlemen, do not disturb yourselves. I will leave this house. I will go away, because"—he accused them dramatically with his glance—"because I do not want to be killed."

Scully was furious with his son. "Will you tell me what is the matter, you young divil? What's the matter, anyhow? Speak out!"

"Blame it!" cried Johnnie in despair, "don't I tell you I don't know? He—he says we want to kill him, and that's all I know. I can't tell what ails him."

The Swede continued to repeat: "Never mind, Mr Scully; never mind. I will leave this house. I will go away, because I do not wish to be killed. Yes, of course, I am crazy—yes. But I know one thing! I will go away. I will leave this house. Never mind, Mr Scully; never mind. I will go away."

"You will not go 'way," said Scully. "You will not go 'way until I hear the reason of this business. If anybody has troubled you I will take care of him. This is my house. You are under my roof, and I will not allow any peaceable man to be troubled here." He cast a terrible eye upon Johnnie, the cowboy, and the Easterner.

"Never mind, Mr Scully; never mind. I will go away. I do not wish to be killed." The Swede moved toward the door which opened upon the stairs. It was evidently his intention to go at once for his baggage.

"No, no," shouted Scully peremptorily; but the white-faced man slid by him and disappeared. "Now," said Scully severely, "what does this mane?"

Johnnie and the cowboy cried together: "Why, we didn't do nothin' to 'im!"

Scully's eyes were cold. "No," he said, "you didn't?"

Johnnie swore a deep oath. "Why, this is the wildest loon I ever see. We didn't do nothin' at all. We were jest sittin' here playin' cards, and he—"

The father suddenly spoke to the Easterner. "Mr Blanc," he asked, "what has these boys been doin'?"

The Easterner reflected again. "I didn't see anything wrong at all," he said at last, slowly.

Scully began to howl. "But what does it mane?" He stared ferociously at his son. "I have a mind to lather you for this, me boy."

Johnnie was frantic. "Well, what have I done?" he bawled at his father.

III

"I think you are tongue-tied," said Scully finally to his son, the cowboy, and the Easterner; and at the end of this scornful sentence he left the room.

Upstairs the Swede was swiftly fastening the straps of his great valise. Once his back happened to be half turned toward the door, and, hearing a noise there, he wheeled and sprang up, uttering a loud cry. Scully's wrinkled visage showed grimly in the light of the small lamp he carried. This yellow effulgence, streaming upward, coloured only his prominent features, and left his eyes, for instance, in mysterious shadow. He resembled a murderer.

"Man! man!" he exclaimed, "have you gone daffy?"

"Oh, no! Oh, no!" rejoined the other. "There are people in this world who know pretty nearly as much as you do—understand?"

For a moment they stood gazing at each other. Upon the Swede's deathly pale cheeks were two spots brightly crimson and sharply edged, as if they had been carefully painted.

Scully placed the light on the table and sat himself on the edge of the bed. He spoke ruminatively. "By cracky, I never heard of such a thing in my life. It's a complete muddle. I can't, for the soul of me, think how you ever got this idea into your head." Presently he lifted his eyes and asked: "And did you sure think they were going to kill you?"

The Swede scanned the old man as if he wished to see into his mind. "I did," he said at last. He obviously suspected that this answer might precipitate an outbreak. As he pulled on a strap his whole arm shook, the elbow wavering like a bit of paper.

Scully banged his hand impressively on the footboard of the bed. "Why, man, we're goin' to have a line of ilictric street-cars in this town next spring."

"'A line of electric street-cars,'" repeated the Swede, stupidly.

"And," said Scully, "there's a new railroad goin' to be built down from Broken Arm to here. Not to mintion the four churches and the smashin' big brick school-house. Then there's the big factory, too. Why, in two years Romper'll be a met-tro-*pol*-is."

Having finished the preparation of his baggage, the Swede straightened himself. "Mr Scully," he said, with sudden hardihood, "how much do I owe you?"

"You don't owe me anythin'," said the old man, angrily.

"Yes, I do," retorted the Swede. He took seventy-five cents from his pocket and tendered it to Scully; but the latter snapped his fingers in disdainful refusal. However, it happened that they both stood gazing in a strange fashion at three silver pieces on the Swede's open palm.

"I'll not take your money," said Scully at last. "Not after what's been goin' on here." Then a plan seemed to strike him. "Here," he cried, picking up his lamp and moving toward the door. "Here! Come with me a minute."

"No," said the Swede, in overwhelming alarm.

"Yes," urged the old man. "Come on! I want you to come and see a picter—just across the hall—in my room."

The Swede must have concluded that his hour was come. His jaw dropped and his teeth showed like a dead man's. He ultimately followed Scully across the corridor, but he had the step of one hung in chains.

Scully flashed the light high on the wall of his own chamber. There was revealed a ridiculous photograph of a little girl. She was leaning against a balustrade of gorgeous decoration, and the formidable bang to her hair was prominent. The figure was as graceful as an upright sled-stake, and, withal, it was of the hue of lead. "There," said Scully, tenderly, "that's the picter of my little girl that died. Her name was Carrie. She had the purtiest hair you ever saw! I was that fond of her, she—"

Turning then, he saw that the Swede was not contemplating the picture at all, but, instead, was keeping keen watch on the gloom in the rear.

"Look, man!" cried Scully, heartily. "That's the picter of my little gal that died. Her name was Carrie. And then here's the picter of my oldest boy, Michael. He's a lawyer in Lincoln, an' doin' well. I gave that boy a grand eddication, and I'm glad for it now. He's a fine boy. Look at 'im now. Ain't he bold as blazes, him there in Lincoln, an honoured an' respicted gintleman! An honoured and respicted gintleman," concluded Scully with a flourish. And, so saying, he smote the Swede jovially on the back.

The Swede faintly smiled.

"Now," said the old man, "there's only one more thing." He dropped suddenly to the floor and thrust his head beneath the bed. The Swede could hear his muffled voice. "I'd keep it under me piller if it wasn't for that boy Johnnie. Then there's the old woman—Where is it now? I never put it twice in the same place. Ah, now come out with you!"

Presently he backed clumsily from under the bed, dragging with him an old coat rolled into a bundle. "I've fetched him," he muttered. Kneeling on the floor, he unrolled the coat and extracted from its heart a large yellow-brown whisky-bottle.

His first manœuvre was to hold the bottle up to the light. Reassured, apparently, that nobody had been tampering with it, he thrust it with a generous movement toward the Swede.

The weak-kneed Swede was about to eagerly clutch this element of strength, but he suddenly jerked his hand away and cast a look of horror upon Scully.

"Drink," said the old man affectionately. He had risen to his feet, and now stood facing the Swede.

There was a silence. Then again Scully said: "Drink!"

The Swede laughed wildly. He grabbed the bottle, put it to his mouth; and as his lips curled absurdly around the opening and his throat worked, he kept his glance, burning with hatred, upon the old man's face.

IV

After the departure of Scully the three men, with the card-board still upon their knees, preserved for a long time an astounded silence. Then Johnnie said: "That's the doddangedest Swede I ever see."

"He ain't no Swede," said the cowboy, scornfully.

"Well, what is he then?" cried Johnnie. "What is he then?"

"It's my opinion," replied the cowboy deliberately, "he's some kind of a Dutchman." It was a venerable custom of the country to entitle as Swedes all light-haired men who spoke with a heavy tongue. In consequence the idea of the cowboy was not without its daring. "Yes, sir," he repeated. "It's my opinion this feller is some kind of a Dutchman."

"Well, he says he's a Swede, anyhow," muttered Johnnie, sulkily. He turned to the Easterner: "What do you think, Mr Blanc?"

"Oh, I don't know," replied the Easterner.

"Well, what do you think makes him act that way?" asked the cowboy.

"Why, he's frightened." The Easterner knocked his pipe against a rim of the stove. "He's clear frightened out of his boots."

"What at?" cried Johnnie and the cowboy together.

The Easterner reflected over his answer.

"What at?" cried the others again.

"Oh, I don't know, but it seems to me this man has been reading dime novels, and he thinks he's right out in the middle of it—the shootin' and stabbin' and all."

"But," said the cowboy, deeply scandalized, "this ain't Wyoming, ner none of them places. This is Nebrasker."

"Yes," added Johnnie, "an' why don't he wait till he gits *out West*?"

The travelled Easterner laughed. "It isn't different there even—not in these days. But he thinks he's right in the middle of hell."

Johnnie and the cowboy mused long.

"It's awful funny," remarked Johnnie at last.

"Yes," said the cowboy. "This is a queer game. I hope we don't git snowed in, because then we'd have to stand this here man bein' around with us all the time. That wouldn't be no good."

"I wish pop would throw him out," said Johnnie.

Presently they heard a loud stamping on the stairs, accompanied by ringing jokes in the voice of old Scully, and laughter, evidently from the Swede. The men around the stove stared vacantly at each other. "Gosh!" said the cowboy. The door flew open, and old Scully, flushed and anecdotal, came into the room. He was jabbering at the Swede, who followed him, laughing bravely. It was the entry of two roisterers from a banquet hall.

"Come now," said Scully sharply to the three seated men, "move up and give us a chance at the stove." The cowboy and the Easterner obediently sidled their chairs to make room for the newcomers. Johnnie, however, simply arranged himself in a more indolent attitude, and then remained motionless.

"Come! Git over, there," said Scully.

"Plenty of room on the other side of the stove," said Johnnie.

"Do you think we want to sit in the draught?" roared the father.

But the Swede here interposed with a grandeur of confidence. "No, no. Let the boy sit where he likes," he cried in a bullying voice to the father.

"All right! All right!" said Scully, deferentially. The cowboy and the Easterner exchanged glances of wonder.

The five chairs were formed in a crescent about one side of the stove. The Swede began to talk; he talked arrogantly, profanely, angrily. Johnnie, the cowboy, and the Easterner maintained a morose silence, while old Scully appeared to be receptive and eager, breaking in constantly with sympathetic ejaculations.

Finally the Swede announced that he was thirsty. He moved in his chair, and said that he would go for a drink of water.

"I'll git it for you," cried Scully at once.

"No," said the Swede, contemptuously. "I'll get it for myself." He arose and stalked with the air of an owner off into the executive parts of the hotel.

As soon as the Swede was out of hearing Scully sprang to his feet and whispered intensely to the others: "Upstairs he thought I was tryin' to poison 'im."

"Say," said Johnnie, "this makes me sick. Why don't you throw 'im out in the snow?"

"Why, he's all right now," declared Scully. "It was only that he was from the East, and he thought this was a tough place. That's all. He's all right now."

The cowboy looked with admiration upon the Easterner. "You were straight," he said. "You were on to that there Dutchman."

"Well," said Johnnie to his father, "he may be all right now, but I don't see it. Other time he was scared, but now he's too fresh."

Scully's speech was always a combination of Irish brogue and idiom, Western twang and idiom, and scraps of curiously formal diction taken from the story-books and newspapers. He now hurled a strange mass of language at the head of his son. "What do I keep? What do I keep? What do I keep?" he demanded, in a voice of thunder. He slapped his knee impressively, to indicate that he himself was going to make reply, and that all should heed. "I keep a hotel," he shouted. "A hotel, do you mind? A guest under my roof has sacred privileges. He is to be intimidated by none. Not one word shall he hear that would prijudice him in favour of goin' away. I'll not have it. There's no place in this here town where they can say they iver took in a guest of mine because he was afraid to stay here." He wheeled suddenly upon the cowboy and the Easterner. "Am I right?"

"Yes, Mr Scully," said the cowboy, "I think you're right."

"Yes, Mr Scully," said the Easterner, "I think you're right."

V

At six-o'clock supper, the Swede fizzed like a fire-wheel. He sometimes seemed on the point of bursting into riotous song, and in all his madness he was encouraged by old Scully. The Easterner was encased in reserve; the cowboy sat in wide-mouthed amazement, forgetting to eat, while Johnnie wrathily demolished great plates of food. The daughters of the house, when they were obliged to replenish the biscuits, approached as warily as Indians, and, having succeeded in their purpose, fled with ill-concealed trepidation. The Swede domineered the whole feast, and he gave it the appearance of a cruel bacchanal. He seemed to have grown suddenly taller; he gazed, brutally disdainful, into every face. His voice rang through the room. Once when he jabbed out harpoon-fashion with his fork to pinion a biscuit, the weapon nearly impaled the hand of the Easterner, which had been stretched quietly out for the same biscuit.

After supper, as the men filed toward the other room, the Swede smote Scully ruthlessly on the shoulder. "Well, old boy, that was a good, square meal." Johnnie looked hopefully at his father; he knew that shoulder was tender from an old fall; and, indeed, it appeared for a moment as if Scully was going to flame out over the matter, but in the end he smiled a sickly smile and remained silent. The others understood from his manner that he was admitting his responsibility for the Swede's new view point.

Johnnie, however, addressed his parent in an aside. "Why don't you license somebody to kick you downstairs?" Scully scowled darkly by way of reply.

When they were gathered about the stove, the Swede insisted on another game of High-Five. Scully gently deprecated the plan at first, but the Swede turned a wolfish glare upon him. The old man subsided, and the Swede canvassed the others. In his tone there was always a great threat. The cowboy and the Easterner both remarked indifferently that they would play. Scully said that he would presently have to go to meet the 6.58 train, and so the Swede turned menacingly upon Johnnie. For a moment their glances crossed like blades, and then Johnnie smiled and said, "Yes, I'll play."

They formed a square, with the little board on their knees. The Easterner and the Swede were again partners. As the play went on, it was noticeable that the cowboy was not board-whacking as usual. Meanwhile, Scully, near the lamp, had put on his spectacles and, with an appearance curiously like an old priest, was reading a newspaper. In time he went out to meet the 6.58 train, and, despite his precautions, a gust of polar wind whirled into the room as he opened the door. Besides scattering the cards, it chilled the players to the marrow. The Swede cursed frightfully. When Scully returned, his entrance disturbed a cosy and friendly scene. The Swede again cursed. But presently they were once more intent, their heads bent forward and their hands moving swiftly. The Swede had adopted the fashion of board-whacking.

Scully took up his paper and for a long time remained immersed in matters which were extraordinarily remote from him. The lamp burned badly, and once he stopped to adjust the wick. The newspaper, as he turned from page to page, rustled with a slow and comfortable sound. Then suddenly he heard three terrible words: "You are cheatin'!"

Such scenes often prove that there can be little of dramatic import in environment. Any room can present a tragic front;

any room can be comic. This little den was now hideous as a torture-chamber. The new faces of the men themselves had changed it upon the instant. The Swede held a huge fist in front of Johnnie's face, while the latter looked steadily over it into the blazing orbs of his accuser. The Easterner had grown pallid; the cowboy's jaw had dropped in that expression of bovine amazement which was one of his important mannerisms. After the three words, the first sound in the room was made by Scully's paper as it floated forgotten to his feet. His spectacles had also fallen from his nose, but by a clutch he had saved them in air. His hand, grasping the spectacles, now remained poised awkwardly and near his shoulder. He stared at the card-players.

Probably the silence was while a second elapsed. Then, if the floor had been suddenly twitched out from under the men they could not have moved quicker. The five had projected themselves head-long toward a common point. It happened that Johnnie, in rising to hurl himself upon the Swede, had stumbled slightly because of his curiously instinctive care for the cards and the board. The loss of the moment allowed time for the arrival of Scully, and also allowed the cowboy time to give the Swede a great push which sent him staggering back. The men found tongue together, and hoarse shouts of rage, appeal, or fear burst from every throat. The cowboy pushed and jostled feverishly at the Swede, and the Easterner and Scully clung wildly to Johnnie; but through the smoky air, above the swaying bodies of the peace-compellers, the eyes of the two warriors ever sought each other in glances of challenge that were at once hot and steely.

Of course the board had been overturned, and now the whole company of cards was scattered over the floor, where the boots of the men trampled the fat and painted kings and queens as they gazed with their silly eyes at the war that was waging above them.

Scully's voice was dominating the yells. "Stop now! Stop, I say! Stop, now—"

Johnnie, as he struggled to burst through the rank formed by Scully and the Easterner, was crying, "Well, he says I cheated! He says I cheated! I won't allow no man to say I cheated! If he says I cheated, he's a——!"

The cowboy was telling the Swede, "Quit, now! Quit, d'ye hear—"

The screams of the Swede never ceased: "He did cheat! I saw him! I saw him—"

As for the Easterner, he was importuning in a voice that was not heeded: "Wait a moment, can't you? Oh, wait a moment. What's the good of a fight over a game of cards? Wait a moment—"

In this tumult no complete sentences were clear. "Cheat"—"Quit"—"He says"—these fragments pierced the uproar and rang out sharply. It was remarkable that, whereas Scully undoubtedly made the most noise, he was the least heard of any of the riotous band.

Then suddenly there was a great cessation. It was as if each man had paused for breath; and although the room was still lighted with the anger of men, it could be seen that there was no danger of immediate conflict, and at once Johnnie, shouldering his way forward, almost succeeded in confronting the Swede. "What did you say I cheated for? What did you say I cheated for? I don't cheat, and I won't let no man say I do!"

The Swede said, "I saw you! I saw you!"

"Well," cried Johnnie, "I'll fight any man what says I cheat!"

"No, you won't," said the cowboy. "Not here."

"Ah, be still, can't you?" said Scully, coming between them.

The quiet was sufficient to allow the Easterner's voice to be heard. He was repeating, "Oh, wait a moment, can't you? What's the good of a fight over a game of cards? Wait a moment!"

Johnnie, his red face appearing above his father's shoulder, hailed the Swede again. "Did you say I cheated?"

The Swede showed his teeth. "Yes."

"Then," said Johnnie, "we must fight."

"Yes, fight," roared the Swede. He was like a demoniac. "Yes, fight! I'll show you what kind of a man I am! I'll show you who you want to fight! Maybe you think I can't fight! Maybe you think I can't! I'll show you, you skin, you card-sharp! Yes, you cheated! You cheated! You cheated!"

"Well, let's go at it, then, mister," said Johnnie, coolly.

The cowboy's brow was beaded with sweat from his efforts in intercepting all sorts of raids. He turned in despair to Scully. "What are you goin' to do now?"

A change had come over the Celtic visage of the old man. He now seemed all eagerness; his eyes glowed.

"We'll let them fight," he answered, stalwartly. "I can't put up with it any longer. I've stood this damned Swede till I'm sick. We'll let them fight."

VI

The men prepared to go out of doors. The Easterner was so nervous that he had great difficulty in getting his arms into the sleeves of his new leather coat. As the cowboy drew his fur cap down over his ears his hands trembled. In fact, Johnnie and old Scully were the only ones who displayed no agitation. These preliminaries were conducted without words.

Scully threw open the door. "Well, come on," he said. Instantly a terrific wind caused the flame of the lamp to struggle at its wick, while a puff of black smoke sprang from the chimney-top. The stove was in mid-current of the blast, and its voice swelled to equal the roar of the storm. Some of the scarred and bedabbled cards were caught up from the floor and dashed helplessly against the farther wall. The men lowered their heads and plunged into the tempest as into a sea.

No snow was falling, but great whirls and clouds of flakes, swept up from the ground by the frantic winds, were streaming southward with the speed of bullets. The covered land was blue with the sheen of an unearthly satin, and there was no other hue save where, at the low, black railway station—which seemed incredibly distant—one light gleamed like a tiny jewel. As the men floundered into a thigh-deep drift, it was known that the Swede was bawling out something. Scully went to him, put a hand on his shoulder, and projected an ear. "What's that you say?" he shouted.

"I say," bawled the Swede again, "I won't stand much show against this gang. I know you'll all pitch on me."

Scully smote him reproachfully on the arm. "Tut, man!" he yelled. The wind tore the words from Scully's lips and scattered them far alee.

"You are all a gang of—" boomed the Swede, but the storm also seized the remainder of this sentence.

Immediately turning their backs upon the wind, the men had swung around a corner to the sheltered side of the hotel. It was the function of the little house to preserve here, amid this great devastation of snow, an irregular V-shape of heavily encrusted grass, which crackled beneath the feet. One could imagine the great drifts piled against the windward side. When the party reached the comparative peace of this spot it was found that the Swede was still bellowing.

"Oh, I know what kind of a thing this is! I know you'll all pitch on me. I can't lick you all!"

Scully turned upon him panther-fashion. "You'll not have to whip all of us. You'll have to whip my son Johnnie. An' the man what troubles you durin' that time will have me to dale with."

The arrangements were swiftly made. The two men faced each other, obedient to the harsh commands of Scully, whose face, in the subtly luminous gloom, could be seen set in the austere impersonal lines that are pictured on the countenances of the Roman veterans. The Easterner's teeth were chattering, and he was hopping up and down like a mechanical toy. The cowboy stood rock-like.

The contestants had not stripped off any clothing. Each was in his ordinary attire. Their fists were up, and they eyed each other in a calm that had the elements of leonine cruelty in it.

During this pause, the Easterner's mind, like a film, took lasting impressions of three men—the iron-nerved master of the ceremony; the Swede, pale, motionless, terrible; and

Johnnie, serene yet ferocious, brutish yet heroic. The entire prelude had in it a tragedy greater than the tragedy of action, and this aspect was accentuated by the long, mellow cry of the blizzard, as it sped the tumbling and wailing flakes into the black abyss of the south.

"Now!" said Scully.

The two combatants leaped forward and crashed together like bullocks. There was heard the cushioned sound of blows, and of a curse squeezing out from between the tight teeth of one.

As for the spectators, the Easterner's pent-up breath exploded from him with a pop of relief, absolute relief from the tension of the preliminaries. The cowboy bounded into the air with a yowl. Scully was immovable as from supreme amazement and fear at the fury of the fight which he himself had permitted and arranged.

For a time the encounter in the darkness was such a perplexity of flying arms that it presented no more detail than would a swiftly revolving wheel. Occasionally a face, as if illumined by a flash of light, would shine out, ghastly and marked with pink spots. A moment later, the men might have been known as shadows, if it were not for the involuntary utterance of oaths that came from them in whispers.

Suddenly a holocaust of warlike desire caught the cowboy, and he bolted forward with the speed of a broncho. "Go it, Johnnie! go it! Kill him! Kill him!"

Scully confronted him. "Kape back," he said; and by his glance the cowboy could tell that this man was Johnnie's father.

To the Easterner there was a monotony of unchangeable fighting that was an abomination. This confused mingling was eternal to his sense, which was concentrated in a longing for the end, the priceless end. Once the fighters lurched near him, and as he scrambled hastily backward he heard them breathe like men on the rack.

"Kill him, Johnnie! Kill him! Kill him! Kill him!" The cowboy's face was contorted like one of those agony masks in museums.

"Keep still," said Scully, icily.

Then there was a sudden loud grunt, incomplete, cut short, and Johnnie's body swung away from the Swede and fell with sickening heaviness to the grass. The cowboy was barely in time to prevent the mad Swede from flinging himself upon his prone adversary. "No, you don't," said the cowboy, interposing an arm. "Wait a second."

Scully was at his son's side. "Johnnie! Johnnie, me boy!" His voice had a quality of melancholy tenderness. "Johnnie! Can you go on with it?" He looked anxiously down into the bloody, pulpy face of his son.

There was a moment of silence, and then Johnnie answered in his ordinary voice, "Yes, I—it—yes."

Assisted by his father he struggled to his feet. "Wait a bit now till you git your wind," said the old man.

A few paces away the cowboy was lecturing the Swede. "No, you don't! Wait a second!"

The Easterner was plucking at Scully's sleeve. "Oh, this is enough," he pleaded. "This is enough! Let it go as it stands. This is enough!"

"Bill," said Scully, "git out of the road." The cowboy stepped aside. "Now." The combatants were actuated by a new caution as they advanced toward collision. They glared at each other, and then the Swede aimed a lightning blow that carried with it his entire weight. Johnnie was evidently half-stupid from weakness, but he miraculously dodged, and his fist sent the overbalanced Swede sprawling.

The cowboy, Scully, and the Easterner burst into a cheer that was like a chorus of triumphant soldiery, but before its conclusion the Swede had scuffled agilely to his feet and come in berserk abandon at his foe. There was another perplexity of flying arms, and Johnnie's body again swung away and fell, even as a bundle might fall from a roof. The Swede instantly staggered to a little wind-waved tree and leaned upon it, breathing like an engine, while his savage and flame-lit eyes roamed from face to face as the men bent over Johnnie. There was a splendour of isolation in his situation at this time which the Easterner felt once when, lifting his eyes from the man on the ground, he beheld that mysterious and lonely figure, waiting.

"Are you any good yet, Johnnie?" asked Scully in a broken voice.

The son gasped and opened his eyes languidly. After a moment he answered, "No—I ain't—any good—any—more." Then, from shame and bodily ill, he began to weep, the tears furrowing down through the blood-stains on his face. "He was too—too—too heavy for me."

Scully straightened and addressed the waiting figure. "Stranger," he said, evenly, "it's all up with our side." Then his voice changed into that vibrant huskiness which is commonly the tone of the most simple and deadly announcements. "Johnnie is whipped."

Without replying, the victor moved off on the route to the front door of the hotel.

The cowboy was formulating new and unspellable blasphemies. The Easterner was startled to find that they were out in a wind that seemed to come direct from the shadowed arctic floes. He heard again the wail of the snow as it was flung to its grave in the south. He knew now that all this time the cold had been sinking into him deeper and deeper, and he wondered that he had not perished. He felt indifferent to the condition of the vanquished man.

"Johnnie, can you walk?" asked Scully.

"Did I hurt—hurt him any?" asked the son.

"Can you walk, boy? Can you walk?"

Johnnie's voice was suddenly strong. There was a robust impatience in it. "I asked you whether I hurt him any!"

"Yes, yes, Johnnie," answered the cowboy, consolingly; "he's hurt a good deal."

They raised him from the ground, and as soon as he was on his feet he went tottering off, rebuffing all attempts at assistance. When the party rounded the corner they were fairly blinded by the pelting of the snow. It burned their faces like fire. The cowboy carried Johnnie through the drift to the door. As they entered, some cards again rose from the floor and beat against the wall.

The Easterner rushed to the stove. He was so profoundly chilled that he almost dared to embrace the glowing iron. The Swede was not in the room. Johnnie sank into a chair and, folding his arms on his knees, buried his face in them. Scully, warming one foot and then the other at a rim of the stove, muttered to himself with Celtic mournfulness. The cowboy had removed his fur cap, and with a dazed and rueful air he was running one hand through his tousled locks. From overhead they could hear the creaking of boards, as the Swede tramped here and there in his room.

The sad quiet was broken by the sudden flinging open of a door that led toward the kitchen. It was instantly followed by an inrush of women. They precipitated themselves upon Johnnie amid a chorus of lamentation. Before they carried their prey off to the kitchen, there to be bathed and harangued with that mixture of sympathy and abuse which is a feat of their sex, the mother straightened herself and fixed old Scully with an eye of stern reproach. "Shame be upon you, Patrick Scully!" she cried. "Your own son, too. Shame be upon you!"

"There, now! Be quiet, now!" said the old man, weakly.

"Shame be upon you, Patrick Scully!" The girls, rallying to this slogan, sniffed disdainfully in the direction of those trembling accomplices, the cowboy and the Easterner. Presently they bore Johnnie away, and left the three men to dismal reflection.

VII

"I'd like to fight this here Dutchman myself," said the cowboy, breaking a long silence.

Scully wagged his head sadly. "No, that wouldn't do. It wouldn't be right. It wouldn't be right."

"Well, why wouldn't it?" argued the cowboy. "I don't see no harm in it."

"No," answered Scully, with mournful heroism. "It wouldn't be right. It was Johnnie's fight, and now we mustn't whip the man just because he whipped Johnnie."

"Yes, that's true enough," said the cowboy; "but—he better not get fresh with me, because I couldn't stand no more of it."

"You'll not say a word to him," commanded Scully, and even then they heard the tread of the Swede on the stairs. His entrance was made theatric. He swept the door back with a bang and swaggered to the middle of the room. No one looked at him. "Well," he cried, insolently, at Scully, "I s'pose you'll tell me now how much I owe you?"

The old man remained stolid. "You don't owe me nothin'."

"Huh!" said the Swede, "huh! Don't owe 'im nothin'."

The cowboy addressed the Swede. "Stranger, I don't see how you come to be so gay around here."

Old Scully was instantly alert. "Stop!" he shouted, holding his hand forth, fingers upward. "Bill, you shut up!"

The cowboy spat carelessly into the sawdust-box. "I didn't say a word, did I?" he asked.

"Mr Scully," called the Swede, "how much do I owe you?" It was seen that he was attired for departure, and that he had his valise in his hand.

"You don't owe me nothin'," repeated Scully in the same imperturbable way.

"Huh!" said the Swede. "I guess you're right. I guess if it was any way at all, you'd owe me somethin'. That's what I guess." He turned to the cowboy. "'Kill him! Kill him! Kill him!'" he mimicked, and then guffawed victoriously. "'Kill him!'" He was convulsed with ironical humour.

But he might have been jeering the dead. The three men were immovable and silent, staring with glassy eyes at the stove.

The Swede opened the door and passed into the storm, giving one derisive glance backward at the still group.

As soon as the door was closed, Scully and the cowboy leaped to their feet and began to curse. They trampled to and fro, waving their arms and smashing into the air with their fists. "Oh, but that was a hard minute!" wailed Scully. "That was a hard minute! Him there leerin' and scoffin'!

One bang at his nose was worth forty dollars to me that minute! How did you stand it, Bill?"

"How did I stand it?" cried the cowboy in a quivering voice. "How did I stand it? Ch!"

The old man burst into sudden brogue. "I'd loike to take that Swade," he wailed, "and hould 'im down on a shtone flure and bate 'im to a jelly wid a shtick!"

The cowboy groaned in sympathy. "I'd like to git him by the neck and ha-ammer him"—he brought his hand down on a chair with a noise like a pistol-shot—"hammer that there Dutchman until he couldn't tell himself from a dead coyote!"

"I'd bate 'im until he—"

"I'd show *him* some things—"

And then together they raised a yearning, fanatic cry—"Oh-o-oh! if we only could—"

"Yes!"

"Yes!"

"And then I'd—"

"O-o-oh!"

VIII

The Swede, tightly gripping his valise, tacked across the face of the storm as if he carried sails. He was following a line of little naked, grasping trees which, he knew, must mark the way of the road. His face, fresh from the pounding of Johnnie's fists, felt more pleasure than pain in the wind and the driving snow. A number of square shapes loomed upon him finally, and he knew them as the houses of the main body of the town. He found a street and made travel along it, leaning heavily upon the wind whenever, at a corner, a terrific blast caught him.

He might have been in a deserted village. We picture the world as thick with conquering and elate humanity, but here, with the bugles of the tempest pealing, it was hard to imagine a peopled earth. One viewed the existence of man then as a marvel, and conceded a glamour of wonder to these lice which were caused to cling to a whirling, fire-smitten, ice-locked, disease-stricken, space-lost bulb. The conceit of man was explained by this storm to be the very engine of life. One was a coxcomb not to die in it. However, the Swede found a saloon.

In front of it an indomitable red light was burning, and the snowflakes were made blood-colour as they flew through the circumscribed territory of the lamp's shining. The Swede pushed open the door of the saloon and entered. A sanded expanse was before him, and at the end of it four men sat about a table drinking. Down one side of the room extended a radiant bar, and its guardian was leaning upon his elbows listening to the talk of the men at the table. The Swede dropped his valise upon the floor, and smiling fraternally upon the barkeeper, said, "Gimme some whisky, will you?" The man placed a bottle, a whisky-glass, and a glass of ice-thick water upon the bar. The Swede poured himself an abnormal portion of whisky and drank it in three gulps. "Pretty bad night," remarked the bartender, indifferently. He was making the pretension of blindness which is usually a distinction of his class; but it could have been seen that he was furtively studying the half-erased blood-stains on the face of the Swede. "Bad night," he said again.

"Oh, it's good enough for me," replied the Swede, hardily, as he poured himself some more whisky. The barkeeper took his coin and manœuvred it through its reception by the highly nickelled cash-machine. A bell rang; a card labelled "20 cts." had appeared.

"No," continued the Swede, "this isn't too bad weather. It's good enough for me."

"So?" murmured the barkeeper languidly.

The copious drams made the Swede's eyes swim, and he breathed a trifle heavier. "Yes, I like this weather. I like it. It suits me." It was apparently his design to impart a deep significance to these words.

"So?" murmured the bartender again. He turned to gaze dreamily at the scroll-like birds and bird-like scrolls which had been drawn with soap upon the mirrors in back of the bar.

"Well, I guess I'll take another drink," said the Swede, presently. "Have something?"

"No, thanks; I'm not drinkin'," answered the bartender. Afterward he asked, "How did you hurt your face?"

The Swede immediately began to boast loudly. "Why, in a fight. I thumped the soul out of a man down here at Scully's hotel."

The interest of the four men at the table was at last aroused.

"Who was it?" said one.

"Johnnie Scully," blustered the Swede. "Son of the man what runs it. He will be pretty near dead for some weeks, I can tell you. I made a nice thing of him, I did. He couldn't get up. They carried him in the house. Have a drink?"

Instantly the men in some subtle way encased themselves in reserve. "No, thanks," said one. The group was of curious formation. Two were prominent local business men; one was the district attorney; and one was a professional gambler of the kind known as "square": But a scrutiny of the group would not have enabled an observer to pick the gambler from the men of more reputable pursuits. He was, in fact, a man so delicate in manner, when among people of fair class, and so judicious in his choice of victims, that in the strictly masculine part of the town's life he had come to be explicitly trusted and admired. People called him a thoroughbred. The fear and contempt with which his craft was regarded were undoubtedly the reason why his quiet dignity shone conspicuous above the quiet dignity of men who might be merely hatters, billiard-markers, or grocery clerks. Beyond an occasional unwary traveller who came by rail, this gambler was supposed to prey solely upon reckless and senile farmers, who, when flush with good crops, drove into town in all the pride and confidence of an absolutely invulnerable stupidity. Hearing at times in circuitous fashion of the despoilment of such a farmer, the important men of Romper invariably laughed in contempt of the victim, and if they thought of the wolf at all, it was with a kind of pride at the knowledge that he would never dare think of attacking their wisdom and courage. Besides, it was popular that this gambler had a real wife and two real children in a neat cottage in a suburb, where he led an exemplary home life; and when any one even suggested a discrepancy in his character, the crowd immediately vociferated descriptions of this virtuous family circle. Then men who led exemplary home lives, and men who did not lead exemplary home lives, all subsided in a bunch, remarking that there was nothing more to be said.

However, when a restriction was placed upon him—as, for instance, when a strong clique of members of the new Pollywog Club refused to permit him, even as a spectator, to appear in the rooms of the organization—the candour and gentleness with which he accepted the judgement disarmed many of his foes and made his friends more desperately partisan. He invariably distinguished between himself and a respectable Romper man so quickly and frankly that his manner actually appeared to be a continual broadcast compliment.

And one must not forget to declare the fundamental fact of his entire position in Romper. It is irrefutable that in all affairs outside his business, in all matters that occur eternally and commonly between man and man, this thieving card-player was so generous, so just, so moral, that, in a contest, he could have put to flight the consciences of nine-tenths of the citizens of Romper.

And so it happened that he was seated in this saloon with the two prominent local merchants and the district attorney.

The Swede continued to drink raw whisky, meanwhile babbling at the barkeeper and trying to induce him to indulge in potations. "Come on. Have a drink. Come on. What—no? Well, have a little one, then. By gawd, I've whipped a man tonight, and I want to celebrate. I whipped him good, too. Gentlemen," the Swede cried to the men at the table, "have a drink?"

"Ssh!" said the barkeeper.

The group at the table, although furtively attentive, had been pretending to be deep in talk, but now a man lifted his eyes toward the Swede and said, shortly, "Thanks. We don't want any more."

At this reply the Swede ruffled out his chest like a rooster. "Well," he exploded, "it seems I can't get anybody to drink with me in this town. Seems so, don't it? Well!"

"Ssh!" said the barkeeper.

"Say," snarled the Swede, "don't you try to shut me up. I won't have it. I'm a gentleman, and I want people to drink with me. And I want 'em to drink with me now. *Now*—do you understand?" He rapped the bar with his knuckles.

Years of experience had calloused the bartender. He merely grew sulky. "I hear you," he answered.

"Well," cried the Swede, "listen hard then. See those men over there? Well, they're going to drink with me, and don't you forget it. Now you watch."

"Hi!" yelled the barkeeper, "this won't do!"

"Why won't it?" demanded the Swede. He stalked over to the table, and by chance laid his hand upon the shoulder of the gambler. "How about this?" he asked wrathfully. "I asked you to drink with me."

The gambler simply twisted his head and spoke over his shoulder. "My friend, I don't know you."

"Oh, hell!" answered the Swede, "come and have a drink."

"Now, my boy," advised the gambler, kindly, "take your hand off my shoulder and go 'way and mind your own business." He was a little, slim man, and it seemed strange to hear him use this tone of heroic patronage to the burly Swede. The other men at the table said nothing.

"What! You won't drink with me, you little dude? I'll make you, then! I'll make you!" The Swede had grasped the gambler frenziedly at the throat, and was dragging him from his chair. The other men sprang up. The barkeeper dashed around the corner of his bar. There was a great tumult, and then was seen a long blade in the hand of the gambler. It shot forward, and a human body, this citadel of virtue, wisdom, power, was pierced as easily as if it had been a melon. The Swede fell with a cry of supreme astonishment.

The prominent merchants and the district attorney must have at once tumbled out of the place backward. The bartender found himself hanging limply to the arm of a chair and gazing into the eyes of a murderer.

"Henry," said the latter, as he wiped his knife on one of the towels that hung beneath the bar rail, "you tell 'em where to find me. I'll be home, waiting for 'em." Then he vanished. A moment afterward the barkeeper was in the street dinning through the storm for help and, moreover, companionship.

The corpse of the Swede, alone in the saloon, had its eyes fixed upon a dreadful legend that dwelt atop of the cash-machine: "This registers the amount of your purchase."

IX

Months later, the cowboy was frying pork over the stove of a little ranch near the Dakota line, when there was a quick thud of hoofs outside, and presently the Easterner entered with the letters and the papers.

"Well," said the Easterner at once, "the chap that killed the Swede has got three years. Wasn't much, was it?"

"He has? Three years?" The cowboy poised his pan of pork, while he ruminated upon the news. "Three years. That ain't much."

"No. It was a light sentence," replied the Easterner as he unbuckled his spurs. "Seems there was a good deal of sympathy for him in Romper."

"If the bartender had been any good," observed the cowboy, thoughtfully, "he would have gone in and cracked that there Dutchman on the head with a bottle in the beginnin' of it and stopped all this here murderin'."

"Yes, a thousand things might have happened," said the Easterner, tartly.

The cowboy returned his pan of pork to the fire, but his philosophy continued. "It's funny, ain't it? If he hadn't said Johnnie was cheatin' he'd be alive this minute. He was an awful fool. Game played for fun, too. Not for money. I believe he was crazy."

"I feel sorry for that gambler," said the Easterner.

"Oh, so do I," said the cowboy. "He don't deserve none of it for killin' who he did."

"The Swede might not have been killed if everything had been square."

"Might not have been killed?" exclaimed the cowboy. "Everythin' square? Why, when he said that Johnnie was cheatin' and acted like such a jackass? And then in the saloon he fairly walked up to git hurt?" With these arguments the cowboy browbeat the Easterner and reduced him to rage.

"You're a fool!" cried the Easterner, viciously. "You're a bigger jackass than the Swede by a million majority. Now let me tell you one thing. Let me tell you something. Listen! Johnnie *was* cheating!"

"'Johnnie,'" said the cowboy, blankly. There was a minute of silence, and then he said, robustly, "Why, no. The game was only for fun."

"Fun or not," said the Easterner, "Johnnie was cheating. I saw him. I know it. I saw him. And I refused to stand up and be a man. I let the Swede fight it out alone. And you—you were simply puffing around the place and wanting to fight. And then old Scully himself! We are all in it! This poor gambler isn't even a noun. He is a kind of an adverb. Every sin is the result of a collaboration. We, five of us, have collaborated in the murder of this Swede. Usually there are from a dozen to forty women really involved in every murder, but in this case it seems to be only five men—you, I, Johnnie, old Scully; and that fool of an unfortunate gambler came merely as a culmination, the apex of a human movement, and gets all the punishment."

The cowboy, injured and rebellious, cried out blindly into this fog of mysterious theory: "Well, I didn't do anythin', did I?"

WILLA CATHER
On the Divide

Willa Cather (1873–1947) was born in Virginia, but moved to Nebraska with her family when she was six. Her talent for writing showed itself while she was a student at Nebraska University, and after graduating she moved to New York (via Pittsburgh) to work as a journalist, eventually editing *McClure's* magazine. Her first novel, *Alexander's Bridge*, was published in 1912, but her career as a writer of fiction really began when she started writing stories about the Nebraska of her childhood and the European immigrants who scratched a living on its prairie landscape. Among the results were her great novels *O Pioneers!* (1913), *My Antonia* (1918), *The Lost Lady* (1925), and the short stories collected in *Obscure Destinies* (1932).

'On the Divide' is from *Overland Monthly*, 1896, and portrays the lives of its pioneer subjects with a vividness and compassion typical of Cather's Western fiction.

NEAR RATTLESNAKE CREEK, on the side of a little draw, stood Canute's shanty. North, east, south, stretched the level Nebraska plain of long rust-red grass that undulated constantly in the wind. To the west the ground was broken and rough, and a narrow strip of timber wound along the turbid, muddy little stream that had scarcely ambition enough to crawl over its black bottom. If it had not been for the few stunted cottonwoods and elms that grew along its banks, Canute would have shot himself years ago. The Norwegians are a timber-loving people, and if there is even a turtle pond with a few plum bushes around it they seem irresistibly drawn toward it.

As to the shanty itself, Canute had built it without aid of any kind, for when he first squatted along the banks of Rattlesnake Creek there was not a human being within twenty miles. It was built of logs split in halves, the chinks stopped with mud and plaster. The roof was covered with earth and was supported by one gigantic beam curved in the shape of a round arch. It was almost impossible that any tree had ever grown in that shape. The Norwegians used to say that Canute had taken the log across his knee and bent it into the shape he wished. There were two rooms, or rather there was one room with a partition made of ash saplings inter-woven and bound together like big straw basket work. In one corner there was a cook stove, rusted and broken. In the other a bed made of unplaned planks and poles. It was fully eight feet long, and upon it was a heap of dark bed clothing. There was a chair and a bench of colossal proportions. There was an ordinary kitchen cupboard with a few cracked dirty dishes in it, and beside it on a tall box a tin washbasin. Under the bed was a pile of pint flasks, some broken, some whole, all empty. On the wood box lay a pair of shoes of almost incredible dimensions. On the wall hung a saddle, a gun, and some ragged clothing, conspicuous among which was a suit of dark cloth, apparently new, with a paper collar carefully wrapped in a red silk handkerchief and pinned to the sleeve. Over the door hung a wolf and a badger skin, and on the door itself a brace of thirty or forty snake skins whose noisy tails rattled ominously every time it opened. The strangest things in the shanty were the wide window sills. At first glance they looked as though they had been ruthlessly hacked and mutilated with a hatchet, but on closer inspection all the notches and holes in the wood took form and shape. There seemed to be a series of pictures. They were, in a rough way, artistic, but the figures were heavy and labored, as though they had been cut very slowly and with very awkward instruments. There were men plowing with little horned imps sitting on their shoulders and on their horses' heads. There were men praying with a skull hanging over their heads and little demons behind them mocking their attitudes. There were men fighting with big serpents, and skeletons dancing together. All about these pictures were blooming vines and foliage such as never grew in this world, and coiled among the branches of the vines there was always the scaly body of a serpent, and behind every flower there was a serpent's head. It was a veritable Dance of Death by one who had felt its sting. In the wood box lay some boards, and every inch of them was cut up in the same manner. Sometimes the work was very rude and careless, and looked as though the hand of the workman had trembled. It would sometimes have been hard to distinguish the men from their evil geniuses but for one fact, the men were always grave and were either toiling or praying, while the devils were always smiling and dancing. Several of these boards had been split for kindling and it was evident that the artist did not value his work highly.

It was the first day of winter on the Divide. Canute stumbled into his shanty carrying a basket of cobs, and after filling the stove, sat down on a stool and crouched his seven foot frame over the fire, staring drearily out of the window at the wide gray sky. He knew by heart every individual clump of bunch grass in the miles of red shaggy prairie that stretched before his cabin. He knew it in all the deceitful loveliness of its early summer, in all the bitter barrenness of its autumn. He had seen it smitten by all the plagues of Egypt. He had seen it parched by drought, and sogged by rain, beaten by hail, and swept by fire, and in the grasshopper years he had seen it eaten as bare and clean as bones that the vultures have left. After the great fires he had seen it stretch for miles and miles, black and smoking as the floor of hell.

He rose slowly and crossed the room, dragging his big feet heavily as though they were burdens to him. He looked out of the window into the hog corral and saw the pigs burying themselves in the straw before the shed. The leaden gray clouds were beginning to spill themselves, and the snow-flakes were settling down over the white leprous patches of frozen earth where the hogs had gnawed even the sod away. He shuddered and began to walk, trampling heavily with his ungainly feet. He was the wreck of ten winters on the Divide and he knew what they meant. Men fear the winters of the Divide as a child fears night or as men in the North Seas fear the still dark cold of the polar twilight.

His eyes fell upon his gun, and he took it down from the wall and looked it over. He sat down on the edge of his bed and held the barrel towards his face, letting his forehead rest upon it, and laid his finger on the trigger. He was perfectly calm, there was neither passion nor despair in his face, but the thoughtful look of a man who is considering. Presently he laid down the gun, and reaching into the cupboard, drew out a pint bottle of raw white alcohol. Lifting it to his lips, he drank greedily. He washed his face in the tin basin and combed his rough hair and shaggy blond beard. Then he stood in uncertainty before the suit of dark clothes that hung on the wall. For the fiftieth time he took them in his hands and tried to summon courage to put them on. He took the paper collar that was pinned to the sleeve of the coat and cautiously slipped it under his rough beard, looking with timid expectancy into the cracked, splashed glass that hung over the bench. With a short laugh he threw it down on the bed, and pulling on his old black hat, he went out, striking off across the level.

It was a physical necessity for him to get away from his cabin once in a while. He had been there for ten years, digging and plowing and sowing, and reaping what little the hail and the hot winds and the frosts left him to reap. Insanity and suicide are very common things on the Divide.

They come on like an epidemic in the hot wind season. Those scorching dusty winds that blow up over the bluffs from Kansas seem to dry up the blood in men's veins as they do the sap in the corn leaves. Whenever the yellow scorch creeps down over the tender inside leaves about the ear, then the coroners prepare for active duty; for the oil of the country is burned out and it does not take long for the flame to eat up the wick. It causes no great sensation there when a Dane is found swinging to his own windmill tower, and most of the Poles after they have become too careless and discouraged to shave themselves keep their razors to cut their throats with.

It may be that the next generation on the Divide will be very happy, but the present one came too late in life. It is useless for men that have cut hemlocks among the mountains of Sweden for forty years to try to be happy in a country as flat and gray and as naked as the sea. It is not easy for men that have spent their youths fishing in the Northern seas to be content with following a plow, and men that have served in the Austrian army hate hard work and coarse clothing and the loneliness of the plains, and long for marches and excitement and tavern company and pretty barmaids. After a man has passed his fortieth birthday it is not easy for him to change the habits and conditions of his life. Most men bring with them to the Divide only the dregs of the lives that they have squandered in other lands and among other peoples.

Canute Canuteson was as mad as any of them, but his madness did not take the form of suicide or religion but of alcohol. He had always taken liquor when he wanted it, as all Norwegians do, but after his first year of solitary life he settled down to it steadily. He exhausted whisky after a while, and went to alcohol, because its effects were speedier and surer. He was a big man with a terrible amount of resistant force, and it took a great deal of alcohol even to move him. After nine years of drinking, the quantities he could take would seem fabulous to an ordinary drinking man. He never let it interfere with his work, he generally drank at night and on Sundays. Every night, as soon as his chores were done, he began to drink. While he was able to sit up he would play on his mouth harp or hack away at his window sills with his jackknife. When the liquor went to his head he would lie down on his bed and stare out of the window until he went to sleep. He drank alone and in solitude not for pleasure or good cheer, but to forget the awful loneliness and level of the Divide. Milton made a sad blunder when he put mountains in hell. Mountains postulate faith and aspiration. All mountain peoples are religious. It was the cities of the plains that, because of their utter lack of spirituality and the mad caprice of their vice, were cursed of God.

Alcohol is perfectly consistent in its effects upon man. Drunkenness is merely an exaggeration. A foolish man drunk becomes maudlin; a bloody man, vicious; a coarse man, vulgar. Canute was none of these, but he was morose and gloomy, and liquor took him through all the hells of Dante. As he lay on his giant's bed all the horrors of this world and every other were laid bare to his chilled senses. He was a man who knew no joy, a man who toiled in silence and bitterness. The skull and the serpent were always before him, the symbols of eternal futileness and of eternal hate.

When the first Norwegians near enough to be called neighbors came, Canute rejoiced, and planned to escape from his bosom vice. But he was not a social man by nature and had not the power of drawing out the social side of other people. His new neighbors rather feared him because of his great strength and size, his silence and his lowering brows. Perhaps, too, they knew that he was mad, mad from the eternal treachery of the plains, which every spring stretch green and rustle with the promises of Eden, showing long grassy lagoons full of clear water and cattle whose hoofs are stained with wild roses. Before autumn the lagoons are dried up, and the ground is burnt dry and hard until it blisters and cracks open.

So instead of becoming a friend and neighbor to the men that settled about him, Canute became a mystery and a terror. They told awful stories of his size and strength and of the alcohol he drank. They said that one night, when he went out to see to his horses just before he went to bed, his steps were unsteady and the rotten planks of the floor gave way and threw him behind the feet of a fiery young stallion. His foot was caught fast in the floor, and the nervous horse began kicking frantically. When Canute felt the blood trickling down into his eyes from a scalp wound in his head, he roused himself from his kingly indifference, and with the quiet stoical courage of a drunken man leaned forward and wound his arms about the horse's hind legs and held them against his breast with crushing embrace. All through the darkness and cold of the night he lay there, matching strength against strength. When little Jim Peterson went over the next morning at four o'clock to go with him to the Blue to cut wood, he found him so, and the horse was on its foreknees, trembling and whinnying with fear. This is the story the Norwegians tell of him, and if it is true it is no wonder that they feared and hated this Holder of the Heels of Horses.

One spring there moved to the next "eighty" a family that made a great change in Canute's life. Ole Yensen was too drunk most of the time to be afraid of any one, and his wife Mary was too garrulous to be afraid of any one who listened to her talk, and Lena, their pretty daughter, was not afraid of man nor devil. So it came about that Canute went over to take his alcohol with Ole oftener than he took it alone. After a while the report spread that he was going to marry Yensen's daughter, and the Norwegian girls began to tease Lena about the great bear she was going to keep house for. No one could quite see how the affair had come about, for Canute's tactics of courtship were somewhat peculiar. He apparently never spoke to her at all: he would sit for hours with Mary chattering on one side of him and Ole drinking on the other and watch Lena at her work. She teased him, and threw flour in his face and put vinegar in his coffee, but he took her rough jokes with silent wonder, never even smiling. He took her to church occasionally, but the most watchful and curious people never saw him speak to her. He would sit staring at her while she giggled and flirted with the other men.

Next spring Mary Lee went to town to work in a steam laundry. She came home every Sunday, and always ran across to Yensens to startle Lena with stories of ten cent theatres, firemen's dances, and all the other esthetic delights of metropolitan life. In a few weeks Lena's head was completely turned, and she gave her father no rest until he let her go to town to seek her fortune at the ironing board. From the time she came home on her first visit she began to treat Canute with contempt. She had bought a plush cloak and kid gloves, had her clothes made by the dressmaker, and assumed airs and graces that made the other women of the neighborhood cordially detest her. She generally brought with her a young man from town who waxed his mustache and wore a red necktie, and she did not even introduce him to Canute.

The neighbors teased Canute a good deal until he knocked one of them down. He gave no sign of suffering from her neglect except that he drank more and avoided the other Norwegians more carefully than ever. He lay around in his den and no one knew what he felt or thought, but little Jim Peterson, who had seen him glowering at Lena in church one Sunday when she was there with the town man, said that he would not give an acre of his wheat for Lena's life or the town chap's either; and Jim's wheat was so wondrously worthless that the statement was an exceedingly strong one.

Canute had bought a new suit of clothes that looked as nearly like the town man's as possible. They had cost him half a millet crop; for tailors are not accustomed to fitting giants and they charge for it. He had hung those clothes in his shanty two months ago and had never put them on, partly from fear of ridicule, partly from discouragement, and partly because there was something in his own soul that revolted at the littleness of the device.

Lena was at home just at this time. Work was slack in the laundry and Mary had not been well, so Lena stayed at home, glad enough to get an opportunity to torment Canute once more.

She was washing in the side kitchen, singing loudly as she worked. Mary was on her knees, blacking the stove and scolding violently about the young man who was coming out from town that night. The young man had committed the fatal error of laughing at Mary's ceaseless babble and had never been forgiven.

"He is no good, and you will come to a bad end by running with him! I do not see why a daughter of mine should act so. I do not see why the Lord should visit such a punishment upon me as to give me such a daughter. There are plenty of good men you can marry."

Lena tossed her head and answered curtly, "I don't happen to want to marry any man right away, and so long as Dick dresses nice and has plenty of money to spend, there is no harm in my going with him."

"Money to spend? Yes, and that is all he does with it, I'll be bound. You think it very fine now, but you will change your tune when you have been married five years and see your children running naked and your cupboard empty. Did Anne Hermanson come to any good end by marrying a town man?"

"I don't know anything about Anne Hermanson, but I know any of the laundry girls would have Dick quick enough if they could get him."

"Yes, and a nice lot of store clothes huzzies you are too. Now there is Canuteson who has an 'eighty' proved up and fifty head of cattle and—"

"And hair that ain't been cut since he was a baby, and a big dirty beard, and he wears overalls on Sundays, and drinks like a pig. Besides he will keep. I can have all the fun I want, and when I am old and ugly like you he can have me and take care of me. The Lord knows there ain't nobody else going to marry him."

Canute drew his hand back from the latch as though it were red hot. He was not the kind of man to make a good eavesdropper, and he wished he had knocked sooner. He pulled himself together and struck the door like a battering ram. Mary jumped and opened it with a screech.

"God! Canute, how you scared us! I thought it was crazy Lou—he has been tearing around the neighborhood trying to convert folks. I am afraid as death of him. He ought to be sent off, I think. He is just as liable as not to kill us all, or burn the barn, or poison the dogs. He has been worrying even the poor minister to death, and he laid up with the rheumatism, too! Did you notice that he was too sick to preach last Sunday? But don't stand there in the cold—come in. Yensen isn't here, but he just went over to Sorenson's for the mail; he won't be gone long. Walk right in the other room and sit down."

Canute followed her, looking steadily in front of him and not noticing Lena as he passed her. But Lena's vanity would not allow him to pass unmolested. She took the wet sheet she was wringing out and cracked him across the face with it, and ran giggling to the other side of the room. The blow stung his cheeks and the soapy water flew in his eyes, and he involuntarily began rubbing them with his hands. Lena giggled with delight at his discomfiture, and the wrath in Canute's face grew blacker than ever. A big man humiliated is vastly more undignified than a little one. He forgot the sting of his face in the bitter consciousness that he had made a fool of himself. He stumbled blindly into the living room, knocking his head against the door jamb because he forgot to stoop. He dropped into a chair behind the stove, thrusting his big feet back helplessly on either side of him.

Ole was a long time in coming, and Canute sat there, still and silent, with his hands clenched on his knees, and the skin of his face seemed to have shriveled up into little wrinkles that trembled when he lowered his brows. His life had been one long lethargy of solitude and alcohol, but now he was awakening, and it was as when the dumb stagnant heat of summer breaks out into thunder.

When Ole came staggering in, heavy with liquor, Canute rose at once.

"Yensen," he said quietly, "I have come to see if you will let me marry your daughter today."

"Today!" gasped Ole.

"Yes, I will not wait until tomorrow. I am tired of living alone."

Ole braced his staggering knees against the bedstead, and stammered eloquently: "Do you think I will marry my daughter to a drunkard? a man who drinks raw alcohol? a man who sleeps with rattlesnakes? Get out of my house or I will kick you out for your impudence." And Ole began looking anxiously for his feet.

Canute answered not a word, but he put on his hat and went out into the kitchen. He went up to Lena and said without looking at her, "Get your things on and come with me!"

The tone of his voice startled her, and she said angrily, dropping the soap, "Are you drunk?"

"If you do not come with me, I will take you—you had better come," said Canute quietly.

She lifted a sheet to strike him, but he caught her arm roughly and wrenched the sheet from her. He turned to the wall and took down a hood and shawl that hung there, and began wrapping her up. Lena scratched and fought like a wild thing. Ole stood in the door, cursing, and Mary howled and screeched at the top of her voice. As for Canute, he lifted the girl in his arms and went out of the house. She kicked and struggled, but the helpless wailing of Mary and Ole soon died away in the distance, and her face was held down tightly on Canute's shoulder so that she could not see whither he was taking her. She was conscious only of the north wind whistling in her ears, and of rapid steady motion and of a great breast that heaved beneath her in quick, irregular breaths. The harder she struggled the tighter those iron arms that had held the heels of horses crushed about her, until she felt as if they would crush the breath from her, and lay still with fear. Canute was striding across the level fields at a pace at which man never went before, drawing the stinging north wind into his lungs in great gulps. He walked with his eyes half closed and looking straight in front of him, only lowering them when he bent his head to blow away the snow-flakes that settled on her hair. So it was that Canute took her to his home, even as his bearded barbarian ancestors took the fair frivolous women of the South in their hairy arms and bore them down to their war ships. For ever and anon the soul becomes weary of the conventions that are not of it, and with a single stroke shatters the civilized lies with which it is unable to cope, and the strong arm reaches out and takes by force what it cannot win by cunning.

When Canute reached his shanty he placed the girl upon a chair, where she sat sobbing. He stayed only a few minutes. He filled the stove with wood and lit the lamp, drank a huge swallow of alcohol and put the bottle in his pocket. He paused a moment, staring heavily at the weeping girl, then he went off and locked the door and disappeared in the gathering gloom of the night.

Wrapped in flannels and soaked with turpentine, the little Norwegian preacher sat reading his Bible, when he heard a thundering knock at his door, and Canute entered, covered with snow and with his beard frozen fast to his coat.

"Come in, Canute, you must be frozen," said the little man, shoving a chair towards his visitor.

Canute remained standing with his hat on and said quietly, "I want you to come over to my house tonight to marry me to Lena Yensen."

"Have you got a license, Canute?"

"No, I don't want a license. I want to be married."

"But I can't marry you without a license, man. It would not be legal."

A dangerous light came in the big Norwegian's eye. "I want you to come over to my house to marry me to Lena Yensen."

"No, I can't, it would kill an ox to go out in a storm like this, and my rheumatism is bad tonight."

"Then if you will not go I must take you," said Canute with a sigh.

He took down the preacher's bearskin coat and bade him put it on while he hitched up his buggy. He went out and closed the door softly after him. Presently he returned and found the frightened minister crouching before the fire with his coat lying beside him. Canute helped him put it on and gently wrapped his head in his big muffler. Then he picked him up and carried him out and placed him in his buggy. As he tucked the buffalo robes around him he said: "Your horse is old, he might flounder or lose his way in this storm. I will lead him."

The minister took the reins feebly in his hands and sat shivering with the cold. Sometimes when there was a lull in the wind, he could see the horse struggling through the snow with the man plodding steadily beside him. Again the blowing snow would hide them from him altogether. He had no idea where they were or what direction they were going. He felt as though he were being whirled away in the heart of the storm, and he said all the prayers he knew. But at last the long four miles were over, and Canute set him down in the snow while he unlocked the door. He saw the bride sitting by the fire with her eyes red and swollen as though she had been weeping. Canute placed a huge chair for him, and said roughly,

"Warm yourself."

Lena began to cry and moan afresh, begging the minister to take her home. He looked helplessly at Canute. Canute said simply,

"If you are warm now, you can marry us."

"My daughter, do you take this step of your own free will?" asked the minister in a trembling voice.

"No sir, I don't, and it is disgraceful he should force me into it! I won't marry him."

"Then, Canute, I cannot marry you," said the minister, standing as straight as his rheumatic limbs would let him.

"Are you ready to marry us now, sir?" said Canute, laying one iron hand on his stooped shoulder. The little preacher was a good man, but like most men of weak body he was a coward and had a horror of physical suffering, although he had known so much of it. So with many qualms of conscience he began to repeat the marriage service. Lena sat sullenly in her chair, staring at the fire. Canute stood beside her, listening with his head bent reverently and his hands folded on his breast. When the little man had prayed and said amen, Canute began bundling him up again.

"I will take you home, now," he said as he carried him out and placed him in his buggy, and started off with him through the fury of the storm, floundering among the snow drifts that brought even the giant himself to his knees.

After she was left alone, Lena soon ceased weeping. She was not of a particularly sensitive temperament, and had little pride beyond that of vanity. After the first bitter anger wore itself out, she felt nothing more than a healthy sense of humiliation and defeat. She had no inclination to run away, for she was married now, and in her eyes that was final and all rebellion was useless. She knew nothing about a license, but she knew that a preacher married folks. She consoled herself by thinking that she had always intended to marry Canute someday, anyway.

She grew tired of crying and looking into the fire, so she got up and began to look about her. She had heard queer tales about the inside of Canute's shanty, and her curiosity soon got the better of her rage. One of the first things she noticed was the new black suit of clothes hanging on the wall. She was dull, but it did not take a vain woman long to interpret anything so decidedly flattering, and she was pleased in spite of herself. As she looked through the cupboard, the general air of neglect and discomfort made her pity the man who lived there.

"Poor fellow, no wonder he wants to get married to get somebody to wash up his dishes. Batchin's pretty hard on a man."

It is easy to pity when once one's vanity has been tickled. She looked at the window sill and gave a little shudder and wondered if the man were crazy. Then she sat down again and sat a long time wondering what her Dick and Ole would do.

"It is queer Dick didn't come right over after me. He surely came, for he would have left town before the storm began and he might just as well come right on as go back. If he'd hurried he would have gotten here before the preacher came. I suppose he was afraid to come, for he knew Canuteson could pound him to jelly, the coward!" Her eyes flashed angrily.

The weary hours wore on and Lena began to grow horribly lonesome. It was an uncanny night and this was an uncanny place to be in. She could hear the coyotes howling hungrily a little way from the cabin, and more terrible still were all the unknown noises of the storm. She remembered the tales they told of the big log overhead and she was afraid of those snaky things on the window sills. She remembered the man who had been killed in the draw, and she wondered what she would do if she saw crazy Lou's white face glaring into the window. The rattling of the door became unbearable, she thought the latch must be loose and took the lamp to look at it. Then for the first time she saw the ugly brown snake skins whose death rattle sounded every time the wind jarred the door.

"Canute, Canute!" she screamed in terror.

Outside the door she heard a heavy sound as of a big dog getting up and shaking himself. The door opened and Canute stood before her, white as a snow drift.

"What is it?" he asked kindly.

"I am cold," she faltered.

He went out and got an armful of wood and a basket of cobs and filled the stove. Then he went out and lay in the snow before the door. Presently he heard her calling again.

"What is it?" he said, sitting up.

"I'm so lonesome, I'm afraid to stay in here all alone."

"I will go over and get your mother." And he got up.

"She won't come."

"I'll bring her," said Canute grimly.

"No, no. I don't want her, she will scold all the time."

"Well, I will bring your father."

She spoke again and it seemed as though her mouth was close up to the key hole. She spoke lower than he had ever heard her speak before, so low that he had to put his ear up to the lock to hear her.

"I don't want him either, Canute—I'd rather have you."

For a moment she heard no noise at all, then something like a groan. With a cry of fear she opened the door, and saw Canute stretched in the snow at her feet, his face in his hands, sobbing on the door step.

B.M. BOWER
Bad Penny

B. M. Bower (1871–1940) was a leading writer of Westerns during the early part of the century. The initials hid the identity of a woman: Bertha Muzzy Bower. She was born in Minnesota, but later experienced the West firsthand when she moved to Montana. Over the course of her career—she was the first woman to make a living from writing popular Westerns—Bower wrote 72 Western novels, the most famous of which is *Chip, Of the Flying U* (1906). As well as Western stories, Bower wrote the screenplay for several silent Western films, including *King of the Rodeo* (1929). Her own stories were widely adapted by Hollywood in the 1910s and 1920s.

The story 'Bad Penny' (1933) is from *Argosy* and features Chip and the cowboys of the Flying U on a cattle drive. As with much of Bower's Western fiction the picture it presents of the West is a romantic one. The character of Chip is reputedly based on the famous Western painter, Charles Russell, who illustrated several of Bower's books.

THE FLYING U BEEF HERD toiled up the last heart-breaking hill and crawled slowly out upon the bench. Under the low-hanging dust cloud which trailed far out behind, nothing much could be seen of the herd save the big, swaying bodies and the rhythmically swinging heads of the leaders. Stolid as they looked, steadily as they plodded forward under the eagle eye of the point man, the steers were tired. Dust clogged blinking eyelashes, dust was in their nostrils, dust lay deep along their backs. The boys on left flank rode with neckerchiefs pulled up over their noses, yet they were not the most unfortunate riders on the drive, for the fitful gusts of wind lifted the gray cloud occasionally and gave them a few clean breaths.

Back on the drag where the dust was thickest, the man they called Penny choked, gasped, and spat viciously at the hind-most steer. He pulled off a glove and rubbed his aching, blood-shot eyes with bare fingertips, swearing a monotonous litany meanwhile, praying to be delivered from his present miseries and from any and all forms of cowpunching. Let him once live through this damnable day and he promised—nay, swore by all the gods he could name—that he'd chase himself into town and buy himself a barrel of whiskey and a barrel of beer and camp between the two of them until he had washed the dust out of his system.

Shorty, who was wagon boss during beef roundup for Jim Whitmore and had stopped half a mile back to gossip with a rancher out hunting his horses, galloped up in time to hear this last picturesque conception of a heaven on earth.

"Make it two barrels while you're about it," he advised unsympathetically. "You'll get 'em just as easy as you will a bottle." He laughed at his own humor—a thing Penny hated in any man—and rode on up to the point where he could help swing the herd down off the bench to the level creek bottom that was their present objective.

Penny renewed his cussing and his coughing and looked across at Chip Bennett, who was helping to push the tired drag along.

"You hear what that damn son-of-a-gun told me?" he called out. And when Chip nodded with the brief grin that he frequently gave a man instead of words, Penny swung closer. "You know what he done to me, don't yuh? Put me on day herd outa my turn—and don't ever think I don't see why he done it. So's I wouldn't get a chance to ride into town tonight. Gone temperance on me, the damn double-crosser. You heard him make that crack about me not gettin' a bottle uh beer, even? Runnin' a wagon has sure went to Shorty's head!"

"I don't think it's that altogether." Chip tried to soothe him. "You want to remember—"

Penny cut in on the sentence. "Remember what happened last time we shipped, I s'pose. Well, that ain't got nothin' to do with this time. I ain't planning to get owl-eyed this time and raise hell like I done before. I swore off three weeks ago, and Shorty knows it. I ain't had a drop fer three weeks."

Chip wheeled his horse to haze a laggard steer into line, and so hid his grin. Penny's swearing off liquor three weeks ago was a joke with the Flying U outfit. The pledge had followed a spree which no one would soon forget. For Penny had not only shot up the new little cow town of Dry Lake and stood guard in the street afterward watching for someone to show his nose outside—to be scared out of his senses by Penny's reckless shooting and his bloodcurdling war whoops—but he had been hauled to camp in the bed wagon next day, hog-tied to prevent his throwing himself out and maybe breaking his neck.

It was after he had recovered that he swore he never would touch another drop of anything stronger than Patsy's coffee. Those who had known him the longest laughed the loudest at that vow, and Shorty was one of them; though he, being lord of the roundup, had to preserve discipline and do his laughing in secret.

"It sure is tough back here," Chip conceded when the cattle were once more strung out and the two rode alongside again. "Cheer up, Penny. It'll be all the same a hundred years from now." And he added, when he saw signs of another outbreak in the grimed face of Penny, "Anyway, we'll all be in town tomorrow."

"If not before," Penny said darkly. "T'morra don't help me none right now." He whacked a dusty red steer into line with his quirt. "What grinds me is to have Shorty take the stand he does; slappin' me on herd outa my turn, like as if he was scared I might break out agin—Why, blast his lousy hide, I ain't got any idee of goin' in to town before t'morra when we load out. Er, I didn't have," he amended querulously. "Not till he went to work and shoved me on herd, just to keep me outa sight of the damn burg as long as he could." He stood in the saddle to ease the cramp in his legs. "Why, hell! If I wanted to go get me a snootful, it'd take more'n that to stop me!"

Still standing in the stirrups, he gazed longingly ahead over the rippling sea of dusty, marching cattle and swore again because the dust shut out the town from his straining sight. Miles away though it was, from this high benchland it would be clearly visible under normal conditions. The men on point could see the little huddle of black dots alongside the pencil line of railroad, he knew that.

"You know damn well, Chip," he complained, settling down off-center in the saddle so that one foot swung free, "that ain't no way to treat a man that's reformed and swore off drinkin'."

"Well, you don't have to stay back here on the drag eating dust," Chip pointed out. "Why don't you get up front awhile? You can probably see town if you ride point awhile, Penny. And another thing; you don't want to take this day-herding too personal. With Jack sick, somebody had to go on outa turn."

"Sick nothin'!" Penny snorted. "I know when a man's playin' off. Jack shore ain't foolin' me a damn bit. And, anyway, Shorty didn't have to go and pick on me."

Chip gave up the argument and swung back to bring up a straggler. Today they were not grazing the herd along as was their custom. The midsummer dry spell had made many a water hole no more than a wallow of caked mud, and most of the little creeks were bone dry. This was in a sense a forced drive, the day herders pushing the herd twice the usual distance ahead so that they would camp that night on the only creek for miles that had water running in it. That it lay within easy riding distance of town was what worried Penny.

Privately Chip thought Shorty had shown darned good sense in putting Penny on day herd. He'd have to stand guard that night—probably the middle guard, if he were taking Jack Bates's place—and that would keep him out of temptation, at least until after the cattle were loaded, when a little backsliding wouldn't matter so much. Whereas, had he been left to his regular routine, Penny would be lying around camp right now wishing he dared sneak off to town. He would have the short guard at the tail end of the afternoon, and at dusk he would have been relieved from duty until morning. With town so close it was easy to guess what Penny would have done with those night hours.

As it was, Penny would have no idle time save the two or three hours of lying around camp after the herd had been thrown on water. Then he'd have to sleep until he was called for middle guard. In the morning the whole outfit would be called out, and they'd be hard at it till the last steer was prodded into the last car and the door slid shut and locked. Then there would be more than Penny racing down to where they could wash the dust from their throats. No, Jack did get sick right at the exact time when it would keep Penny from getting drunk when he was most needed. A put-up job, most likely. Shorty wasn't so slow after all.

"We'll be down off the bench and on water in another hour," Chip yelled cheeringly when he came within shouting distance of Penny again.

Penny had turned sullen and he made no reply to that. He rode with both hands clasped upon the saddle horn, one foot swinging free of its stirrup, and a cigarette waggling in the corner of his mouth. His hat was pulled low over his smarting eyes, squinted half shut against the smothering dust that made his face as gray as his hat.

Not once during the remainder of the drive did he open his lips except when he coughed and spat out dust or when he swore briefly at a laggard steer. And Chip, being the tactful young man he was, let him alone to nurse his grudge.

He did not sympathize with it, however, for Chip was still filled with a boyish enthusiasm for the picturesque quality of the drive. Even the discomfort of riding on the drag, with twelve hundred beef cattle kicking dust into his face, could not make him feel himself the martyr that Penny did.

For that reason and the fact that he never had felt the drunkard's torment of thirst, Chip certainly failed to grasp the full extent of Penny's resentment. He thought it was pretty cute of Shorty to fix it so that Penny couldn't get to town ahead of the herd. He had simply saved Penny from making seventeen kinds of a fool of himself and maybe kept him from losing his job as well. Let him sulk if he wanted to. He'd see the point when it was all over with and they were headed back onto the range again after another herd.

So they rode in the heat and the dust, each thinking his own thoughts. The herd plodded on in the scorching, windless heat, stepping more briskly as they neared the edge of the bench.

Bellowing thirstily, the cattle poured down the long, steep slope to the sluggish creek at the mouth of the narrow coulee. As the drag dipped down from the level, even Penny could see the long, level valley beyond and the little huddle of houses squatting against the farther hill. Two hundred yards up the creek and inside the coulee, the tents of the Flying U showed their familiar, homey blotches of gray-white against the brown grass. Behind them a line of green willows showed where the creek snaked away up the coulee. Never twice in the same setting, flitting like huge birds over the range to alight where water and feed were best, those two tents were home to the Flying U boys—a welcome sight when a long day's work was done.

Chip's eyes brightened at the sight, and he cleared his throat of the last clinging particles of dust. With a whoop he hailed the two men ambling out from camp to relieve them. Others would follow—were following even as he looked—to take charge of the tired, thirsty cattle already blotting the creek altogether from sight where they crowded to drink. Cal Emmett and Slim rode straight on to meet Chip and Penny.

"Gosh, ain't it hot!" Cal greeted them, voicing an obvious fact as is the way of men who have nothing important to say. "Weather breeder, if yuh ask me."

"Well, if it holds off till we get these cattle in the cars it can rain all it damn pleases," Chip replied carelessly. "I want to get caught up on my sleep, anyway."

"Don't you ever think it'll hold off! Bet you'll be huntin' buttons on your slicker tonight." Cal grinned. "Sure glad I don't have to stand guard t'night!"

"By golly, that's right," Slim agreed. "If it don't cut loose an' rain t'night I miss my guess."

Penny scowled at him, grunted, and rode on past. "Let 'er rain and be damned to it!" he muttered as he pricked his horse into a lope. But Chip had also put his horse into a gallop and failed to hear anything Penny might say.

At the rope corral as they rode up, Shorty was speaking to someone over across the *remuda*, judging from the pitch of his voice.

"No, sir! The man that rides to town before this beef is loaded can take his bed along with him. The cars'll be spotted sometime tonight, ready for us to start loadin' whenever we're ready tomorrow. I shore as hell ain't goin' to stop and round up a bunch of drunken punchers before I start workin' the herd in the mornin'."

Penny muttered an unprintable sentence as he dismounted and began loosening the *latigo*, and Chip gave him a quick questioning glance as he stepped down from his saddle close by. He glanced at Shorty, let his eyes go questing for the man he had been speaking to, and returned his glance to Penny.

"That's him every time, hittin' yuh over another man's back," Penny grumbled and shot an angry, sidelong glance at the wagon boss. "If he's got anything to say to me, why don't he spit it out to my face?"

"Ah, he wasn't talking to you," Chip protested, biting the words off short as Shorty turned and walked toward them.

The wagon boss gave them a sharp glance as he passed, almost as if he had overheard them. But he did not say anything and Penny did not look up.

Though other men chatted around him, Penny ate his supper in silence, scowling over his plate. Afterward he lay in the shade of the bed tent and smoked moodily until it was time to catch his night horse. No one paid any attention to him, for tempers were quite likely to be short at the end of a beef roundup, when sleep was broken with night-guarding a herd as temperamental as rival prima donnas are said to be and almost as valuable. If a man went into the sulks it was just as well to let him alone while the mood lasted. Which did not mean, however, that no one knew the state of mind he was in.

By the set of his head and the stiffness of his neck while he saddled his horse Penny proclaimed to his world that he was plenty mad. He looped up the long free end of the *latigo*, unhooked the stirrup from the horn, and let it drop with a snap that sent his horse ducking sidewise. He jerked him to a snorting stand, fixing a stern and warning eye upon him, hesitated just a second or two, and instead of tying him to the wagon as he should have done he jerked down his hat for swift riding, thrust his toe in the stirrup, and mounted.

"Here! Where you think you're goin'?" Shorty called out in surprise, leaping up from the ground.

"Goin' after my mail! Be right back." Penny grinned impudently over his shoulder as he wheeled his horse toward the open land. He was off, galloping down the coulee before Shorty could get the slack out of his jaw.

"His mail! Hell!" Shorty spluttered angrily, glaring after the spurts of dust Penny left behind him. "He ain't had a letter in all the two years I've knowed him." He stood irresolute, plainly tempted to give chase. Then he relaxed with a snort. "Think I'll hog-tie him and haul him out in the wagon again and sober him up?" he said disgustedly. "I'll fire the son-of-a-gun—"

Then he remembered that he was no longer just one of the Happy Family, free to speak his mind, but a full-fledged roundup foreman who had the dignity of his position to maintain. He stalked off to the cook tent and unrolled his bed, knowing full well that Penny would be howling drunk before midnight, and that by morning he would be unable to sit in the saddle—to say nothing of reading brands and helping work the herd and weed out strays before loading the cattle. The Flying U was already working shorthanded. He'd just have to consider himself shy another man, which went against the grain. Penny sober was a top hand—and, darn the luck, Shorty liked him.

He spread his blankets and started to get ready to crawl in, then decided that the air was too sultry inside and dragged his bed out under the mess wagon. Other men were deserting their canvas shelter in spite of the threatening clouds. For even at dusk the air was stifling. If it busted loose and rained they could move inside, but they'd be darned if they were going to suffocate in the meantime.

"Saddle yourselves a night horse before you turn in, boys." Shorty made a sudden decision as a whiff of cool air struck his face. "We can't take any chances at this stage of the game." And he went off to practice what he preached.

It was a sensible precaution, for if the storm did strike before morning there was no telling how bad it might be or how the herd would take it. Shorty had seen beef herds stampede in a thunderstorm and he hoped never to see another one—certainly not while he was responsible for the safety of the cattle. So, having done what he could to prepare for an emergency, Shorty crawled into his blankets and was snoring inside five minutes. And presently the dim bulks on the ground nearby were likewise sleeping with the deep, unheeding slumber of work-weary men untroubled by conscience or care.

Down beyond the coulee mouth the night guard rode slowly round and round the sleeping herd. By sound they rode mostly, and by that unerring instinct that comes of long habit and the intimate knowledge it brings. As the sullen clouds crept closer it was so dark they could not see one another as they met and passed on. But the droning lullaby tones of their voices met and blended for a minute or so in pleasant companionship and understanding. Then the voices would draw apart and recede into the suffocating blackness. The whisper of saddle leather, the mouthing of a bit, the faint rattle of bridle chains grew faint and finally were lost until, minutes later, the meeting came again.

Chip was young, and his imagination never slept. He liked the velvet blackness, the brooding mystery that descended upon the land with the dusk. Even the frogs over in the creek did their croaking tonight with bashful hesitation, as if they, too, felt the silence weigh upon them and only croaked because the habit was too strong for them. Chip thought of this breathless night as a curtained dome where some gigantic goddess walked and trailed her velvet robes, treading softly with her finger on her lips. Which only proves how young and imaginative he could be on night guard.

Away across the herd came the plaintive notes of a melancholy song that Weary Willie seemed to favor lately, for no good reason save that it had many verses and a tune that lent itself to melodious crooning. Chip hushed his own low singing to listen. In that breathless air, across twelve hundred sleeping steers, the words came clear.

"Oh, bury me not on the lone prairee
Where the wild coyotes will howl o'er me,
Where the rattlesnakes hiss and the wind blows free—
Oh-h, bury me not on the lone prairee."

Chip wondered who had written those words, anyway. Not a real cowboy, he'd bank on that. They'd sing it, of course, with that same wailing chorus plaintively making its sickish plea between the verses. But he didn't believe any real cowpuncher ever felt that way, when you came right down to it.

When a cowboy's light went out—according to the opinion of all the fellows he had ever heard discoursing on the subject—he didn't give a damn where they laid his carcass. They were quite likely to say, with unpleasant bluntness, "Just drag me off where I won't stink." But when they stood guard, like Weary tonight, nine times in ten they'd sing that maudlin old song. And though Chip would never admit it, over there in the dark the words lost their sickish sentimentality and seemed to carry a pulsing tremor of feeling.

"Oh, bury me where a mother's prayer
And a sister's tears may linger there!
Where my friends may come and weep o'er me—
Oh, bury me not on the lone prairee!"

In daylight Chip would have hooted at the lugubrious tones with which Weary Willie sang those words, but now he did not even smile to himself. The night like that and with sheet lightning playing along the skyline with the vague and distant mutter of thunder miles away, death and the tears and prayers of loved ones did not seem so incongruous.

"Oh, bury me not—but his voice failed there.
And they gave no heed to his dying prayer.
In a narrow grave just six by three-e.
They-y buried him there on the lone prairee—"

The singer was riding toward him, the soft thud of his horse's feet and the faint saddle sounds once more audible. A steer close to Chip blew a snorting breath, grunted and got to his feet, his horns rattling against the horns of his nearest neighbor. Chip forgot Weary and his song and began a soothing melody of his own. Another steer got up, and another. Black as it was, he sensed their uneasy, listening attitudes.

It couldn't have been Weary who wakened them. Weary had circled the herd many times with his melancholy ditty, his presence carrying reassurance. Chip dared not quicken his pace, dared not call a warning. Instead he began singing in his clear young tenor, hoping to override whatever fear was creeping on among the cattle.

"Come, love, come, the boat lies low—
The moon shines bright on the old bayou—"

Almost overhead the clouds brightened with the sudden flare of lightning, but the rumble that followed was slow and deep and need not have been disquieting to animals that had grown up in the land of sudden storms.

"Come, love, come, oh come along with me,
I'll take you down-n to Tenn—"

Off in the night there came the drumming of hoofs—some strange horseman coming at a swift gallop straight toward the herd. A chill prickled up Chip's neck. Slowly, carefully as a mother tiptoeing away from her sleeping baby, he reined aside and walked his horse out to meet and warn the approaching rider.

"Slow down!" he called cautiously when another lightning flare revealed the rider. "You'll be on top of the herd in another minute, you damn fool!"

A shrill, reckless yell from just ahead answered him: "Ayee-ee—Yipee! Them's the babies I'm a-lookin' for! Gotta stand guard! *Whee-ee!* Bossies, here's yer—what the hell?"

With an indescribable sound of clashing horns and great bodies moving in unison, the herd was up and away like flushed quail. There was no more warning than that first great swoosh of sound. Here and there steers bawled throatily—caught in the act of getting to their feet. Now they were battered back to earth as the herd lunged over them. For the cattle had taken fright on the outer fringe nearest camp and the open valley, and were stampeding across their own bed ground toward the bench.

The night was no longer silent under a velvety blackness. It was a roaring tumult of sound, the never-to-be-forgotten clamor of a stampede in full flight. Weary Willie, by God's mercy out of their path as he swung round the side toward the valley, yelled to Chip above the uproar.

"What started 'em? Y'all right, Chip?"

And Penny, with a pint or more of whiskey inside him and two quart flasks in his pockets, answered with another yell, "I did! Jus' sayin' hello—the damn things've fergot me a'ready!" He gave a whoop and emptied his six-shooter into the air as he galloped.

"Go it like hell!" he jeered, racing jubilantly after them. "Git a move on! *You* don't need no sleep, anyhow! What you want's—ex-ercise! Dammit, ex-ercise, you rip-pety-rip—"

Cursing, laughing, shooting, he rode like a wild man, urging them on up and over the hill.

Up in camp Shorty lifted his head as the distant yelling came faint on the still air. Then came the shots and the vibrant roar of the stampede, but that was when Shorty had already jumped to his feet.

"Pile out!" he yelled. "The cattle's runnin'!"

Five words only, but they brought every man in camp out of his blankets, and grabbing for his clothes. Not much behind Shorty's hurried dressing they jerked on their boots, stamping their feet in on their way to their horses. They untied their mounts by the sense of touch alone, felt for stirrups in the inky blackness between lightning flashes, mounted, and were off, streaming down the coulee at a dead run. Even Patsy the cook was up and dressed and standing outside listening and swearing and trying to guess which way the cattle were running. Patsy had been almost caught in a stampede once when a herd had run past camp, and since then he took no chance if he could help himself.

To have a beef herd stampede in the night is a catastrophe at any time. To have it happen on the last night before they are crowded into cars and sent lurching away to market is next to the worst luck that can happen to a range man at shipping time. The ultimate disaster, of course, would be to have the herd wiped out entirely.

Shorty looked at the clouds, quiet yet as approaching storms go, and wondered what had started the cattle. The shooting, he guessed, had been done in the hope of turning the herd. Then, above the fast decreasing rumble of the stampede, he heard a shrill yell he knew of old.

"Penny, by thunder!" He dug his heels into the flanks of his horse and swore aloud in his wrath. Certain broken phrases whipped backward on the wind he made in his headlong flight. "If I ever git my hands on the—" And again: "A man like him had oughta be strung up by the heels!—any damn fool that will go yellin' and shootin' into a beef herd bedded down—"

Shorty was not even aware that he was speaking. His horse stumbled over a loose rock, recovered himself with a lurch, and went pounding on across the creek and up the steep slope to the bench beyond. The horse knew and followed the sounds without a touch on the reins, would follow until he dropped or overtook the herd.

Around and behind him the riders were tearing along, their horses grunting as they took the steep hill in rabbit jumps. Good thing the cattle headed along the back trail, Shorty thought as his horse strained up the last bitter climb and lengthened his stride on the level. That hill would slow the herd down, maybe. Give the boys a chance to turn them. But with that drunken maniac still whooping up ahead, the prospect didn't look very bright.

On the left flank of the herd the night guard were racing, yelling, and shooting to turn the cattle. But they could not cover the unmistakable bellowing chant of Penny riding behind and to the right of the maddened herd and undoing the work of the left-flank boys. Shorty was so incensed that he actually turned that way with the full intention of overtaking Penny and shooting him off his horse. It seemed the only way to silence him. He didn't want to kill the cussed lunatic, but if he had to do it to shut him up no jury of range men would call it murder.

The storm clouds, too, were moving overhead, the lightning playing behind the tumbling thunderheads and turning them a golden yellow, with an occasional sword thrust of vivid flame. But still the rain did not come down upon the thirsty land. The bulk of the storm, as Shorty saw with one quick backward glance, was swinging around to throw itself bodily against the rugged steeps of the mountains beyond.

Out upon the level, as the lightning brightened for an instant the whole landscape, they saw the herd a black blotch in the distance. With the cattle they glimpsed the night herders riding alongside the left flank, swinging the galloping herd more and more to the right. Of Penny they saw nothing. There was no more shooting, no more yelling.

"He's cooled down mighty sudden," Shorty gritted unforgivingly. "But that won't do him a damn bit of good when I get my hands on him. I'll sure as hell make him wish his mother'd been a man. He's through with this outfit, the rippety-rip—"

Away on the ragged fringe of the herd rode Chip and two other herders, with voices and swinging loops forcing the leaders around until they were running back the way they had come. As the bulk of the herd followed blindly where the others led, they too changed the course of their flight. In ten minutes or less the entire herd ran in a huge circle that slowed to a trot, then to a walk. "Milling," the cowboys called that uneasy circling round and round.

Within a mile or so the stampede was stopped, and except for one top hand forever disgraced and banished from the Flying U—and from the range, wherever the story seeped out—and a few broken-legged steers that would have to be shot, no harm had been done. The herd, at least, was intact. They had lost weight. Shorty would delay the shipping as long as he could hold the cars, to bring the cattle up to the best condition he could. A day, maybe—he'd ride in and see how much time he could have. Bad enough, but it could have been worse.

He rode over to where the lightning showed him Chip and Weary, meeting and halting a minute to compare notes and breathe their winded mounts.

"Good work, boys. Where's that—?" With as many unprintable epithets as he could string together he named the name of Penny.

"Search me, Shorty." Chip replied with a note of excitement still in his voice. "We dropped him right after we got out on the bench. He'd of had us clear down to the Missouri if he hadn't quit trying to shoot the tails off the drag. He's drunk as forty dollars."

"He'll be sober when I git through with him," Shorty promised darkly. "Bed the cattle right here if they'll settle down. Storm's goin' round us, I guess. You boys stand another hour and come on in. Have to double the guard from now till mornin'."

"Hell, listen to that wind!" Cal Emmett called out as he rode up. Men drew rein and turned in their saddles to look and listen. The clouds were thinning, drifting off to the north where the lightning jagged through the dark, but a great roaring came out of the nearer distance.

"That ain't wind," Shorty contradicted, and swung his horse around to stare at the inky blackness, until now utterly disregarded, in the east. "It's comin' from off that way." And suddenly he jumped his horse into a run toward the valley. "My God, it's water!" he yelled as he rode, and all save the night guard, doubled now to six, followed him at top speed.

At the brink of the steep hillside they pulled up short and looked below. With the tremendous roaring in their ears they scarcely needed the flickering light of the distant storm or the feeble moon struggling through the clouds overhead. They could not see much, but they saw quite enough and they could guess the rest.

Down below, where the creek had meandered languidly through the willows, there was a solid, swirling wall of water. Down the coulee it pushed its resistless way, and they heard it go ravening out across the valley. The horses snorted and tried to bolt, though up there on the bench's rim they were safe. But where the herd had bedded for the night, down there beside the creek, there pushed a raging flood. Where the night hawk had taken the *remuda* none of them knew. Out into the valley, probably. If he heard and heeded he could run his horses to safety on high ground.

But the camp—"Patsy's caught!" yelled Shorty, and reined his horse up along the hillside. They raced up the coulee side to where they could look down upon the camp—or where the camp had stood. A smooth brown plane of water flowed swiftly there, the willow tops trailing on the surface like the hair of drowned women.

No one mentioned Patsy again. Without a word they turned and rode back to the cattle. There was nothing else that they could do until daylight.

By sunrise the flood waters had passed on, and they rode down to search for the body of their cook and to retrieve what they could of the camp outfit. They passed the wagons, over-turned and carried down to the mouth of the coulee where both had lodged in the bedraggled willows.

"We'll get them later on," said Shorty, and rode on. Without putting into words the thought in the minds of them all, they knew that Patsy came first.

He did. Waddling down the muddy flat with a lantern long burned dry, he met them with his bad news.

"Poys! Der vagon iss over!" he shouted excitedly as they rode up.

"Over where, Patsy?" Shorty asked gravely with a relieved twinkle in his eye.

"On his pack, you tamn fool!" snorted Patsy. "Der vater iss take him to hell and der stove mit. I cooks no preakfast, py tamn!"

They crowded around him, plying him with questions. Patsy, it appeared, had lighted the lantern and listened with both ears, ready to run if the cattle came up the coulee. The rush of water he had mistaken for the stampede coming, and he had run clumsily to the nearest coulee wall and climbed as high as he could. He had seen the wagons lifted and rolled over and carried off down the coulee. The demolition of the tents had not impressed him half so much, nor the loss of all their beds and gear.

There was nothing to do there, then. They rode back down the coulee hunting their belongings. One man was sent to town for grub and a borrowed outfit to cook it on, together with dishes and such. Hungry as when they had left the bench, the relief rode back to the herd.

Free for the moment, Chip started up the hill alone. "Where yuh goin'?" Shorty yelled after him irritably, his nerves worn ragged with the night's mishaps.

"Going to find Penny." Chip yelled back. "You've cussed him and called him everything you could lay your tongue to—but it never seemed to occur to you that Penny saved the cattle—and a lot of your necks, too. What if you'd been asleep when that cloudburst—"

"Aw, don't be so damn mouthy!" Shorty cut him off. "I'll tend to Penny's case."

"Well, time you were doing it then," snapped Chip, just as if Shorty were still one of the boys with no authority whatever. "Me, I don't like the way he choked off his yelling so sudden, last night. I was on guard or I'd have looked for him then. The rest of you don't seem to give a damn."

"Now that'll be enough outa you." growled Shorty. "I guess I'm still boss around here." He spurred his horse up the hill and disappeared over the top.

And Chip, with Weary Willie at his heels as usual, followed him, grinning a little to himself.

"Mamma! You want to get yourself canned?" Weary protested as their horses climbed. "Shorty's went through a lot, remember."

"Well, he ain't through yet," replied Chip, grinning. "He'll go through a change of heart, if I ain't mistaken." And he added cryptically, "He's going to find Penny." And when Weary looked at him questioningly, he only shook his head. "I got there first, as it happens. On my way down. You wait."

So Shorty found Penny. He was lying almost as he fell when his horse stepped in a hole last night. Where the horse was now a systematic search might reveal; certainly he was nowhere in sight. A faint aroma of whiskey still lingered around the prone figure, but there were no bottles. Chip had seen to that.

Penny had a broken collarbone and an ear half torn off and one twisted ankle, but he was conscious and he managed to suppress a groan when Shorty piled off and knelt beside him.

"Yuh hurt, Penny?" A foolish question, but one invariably asked at such moments.

Penny bit back another groan. "The herd—did I git here—in time? Did I save—the cattle?" he murmured weakly, just as Chip had told him he must do.

"The cattle? Yeah, they're all right. Safe as hell, Penny. How—"

"Then—I got here—in time," muttered Penny, and went limp in his foreman's arms.

"And I was goin' to fire the son-of-a-gun!" said Shorty brokenly, looking up blur-eyes into Chip's face as he and Weary rode up.

JACK LONDON
All Gold Canyon

Jack London (1876–1916) was born in San Francisco. His personal experience of hardship made him a convinced radical, and he was a member of the Socialist Labour Party for many years. In 1897 London participated in the gold rush to the Klondike (then the last North American frontier), returning a year later with the raw material for a vast amount of fiction, including the famous dog novels, *Call of the Wild* (1903) and *White Fang* (1906). London's gripping, naturalistic Alaska stories were so successful that they virtually created a sub-division of the Western, the 'Northern'. As well as frontier fiction, London wrote such modern classics as *The Iron Heel*, *Martin Eden* and *The Sea Wolf*. Like Ernest Hemingway, an author with whom he is sometimes compared, London committed suicide.

The story 'All Gold Canyon' is from London's 1901 collection, *Moon Face*.

IT WAS THE GREEN HEART of the canyon, where the walls swerved back from the rigid plan and relieved their harshness of line by making a little sheltered nook and filling it to the brim with sweetness and roundness and softness. Here all things rested. Even the narrow stream ceased its turbulent down-rush long enough to form a quiet pool. Knee-deep in the water, with drooping head and half-shut eyes, drowsed a red-coated, many-antlered buck.

On one side, beginning at the very lip of the pool, was a tiny meadow, a cool, resilient surface of green that extended to the base of the frowning wall. Beyond the pool a gentle slope of earth ran up and up to meet the opposing wall. Fine grass covered the slope—grass that was spangled with flowers, with here and there patches of color, orange and purple and golden. Below, the canyon was shut in. There was no view. The walls leaned together abruptly and the canyon ended in a chaos of rocks, moss-covered and hidden by a green screen of vines and creepers and boughs of trees. Up the canyon rose far hills and peaks, the big foothills, pine-covered and remote. And far beyond, like clouds upon the border of the sky, towered minarets of white, where the Sierra's eternal snows flashed austerely the blazes of the sun.

There was no dust in the canyon. The leaves and flowers were clean and virginal. The grass was young velvet. Over the pool three cottonwoods sent their snowy fluffs fluttering down the quiet air. On the slope the blossoms of the wine-wooded manzanita filled the air with springtime odors, while the leaves, wise with experience, were already beginning their vertical twist against the coming aridity of summer. In the open spaces on the slope, beyond the farthest shadow-reach of the manzanita, poised the mariposa lilies, like so many flights of jewelled moths suddenly arrested and on the verge of trembling into flight again. Here and there that woods harlequin, the madrone, permitting itself to be caught in the act of changing its pea-green trunk to madder-red, breathed its fragrance into the air from great clusters of waxen bells. Creamy white were these bells, shaped like lilies-of-the-valley, with the sweetness of perfume that is of the springtime.

There was not a sigh of wind. The air was drowsy with its weight of perfume. It was a sweetness that would have been cloying had the air been heavy and humid. But the air was sharp and thin. It was as starlight transmuted into atmosphere, shot through and warmed by sunshine, and flower-drenched with sweetness.

An occasional butterfly drifted in and out through the patches of light and shade. And from all about rose the low and sleepy hum of mountain bees—feasting Sybarites that jostled one another good-naturedly at the board, nor found time for rough discourtesy. So quietly did the little stream drip and ripple its way through the canyon that it spoke only in faint and occasional gurgles. The voice of the stream was as a drowsy whisper, ever interrupted by dozings and silences, ever lifted again in the awakenings.

The motion of all things was a drifting in the heart of the canyon. Sunshine and butterflies drifted in and out among the trees. The hum of the bees and the whisper of the stream were a drifting of sound. And the drifting sound and drifting color seemed to weave together in the making of a delicate and intangible fabric which was the spirit of the place. It was a spirit of peace that was not of death, but of smooth-pulsing life, of quietude that was not silence, of movement that was not action, of repose that was quick with existence without being violent with struggle and travail. The spirit of the place was the spirit of the peace of the living, somnolent with the easement and content of prosperity, and undisturbed by rumors of far wars.

The red-coated, many-antlered buck acknowledged the lordship of the spirit of the place and dozed knee-deep in the cool, shaded pool. There seemed no flies to vex him and he was languid with rest. Sometimes his ears moved when the stream awoke and whispered; but they moved lazily, with fore-knowledge that it was merely the stream grown garrulous at discovery that it had slept.

But there came a time when the buck's ears lifted and tensed with swift eagerness for sound. His head was turned down the canyon. His sensitive, quivering nostrils scented the air. His eyes could not pierce the green screen through which the stream rippled away, but to his ears came the voice of a man. It was a steady, monotonous, singsong voice. Once the buck heard the harsh clash of metal upon rock. At the sound he snorted with a sudden start that jerked him through the air from water to meadow, and his feet sank into the young velvet, while he pricked his ears and again scented the air. Then he stole across the tiny meadow, pausing once and again to listen, and faded away out of the canyon like a wraith, soft-footed and without sound.

The clash of steel-shod soles against the rocks began to be heard, and the man's voice grew louder. It was raised in a sort of chant and became distinct with nearness, so that the words could be heard:

"Tu'n around an' tu'n yo' face
Untoe them sweet hills of grace
(D' pow'rs of sin yo' am scornin'!).
Look about an' look aroun'
Fling yo' sin-pack on d' groun'
(Yo' will meet wid d' Lord in d' mornin'!)."

A sound of scrambling accompanied the song, and the spirit of the place fled away on the heels of the red-coated buck. The green screen was burst asunder, and a man peered out at the meadow and the pool and the sloping side-hill. He was a deliberate sort of man. He took in the scene with one embracing glance, then ran his eyes over the details to verify the general impression. Then, and not until then, did he open his mouth in vivid and solemn approval:

"Smoke of life an' snakes of purgatory! Will you just look at that! Wood an' water an' grass an' a side-hill! A pocket-hunter's delight an' a cayuse's paradise! Cool green for tired eyes! Pink pills for pale people's ain't in it. A secret pasture for prospectors and a resting-place for tired burros. It's just booful!"

He was a sandy-complexioned man in whose face geniality and humor seemed the salient characteristics. It was a mobile face, quick-changing to inward mood and thought. Thinking was in him a visible process. Ideas chased across his face like wind-flaws across the surface of a lake. His hair, sparse and unkempt of growth, was as indeterminate and colorless as his complexion. It would seem that all the color of his frame had gone into his eyes, for they were startlingly blue. Also, they were laughing and merry eyes, within them much of the naiveté and wonder of the child; and yet, in an unassertive way, they contained much of calm self-reliance and strength of purpose founded upon self-experience and experience of the world.

From out the screen of vines and creepers he flung ahead of him a miner's pick and shovel and gold-pan. Then he crawled out himself into the open. He was clad in faded overalls and black cotton shirt, with hobnailed brogans on his feet, and on his head a hat whose shapelessness and stains advertised the rough usage of wind and rain and sun and camp-smoke. He stood erect, seeing wide-eyed the secrecy of the scene and sensuously inhaling the warm, sweet breath of the canyon-garden through nostrils that dilated and quivered with delight. His eyes narrowed to laughing slits of blue, his face wreathed itself in joy, and his mouth curled in a smile as he cried aloud:

"Jumping dandelions and happy hollyhocks, but that smells good to me! Talk about your attar o' roses an' cologne factories! They ain't in it!"

He had the habit of soliloquy. His quick-changing facial expressions might tell every thought and mood, but the tongue, perforce, ran hard after, repeating, like a second Boswell.

The man lay down on the lip of the pool and drank long and deep of its water. "Tastes good to me," he murmured, lifting his head and gazing across the pool at the side-hill, while he wiped his mouth with the back of his hand. The side-hill attracted his attention. Still lying on his stomach, he studied the hill formation long and carefully. It was a practised eye that traveled up the slope to the crumbling canyon-wall and back down again to the edge of the pool. He scrambled to his feet and favored the side-hill with a second survey.

"Looks good to me," he concluded, picking up his pick and shovel and gold-pan.

He crossed the stream below the pool, stepping agilely from stone to stone. Where the side-hill touched the water he dug up a shovelful of dirt and put it into the gold-pan. He squatted down, holding the pan in his two hands, and partly immersing it in the stream. Then he imparted to the pan a deft circular motion that sent the water sluicing in and out through the dirt and gravel. The larger and the lighter particles worked to the surface, and these, by a skilful dipping movement of the pan, he spilled out and over the edge. Occasionally, to expedite matters, he rested the pan and with his fingers raked out the large pebbles and pieces of rock.

The contents of the pan diminished rapidly until only fine dirt and the smallest bits of gravel remained. At this stage he began to work very deliberately and carefully. It was fine washing, and he washed fine and finer, with a keen scrutiny and delicate and fastidious touch. At last the pan seemed empty of everything but water; but with a quick semi-circular flirt that sent the water flying over the shallow rim into the stream, he disclosed a layer of black sand on the bottom of the pan. So thin was this layer that it was like a streak of paint. He examined it closely. In the midst of it was a tiny golden speck. He dribbled a little water in over the depressed edge of the pan. With a quick flirt he sent the water sluicing across the bottom, turning the grains of black sand over and over. A second tiny golden speck rewarded his effort.

The washing had now become very fine—fine beyond all need of ordinary placer mining. He worked the black sand, a small portion at a time, up the shallow rim of the pan. Each small portion he examined sharply, so that his eyes saw every grain of it before he allowed it to slide over the edge and away. Jealously, bit by bit, he let the black sand slip away. A golden speck, no larger than a pin-point, appeared on the rim, and by his manipulation of the water it returned to the bottom of the pan. And in such fashion another speck was disclosed, and another. Great was his care of them. Like a shepherd he herded his flock of golden specks so that not one should be lost. At last, of the pan of dirt nothing remained but his golden herd. He counted it, and then, after all his labor, sent it flying out of the pan with one final swirl of water.

But his blue eyes were shining with desire as he rose to his feet. "Seven," he muttered aloud, asserting the sum of the specks for which he had toiled so hard and which he had so wantonly thrown away. "Seven," he repeated, with the emphasis of one trying to impress a number on his memory.

He stood still a long while, surveying the hillside. In his eyes was a curiosity, new-aroused and burning. There was an exultance about his bearing and a keenness like that of a hunting animal catching the fresh scent of game.

He moved down the stream a few steps and took a second panful of dirt.

Again came the careful washing, the jealous herding of the golden specks, and the wantonness with which he sent them flying into the stream. His golden herd diminished. "Four, five," he muttered, and repeated, "five."

He could not forbear another survey of the hill before filling the pan farther down the stream. His golden herds diminished. "Four, three, two, two, one," were his memory tabulations as he moved down the stream. When but one speck of gold rewarded his washing, he stopped and built a fire of dry twigs. Into this he thrust the gold-pan and burned it till it was blue-black. He held up the pan and examined it critically. Then he nodded approbation. Against such a color-background he could defy the tiniest yellow speck to elude him.

Still moving down the stream, he panned again. A single speck was his reward. A third pan contained no gold at all. Not satisfied with this, he panned three times again, taking his shovels of dirt within a foot of one another. Each pan proved empty of gold, and the fact, instead of discouraging him, seemed to give him satisfaction. His elation increased with each barren washing, until he arose, exclaiming jubilantly:

"If it ain't the real thing, may God knock off my head with sour apples!"

Returning to where he had started operations, he began to pan up the stream. At first his golden herds increased—increased prodigiously. "Fourteen, eighteen, twenty-one, twenty-six," ran his memory tabulations. Just above the pool he struck his richest pan—thirty-five colors.

"Almost enough to save," he remarked regretfully as he allowed the water to sweep them away.

The sun climbed to the top of the sky. The man worked on. Pan by pan, he went up the stream, the tally of results steadily decreasing.

"It's just booful, the way it peters out," he exulted when a shovelful of dirt contained no more than a single speck of gold.

And when no specks at all were found in several pans, he straightened up and favored the hillside with a confident glance.

"Ah, ha! Mr Pocket!" he cried out, as though to an auditor hidden somewhere above him beneath the surface of the slope. "Ah, ha! Mr Pocket! I'm a-comin', I'm a-comin', an' I'm shorely gwine to get yer! You heah me, Mr Pocket? I'm gwine to get yer as shore as punkins ain't cauliflowers!"

He turned and flung a measuring glance at the sun poised above him in the azure of the cloudless sky. Then he went down the canyon, following the line of shovel-holes he had made in filling the pans. He crossed the stream below the pool and disappeared through the green screen. There was little opportunity for the spirit of the place to return with its quietude and repose, for the man's voice, raised in ragtime song, still dominated the canyon with possession.

After a time, with a greater clashing of steel-shod feet on rock, he returned. The green screen was tremendously agitated. It surged back and forth in the throes of a struggle. There was a loud grating and clanging of metal. The man's voice leaped to a higher pitch and was sharp with imperativeness. A large body plunged and panted. There was a snapping and ripping and rending, and amid a shower of falling leaves a horse burst through the screen. On its back was a pack, and from this trailed broken vines and torn creepers. The animal gazed with astonished eyes at the scene into which it had been precipitated, then dropped its head to the grass and began contentedly to graze. A second horse scrambled into view, slipping once on the mossy rocks and regaining equilibrium when its hoofs sank into the yielding surface of the meadow. It was riderless, though on its back was a high-horned Mexican saddle, scarred and discolored by long usage.

The man brought up the rear. He threw off pack and saddle, with an eye to camp location, and gave the animals their freedom to graze. He unpacked his food and got out frying-pan and coffee-pot. He gathered an armful of dry wood, and with a few stones made a place for his fire.

"My!" he said, "but I've got an appetite. I could scoff iron-filings an' horseshoe nails an' thank you kindly, ma'am, for a second helpin'."

He straightened up, and, while he reached for matches in the pocket of his overalls, his eyes traveled across the pool to the side-hill. His fingers had clutched the match-box, but they relaxed their hold and the hand came out empty. The man wavered perceptibly. He looked at his preparations for cooking and he looked at the hill.

"Guess I'll take another whack at her," he concluded, starting to cross the stream.

"They ain't no sense in it, I know," he mumbled apologetically. "But keepin' grub back an hour ain't goin' to hurt none, I reckon."

A few feet back from his first of test-pans he started a second line. The sun dropped down the western sky, the shadows lengthened, but the man worked on. He began a third line of test-pans. He was cross-cutting the hillside, line by line, as he ascended. The center of each line produced the richest pans, while the ends came where no colors showed in the pan. And as he ascended the hillside the lines grew perceptibly shorter. The regularity with which their length diminished served to indicate that somewhere up the slope the last line would be so short as to have scarcely length at all, and that beyond could come only a point. The design was growing into an inverted "V". The converging sides of this "V" marked the boundaries of the gold-bearing dirt.

The apex of the "V" was evidently the man's goal. Often he ran his eye along the converging sides and on up the hill, trying to divine the apex, the point where the gold-bearing dirt must cease. Here resided "Mr Pocket" —for so the man familiarly addressed the imaginary point above him on the slope, crying out:

"Come down out o' that, Mr Pocket! Be right smart an' agreeable, an' come down!"

"All right," he would add later, in a voice resigned to determination. "All right, Mr Pocket. It's plain to me I got to come right up an' snatch you out bald-headed. An' I'll do it! I'll do it!" he would threaten still later.

Each pan he carried down to the water to wash, and as he went higher up the hill the pans grew richer, until he began to save the gold in an empty baking powder can which he carried carelessly in his hip-pocket. So engrossed was he in his toil that he did not notice the long twilight of oncoming night. It was not until he tried vainly to see the gold colors in the bottom of the pan that he realized the passage of time. He straightened up abruptly. An expression of whimsical wonderment and awe overspread his face as he drawled:

"Gosh darn my buttons! if I didn't plumb forget dinner!"

He stumbled across the stream in the darkness and lighted his long-delayed fire. Flapjacks and bacon and warmed-over beans constituted his supper. Then he smoked a pipe by the smouldering coals, listening to the night noises and watching the moonlight stream through the canyon. After that he unrolled his bed, took off his heavy shoes and pulled the blankets up to his chin. His face showed white in the moonlight, like the face of a corpse. But it was a corpse that knew its resurrection, for the man rose suddenly on one elbow and gazed across at his hillside.

"Good night, Mr Pocket," he called sleepily. "Good night."

He slept through the early gray of morning until the direct rays of the sun smote his closed eyelids, when he awoke with a start and looked about him until he had established the continuity of his existence and identified his present self with the days previously lived.

To dress, he had merely to buckle on his shoes. He glanced at his fireplace and at his hillside, wavered, but fought down the temptation and started the fire.

"Keep yer shirt on, Bill; keep yer shirt on," he admonished himself. "What's the good of rushin'? No use in gettin' all het up an' sweaty. Mr Pocket 'll wait for you. He ain't a-runnin' away before you can get your breakfast. Now, what you want, Bill, is something fresh in yer bill o'fare. So it's up to you to go an' get it."

He cut a short pole at the water's edge and drew from one of his pockets a bit of line and a draggled fly that had once been a royal coachman.

"Mebbe they'll bite in the early morning," he muttered, as he made his first cast into the pool. And a moment later he was gleefully crying: "What 'd I tell you, eh? What 'd I tell you?"

He had no reel, nor any inclination to waste time, and by main strength, and swiftly, he drew out of the water a flashing ten-inch trout. Three more, caught in rapid succession, furnished his breakfast. When he came to the stepping-stones on his way to his hillside, he was struck by a sudden thought, and paused.

"I'd just better take a hike down-stream a ways," he said. "There's no tellin' who may be snoopin' around."

But he crossed over on the stones, and with a "I really oughter take that hike," the need of the precaution passed out of his mind and he fell to work.

At nightfall he straightened up. The small of his back was stiff from stooping toil, and as he put his hand behind him to soothe the protesting muscles, he said:

"Now what d'ye think of that? I clean forgot my dinner again! If I don't watch out, I'll be degeneratin' into a two-meal-a-day crank."

"Pockets is the hangedest things I ever see for makin' a man absent-minded," he communed that night, as he crawled into his blankets. Nor did he forget to call up the hillside, "Good night, Mr Pocket! Good night!"

Rising with the sun, and snatching a hasty breakfast, he was early at work. A fever seemed to be growing in him, nor did the increasing richness of the test-pans allay this fever. There was a flush in his cheek other than that made by the heat of the sun, and he was oblivious to fatigue and the passage of time. When he filled a pan with dirt, he ran down the hill to wash it; nor could he forbear running up the hill again, panting and stumbling profanely, to refill the pan.

He was now a hundred yards from the water, and the inverted "V" was assuming definite proportions. The width of the pay-dirt steadily decreased, and the man extended in his mind's eye the sides of the "V" to their meeting place far up the hill. This was his goal, the apex of the "V", and he panned many times to locate it.

"Just about two yards above that manzanita bush an' a yard to the right," he finally concluded.

Then the temptation seized him. "As plain as the nose on your face," he said, as he abandoned his laborious cross-cutting and climbed to the indicated apex. He filled a pan and carried it down the hill to wash. It contained no trace of gold. He dug deep, and he dug shallow, filling and washing a dozen pans, and was unrewarded even by the tiniest golden speck. He was enraged at having yielded to the temptation, and berated himself blasphemously and pridelessly. Then he went down the hill and took up the cross-cutting.

"Slow an' certain, Bill; slow an' certain," he crooned. "Short-cuts to fortune ain't in your line, an' it's about time you know it. Get wise, Bill; get wise. Slow an' certain's the only hand you can play; so get to it, an' keep to it, too."

As the cross-cuts decreased, showing that the sides of the "V" were converging, the depth of the "V" increased. The gold-trace was dipping into the hill. It was only at thirty inches beneath the surface that he could get colors in his pan. The dirt he found at twenty-five inches from the surface, and at thirty-five inches yielded barren pans. At the base of the "V", by the water's edge, he had found the gold colors at the grass roots. The higher he went up the hill, the deeper the gold dipped. To dig a hole three feet deep in order to get one test-pan was a task of no mean magnitude; while between the man and the apex intervened an untold number of such holes to be dug. "An' there's no tellin' how much deeper it'll pitch," he sighed, in a moment's pause, while his fingers soothed his aching back.

Feverish with desire, with aching back and stiffening muscles, with pick and shovel gouging and mauling the soft brown earth, the man toiled up the hill. Before him was the smooth slope, spangled with flowers and made sweet with their breath. Behind him was devastation. It looked like some terrible eruption breaking out on the smooth skin of the hill. His slow progress was like that of a slug, befouling beauty with a monstrous trail.

Though the dipping gold-trace increased the man's work, he found consolation in the increasing richness of the pans. Twenty cents, thirty cents, fifty cents, sixty cents, were the values of the gold found in the pans, and at nightfall he washed his banner pan, which gave him a dollar's worth of gold-dust from a shovelful of dirt.

"I'll just bet it's my luck to have some inquisitive one come buttin' in here on my pasture," he mumbled sleepily that night as he pulled the blankets up to his chin.

Suddenly he sat upright. "Bill!" he called sharply. "Now, listen to me, Bill; d'ye hear! It's up to you, tomorrow mornin', to mosey round an' see what you can see. Understand? Tomorrow morning, an' don't you forget it!"

He yawned and glanced across at his side-hill. "Good night, Mr Pocket," he called.

In the morning he stole a march on the sun, for he had finished breakfast when its first rays caught him, and he was climbing the wall of the canyon where it crumbled away and gave footing. From the outlook at the top he found himself in the midst of loneliness. As far as he could see, chain after chain of mountains heaved themselves into his vision. To the east his eyes, leaping the miles between range and range and between many ranges, brought up at last against the white-peaked Sierras—the main crest, where the backbone of the Western world reared itself against the sky. To the north and south he could see more distinctly the cross-systems that broke through the main trend of the sea of mountains. To the west the ranges fell away, one behind the other, diminishing and fading into the gentle foothills that, in turn, descended into the great valley which he could not see.

And in all that mighty sweep of earth he saw no sign of man nor of the handiwork of man—save only the torn bosom of the hillside at his feet. The man looked long and carefully. Once, far down his own canyon, he though he saw in the air a faint hint of smoke. He looked again and decided that it was the purple haze of the hills made dark by a convolution of the canyon wall at its back.

"Hey, you Mr Pocket!" he called down into the canyon. "Stand out from under! I'm a-comin', Mr Pocket! I'm a-comin'!"

The heavy brogans on the man's feet made him appear clumsy-footed, but he swung down from the giddy height as lightly and airily as a mountain goat. A rock, turning under his foot on the edge of the precipice, did not disconcert him. He seemed to know the precise time required for the turn to culminate in disaster, and in the meantime he utilized the false footing itself for the momentary earth-contact necessary to carry him on into safety. Where the earth sloped so steeply that it was impossible to stand for a second upright, the man did not hesitate. His foot pressed the impossible surface for but a fraction of the fatal second and gave him the bound that carried him onward. Again, where even the fraction of a second's footing was out of the question, he would swing his body past by a moment's hand-grip on a jutting knob of rock, a crevice, or a precariously rooted shrub. At last, with a wild leap and yell, he exchanged the face of the wall for an earth-slide and finished the descent in the midst of several tons of sliding earth and gravel.

His first pan of the morning washed out over two dollars in coarse gold. It was from the centre of the "V". To either side the diminution in the values of the pans was swift. His lines of cross-cutting holes were growing very short. The converging sides of the inverted "V" were only a few yards apart. Their meeting-point was only a few yards above him. But the pay-streak was dipping deeper and deeper into the earth. By early afternoon he was sinking the test-holes five feet before the pans could show the gold-trace.

For that matter, the gold-trace had become something more than a trace; it was a placer mine in itself, and the man resolved to come back after he had found the pocket and work over the ground. But the increasing richness of the pans began to worry him. By late afternoon the worth of the pans had grown to three and four dollars. The man scratched his head perplexedly and looked a few feet up the hill at the manzanita bush that marked approximately the apex of the "V". He nodded his head and said oracularly:

"It's one o' two things, Bill: one o' two things. Either Mr Pocket's spilled himself all out an' down the hill, or else Mr Pocket's so rich you maybe won't be able to carry him all away with you. And that 'd be an awful shame, wouldn't it, now?" He chuckled at contemplation of so pleasant a dilemma.

Nightfall found him by the edge of the stream, his eye wrestling with the gathering darkness over the washing of a five-dollar pan.

"Wisht I had an electric light to go on working," he said.

He found sleep difficult that night. Many times he composed himself and closed his eyes for slumber to overtake him; but his blood pounded with too strong desire, and as many times his eyes opened and he murmured wearily, "Wisht it was sun-up."

Sleep came to him in the end, but his eyes were open with the first paling of the stars, and the gray of dawn caught him with breakfast finished and climbing the hillside in the direction of the secret abiding-place of Mr Pocket.

The first cross-cut the man made, there was space for only three holes, so narrow had become the pay-streak and so close was he to the fountainhead of the golden stream he had been following for four days.

"Be ca'm, Bill; be ca'm," he admonished himself, as he broke ground for the final hole where the sides of the "V" had at last come together in a point.

"I've got the almighty cinch on you, Mr Pocket, an' you can't lose me," he said many times as he sank the hole deeper and deeper.

Four feet, five feet, six feet, he dug his way down into the earth. The digging grew harder. His pick grated on broken rock. He examined the rock. "Rotten quartz," was his conclusion as, with the shovel, he cleared the bottom of the hole of loose dirt. He attacked the crumbling quartz with the pick, bursting the disintegrating rock asunder with every stroke.

He thrust his shovel into the loose mass. His eye caught a gleam of yellow. He dropped the shovel and squatted suddenly on his heels. As a farmer rubs the clinging earth from fresh-dug potatoes, so the man, a piece of rotten quartz held in both hands, rubbed the dirt away.

"Sufferin' Sardanopolis!" he cried. "Lumps an' chunks of it! Lumps an' chunks of it!"

It was only half rock he held in his hand. The other half was virgin gold. He dropped it into his pan and examined another piece. Little yellow was to be seen, but with his strong fingers he crumbled the rotten quartz away till both hands were filled with glowing yellow. He rubbed the dirt away from fragment after fragment, tossing them into the gold-pan. It was a treasure-hole. So much had the quartz rotten away that there was less of it than there was of gold. Now and again he found a piece to which no rock clung—a piece that was all gold. A chunk, where the pick had laid open the heart of the gold, glittered like a handful of yellow jewels, and he cocked his head at it and slowly turned it around and over to observe the rich play of the light upon it.

"Talk about yer Too Much Gold diggin's!" the man snorted contemptuously. "Why, this diggin' 'd make it look like thirty cents. This diggin' is All Gold. An' right here an' now I name this yere canyon 'All Gold Canyon', b' gosh!"

Still squatting on his heels, he continued examining the fragments and tossing them into the pan. Suddenly there came to him a premonition of danger. It seemed a shadow had fallen upon him. But there was no shadow. His heart had given a great jump up into his throat and was choking him. Then his blood slowly chilled and he felt the sweat of his shirt cold against his flesh.

He did not spring up nor look around. He did not move. He was considering the nature of the premonition he had received, trying to locate the source of the mysterious force that had warned him, striving to sense the imperative presence of the unseen thing that threatened him. There is an aura of things hostile, made manifest by messengers too refined for the senses to know; and this aura he felt, but knew not how he felt it. His was the feeling as when a cloud passes over the sun. It seemed that between him and life had passed something dark and smothering and menacing; a gloom, as it were, that swallowed up life and made for death—his death.

Every force of his being impelled him to spring up and confront the unseen danger, but his soul dominated the panic, and he remained squatting on his heels, in his hands a chunk of gold. He did not dare to look around, but he knew by now that there was something behind him and above him. He made believe to be interested in the gold in his hand. He examined it critically, turned it over and over, and rubbed the dirt from it. And all the time he knew that something behind him was looking at the gold over his shoulder.

Still feigning interest in the chunk of gold in his hand, he listened intently and he heard the breathing of the thing behind him. His eyes searched the ground in front of him for a weapon, but they saw only the uprooted gold, worthless to him now in his extremity. There was his pick, a handy weapon on occasion; but this was not such an occasion. The man realized his predicament. He was in a narrow hole that was seven feet deep. His head did not come to the surface of the ground. He was in a trap.

He remained squatting on his heels. He was quite cool and collected; but his mind, considering every factor, showed him only his helplessness. He continued rubbing the dirt from the quartz fragments and throwing the gold into the pan. There was nothing else for him to do. Yet he knew that he would have to rise up, sooner or later, and face the danger that breathed at his back. The minutes passed, and with the passage of each minute he knew that by so much he was nearer the time when he must stand up, or else—and his wet shirt went cold against his flesh again at the thought—or else he might receive death as he stooped there over his treasure.

Still he squatted on his heels, rubbing dirt from gold and debating in just what manner he should rise up. He might rise up with a rush and claw his way out of the hole to meet whatever threatened on the even footing above ground. Or he might rise up slowly and carelessly, and feign casually to discover the thing that breathed at his back. His instinct and every fighting fibre of his body favored the mad, clawing rush to the surface. His intellect, and the craft thereof, favored the slow and cautious meeting with the thing that menaced and which he could not see. And while he debated, a loud, crashing noise burst on his ear. At the same instant he received a stunning blow on the left side of his back, and from the point of impact felt a rush of flame through his flesh. He sprang up in the air, but halfway to his feet collapsed. His body crumpled in like a leaf withered in sudden heat, and he came down, his chest across his pan of gold, his face in the dirt and rock, his legs tangled and twisted because of the restricted space at the bottom of the hole. His legs twitched convulsively several times. His body was shaken with a mighty ague. There was a slow expansion of the lungs, accompanied by a deep sigh. Then the air was slowly, very slowly, exhaled, and his body as slowly flattened itself down into inertness.

Above, revolver in hand, a man was peering down over the edge of the hole. He peered for a long time at the prone and motionless body beneath him. After a while the stranger sat down on the edge of the hole so that he could see into it, and rested the revolver on his knee. Reaching his hand into a pocket, he drew out a wisp of brown paper. Into this he dropped a few crumbs of tobacco. The combination became a cigarette, brown and squat, with the ends turned in. Not once did he take his eyes from the body at the bottom of the hole. He lighted the cigarette and drew its smoke into his lungs with a caressing intake of the breath. He smoked slowly. Once the cigarette went out and he relighted it. And all the while he studied the body beneath him.

In the end he tossed the cigarette stub away and rose to his feet. He moved to the edge of the hole. Spanning it, a hand resting on each edge, and with the revolver still in the right hand, he muscled his body down into the hole. While his feet were yet a yard from the bottom he released his hands and dropped down.

At the instant his feet struck bottom he saw the pocket-miner's arm leap out, and his own legs knew a swift, jerking grip that overthrew him. In the nature of the jump his revolver-hand was above his head. Swiftly as the grip had flashed about his legs, just as swiftly he brought the revolver down. He was still in the air, his fall in process of completion, when he pulled the trigger. The explosion was deafening in the confined space. The smoke filled the hole so that he could see nothing. He struck the bottom on his back, and like a cat's the pocket-miner's body was on top of him. Even as the miner's body passed on top, the stranger crooked in his right arm to fire; and even in that instant the miner, with a quick thrust of elbow, struck his wrist. The muzzle was thrown up and the bullet thudded into the dirt of the side of the hole.

The next instant the stranger felt the miner's hand grip his wrist. The struggle was now for the revolver. Each man strove to turn it against the other's body. The smoke in the hole was clearing. The stranger, lying on his back, was beginning to see dimly. But suddenly he was blinded by a handful of dirt deliberately flung into his eyes by his antagonist. In that moment of shock his grip on the revolver was broken. In the next moment he felt a smashing darkness descend upon his brain, and in the midst of the darkness even the darkness ceased.

But the pocket-miner fired again and again, until the revolver was empty. Then he tossed it from him and, breathing heavily, sat down on the dead man's legs.

The miner was sobbing and struggling for breath. "Measly skunk!" he panted; "a-campin' on my trail an' lettin' me do the work, an' then shootin' me in the back!"

He was half crying from anger and exhaustion. He peered at the face of the dead man. It was sprinkled with loose dirt and gravel, and it was difficult to distinguish the features.

"Never laid eyes on him before," the miner concluded his scrutiny. "Just a common an' ordinary thief, hang him! An' he shot me in the back! He shot me in the back!"

He opened his shirt and felt himself, front and back, on his left side.

"Went clean through, and no harm done!" he cried jubilantly. "I'll bet he aimed all right all right; but he drew the gun over when he pulled the trigger—the cur! But I fixed 'm! Oh, I fixed 'm!"

His fingers were investigating the bullet-hole in his side, and a shade of regret passed over his face. "It's goin' to be stiffer'n hell," he said. "An' it's up to me to get mended an' get out o' here."

He crawled out of the hole and went down the hill to his camp. Half an hour later he returned, leading his pack-horse. His open shirt disclosed the rude bandages with which he had dressed his wound. He was slow and awkward with his left-hand movements, but that did not prevent his using the arm.

The bight of the pack-rope under the dead man's shoulders enabled him to heave the body out of the hole. Then he set to work gathering up his gold. He worked steadily for several hours, pausing often to rest his stiffening shoulder and to exclaim:

"He shot me in the back, the measly skunk! He shot me in the back!"

When his treasure was quite cleaned up and wrapped securely into a number of blanket-covered parcels, he made an estimate of its value.

"Four hundred pounds, or I'm a Hottentot," he concluded. "Say two hundred in quartz an' dirt—that leaves two hundred pounds of gold, Bill! Wake up! Two hundred pounds of gold! Forty thousand dollars! An' it's yourn—all yourn!"

He scratched his head delightedly and his fingers blundered into an unfamiliar groove. They quested along it for several inches. It was a crease through his scalp where the second bullet had ploughed.

He walked angrily over to the dead man.

"You would, would you?" he bullied. "You would, eh? Well, I fixed you good an' plenty, an' I'll give you a decent burial, too. That's more'n you'd have done for me."

He dragged the body to the edge of the hole and toppled it in. It struck the bottom with a dull crash, on its side, the face twisted up to the light. The miner peered down at it.

"An' you shot me in the back!" he said accusingly.

With pick and shovel he filled the hole. Then he loaded the gold on his horse. It was too great a load for the animal, and when he had gained his camp he transferred part of it to his saddle-horse. Even so, he was compelled to abandon a portion of his outfit—pick and shovel and gold-pan, extra food and cooking utensils, and divers odds and ends.

The sun was at the zenith when the man forced the horses at the screen of vines and creepers. To climb the huge boulders the animals were compelled to uprear and struggle blindly through the tangled mass of vegetation. Once the saddle-horse fell heavily and the man removed the pack to get the animal on its feet. After it started on its way again the man thrust his head out from among the leaves and peered up at the hillside.

"The measly skunk!" he said, and disappeared.

There was a ripping and tearing of vines and boughs. The trees surged back and forth, marking the passage of the animals through the midst of them. There was a clashing of steel-shod hoofs on stone, and now and again a sharp cry of command. Then the voice of the man was raised in song:—

"Tu'n around an' tu'n yo' face
Untoe them sweet hills of grace
(D'pow'rs of sin yo' am scornin'!).
Look about an' look aroun'
Fling yo' sin-pack on d' groun'
(Yo' will meet wid d' Lord in d' mornin'!)."

The song grew fainter and fainter, and through the silence crept back the spirit of the place. The stream once more drowsed and whispered; the hum of the mountain bees rose sleepily. Down through the perfume-weighted air fluttered the snowy fluffs of the cottonwoods. The butterflies drifted in and out among the trees, and over all blazed the quiet sunshine. Only remained the hoof-marks in the meadow and the torn hillside to mark the boisterous trail of the life that had broken the peace of the place and passed on.

JOHN G. NEIHARDT
The Last Thunder Song

John Gneisenau Neihardt (1881–1973) was brought up in a pioneer sod house in Kansas. He graduated from Nebraska Normal College at the age of sixteen, and took a variety of jobs before devoting himself to writing, eventually becoming Professor of Poetry at the University of Nebraska. For a number of years he lived amongst the Omahas and Sioux, and later served on the Bureau of Indian Affairs. American Indians are at the centre of his Western fiction, and he was amongst the very first to portray them sympathetically. In the Western genre, Neihardt published three novels, *The Dawn Builder* (1911), *Life's a Love* (1914), *When the Tree Flowered* (1951), and two collections of short stories, *The Lonesome Trail* (1907) and *Indian Tales and Others* (1926). Neihardt also worked as secretary to the Sioux medicine man, Black Elk, a collaboration which led to *Black Elk Speaks* (1932), one of the most important books published about Amerindians. As a poet, Neihardt is most famous for his five-part *Cycle of the West*.

'The Last Thunder Song' is from *The Lonesome Trail* collection.

IT IS AN ANCIENT CUSTOM to paint tragedy in blood tints. This is because men were once merely animals, and have not as yet been able to live down their ancestry. Yet the stroke of a dagger is a caress beside the throb of hopeless days.

Life can ache; the living will tell you this. But the dead make no complaint.

There is no greater tragedy than the fall of a dream! Napoleon dreamed; so did a savage. It is the same. I know of the scene of a great tragedy. Very few have recognized it as such; there was so little noise along with it. It happened at the Omaha Agency, which is situated on the Missouri River some seventy miles above Omaha.

The summer of 1900 debilitated all thermal adjectives. It was not hot; it was *Saharical!* It would hardly have been hyperbole to have said that the Old Century lay dying of a fever. The untilled hills of the reservation thrust themselves up in the August sunshine like the emaciated joints of one bedridden. The land lay as yellow as the skin of a fever patient, except in those rare spots where the melancholy corn struggled heartlessly up a hillside, making a blotch like a bedsore!

The blood of the prairie was impoverished, and the sky would give no drink with which to fill the dwindling veins. When one wished to search the horizon for the cloud that was not there, he did it from beneath an arched hand. The small whirlwinds that awoke like sudden fits of madness in the sultry air, rearing yellow columns of dust into the sky—these alone relieved the monotony of dazzle.

Every evening the clouds rolled flashing about the horizon and thundered back into the night. They were merely taunts, like the holding of a cool cup just out of reach of a fevered mouth; and the clear nights passed, bringing dewless dawns, until the ground cracked like a parched lip!

The annual Indian powwow was to be ended prematurely that year, for the sun beat uninvitingly upon the flat bottom where the dances were held, and the Indians found much comfort in the shade of their summer tepees. But when it was noised about that, upon the next day, the old medicine-man

Mahowari (Passing Cloud) would dance potent dances and sing a thunder song with which to awaken the lazy thunder spirits to their neglected duty of rain-making, then the argument of the heat became feeble.

So the next morning, the bronze head of every Indian tepeehold took his pony, his dogs, his squaw, and his papooses of indefinite number to the powwow ground. In addition to these, the old men carried with them long memories and an implicit faith. The young men, who had been away to Indian school, and had succeeded to some extent in stuffing their brown skins with white souls, carried with them curiosity and doubt, which, if properly united, beget derision.

The old men went to a shrine; the young men went to a show. When a shrine becomes a show, the World advances a step. And *that* is the benevolence of Natural Law!

About the open space in which the dances were held, an oval covering had been built with willow boughs, beneath which the Indians lounged in sweating groups. Slowly about the various small circles went the cumbersome stone pipes.

To one listening, drowsed with the intense sunlight, the buzzle and mutter and snarl of the gossiping Omahas seemed the grotesque echoes from a vanished age. Between the dazzle of the sun and the sharply contrasting blue shade, there was but a line of division; yet a thousand years lay between one gazing into the sun and those dozing in the shadow. It was as if God had flung down a bit of the Young World's twilight into the midst of the Old World's noon. Here lounged the masterpiece of the toiling centuries—a Yankee. There sat the remnant of a race as primitive as Israel. Yet the white man looked on with the contempt of superiority.

Before ten o'clock everybody had arrived and his family with him. A little group, composed of the Indian Agent, the Agency Physician, the Mission Preacher, and a newspaper man, down from the city for reportorial purposes, waited and chatted, sitting upon a ragged patch of available shadow.

"These Omahas are an exceptional race," the preacher was saying in his ministerial tone of voice; "an exceptional race!"

The newspaper man mopped his face, lit a cigarette and nodded assent with a hidden meaning twinkling in his eye.

"Quite exceptional!" he said, tossing his head in the direction of an unusually corpulent bunch of steaming, sweating, bronze men and women. "God, like some lesser master-musicians, has not confined himself to grand opera, it seems!"

He took a long pull at his cigarette, and his next words came out in a cloud of smoke.

"This particular creation savours somewhat of opera bouffe!"

With severe unconcern the preacher mended the broken thread of his discourse. "Quite an exceptional race in many ways. The Omaha is quite as honest as the white man."

"That is a truism!" The pencil-pusher drove this observation between the minister's words like a wedge.

"In his natural state he was much more so," uninterruptedly continued the preacher; he was used to continuous discourse. "I have been told by many of the old men that in the olden times an Indian could leave his tepee for months at a time, and on his return would find his most valuable possessions untouched. I tell you, gentlemen, the Indian is like a prairie flower that has been transplanted from the blue sky and the summer sun and the pure winds into the steaming, artificial atmosphere of the hothouse! A glass roof is not the blue sky! Man's talent is not God's genius! That is why you are looking at a perverted growth.

"Look into an Indian's face and observe the ruins of what was once manly dignity, indomitable energy, masterful prowess! When I look upon one of these faces, I have the same thought as, when travelling in Europe, I looked upon the ruins of Rome.

"Everywhere broken arches, fallen columns, tumbled walls! Yet through these as through a mist one can discern the magnificence of the living city. So in looking upon one of these faces, which are merely ruins in another sense. They were once as noble, as beautiful as—"

In his momentary search for an eloquent simile, the minister paused.

"As pumpkin pies!" added the newspaper man with a chuckle; and he whipped out his notebook and pencil to jot down his brilliant thought, for he had conceived a very witty "story" which he would pound out for the Sunday edition.

"Well," said the Agency Physician, finally sucked into the whirlpool of discussion, "it seems to me that there is no room for crowding on either side. Indians are pretty much like white men; liver and kidneys and lungs, and that sort of thing; slight difference in the pigment under the skin. I've looked into the machinery of both species and find just as much room in one as the other for a soul!"

"And both will go upward," added the minister.

"Like different grades of tobacco," observed the Indian Agent, "the smoke of each goes up in the same way."

"Just so," said the reporter; "but let us cut out the metaphysics. I wonder when this magical *cuggie* is going to begin his humid evolutions. Lamentable, isn't it, that such institutions as rain prayers should exist on the very threshold of the Twentieth Century?"

"I think," returned the minister, "that the Twentieth Century has no intention of eliminating God! This medicine-man's prayer, in my belief, is as sacred as the prayer of any churchman. The difference between Wakunda and God is merely orthographical."

"But," insisted the cynical young man from the city, "I had not been taught to think of God as of one who forgets! Do you know what I would do if I had no confidence in the executive ability of my God?"

Taking the subsequent silence as a question, the young man answered: "Why, I would take a day off and whittle one out of wood!"

"A youth's way is the wind's way," quoted the preacher, with a paternal air.

"And the thoughts of youth are long, long thoughts; but what is all this noise about?" returned the reporter.

A buzz of expectant voices had grown at one end of the oval, and had spread contagiously throughout the elliptical strip of shade. For with slow, majestic steps the medicine-man, Mahowari, entered the enclosure and walked towards the centre. The fierce sun emphasized the brilliancy of the old man's garments and glittered upon the profusion of trinkets, the magic heirlooms of the medicine-man. It was not the robe nor the dazzling trinkets that caught the eye of one acquainted with Mahowari. It was the erectness of his figure, for he had been bowed with years, and many vertical suns had shone upon the old man's back since his face had been turned toward the ground. But now with firm step and form rigidly erect he walked.

Any sympathetic eye could easily read the thoughts that passed through the old man's being like an elixir infusing youth. Now in his feeble years would come his greatest triumph! Today he would sing with greater power than ever he had sung. Wakunda would hear the cry. The rains would come! Then the white men would be stricken with belief!

Already his heart sang before his lips. In spite of the hideous painting of his face, the light of triumph shone there like the reflection of a great fire.

Slowly he approached the circle of drummers who sat in the glaring centre of the ellipse of sunlight. It was all as though the First Century had awakened like a ghost and stood in the very doorway of the Twentieth!

When Mahowari had approached within a yard of the drums, he stopped, and raising his arms and his eyes to the cloudless sky, uttered a low cry like a wail of supplication. Then the drums began to throb with that barbaric music as old as the world; a sound like the pounding of a fever temple, with a recurring snarl like the warning of a rattlesnake.

Every sound of the rejoicing and suffering prairie echoes in the Indian's drum.

With a slow, majestic bending of the knees and an alternate lifting of his feet, the medicine-man danced in a circle about the snarling drums. Then like a faint wail of winds toiling up a wooded bluff, his thunder song began.

The drone and whine of the mysterious, untranslatable words pierced the drowse of the day, lived for a moment with the echoes of the drums among the surrounding hills, and languished from a whisper into silence. At intervals the old man raised his face, radiant with fanatic ecstasy, to the meridian glare of the sun, and the song swelled to a supplicating shout.

Faster and faster the old man moved about the circle; louder and wilder grew the song. Those who watched from the shade were absorbed in an intense silence, which, with the drowse of the sultry day, made every sound a paradox! The old men forgot their pipes and sat motionless.

Suddenly, at one end of the covering, came the sound of laughter! At first an indefinite sound like the spirit of merriment entering a capricious dream of sacred things; then it grew and spread until it was no longer merriment, but a loud jeer of derision! It startled the old men from the intenseness of their watching. They looked up and were stricken with awe. The young men were jeering this, the holiest rite of their fathers!

Slower and slower the medicine-man danced; fainter and fainter grew the song and ceased abruptly. With one quick glance, Mahowari saw the shattering of his hopes. He glanced at the sky; but saw no swarm of black spirits to avenge such sacrilege. Only the blaze of the sun, the glitter of the arid zenith!

In that one moment, the temporary youth of the old man died out. His shoulders drooped to their wonted position. His limbs tottered. He was old again.

It was the Night stricken heart-sick with the laughter of the Dawn. It was the audacious Present jeering at the Past, tottering with years. At that moment, the impudent, cruel, brilliant youth called Civilisation snatched the halo from the grey hairs of patriarchal Ignorance. Light flouted the rags of Night. A clarion challenge shrilled across the years.

Never before in all the myriad moons had such a thing occurred. It was too great a cause to produce an effect of grief or anger. It stupefied. The old men and women sat motionless. They could not understand.

With uneven step and with eyes that saw nothing, Mahowari passed from among his kinsmen and tottered up the valley toward his lonesome shack and tepee upon the hillside. It was far past noon when the last of the older Omahas left the scene of the dance.

The greatest number of the white men who had witnessed the last thunder dance of the Omahas went homeward much pleased. The show had turned out quite funny indeed. "Ha, ha, ha! Did you see how surprised the old *cuggie* looked? He, he, he!" Life, being necessarily selfish, argues from its own standpoint.

But as the minister rode slowly toward his home there was no laughter in his heart. He was saying to himself: "If the whole fabric of my belief should suddenly be wrenched from me, what then?" Even this question was born of selfishness, but it brought pity.

In the cool of the evening the minister mounted his horse and rode to the home of Mahowari, which was a shack in the winter and a tepee in the summer. Dismounting, he threw the bridle reins upon the ground and raised the door flap of the tepee. Mahowari sat cross-legged upon the ground, staring steadily before him with unseeing eyes.

"How!" said the minister.

The old Indian did not answer. There was no expression of grief or anger or despair upon his face. He sat like a statue. Yet, the irregularity of his breathing showed where the pain lay. An Indian suffers in his breast. His face is a mask.

The minister sat down in front of the silent old man and, after the immemorial manner of ministers, talked of a better world, of a pitying Christ, and of God, the Great Father. For the first time the Indian raised his face and spoke briefly in English:

"God? He dead, guess!"

Then he was silent again for some time.

Suddenly his eyes lit up with a light that was not the light of age. The heart of his youth had awakened. The old memories came back and he spoke fluently in his own tongue, which the minister understood.

"These times are not like the old times. The young men have caught some of the wisdom of the white man. Nothing is sure. It is not good. I cannot understand. Everything is young and new. All old things are dead. Many moons ago, the wisdom of Mahowari was great. I can remember how my father said to me one day when I was yet young and all things lay new before me: 'Let my son go to a high hill and dream a great dream'; and I went up in the evening and cried out to Wakunda and I slept and dreamed.

"I saw a great cloud sweeping up from under the horizon, and it was terrible with lightning and loud thunder. Then it passed over me and rumbled down the sky and disappeared. And when I awoke and told my people of my dream, they rejoiced and said: 'Great things are in store for this youth. We shall call him the Passing Cloud, and he shall be a thunder man, keen and quick of thought, with the keenness and quickness of the lightning; and his name shall be as thunder in the ears of men.' And I grew and believed in these sayings and I was strong. But now I can see the meaning of the dream—a great light and a great noise and a passing."

The old man sighed, and the light passed out of his eyes. Then he looked searchingly into the face of the minister and said, speaking in English:

"You white medicine-man. You pray?"

The minister nodded.

Mahowari turned his gaze to the ground and said wearily:

"White God dead too, guess."

EUGENE MANLOVE RHODES
The Bird in the Bush

Eugene Manlove Rhodes (1869–1934) was born in Nebraska, but in 1881 his father moved the family to New Mexico. After working as a cowboy, Rhodes migrated to Apalachin, New York, taking a job as a farm labourer to support his wife and her extended family. In Apalachin, Rhodes longed for New Mexico, and began writing Western stories set in that state as a means of dealing with his homesickness. Not unsurprisingly, the Far West which appears in Rhodes's stories is a place of rose-tinted romance. Rhodes wrote nine Western novels in all, starting with *Good Men and True* (1910) and finishing with *The Proud Sheriff* (1935), the best-known of which is the short novel *Paso Por Aqui* (1927)—which many consider to be the finest Western story ever written. Rhodes's fictional style is somewhat overblown, but his writing, at its best, is of a rare intensity.

'Bird in the Bush' is from *Redbook*, 1917.

I LIKED THE BIG SANDY, and I liked the people. But I saw what was coming. Good rains—high grass—double your herds every washday—everything lovely! Then along comes old Mr Drought. *Bing!* There you are, busted. It's like playing double or quits; if you don't pinch your bets, you're going home talking to yourself. It's got to be that way. So I sold out.

Then I went off alone and tried to establish communication with myself. "Look here, Andy," says I, "are you going to be a dern fool all your whole life? You're getting old, and you're getting bald, and those that know you best, they love you most—but they put up quarantine signs against you. It's time to quit your wild, fool ways and settle down."

"But, still, yet," I rejoins, "you can't never be satisfied in town, planted in rows, or packed in cans or stacked on shelves. And you'll never be anything more than a bald-headed boy so long as you stay on the free range. With that rep' you got, people wouldn't let you behave if you wanted to. Your poor old dad tried to hammer some farmin' into your head," says I. "Why not try that?"

"But, again, then," says I, "you got to jar loose from the cow-business gradual. A little bunch of bossies fenced safe from the depredations of unprincipled men—that's what you want, to tide you over till you get the hang of farming."

Good scheme, wasn't it? I thought so. I'd held onto some of my wisest cow-ponies. So now I picked out two and sold the rest. Deacon was experienced and observing and level-headed; Quaker didn't have near such good judgment, but he was Deacon's pardner. I fixed me up a pack, and we went projecting off, still-huntin' a home for our declining years.

We skipped Prescott. Prescott had forgiven me, all right, allowing I was as much sinned against as sinning; but they was likewise strong of the opinion that if I ever came back, they'd sin against me some more. They was mighty explicit about that.

We shunned Tonto Basin too, where cattle- and sheep-men was enjoyin' a war. I wasn't in any hurry. I reckon we put in three or four months on that search. But I hadn't found nothing quite to fit me.

I'd been climbing uphill two or three days—hadn't seen a man since I left Salt River, and mighty few sheep-herders—just a steady up, up, up, through a crooked, winding, wavy, hazy, cold, blue-black piny-woods country, and at last I came out on the big top. Oh, man!

The mountain dropped off in fifteen minutes all I'd climbed up in three days. Right under me was a mesa of low, red foothills; then came a great, round, gray-greenish-yellow basin, thirty or fifty miles across any which way, saucer-shaped, heaped high with sunshine. There was big mountains all around it; where I sat, on the south, they made a level black wall with one gate-way off to my left. The eastern curve was piny-black too, broken hills, round, rolling and low. Across in the southwest, maybe forty mile away, was a stretch of bare gray cliffs, straight upandicular, ending in a limestone elephant with one eye and a granite trunk six miles long. He looked mighty curious. He kept that one eye on me, and I felt little cold shivers playing up and down my backbone.

Running catawampus across the basin, like a crack in the saucer, was a cañon. It headed in a gap in the northeast and slipped off to the Pacific through a fold in the cliffs this side of that elephant. He had a mean eye.

It was wide and deep and crooked, that cañon. My side of the basin was wavy; north of the cañon-crack it rose in benches; and 'way beyond and above the last bench was a half-circle of misty, pinky granite knobs and spikes and spires, notched and jagged, domes and turrets and things. They took my eye. Seems like the nicest places to live are where you find that worn-down granite for soil. It's so clean and cheerful.

Down under us I saw a big white road striking across to the front gate at my left. Only for the road, I'd 'a' thought I was the first man on the job.

I'd been pursuing around at random, and there wasn't rightly any way to get down from where I was. But we made it sliding, somehow. It took us half a day. Down in the red feethills we found mines and things, all nailed up and abandoned. We found a little spring and made camp.

Soon in the morning we was out on the plain. Prettiest rolling mesa you ever see—black grama and crowfoot; plenty slick fat cattle, mostly branded J.B.; antelope, and too many bands of wild horses. Presently we hit an old wagon-track, rutted deep but grown up with grass. More old roads comes anglin' in, and at last we come to the big white road I'd seen from the summit.

It had been traveled a heap once, but not lately. It was ruler-straight across the mesa, till we pitched off into the breaks of a draw that led down to the main big cañon, getting deeper and deeper. Directly we come to the jump-off place, and the wagon-road took to the side-hill. It was dug out two or three thousand years ago and hadn't been repaired since—ribbed and gullied—rubble, with the soil all washed away. We twisted down and down and down some more, till at last we come out on the cañon-floor to orchards and ditches and a white town asleep in the sun.

Yessir! Every man I see was asleep, under the trees or on the porches; and they was all old, old men. I followed along between vineyards and open doors and alfalfa and cottonwood trees to a shady plaza with a *'cequia* tinklin' down beside, mighty pleasant. I let the horses drink. There was a 'dobe store squandering around under the oldest cottonwood in the world, and in front sets an old jasper with a long, gray beard, sound asleep. I woke him up.

"Good evening," says I. "Can you tell me where I can find *Allan Quatermain?*"

He didn't get me. He wasn't literary. "Never heard of him," says he.

I heard some one laugh behind me. It was a cool, ripply little laugh, tuned to a little waterfall in the *'cequia*. I looked around and saw a girl in a streak of dancing sun that smuggled through the branches.

"S-sh! *Allan Quatermain* escaped—three years ago—across the mountain—and the forest—and the desert—toward Zanzibar! Hush-sh!" She put her finger to her lip and tiptoed across to me. She gave the old geezer a side-look and held her hand up, palm out. "S-sh!" she says again. . . .

Sometimes I dream of going back. I ride along dim old roads that never were, to old houses that couldn't be—great, ramshackle old barracks, doors open and sagging, shutters that swing and squeak over broken—dim and dark inside, old moldy pictures on the wall, dust on the tables and chairs and drifted in the fireplace. And I can't remember—quite. So I follow the old road, windin' and windin' through a level, brushy country. There's no tracks turning off, but the road gets dimmer and dimmer, and at last it plays out. So I go on and on to look for ranches I can almost remember, and a little swift river that ought to be somewhere: but the mountains are wrong, and all the gaps are in the wrong places, and everything is changed—except Minnie. She is just the same; she isn't any older; her eyes are sunny; she comes dancing and laughing to meet me through a deep shade. And—this is curious—she brings the sunlight with her, always the warm, clear sunshine rippling about her as she comes. I wasn't expecting her: I try to tell her so—and then I wake up.

I hopped down as she came—the really time, I mean, not the dream. Deacon stretched out his nose, and she pets him. "It is the custom of the valley," she says, "for strangers from the outside world to stay at the—at the palace—until their fate is decided."

She was just a little trick. There was a dimple in her cheek that come and went as she spoke; her eyes were brown, and down in each one lived a little, merry, dancing gold devil—you could see him when she laughed at you. Quaker come up alongside and crowded old Deacon off—he wanted to be petted too. So I pushed his head away, just like he done to Deacon—and then she laughed again. "Got to keep pack-horses in their places," says I.

"They want their dinner," said the girl. "So do you. Come along."

"That's right," said the old geezer, settlin' back for another snooze. "Cow-men, they all stop with her dad—he owns the J.B. You go along with her."

So we walked on down the street; the *'cequia* sung along beside us, Deacon and Quaker looking around, mighty interested, sizing things up.

"Who, which, why, when, where, what, how?" says I. "Where am I? Why is everyone asleep? And why are the mines closed down? Why doesn't no one ever travel the roads? Why hasn't no one ever heard of this place before? Why did the elephant try to scare me back? Why everything?"

So she told me why. "We're waiting for the railroad. It's our sole occupation. That's the answer to all the questions. And now it's your turn, isn't it? Who, where, how? Explain! No wanderer has found his way here since —"

"Allan Quatermain?" says I. "For me, Miss—why, I guess I couldn't have stayed away if I'd tried. It was predestined and foreordained that I was comin' here—to wait for the railroad."

"Here's the J.B. house," she said. "Father isn't at home, but Anselmo will show you where to put your horses." She give both of 'em a little pat. "Then come on in. Mother and I will have dinner ready for you."

I turned the horses to an alfalfa stack and went in. Mrs Briscoe was a nice, motherly old lady, but she acted kinder worn-out road-weary. After I met old man Briscoe, I knew why. He was a mean old whelp—just naturally cussed. The house was fixed up nice.

That evenin' Minnie sat out on the gallery with me, explainin'. The basin was called the Butterbowl—'member the Butterbowl on Rainbow? I named that myself, after this place. The river was San Lucas; the big range I'd crossed was Black Mountain, and my nice pinky hills was Dream Mountain.

In and around Butterbowl was everything a man could want—grass, lumber-woods, mines, water and soil to grow anything: but it took three days' hard riding in that direction to reach a given point. The early settlers saw that a railroad was bound to tap this country—some time. So they made 'em a town, Central, built them wagon-roads out to the tributary mines and lumber, built orchards and ditches and set down to wait for the whistle. Meantime they raised cattle.

There was one big cattle-company, the J.B., and a lot of little outfits beside. Leastwise, they called it a company, though Minnie's dad, he owned most of it. They hadn't overstocked yet, but they was fixin' to; they hadn't got to stealin' much yet, but they was practicing; and old J. Briscoe allowed the little cow-men was all worthless and not fit company for his daughter: so they had all the makin's of trouble. I thought I'd stay.

In the morning I struck out for my pinky mountains. One of them nice little Southwest spring winds, like we got here, was beating in my face, mighty raw. Once I climbed the mesa, I quit the road and sidled off, so's to split the difference between the one-eyed elephant and the stage-road gap, Holbrook way. I was needin' a place where I wouldn't be in nobody's way, d'yuh see—an' likewise, where nobody'd be in my way. I passed all the cattle, and I passed all the cattle-tracks; I got up on the last bench, level as a billiard-table, right under them pinky mountains: I put in between two of them back-bones and run spang onto exactly what I wanted.

I heard the wind ravin' and howlin' up overhead, but in between them two spurs of hill it was still as a Monday meetin'-house. After facing that wind all day, it seemed like a box-seat in Paradise, complimentary. I named it Shelter, right off.

I guess Adam had the best time anybody ever did, namin' things. Ever notice what good names you find in a thin-settled country? That's cause they didn't have no prominent citizens to call things after.

There was a narrow box between the hills for about a quarter, and a big gravel wash. Then we came out in a wide open valley with a big granite fence about two thousand foot high all around it, and I knowed Andrew Jackson Bates had found him a home.

Come to find out afterward, the Butterbowl folks called the place Bottle Basin. That was the shape of it, maybe five miles across from rim-rock to rim-rock, and about six the long way. There was crowfoot, black grama and short, curly, yellow buffalo-grass, and mesquite beans; plenty cedar, juniper and live-oak on the ridges. Put a little fence across the mouth of the bottle, and there I was, snug, my cows fenced in and other people's fenced out. I made camp and went a-prospectin'.

There wasn't any living water, as I knowed before, by there being no fresh cow-tracks, but I could see by the wash that a heap of water come down the draw when it rained. My play was to build tanks and store flood-water—see? By sundown I had it all figured out. Here I was to build a little tank, to hold water for my teams, whilst I was weavin' a big one. Both was to be in a smooth side-draw, where there was first a wide place to hold a world of water, and then a narrow place to make a dam. I was going to put a wing-dam in on the main cañon, and carry flood-water to my tanks in a ditch through a little saddle—so too much heap flood would never break my dams; I was going to make my waste-ways first, make 'em twice as big as they'd ever need to be, and then make 'em bigger. I'd seen dams built before.

It was full moon, that night. I prowled around, a-plannin', proud as a pawn in the king-row. I reckon that was about the happiest one time I ever put in. "Andrew Jackson, I sure made a stake to-morrow," says I. Here I was to build my big dam, and here my spillway; here was to be my corrals, and here my orchard; I began farmin' by breaking in a little flat and edged a little further down every year.

Next day we ambled around looking for water. I followed the dim cow-trails till they got plain, and the plain ones till they got dusty, and we struck a spring, fifteen miles away, where a fellow named Hall held out—give the Bow-and-Arrow brand. Come dinner, I found this was the nearest place for me to haul water from to begin my work. Of course, I didn't tip my hand. Cow-men sure hate to be crowded.

That night I cached my pack and hiked to Holbrook for a surveyor. He ran out my section numbers for me, and made me plots and plans and estimates and specifications. I didn't want 'em: I built my dam by guess and by golly when I got at it; but the law calls for 'em.

Then I wandered over and broke the news gently to old man Hall and asked him if I could borrow some water to haul over to Shelter. He fought his head right smart at first, till he found out what my name was. Then he come to his feet. He'd heard of me. And he judged I'd come in handy to hold the J.B. outfit level. So I got him and his boy Bill to slip down to Globe with me as witnesses when I filed on my claim.

I got a wagon in Globe, a darky named Eph and a span of mules, a Mex boy and a span of big horses, a plow and two scrapers, water-barrels, tools and a tent and such. We took rounders on the Butterbowl and pussy-footed into Shelter unbeknownst.

Hall drawed me over a first load of water on his wagon, for a starter. I set Eph and Esteban to tanking while I broke Deacon and Quaker to the water-wagon. They was dead set against it. It was some comedown from bein' crack cowhorses. I reckon they thought I'd put 'em on the scraper next.

I see they wasn't going to be satisfied, and we hadn't brought much corn up from Globe; so after a few trips I put off down to Central. They was bound to find out about me and Shelter before long, anyway. I dickered for a span of spankin' black mares, Zip and Jezebel, and carried out a load of corn and supplies, with Deacon and Quaker at the tailgate. They were sure tickled. I knew some one would be curious about me. And sure enough, the next day but one, here comes old John Briscoe, just a-snuffin'. I hadn't never seen him before, but I knowed him right off. He looked like a cartoon of himself.

"What's this? What's all this? What you doing here?" he sizzles.

"Just now I'm a-prizing long, wide, hard, heavy, thick, big rocks out o' my spillway with a crowbar," says I. "And directly I'm going to compound the finest dinner you ever flopped your lip over. Get down and look at your saddle a spell."

"Of all the gall!" says J.B. "We'll fix *your* clock! You'll be glad to get out o' here, quicker than you came—crowdin' yourself in where you ain't wanted. If you're hunting trouble, you've come to the right shop. You'll get it, and you'll get it good!"

Wasn't that a nice crack to make? That's what a man gets himself by going where he's not known.

"Did you ever chance to hear the honored name of Aforesaid Andrew Jackson Bates?" I asked him.

"The pleasure is mine," he says, mighty sneerin'. "I have not. Desperado, I reckon?"

"Worse than that," says I. "A heap worse. I'm a stayer. I've got a positive genius for bad luck—witness them opprobrious syllables, Aforesaid, wished onto me by acclamation of five States and Territories. Fair sir," says I, "you was mentionin' trouble to me. I've had all kinds of trouble a mere single man can have, and most generally got the worst of it; but let me tell you, beloved, none of my victorious and laurel-wreathed antagonists has ever bragged about it any, and that includes the sovereign State of California, the Republic of Mexico, the Espee Railroad, the Diamond-A Cattle Company, Yavapai County, Prescott, Bucky O'Neill and the Arizona House of Reprobates, besides Montana and some few other commonwealths whose memory is now fadin' in the mists that rise down the River of Time. So far, I've had no mix-up with the United States or the Daughters of the Revolution," says I, "but outside o' that, I've met everything in the shape of man or beast that the umpire could furnish and have never yet lowered my arm.

"Trouble?" says I. "Trouble? Before you come talking trouble to me, you'd better read the history of your country. Pending them investigations," says I, "don't you try to run any blazers on me, and likewise smooth your wrinkled front. You may not know it, but you're allowin' yourself to make horrid frowns at me, and I won't have it. I like smilin' faces and cheerful words and happy laughter around me, and I'm goin' to have 'em. I came here seekin' a quiet and peaceful spot to while away the Indian summer of my soul, and if you pester me any, I'm going to do you a great personal injury, forthwith, at once, *ahorita, immediatamente* and now! Declare yourself, Marmaduke Mortimer—a gold chain or a wooden leg?"

J.B. was some impressed by them remarks. He come back at me easy. "But it wouldn't be right for you to turn no cattle loose on this range," says he. "You ain't got no water-right. And you can't get no water by digging—not around here. I've drilled a well five hundred foot, right here in Bottom Basin."

"Shelter," I corrects him.

He was right on! "And this mizzable little tank you're making won't have a drop of water in it three months after the rains. You can't—I mean, it wouldn't be the square thing to turn a herd in the Butterbowl on the strength of that."

"The audience will kindly retain their rompers," says I. "I ain't goin' to turn any cattle loose on your range. This is only my family cistern, to water my horses whilst we collaborate on a big he-tank. I'm goin' to make the desert do that blossom thing; I'm goin' to be a bold yeomanry, my country's pride, and sit under my own vine and fig-tree. I'm going to raise Early Martyr potatoes; I'm going to walk abroad and view the fields where oats, peas, beans and barley grows. You cast your eagle eye down the hollow betwixt them two hills," says I. "Right there, in about ten months or two years, I'm goin' to have me a tame ten-acre lake."

"Huh! There ain't watershed enough, in this little draw," says he.

"Goin' to tap the main draw and lead it through yonder little saddle," I explains to him.

He looks kinder interested. "Why—I believe that would work," says he. "But if you want to farm, why don't you buy a place down on the San Lucas?"

"Me? Shucks, I never could see any good times herdin' with them sleep-walkin' nesters," says I. "Dern a granger, anyhow!"

"Why—why—why, you're going to be one yourself!" says Briscoe.

He had me there. I hadn't thought o' that. It struck me all in a heap.

"Well, not so's you can notice it. I may irrigate the soil a little, as a gentlemanly relaxation—but do I look anyways like a splay-footed, sod-hopping, apple-grafting granger? I'm as good a cow-man as ever throwed a loop by moonlight," says I.

"But you said you wouldn't turn no cattle loose on my range," said Briscoe, stuttering.

"Ain't it the truth?" says I. "What's the matter with my range—*m-y, my?* Throw a little fence across that cañon, like a stopper in a bottle —"

I didn't finish, 'cause Briscoe, he was carryin' on something fierce. He was a natural-born hawg, that man was.

I let him rave a spell, till I see that I might as well stop him first as last. "See here, Aloysius," says I, "you're talking pretty brash. I wonder at myself that I ain't bent this crowbar over your old hard head."

He reined his horse around. "Where you goin'?" says I, and I grabbed up a rock. "I'm a patient man," says I, "but if you don't light off that cayuse and stay to dinner, I'm goin' to bounce a pebble off your medulla obligato. It isn't anywise neighborly to go off that way just as dinner's ready; it casts reflections on my cookin'. Welcome, little stranger!" I says, as he climbs off. "Welcome to Shelter!"

I tried to rib him up with a jolly whilst I was wrangling chuck. "I know what makes your sorrows grieve you so, Montmorency," says I. "You tot it up that because I've got a pasture I'm goin' to get implicated with your calves. I been all along that road, same as you have—we won't deny it, Epaminondas; but I wouldn't choose any more of the pie. Honesty is the best policy, as who should know better than me? You and the J.B. punchers is welcome to prowl around in here, auditing, any time, and there'll always be a meal's victuals for you and a nice level place to sleep."

But he wouldn't mellow up and he went away dissatisfied. That old man never did like me.

Next time I went to town, old J.B. had me over to the house and offered me five hundred to quit-claim Shelter to him. Seems like he'd set his heart on it, and he couldn't forgive me for him not thinkin' of buildin' a tank there first. That night I met Minnie's cousin Jane, who was the Central school-ma'am, and old man Duffy, Methodist preacher from St Johns, and Dee Macfarlane. Dee had sunny hair, the rascal—wavy and sunny. He owned a nice little bunch of cattle, but he didn't 'tend to his business very close, *I* thought. He was settin' around up to Minnie's nearly every time I went near there. That's no way to run cattle. You got to be out amongst 'em.

Well, there come an early rain that year, along in April. That filled my cistern so I got shut of water-hauling. So long as I had a township for pasture, ready-made all but the gate, I thought we'd better fix the gate. So we strung up the wire fence across the box. After that we could turn our work-horses loose at night, instead of hobbling, and they done better. I got another scraper down to Central, and another Mexican—Eusebio. He wasn't much force, not sized up with Eph and Esteban. He had a Candelaria girl in Central. Candy, she worked for Mamma Briscoe. I didn't mind him going down Sundays so much, though he was lonesome to ride with—but he did sing such long-drawn and mournful despair around the camp-fire after supper:

> *"Tal vez, mi amada, en brazos de otro amor,*
> *Duerme y descansa—ay! sin pensar en mi!"*

We began makin' dirt fly on this new dam. Beat all, what a difference it made not havin' to draw water fifteen mile for six horses and a camp. I tied up Deacon or Quaker, turn about, for night-horse. Every morning I was out wranglin' work-stock before day, while the boys rustled breakfast. I did the rest o' the cookin' and all the pot-walloping and black-smithing. I hauled corn and chuck, and kep' camp in venison, and rustled wood: I jumped in to hold the plow or whatever was needed quick and most, and we inched right along. I hadn't never worked so steady since I was a boy on Staten Island. The plowed dirt smelled good, and the green grass it smelled good, and the chuck tasted good. I felt virtuouser and virtuouser every day, I'd put away childish things: I looked back with pain to them ranikiboo plays I'd hitherto promulgated.

The neighbors took to droppin' in to see me. Nice lot of two-handed punchers, they was—Hall and Billy Hall, Spike and Doc and Squatty Robinson and San Simon—he was a prospector, San Simon was.

J. Briscoe, he mostly flocked by his only, but he come out twice more, raising his offer to fifteen hundred. He sure wanted the Shelter place. Joe Only, the J.B. wagon boss, he happened in pretty frequent, as Chuck Barefoot.

For I began to have other company too. Minnie Briscoe and her cousin Jane, they took to comin' out Saturday nights and stayin over Sunday. I got a new tent for 'em, soon as I see they was formin' the habit. I'd go deer-hunting with Minnie at first—or just go browsing around with both of 'em. Jane was an easy keeper, but she wasn't exciting. Sometimes they brought Minnie's ma along for chaperon, sometimes not. It didn't make no difference. Them girls didn't need no chaperon—not much, anyway.

Did I say that the boys had quit visiting each other and made Shelter the reg'lar Sunday headquarters since the girls took to comin' out? Well, they did. It was bound to be that way. So I wasn't obliged to go huntin' with 'em any more. Somehow I wasn't near as glad as I might 'a' been. But I was the host, and also I wasn't much young any more. The play come for me to take a back seat.

Minnie thought there wasn't no place like Shelter, and she kept coaxin' me to sell out to her father. "If you will, I'll get Poppa to let me homestead it," she says, "and I'll have it for my very own. Poppa has used his homestead right. I think you might, Andrew J."

This was about the thirteenth time she'd named it to me. "Why, yes, so I might, but then will I?" says I. "There ain't another place just like this in the whole dinky world, I don't believe. I've done used my homestead right, too. Your little scheme would mean forfeiting my desert claim—and where would Aforesaid A.J. Bates be then, poor thing?"

"You might buy a place," says Minnie, pouting.

"I want to tell you, Miss Minnie," says I, "that there can't no man buy a place—not if it cost him a million dollars—and get so much solid comfort from it as he can where he was the very first man that ever nested there since the world began, and where he has cut every post and built in every stone and set out every tree with his own fair hands. So I go along with Shelter as an encumbrance. If you're dead set to make your home here—take a chance! A bird in the bush is the noblest work of God," says I. "I'm old and I'm stove-up and I'm unlucky, but I'll do my da—I'll do my best to make it a safe shelter, Minnie," says I.

She flushed all rosy red, and she dropped her eyes, but she shook her head. "I can't," she whispers. "You'd make it a safe shelter, Andy, and maybe it would be better if I could. But I can't."

"Why?" says I. "Don't you like me at all, Minnie, not the least little bit?"

"Oh, I do!" says she. "I do like you, ever so much—but not that way."

"How do you know?" says I.

"I know!" says Minnie.

"Who is it, Minnie? Dee, I reckon?"

"*Don't!* You mustn't!" she says, catchin' her breath short. She let me see her face—my pretty! And there were tears in her eyes. I knowed when she let me see them tears that no matter how much she liked Dee, she might have liked me pretty well too, if the play had come different.

Then she gave me a straight look. "And you don't really want me, Andy—not really! Oh, you think you do—just now! But it's partly because you want to be neighborly, and maybe because you know that I don't have a very good time at home. And you'd always be good and kind to me, I guess. But after a while, you'd be sorry. For there's just two kinds of people in this world," says Minnie. "The kind that thinks a bird in the hand is worth two in the bush—and your kind, Mr Aforesaid Andrew Jackson Bates! Wherever you are, the soil of that place will be burning your foot-soles. You'll always be wondering what is on the other side of the hill, and you'll always be wondering what is on the other side of the world, and wanting to go see: and you'll always be wearyin' for the bird in the bush!"

"Well, then, don't you grieve your pretty head about me, honey," says I. "I'm old, and I'm tough, and I'll winter through some way. Maybe there's a good deal in what you say. But just you remember Shelter, if ever the world don't use you well. I'll be here, waiting."

"I'll remember," says Minnie. "But don't you put on such a long face. You can't fool me much, Andrew Jackson! You're one-half sorry and disappointed, and the other half is glad you've done your duty and no harm come of it. You'll be good as new in no time, and dreamin' about the bird in the bush. Good-by, and good luck!" she says, and turns her pony's head to town.

"You ain't going to let this make no difference about comin' out, when you feel like it?" says I.

"Oh, no! I'll be out, same as usual—after a little." Her face was kind of smily and teary and cheery all at once, and part mischievous, and kind of poutish too. "I know you only want what's best for me," she threw back over her shoulder, "and that's why I know you don't really-truly like me—that way," she says. "If you did, you wouldn't know you was old or unlucky or anything—and you'd be insisting on havin' your own way, whether 'twas best for me or not!"

I spurred up, but she hit her pony a lick and held up her open hand. So I stopped. "It's too late to insist now, Andy J.—after what I just said," says Minnie, reinin' up. "You go on back to your dam-work that you're so all wrapped up in. And say, Andy—" Her pretty face was all mischief now.

"Orders!" says I, touching my hat.

"Don't let your kind heart coax you to ask Jane! If you do, Andrew Jackson, I sha'n't like it one little bit!" And she was gone.

I think of her a heap, sometimes. . . . Say, it's hell to be old! 'Specially when you're not really a little bit old, inside.

I've had a lot of fun; sometimes I think I've had more fun than anyone. But I've missed a heap, too.

Minnie come back, after a few weeks, but it wasn't ever quite the same. She kept Dee or Jane right with her, and she didn't call me Andy J. any more. I was Mr Bates. So I built dam.

We kep' things rockin' along as per usual, Eph and Esteban and me just a-humpin', and Eusebio trifling along, only a little above the average. Lordie, there's a heap of difference in men! My the'ry is that if a man don't earn more than you give him, no matter how much that is, he ain't worth having around. Half the time Eusebio was plumb in our way.

Along late in September, when it was likely there wouldn't be any more rains, I saw a big storm coming up. "Maybe the last of the season," thinks I. So I called the boys out.

"Vacation!" says I. "We'll just fix our ditch to fill up this hole-in-the-ground and see if she'll hold. The teams is pretty well jaded out. Steve, you and 'Sebio take a week's lay-off—more, if you want it."

"You theenk thees tank not break, Meester Bates?" says Esteban.

"I hope not, Steve, old socks," says I. "For if she goes, we're sure a-going with it. It's no more than the square thing for us to put on our slickers and set on the dam—just as a bet that we been doin' good work."

Well, we done so, and she didn't break. My recipe for perpetratin' dams is to make 'em twice-and-a-half as strong and long and deep and wide and high as there is any use of, 'special the spillway, and then to say a little prayer.

The sun come out warm and pleasant, and we all took a big swim. The Mexican men, they went to rustle their horses so's they could pull their freight after supper, and I set there on the dam, seein' things.

Next mornin' Eph and me slep' till the horses woke us up beggin' for corn. Eph, he went off to pluck a venison, and I stayed in camp.

I reckon there was where I made a mistake—quittin' work sudden in the middle of the week. If it had been

Sunday, now, and folks around, maybe things might 'a' come different. All of a sudden, I felt tired out and old and blue and bald and all-alonesome; and I couldn't get seein' things any more. I couldn't see myself makin' *'cequias* and settin' our fruit-trees; I just knowed that soil wouldn't grow alfalfa; my cows would climb out over them pinnacles; I couldn't think of no decent brand for 'em, and I couldn't think of no name for my cussed lake; and as for rip-rappin' that dam when the water got low, it made me fair sick to think of it.

No sir, all I could do was to study about how sad it would be if anything was to happen to Minnie's little boy-doll. I hadn't a thing against Dee, you understand—square and white a kid as ever rode leather. It just broke my heart to think of that hazardous occupation he was following, and nothing ever goin' wrong. He might fall off a horse, or down a shaft, or in my new lake: a steer might butt him, or somebody might shoot him. There was a new man, Petey Simmons, breakin' bronc's for the J.B.; six or seven feet high, no eyebrows or hair on his face, 'count of having had smallpox—mighty ugly man; I wondered if maybe Petey wouldn't do it. Then Dee might get snake-bit or quick consumption. Railroads, too, they was mighty dangerous. I did wish that railroad would hurry up and come.

Before noon I'd about compromised by havin' Dee run off with Jane. But I see that wouldn't do.

"You're getting morbid, Andy," says I. "I know what's the matter with you. You want to take a little horse-ride."

So I caught up old Quaker and went for a *pasear*—not anywhere particular, you know—just riding the curse off. I felt better right straight. Pretty soon I was singing about how once in the saddle I used to be a gay old bird.

About the middle of the evenin' I was 'way up on a pinnacle, when I saw some one chasing a bunch of cattle in the hills just under me. I took a small peep through my field-glasses.

It was old Squatty Robinson on a blue bronco. He caught a big yearlin' and tied it to a saplin'; then he took in after the bunch and fought 'em on up the draw. I knew what he was up to. He'd drive the mammy-cow off up in the hills three or four miles; then he'd hurry back and adopt that yearlin'.

Quaker was prancing; I began to feel frisky, like I was only a big grown-up boy. Quaker was a flighty, hoity-toity horse, anyway—no fit company for a serious-minded man.

"Andrew Jackson," says I, "this is plumb dishonest, and it ought to be discouraged. Be you goin' to allow such goin's-on, or be you not?"

I went down there. I set that calf loose, and I took the rope that was on her and flung it over a limb, so the noose hung down just about high enough to hang a short man, and I tied the other end around the tree-trunk. Squatty was a short man.

I knowned Squatty would be back soon to drive home his foundling. I hid out to watch him. Just as I got myself spotted, here come a bunch of wild mares up the cañon, forty or fifty, and went on up the way Squatty did. They was burnin' the breeze; and behind them, here comes Esteban and Eusebio. That was funny too, because they told me the night before they was goin' to Holbrook. I lay right still.

They come pretty near up to where I was. I had to pinch Quaker's nose to keep him from whinnyin'. They turned out of the cañon opposite me and rode up the hill to a big slick piece of granite below a cliff. They climbed up that afoot, and they hid something in a hole under the cliff. Then they rode back down the cañon.

"I go look-see!" says I, soon as they was out of sight. When I come to the tracks, they was barefoot tracks; yet them horses was fresh shod only yesterday: curious thing! I took away the stones and felt in that hidey-hole. What do you think I found? Two slickers with eye-holes cut in the backs of 'em just below the collar! I tried again and fished out a package. It was little: it had the express-company's seal on it, broken; it had been tied up again. Inside was a bunch of yellow-backs. Them triflin' boys of mine had robbed the stage!

"I'm plumb surprised at Steve," I says. "This ain't honest!" I counted the money. There was twenty-five bills, each for one hundred perfectly good dollars. "Sufferin' Moses!" says I. "I didn't think the stage carried as much as that, all told, in a year." I turned the package over. 'Twas addressed to *J. Briscoe, Central, Arizona.*

"Twenty-five hundred is a heap of cash for the Butter-bowl," I thinks. I tucked it away in my shirt-bosom. "Whatever did J. B. want of that much in cold cash? And when did my enterprisin' young friends know so pat when to get busy? And I thought that triflin' Steve was a pretty good *hombre*, dern him. Say! By Jings, I bet that Candy girl of his has been snoopin' through the letters on Poppa Briscoe's desk—and that's how they knew when the money was comin'! They started up them mares to account for themselves if they run onto anybody—and so they didn't see Squatty's trail, or mine, 'cause the mares had done run over 'em. That part is nearly right. But what I don't see, is what J. B. wanted of all that wad."

I was so absorbed I didn't see that same bunch of mares sky-hootin' back down the hill to my horse that I'd left with his bridle-reins dangling. But I was too late. That ornery Quaker up with his tail and threw in with 'em. They went on down to the plain—and I was afoot!

I was pretty sore. I judged Squatty had met them broom-tails and turned 'em as he was coming back. So I got behind a boulder and waited. I didn't want to walk home—not if I could get Squatty's horse.

Squatty come directly. He was real surprised at not finding no yearling, and he said so. When he got down to get his rope, I cut loose a few shots, puffin' up dust between him and his horse. Squatty, he went to the wild bunch.

I kept foggin' away till I saw him come out of the timber two or three hundred yards up and cross a little glade to the main woods. Then I knowed Squatty had gone to waterin' at night.

I climbed his blue bronc'. I turned across toward home, studying up something real severe to say to Steve. But I never got to Shelter. I looked up, and there was that same bunch of mares quartering along in front of me. Some one had headed 'em off again and turned 'em back. They was almost beat out; they was strung along like a snake, rockin' up and down, noses to the ground, like one of them dream-gallops we have, where we don't get any forwarder. Some of 'em could hardly navigate. That old gray fool of a Quaker was hanging on behind. I could see his saddle shine.

I made a circle and fell in beside, sorter headin' 'em toward the stage-road. I closed in, riding easy, took after old Quaker and hurled my twine. The loop drawed up pretty deep on Quaker's shoulders—and just then my blue stumbled, and down we went!

I kep' out from under, but my foot hung in the stirrup. The blue horse scrambled up before I could kick loose: I grabbed for my gun, but it was jarred out where we fell—and away we went, kicking and bucking and squealing, with Andrew J. Bates, Baron Shelter, Lord of the Lake, dragging by one hind leg, on his back or belly as the case might be, grubbing up cactus and soapweed with himself.

One end of the rope bein' fast to my saddle-horn and the other end on Quaker's neck, Blue Beelzebub had to go round and round like a circus-horse doing tricks, hurdling mesquite bushes and the like.

As luck would have it, little Andrew was dragging on the inside. That was what saved him. When Beezy kicked, he missed my face more'n two inches. Old Quaker gave a little to keep from chokin', so the little geometrical design I was inscribing with my carcass was a free-hand spiral, like the writing-teacher used to show us to develop the whole-arm movement, only more so.

I kep' trying to climb up my leg far enough to grab that rope, but 'twas only as a matter of principle—I really didn't expect to do it. Then—bang! went a gun. Poor old Beelzebub come down on his side and lay there, with only his legs a-quivering.

I could 'a' had a real lovely time, just layin' still a week or two, but I judged it best not. I got my foot out pretty brisk and rolled over on my hands and knees. Beelzebub was shot right through the brainpan. He was mighty dead.

I boosted myself up by the saddle-horn and cantle and set down on the defunct: I poured the sand out o' my mouth and nose and ears and eyes, and looked round. I was considerable dizzy.

We was right beside the wagon-road: Beelzebub had stumbled crossing it. Quaker had got some slack and was getting his breath—head hanging down, legs braced. Then I see a man. It was Petey Simmons, the J. B. bronco-buster. His mouth was open; his eyes was buggin' out, and he had a gun in his hand; he sat there on his horse looking at me, and he was whispering to himself. "Well, *I'll* be damned!" he says. "I will be *damned!*"

I looked at Petey a spell, and Petey looked at me. After a bit things steadied down some, and I remembers my manners.

"Thank you!" says I.

"Oh, I *will* be damned!" whispers Petey again, as if his soul in them few words he would outpour.

I felt considerable nettled. It didn't seem to me that Petey was showin' the proper sort of spirit.

"Doubtless," says I. "But why so confidential about it? And what makes you think it's interesting to me? If you've fully made up your mind, all right—but *I* don't care, I'll tell you those!"

Petey took off his hat. The sweat was starting on his face. He seemed stunned and grieved and discouraged; he hadn't the joyful look a man ought to wear that had just saved a valuable life. It didn't seem much of a compliment to me.

"Petey, that was a pretty fair shot you made," says I.

"Well, I will—" he began again, but I cut him off short at the pockets.

"Petey, I'll give you just one more chance," says I in a firm yet trembling voice. "You hunt around and pick up my gun and my hat and any pieces of my hide you think can be used again," says I. "And compose your mind good' for if you say any more about your future fate, I'm going to shoot you five times in the middle West. You plumb displease me. But first of all, you look in the road and see if there ain't a lot of fresh tracks headin' for the Holbrook Gap."

He done so and nodded his head.

"I thought as much," says I. "Petey, some one robbed the stage out there this morning—two men named Doe and Roe. Central has done waked up and gone to see how about it."

"Hell's bells!" said Petey in a cracked and horrified voice. "Just the one time it's ever carried any money since Heck was a pup! Curse that black-hearted, liver-lipped, whip-sawin' old J. B., I believe he done it himself!"

"How'd you happen along so appropriate?" says I—wondering to myself how Petey knew there was any money on that stage.

"I been out to your place," says Petey, lickin' his dry lips. "You've gone; greasers gone; nigger gone. Comin' back, I see a saddled horse in a bunch of mares. I tried to cut him out, but they outrun me. So I shacked along on their trail, thinking maybe I'd aidge 'em along toward a corral and find some one to help pen 'em. Next I know, I saw a man clearin' off a place with himself for a three-ring circus. I tore off down here to keep him from being dragged to death—and it's *you!* Think of it!" says Petey, exceedin' bitter. "I run hellity-larrup through two miles of dog-holes, sixty miles an hour, hop, skip and jump, till each separate hair on my head stood up like feathers on the fretful concubine—and it's *you!* I'm ha'nted!" says Petey. "That's what is it—I'm ha'nted!"

Any way you look at it, Petey was showin' up mighty ungrateful. He stared at me some more and rode off, muttering, to look for my gun and things.

"Andrew Jackson!" thinks I to myself, "what call has this long, lean, lank son of Satan to show such deep and abiding chagrin because he has been the humble instrument, under Providence, for prolonging your days in the land? Why does he think J. B. had the stage robbed? If he did, wan't it his own money? Who would J. B. be whipsawing by stealing his own money, and why should it stir up Petey's bile? But if so, why? What lot or part did Petey have in that lost and vanished wad?" Here I felt in my shirt-bosom for the money, thinkin' it might have got lost durin' the late exhibition, but it was still there.

"You can't deny it, Mister Bates—you've never been quite reconciled to J. B. sending for that amount of cash. Cash is for people that ain't satisfied with checks. Who ain't satisfied with checks? People that ain't stayin' to have 'em cashed. Pretty big sum, ain't it? About the price of what? Of erasing somebody? Who ain't satisfied? Petey. How else could Petey earn that much so slick? Erasing who? Hey? Who's J. B. got it in for? Answer: Andrew Jackson Bates, of Naboth's vineyard.

"When did this money come? To-day, September 30th. When did Petey Simmons make his first and only visit to Shelter? To-day, September 30th. Was he displeased at the stage being robbed? He was. Why? Was he pleased at me not staying home? He was not. Why should a gentleman stay at home, if he didn't choose to wish to do so? Was Petey Simmons grateful to have saved a valued life? He was not. Last and most convincing of all, who was it you picked for to be poor Dee Macfarlane's murderer? Petey Simmons!

"Andrew Jackson, you ought to be thankful to J. Doe and R. Roe and Squatty. Only for their thoughtfulness there'd be a singin' soon at Shelter—and you'd be there, but you wouldn't hear it. Petey would just about have killed a J. B. beef beside your cold, unconscious clay, and said he caught you stealin' it. . . . I wonder if Minnie would 'a' believed that?" thinks I.

Of course I didn't think it out in words, like that. I just thought it in thoughts, all at once and good deal clearer. Words is mighty poor, slow tools, and they never did a good job in this world.

That wasn't all I sensed, either. There was impressions, little sidewise glances, things like this: Joe Only was boss; it was his to hire and fire. He didn't hire Petey; old Briscoe hired him. 'Twasn't usual, and 'twasn't liked. Nobody's been real pleasant to Petey. The J. B. boys felt they was pretty adequate to break their own broncos.

All this grand and lofty thinkin' took place simultaneous like a sewing-bee. Petey brought me my things. I cleaned the sand out of my good old gun, shoved her in the scabbard and give her a loving pat. Then I cocks one eye at my noble benefactor.

"Petey," says I, "not to be pryin' into your personal affairs, but was the old man to give you all that twenty-five hundred for expurgatin' me?"

Petey just stared at me, choking the horn of the saddle with both hands. I guess he felt that I was kinder vaccinated against him, after him savin' my life; he doesn't make any break for his gun.

"And you figure that he framed up a fake stage-robbin', to saw off the blame on you?" says I. "So you'd either get rubbed out or scared out?"

"Say, I hadn't thought of that!" says Petey, some startled. He give a pretty accurate description of the old man. He was a real powerful talker. "I'll go kill him right now—the old double-crossin' hypocrite!" he says to wind up.

"Now, now, Petey!" says I, soothin' him. "You don't want to do nothing like that. People would talk. The old man has been dealin' 'em to you from the bottom, I can see that. But I wouldn't kill him, exactly. Say, Petey, if I show you how to get that twenty-five hundred to-night, honest and aboveboard, will you come to Squatty's place by sun-up and give me half?"

"Will I?" says Petey. "I'll give you all of it! But how? How? The money's gone."

"I don't know yet," says I. "You just keep your mind off your thoughts whilst I study a spell."

I unsaddled Quaker and felt in the saddle-bags to see if my fieldglass was broke, and it wasn't.

"First off, Petey," says I, "them bold bandit-chasers are going to be back along here about sundown, ain't they?"

He allowed they was, some of 'em, anyway.

"Bueno! Pues," says I, "they're going to see that dead horse, shot by a master hand. Everyone knows my saddle—and you're going to help me put it on the dead horse, right now."

He done so. It was hard to make the change, but we rolled old Beelzebub into my saddle and cinched it on. Then I put the other outfit on Quaker.

"There!" says I. "What with that and the robbery and Squatty missing too, Central will be one wild and nervous uproar. And who so agitated as J. Briscoe? I grieve to think how scared that man will be!" said I. "Too scared to use any daylight judgment at all. So if you drop in and tell him you had the misfortune to kill me and would like to collect, I reckon he'd give you the wealth without asking for no receipt."

"How in blazes," said Petey, "is he going to give me any money, when the money's gone?"

"I meant, if they happen to find the money anywhere," says I. "If they don't get the money, you don't say anything to J. B. But I think maybe they'll find it. So you trot along and come out there to Squatty's soon as you can. Squatty, he ain't there. We'll divide even—you for doing the bloody deed and me for concealin' the body," says I. "You tell the old man the play didn't come out just right, as there wasn't any beef-critter handy, and that you've hid out the corpse. Offer to lead him to me, if he holds back. But he won't. I've took a snubbing-postgratuate-course in psychology, Petey," says I, "and I tell you that J. Briscoe will be scared."

Petey took a long look at me. "I believe you are the devil!" he said. He was sweating again. "Lord, I'd like to! But I'll tell you honest, I lost my nerve when I found out whose life I'd saved. A man can't stand but just so much. Suppose the boys suspect me of killing you and find that money on me? They'll put me to bed with a shovel; they'll hang me and old man Briscoe with one rope."

"It ain't likely," says I. "It seems a pity. But I can't take chances of losing my share of that money. I'll fix you out. Is Dee Macfarlane in town?"

Petey nodded, and I dug up my tally-book. I wrote a note to Dee, dating it September 30, six P.M., telling him not to be alarmed at any reports he might hear about me that night, that I was just having a little innocent relaxation after my arjous toils; and for him to tell Minnie—I wasn't going to have my pretty frightened—but on no account to tell anybody else except to save life. "Please return this note to bearer, who doesn't want to be hung," I adds as a post-script. Petey read it, he grinned and started. He turned around and hollered back at me mighty earnest, "Don't you let anything happen to you, Andrew Jackson Bates!"

Me and Quaker terrapinned up the road a stretch, till I come to a rise that I could watch from a long ways off. Here I built up a little stone monument in the road and put that money on top, still in the original package, address-side up. I tacked off east two or three miles, to a bench where I could keep cases on that money with my fieldglass.

After a while the push fell off down the slope, six or eight of the boys loping along in front. I see them stop at my monument. Then I dug it up a draw for Squatty's. Got in about half-past dark, mighty tired. I drove up a bunch of Squatty's saddle-stock with me, and I caught his sorrel Gold Dollar horse. Then I turned Quaker loose with the bunch, opened up a lot of canned stuff and slept a few lines.

About sun-up Petey shook me. "Get up!" he says. "We got to get out of this!"

"Breakfast first," says I.

"Breakfast, nothing!" says Petey. "You come look at the Butterbowl!"

I took one look, and I see Petey was right. The sun was just peepin' over the hills, and the valley looked cool and pleasant. There was bunches of men scurryin' around everywhere, like drunk ants. I guess about the whole he-population was present. The nearest was eight or ten miles.

Some was following Petey's trail, some on mine, but most of 'em was spreadin' out for general results. They got 'em. Every mess of wile horses they scared up stampeded three more batches, and those bands scared more, and all of 'em stampeded every bunch of cattle they passed, and those cattle scared the next lot, and so on—and on—and on: just like politics. 'Twas a stirrin' scene.

My bosom swelled with pride. "Petey," says I, "did you get it?"

"That's what I went after," said Petey. "Here's yours. You keep the odd hundred."

"Let this be a lesson to you, Petey," says I, pretty severe.

"We'd better take to the hills," says Petey.

"We will not," said I, saddlin' the sorrel horse. "I always wished I was a musician, so I could fiddle at a fight. And this is the day when all my dreams come true. You and me, Petey, will go out on the flat." Then I stopped short and slapped my leg. "Chickens!" says I. "Chickens!"

"What's the matter with you now, you old hag?" said Petey, edgin' off.

"Chickens! I never once thought of keepin' chickens at Shelter till this very now! Come on, Petey," says I. "Let's us go play hare and hounds."

Petey came on, but he didn't like it. "You red hellion," says that interesting beast, "I dassent leave you get an inch away from me till all the Butterbowl knows you're alive. Joe Only suspected me and J. B. right off. Otherwise I'd see you rot first. May my right hand cleave to the roof of my mouth if I don't think you're part fiend!"

We had to go a couple of miles toward the man-hunt to get down out of the hills. They seen us. Then we turned east across the big flat, heading for the big pass, where progress and the railroad was to come in—some time—and the Butterbowl fanned along after us. I reckon the cattle thought it was the Day of Judgement.

We let the boys gain on us, to encourage them—that is, I did. Petey, he was in favor of going on, but I held him back. "I never knowed how popular I was," said I. "Them boys are sure aimin' to avenge the deep damnation of my taking-off. And oh, Petey!" says I, "if you and me could only meet up with J.B. face to face, what a joyful reunion we would have!"

By the time we got in the foothills by the pass, they was pretty close—two of 'em 'way ahead of the others.

"That's Barefoot and Joe Only," says Petey. "They've got the best horses in the works."

And here I got my great surprise. We come out on a ridge above the wagon-road, and there I saw two numbers that wasn't down on my program at all. Right below us, outward bound, was Minnie and Dee, joggin' happily along dead to the world. They'd just climbed out of the San Lucas where the wagon-road quit the Narrows, so missing the glorious and inspirin' panorama being presented on the flats.

I got the idea. Reasonin' from my note that I wasn't dead enough to grieve about, they was makin' the best possible use of the chance the excitement gave 'em.

If so, it was providential; for a little ahead, around a turn, I saw Parson Duffy coming in from St. Johns. I knew his white horses and his little old buckboard.

I called to them, and they jumped their horses apart like I'd thrown a bomb. Then they saw who it was, and they waited.

"Walkin' away to be married, children?" says I. Minnie drooped her head and blushed, and Dee looked foolish. And then I knew that old Andy Jackson was leaving Butterbowl. "'Cause, if you are," says I, "you'd better get to running."

I waved my hand down the pass. The hardy pursuers were just pouring into the scenery. One look was enough. The eloping party began hittin' the high places. There didn't seem to be any call to tell 'em that wasn't the angry father, but just a few friends desiring to lynch me for causing my own death.

"Easy!" I says. "You needn't ride so fast, for you won't have to ride far. You're both of age, and Parson Duffy is coming, Johnny-on-the-spot, up the road a stretch. If you'd like to be married while you are still in peaceful Butterbowl, Petey and I'll be witnesses, and you can be man and wife before you turn over the divide. Does it go?"

They said it went. We slowed down till we met the preacher. I did the explaining.

'Mr Duffy," says, I, "if you'll turn right around, we'd like to have you perform the marriage ceremony for this young couple, short but binding. You know them; they're of age and otherwise unmarried."

The Parson saw the avengers coming, and there's a twinkle in his eye. "You are in some haste, perhaps?" says he as he turns back.

"Oh, no hurry, no hurry at all; just lope right along," says I, as a couple of bullets whanged over our heads. Then we turned a curve out o' range. And by thunder, that old sport stood up in that rocking old buckboard and married them on the run!

I kissed the bride. "Be a good girl, honey," says I. "Lots of happiness to you both. I'm leaving here for keeps, and I'm giving Shelter to you two for a wedding-present—Mr Duffy bein' witness. Good luck, Dee!" says I. "Be good to Deacon and Quaker—yes, and to Minnie too. Here's the summit. I'll stay here to check the maddened parent. No, there won't be any violence, Minnie. I'll give you my word. Just moral suasion. I got a heap of influence with the Butterbowl. Good-by!"

"Good-by!" said Dee, and "Good-by, Andy Jackson," said Minnie. "We'll not forget you. If you ever find the bird in the bush—or if you don't—come back to Shelter. It is always yours. We'll look for you. Good-by!"

We waited, sky-lighted on the summit.

The pass opened up wide; across in the east it framed off a big country I'd never seen. Petey and I got off our horses and let 'em puff and blow: the parson fixed up his tally of the marriage for us to sign. I laid one of my blood-money bills in the buckboard seat, for his fee.

"I'm going to stay just long enough for Joe to see us together," Petey snapped at me. "Then you pick one side of the world and I'll take the other."

"All right, Petey," says I. "I'll sorter fade away over into New Mexico. I have always liked that country."

Then the committee of unsafety arrived. Joe Only set his horse up and looked at me a long time, real sad.

"What in the name of the seven deadly sins have you been up to?" says he. "I made sure Simmons had murdered you. Why didn't he?"

"It's a pretty note," I says to him, real peevish and bitter. "When a couple of white, male, free American citizens can't attend a wedding without such a hullabaloo as this!"

"Weddin'!" says Chuck. "Weddin'?"

"Sure—Miss Minnie Briscoe and Mr Dee Macfarlane. Didn't you get an invite? Petey and I we rode over to be witnesses. Didn't we, Petey?"

"Don't ask me," said Petey. "I have went!" And he did so.

"But what—why—where's Squatty? Who robbed the stage? How'd that money get back?" says Joe.

Outraged citizens was a-burnin' around the bend. I wished I might have seen Poppa once more, but I see this was no place for Andrew J. Bates. "You go back, Joe," says I. "You go back and explain to 'em."

Joe Only was much of a man, but he let his voice go up to a screech. "Explain? Explain! What'll I tell 'em?"

"How should I know?" says I, giving him a little push. "Just explain!" And I came away.

STEWART EDWARD WHITE
The Honk-Honk Breed

Steward Edward White (1873–1946) was born in Grand Rapids, Michigan, and was educated at the University of Michigan, and Columbia Law School. He later worked as a prospector, a packing-house worker, and a bookshop-assistant. During World War One he served as an artillery major in the US Army. His first Western novel was *The Claim Jumpers* (1901), and another eighteen followed, the best of which is *Folded Hills* (1934), part of a Californian-based saga featuring Andy Burnett. White also published a Western short story collection, *Arizona Nights*, in 1907. As well as frontier fiction, White wrote several books of Western history, and was a prolific author of popular adventure novels.

'The Honk-Honk Breed' is from *Arizona Nights*. Most of White's Western fiction was highly realistic and informed by his own knowledge of the West, but this story is more in the tradition of the 'tall tale'.

IT WAS SUNDAY AT THE ranch. For a wonder the weather had been favorable; the windmills were all working, the bogs had dried up, the beef had lasted over, the remuda had not strayed—in short, there was nothing to do. Sang had given us a baked bread-pudding with raisins in it. We filled it in—a wash basin full of it—on top of a few incidental pounds of *chile con*, baked beans, soda biscuits, "air tights" and other delicacies. Then we adjourned with our pipes to the shady side of the blacksmith's shop where we could watch the ravens on top the adobe wall of the corral. Somebody told a story about ravens. They led to road-runners. This suggested rattlesnakes. They started Windy Bill.

"Speakin' of snakes," said Windy, "I mind when they catched the great granddaddy of all the bullsnakes up at Lead in the Black Hills. I was only a kid then. This wasn't no such tur'ble long a snake, but he was more'n a foot thick. Looked just like a sahuaro stalk. Man name of Terwilliger Smith catched it. He named this yere bullsnake Clarence, and got it so plumb gentle it followed him everywhere. One day old P. T. Barnum come along and wanted to buy this Clarence snake—offered Terwilliger a thousand cold—but Smith wouldn't part with the snake nohow. So finally they fixed up a deal so Smith could go along with the show. They shoved Clarence in a box in the baggage car, but after a while Mr Snake gets so lonesome he gnaws out and starts to crawl back to find his master. Just as he is half-way between the baggage car and the smoker, the couplin' give way—right on that heavy grade between Custer and Rocky Point. Well, sir, Clarence wound his head 'round one brake wheel and his tail around the other, and held that train together to the bottom of the grade. But it stretched him twenty-eight feet and they had to advertise him as a boa-constrictor."

Windy Bill's history of the faithful bullsnake aroused to reminiscence the grizzled stranger, who thereupon held forth as follows:

Well, I've seen things and I've heard things, some of them ornery and some you'd love to believe, they was that gorgeous and improbable. Nat'ral history was always my hobby and sportin' events my special pleasure—and this yarn of Windy's reminds me of the only chanst I ever had to ring in business and pleasure and hobby all in one grand merry-go-around of joy. It came about like this:

One day, a few years back, I was sittin' on the beach at Santa Barbara watchin' the sky stay up, and wonderin' what to do with my year's wages, when a little squinch-eye round-face with big bow spectacles came and plumped down beside me.

"Did you ever stop to think," says he, shovin' back his hat, "that if the horse-power delivered by them waves on this beach in one single hour could be concentrated behind washin' machines, it would be enough to wash all the shirts for a city of four hundred and fifty-one thousand and thirty-six people?"

"Can't say I ever did," says I, squintin' at him sideways.

"Fact," says he, "and did it ever occur to you that if all the food a man eats in the course of a natural life could be gathered together at one time, it would fill a wagon-train twelve miles long?"

"You make me hungry," says I.

"And ain't it interestin' to reflect," he goes on, "that if all the finger-nail parin's of the human race for one year was to be collected and subjected to hydraulic pressure it would equal in size the pyramid of Cheops?"

"Look yere," says I, sittin' up, "did *you* ever pause to excogitate that if all the hot air you is dispensin' was to be collected together it would fill a balloon big enough to waft you and me over that Bullyvard of Palms to yonder gin mill on the corner?"

He didn't say nothin' to that—just yanked me to my feet, faced me toward the gin mill above mentioned and exerted considerable pressure on my arm in urgin' me forward.

"You ain't so much of a dreamer, after all," thinks I. "In important matters you are plumb decisive."

We sat down at little tables, and my friend ordered a beer and a chicken sandwich.

"Chickens," says he, gazin' at the sandwich, "is a dollar apiece in this country, and plumb scarce. Did you ever pause to ponder over the returns chickens would give on a small investment? Say you start with ten hens. Each hatches out thirteen aigs, of which allow a loss of say six for childish accidents. At the end of the year you has eighty chickens. At the end of two years that flock has increased to six hundred and twenty. At the end of the third year—"

He had the medicine tongue! Ten days later him and me was occupyin' of an old ranch fifty miles from anywhere. When they run stage-coaches this joint used to be a road-house. The outlook was on about a thousand little brown foothills. A road two miles four rods two foot eleven inches in sight run by in front of us. It come over one foothill and disappeared over another. I know just how long it was, for later in the game I measured it.

Out back was about a hundred little wire chicken corrals filled with chickens. We had two kinds. That was the doin's of Tuscarora. My pardner called himself Tuscarora Maxillary. I asked him once if that was his real name.

"It's the realest little old name you ever heard tell of," says he. "I know, for I made it myself—liked the sound of her. Parents ain't got no rights to name their children. Parents don't have to be called them names."

Well, these chickens, as I said, was of two kinds. The first was these low-set, heavy-weight propositions with feathers on their laigs, and not much laigs at that, called Cochin Chinys. The other was a tall ridiculous outfit made up entire of bulgin' breast and gangle laigs. They stood about two foot and a half tall, and when they went to peck the ground their tail feathers stuck straight up to the sky. Tusky called 'em Japanese Games.

"Which the chief advantage of them chickens is," says he, "that in weight about ninety per cent of 'em is breast meat. Now my idee is, that if we can cross 'em with these Cochin Chiny fowls we'll have a low-hung, heavy-weight chicken runnin' strong on breast meat. These Jap Games is too small, but if we can bring 'em up in size and shorten their laigs, we'll shore have a winner."

That looked good to me, so we started in on that idee. The theery was bully, but she didn't work out. The first broods we hatched growed up with big husky Cochin Chiny bodies and little short necks, perched up on laigs three foot long. Them chickens couldn't reach ground nohow. We had to build a table for 'em to eat off, and when they went out rustlin' for themselves they had to confine themselves to sidehills or flyin' insects. Their breasts was all right, though—"And think of them drumsticks for the boardin' house trade!" says Tusky.

So far things wasn't so bad. We had a good grubstake. Tusky and me used to feed them chickens twict a day, and then used to set around watchin' the playful critters chase grasshoppers up an' down the wire corrals, while Tusky figgered out what'd happen if somebody was dumfool enough to gather up somethin' and fix it in baskets or wagons or such. That was where we showed our ignorance of chickens.

One day in the spring I hitched up, rustled a dozen of the youngsters into coops and druv over to the railroad to make our first sale. I couldn't fold them chickens up into them coops at first, but then I stuck the coops up on aidge and they worked all right, though I will admit they was a comical sight. At the railroad one of them towerist trains had just slowed down to a halt as I come up, and the towerists was paradin' up and down allowin' they was particular enjoyin' of the warm Californy sunshine. One old terrapin, with grey chin whiskers, projected over, with his wife, and took a peek through the slats of my coop. He straightened up like someone had touched him off with a red-hot poker.

"Stranger," said he, in a scared kind of whisper, "what's them?"

"Them's chickens," says I.

He took another long look.

"Marthy," says he to the old woman, "this will be about all! We come out from Ioway to see the Wonders of Californy, but I can't go nothin' stronger than this. If these is chickens, I don't want to see no Big Trees."

Well, I sold them chickens all right for a dollar and two bits, which was better than I expected, and got an order for more. About ten days later I got a letter from the commission house.

"We are returnin' a sample of your Arts and Crafts chickens with the lovin' marks of the teeth still onto him," says they. "Don't send any more till they stops pursuin' of the nimble grasshopper. Dentist bill will foller."

With the letter came the remains of one of the chickens. Tusky and I, very indignant, cooked her for supper. She was tough, all right. We thought she might do better biled, so we put her in the pot over night. Nary bit. Well, then we got interested. Tusky kep' the fire goin' and I rustled greasewood. We cooked her three days and three nights. At the end of that time she was sort of pale and frazzled, but still givin' points to three-year-old jerky on cohesion and other uncompromisin' forces of Nature. We buried her then, and went out back to recuperate.

There we could gaze on the smilin' landscape, dotted by about four hundred long-laigged chickens swoopin' here and there after grasshoppers.

"We got to stop that," says I.

"We can't," murmured Tusky, inspired. "We can't. It's born in 'em; it's a primal instinct, like the love of a mother for her young, and it can't be eradicated! Them chickens is constructed by a divine province for the express purpose of chasin' grasshoppers, jest as the beaver is made for buildin' dams, and the cowpuncher is made for whisky and faro-games. We can't keep 'em from it. If we was to shut 'em in a dark cellar, they'd flop after imaginary grasshoppers in their dreams, and die emaciated in the midst of plenty. Jimmy, we're up against the Cosmos, the oversoul—" Oh, he had the medicine tongue, Tusky had, and risin' on the wings of eloquence that way, he had me faded in ten minutes. In fifteen I was wedded solid to the notion that the bottom had dropped out of the chicken business. I think now that if we'd shut them hens up, we might have—still, I don't know; they was a good deal in what Tusky said.

"Tuscarora Maxillary," says I, "did you ever stop to entertain that beautiful thought that if all the dumfoolishness possessed now by the human race could be gathered together, and lined up alongside of us, the first feller to come along would say to it 'Why, hello, Solomon!'"

We quit the notion of chickens for profit right then and there, but we couldn't quit the place. We hadn't much money, for one thing, and then we kind of liked loafin' around and raisin' a little garden truck, and—oh, well. I might as well say so, we had a notion about placers in the dry wash back of the house—you know how it is. So we stayed on, and kept a-raisin' these long-laigs for the fun of it. I used to like to watch 'em projectin' around, and I fed 'em twic't a day about as usual.

So Tusky and I lived alone there together, happy as ducks in Arizona. About onc't in a month somebody'd pike along the road. She wasn't much of a road, generally more chuck-holes than bumps, though sometimes it was the other way around. Unless it happened to be a man horseback or maybe a freighter without the fear of God in his soul, we didn't have no words with them; they was too busy cussin' the highways and generally too mad for social discourses.

One day early in the year, when the 'dobe mud made ruts to add to the bumps, one of these automobeels went past. It was the first Tusky and me had seen in them parts, so we run out to view her. Owin' to the high spots on the road, she looked like one of these movin' picters, as to blur and wobble; sounded like a cyclone mingled with cuss-words and smelt like hell on housecleanin' day.

"Which them folks don't seem to be enjoyin' of the scenery," says I to Tusky. "Do you reckon that there blue trail is smoke from the machine or remarks from the inhabitants thereof?"

Tusky raised his head and sniffed long and inquirin'.

"It's langwidge," says he. "Did you ever stop to think that all the words in the dictionary hitched end to end would reach—"

But at that minute I catched sight of somethin' brass lyin' in the road. It proved to be a curled-up sort of horn with a rubber bulb on the end. I squoze the bulb and jumped twenty foot over the remark she made.

"Jarred off the machine," says Tusky.

"Oh, did it?" says I, my nerves still wrong. "I thought maybe it had growed up from the soil like a toadstool."

About this time we abolished the wire chicken corrals, because we needed some of the wire. Them long-laigs thereupon scattered all over the flat searchin' out their prey. When feed time come I had to screech my lungs out gettin' of 'em in, and then sometimes they didn't all hear. It was plumb discouragin', and I mighty nigh made up my mind to quit 'em, but they had come to be sort of pets, and I hated to turn 'em down. It used to tickle Tusky almost to death to see me out there hollerin' away like an old bull-frog. He used to come out reg'lar, with his pipe lit, just to enjoy me. Finally I got mad and opened up on him.

"Oh," he explains, "it just plumb amuses me to see the dumfool at his childish work. Why don't you teach 'em to come to that brass horn, and save your voice?"

"Tusky," says I, with feelin', "sometimes you do seem to get a glimmer of real sense."

Well, first off them chickens used to throw back-sommersets over that horn. You have no idea how slow chickens is to learn things. I could tell you things about chickens—say, this yere bluff about roosters bein' gallant is all wrong. I've watched 'em. When one finds a nice feed he gobbles it so fast that the pieces foller down his throat like yearlin's through a hole in the fence. It's only when he scratches up a measly one-grain quick-lunch that he calls up the hens and stands noble and self-sacrificin' to one side. That ain't the point, which is, that after two months I had them long-laigs so they'd drop everythin' and come kitin' at the *honk-honk* of that horn. It was a purty sight to see 'em, sailin' in from all directions twenty foot at a stride. I was proud of em, and named 'em the Honk-honk Breed. We didn't have no others, for by now the coyotes and bob-cats had nailed the straight-breds. There wasn't no wild cat or coyote could catch one of my Honk-honks, no, sir!

We made a little on our placer—just enough to keep interested. Then the supervisors decided to fix our road, and what's more, *they done it*! That's the only part in this yarn that's hard to believe, but, boys, you'll have to take it on faith. They ploughed her, and crowned her, and scraped her and rolled her, and when they moved on we had the fanciest highway in the State of Californy.

That noon—the day they called her a job—Tusky and I sat smokin' our pipes as per usual, when way over the foothills we seen a cloud of dust and faint to our ears was bore a whizzin' sound. The chickens was gathered under the cottonwood for the heat of the day, but they didn't pay no attention. Then faint, but clear, we heard another of them brass horns:

"Honk! honk!" it says, and every one of them chickens woke up, and stood at attention.

"Honk! honk!" it hollered clearer and nearer. Then over the hill come an automobeel, blowin' vigorous at every jump.

"My God!" I yells to Tusky, kickin' over my chair, as I springs to my feet. "Stop 'em! Stop 'em!"

But it was too late. Out the gate sprinted them poor devoted chickens, and up the road they trailed in vain pursuit. The last we seen of 'em was a minglin' of dust and dim figgers goin' thirty mile an hour after a disappearin' automobeel.

That was all we seen for the moment. About three o'clock the first straggler came limpin' in, his wings hangin', his mouth open, his eyes glazed with the heat. By sundown fourteen had returned. All the rest had disappeared utter; we never seen 'em again. I reckon they just naturally run themselves into a sunstroke and died on the road.

It takes a long time to learn a chicken a thing, but a heap longer to unlearn him. After that two or three of these yere automobeeles went by every day, all a-blowin' of their horns, all kickin' up a hell of a dust. And every time them fourteen Honk-honks of mine took along after 'em, just as I'd taught 'em to do, layin' to get to their corn when they caught up. No more of 'em died, but that fourteen did get into elegant trainin'. After a while they got plumb to enjoyin' it. When you come right down to it, a chicken don't have many amusements and relaxations in this life. Searchin' for worms, chasin' grasshoppers and wallerin' in the dust is about the limits of joys for chickens.

It was sure a fine sight to see 'em after they got well into the game. About nine o'clock every mornin' they would saunter down to the rise of the road where they would wait patient until a machine came along. Then it would warm your heart to see the enthusiasm of them. With exultant cackles of joy they'd trail in, reachin' out like quarter-horses, their wings half spread out, their eyes beamin' with delight. At the lower turn they'd quit. Then, after talkin' it over excited-like for a few minutes, they'd calm down and wait for another.

After a few months of this sort of trainin' they got purty good at it. I had one two-year-old rooster that made fifty-four mile an hour behind one of these sixty-horsepower Panhandles. When cars don't come along often enough, they'd all turn out and chase jack-rabbits. They wasn't much fun at that. After a short, brief sprint the rabbit would crouch down plumb terrified, while the Honk-honks pulled off triumphal dances around his shrinkin' form.

Our ranch got to be purty well known them days among automobeelists. The strength of their cars was horse-power, of course, but the speed of them they got to ratin' by chicken-power. Some of them used to come way up from Los Angeles just to try out a new car along our road with the Honk-honks for pace-makers. We charged them a little somethin', and then, too, we opened up the road-house and the bar, so we did purty well. It wasn't necessary to work any longer at the bogus placer. Evenin's we sat around outside and swapped yarns, and I bragged on my chickens. The chickens would gather round close to listen. They liked to hear their praises sung, all right. You bet they *sabe*! The only reason a chicken, or any other critter, isn't intelligent is because he hasn't no chance to expand.

Why, we used to run races with 'em. Some of us would hold two or more chickens back of a chalk line, and the starter'd blow the horn from a hundred yards to a mile away, dependin' on whether it was a sprint or for distance. We had pools on the results, gave odds, made books and kept records. After the thing got knowed we made money hand over fist.

The stranger broke off abruptly and began to roll a cigarette.

"What did you quit it for, then?" ventured Charley, out of the hushed silence.

"Pride," replied the stranger solemnly. "Haughtiness of spirit."

"How so?" urged Charley, after a pause.

"Them chickens," continued the stranger, after a moment, "stood around listenin' to me a-braggin' of what superior fowls they was until they got all puffed up. They wouldn't have nothin' whatever to do with the ordinary chickens we brought in for eatin' purposes, but stood around lookin' bored when there wasn't no sport doin'. They got to be just like that Four Hundred you read about in the papers. It was one continual round of grasshopper balls, race meets and afternoon hen-parties, They got idle and haughty, just like folks. Then come race suicide. They got to feelin' so aristocratic the hens wouldn't have no eggs."

Nobody dared say a word.

"Windy Bill's snake—" began the narrator genially.

"Stranger," broke in Windy Bill, with great emphasis, "as to that snake, I want you to understand this: yereafter in my estimation that snake is nothin' but an ornery angle-worm!"

ZANE GREY
The Ranger

Zane Grey (1872–1939) was born Pearl Zane Grey in Zanesville, an Ohio town named after his great-great-grandfather. He won a baseball scholarship to the University of Pennsylvania, from which he graduated with a degree in dentistry. In 1905 he married Lina Elise Roth. Dolly—as Lina was known—was to be instrumental in Grey's success as a writer: not only did she pay for the trip West that enabled Grey to gather material for his first successful novel, *The Heritage of the Desert* (1910), but throughout his career she corrected his manuscripts and managed his finances. *The Heritage of the Desert* was followed by seventy-seven other Western novels, including the most famous novel of the American West, *Riders of the Purple Sage* (1912), and such classics as *The U.P. Trail* (1918), and *The Vanishing American* (1925). These books made Grey the second best-selling Western writer of all time (only Louis L'Amour has sold more), and his name synonymous with the Western genre. Grey's fiction was often formulaic and sentimental, but he was also capable of the richest fantasy.

The novelette 'The Ranger' is from 1929. Unlike the majority of Grey's tales, which have an Arizona setting, this tale is set in Texas.

PERIODICALLY OF LATE, ESPECIALLY AFTER some bloody affray or other, Vaughn Medill, ranger of Texas, suffered from spells of depression and longing for a ranch and wife and children. The fact that few rangers ever attained these cherished possessions did not detract from their appeal. At such times the long service to his great state, which owed so much to the rangers, was apt to lose its importance.

Vaughn sat in the shade of the adobe house, on the bank of the slow-eddying, muddy Rio Grande, outside the town of Brownsville. He was alone at this ranger headquarters for the very good reason that his chief, Captain Allerton, and two comrades were laid up in the hospital. Vaughn, with his usual notorious luck, had come out of the Cutter rustling fight without a scratch.

He had needed a few days off, to go alone into the mountains and there get rid of the sickness killing always engendered in him. No wonder he got red in the face and swore when some admiring tourist asked him how many men he had killed. Vaughn had been long in the service. Like other Texas youths he had enlisted in this famous and unique state constabulary before he was twenty, and he refused to count the years he had served. He had the stature of the born Texan. And the lined, weathered face, the resolute lips, grim except when he smiled, and the narrowed eyes of cool gray, and the tinge of white over his temples did not begin to tell the truth about his age.

Vaughn watched the yellow river that separated his state from Mexico. He had reason to hate that strip of dirty water and the hot mosquito and cactus land beyond. Like as not, this very day or tomorrow he would have to go across and arrest some renegade native or fetch back a stolen calf or shoot it out with Quinola and his band, who were known to be on American soil again. Vaughn shared in common with all Texans a supreme contempt for people who were so unfortunate as to live south of the border. His father had been a soldier in both Texas wars, and Vaughn had inherited his conviction that all Mexicans were his natural enemies. He knew this was not really true. Villa was an old acquaintance, and he had listed among men to whom he owed his life, Martiniano, one of the greatest of the Texas *vaqueros*.

Brooding never got Vaughn anywhere, except into deeper melancholy. This drowsy summer day he got in very deep indeed, so deep that he began to mourn over the several girls he might—at least he believed he might—have married. It all seemed so long ago, when he was on fire with the ranger spirit and would not have sacrificed any girl to the agony of waiting for her ranger to come home—knowing that some day he would never come again. Since then sentimental affairs of the heart had been few and far between; and the very latest, dating to this very hour, concerned Roseta, daughter of Uvaldo, foreman for the big Glover ranch just down the river.

Uvaldo was a Mexican of quality, claiming descent from the Spanish soldier of that name. He had an American wife, owned many head of stock, and in fact was partner with Glover in several cattle deals. The black-eyed Roseta, his daughter, had been born on the American side of the river, and had shared advantages of school and contact, seldom the lot of most señoritas.

Vaughn ruminated over these few facts as the excuse for his infatuation. For a Texas ranger to fall in love with an ordinary Mexican girl was unthinkable. To be sure, it had happened, but it was something not to think about. Roseta, however, was extraordinary. She was pretty, and slight of stature—so slight that Vaughn felt ludicrous, despite his bliss, while dancing with her. If he had stretched out his long arm and she had walked under it, he would have had to lower his hand considerably to touch her glossy black head. She was roguish and coquettish, yet had the pride of her Spanish forebearers. Lastly she was young, rich, the belle of Las Animas, and the despair of cowboy and *vaquero* alike.

When Vaughn had descended to the depths of his brooding he discovered, as he had many times before, that there were but slight grounds for any hopes which he may have had of winning the beautiful Roseta. The sweetness of a haunting dream was all that could be his. Only this time it seemed to hurt more. He should not have let himself in for such a catastrophe. But as he groaned in spirit and bewailed his lonely state, he could not help recalling Roseta's smiles, her favors of dances when scores of admirers were thronging after her, and the way she would single him out on those occasions. "*Un señor grande*," she had called him, and likewise "handsome gringo," and once, with mystery and fire in her sloe-black eyes, "You Texas ranger—you bloody gunman—killer of Mexicans!"

Flirt Roseta was, of course, and doubly dangerous by reason of her mixed blood, her Spanish lineage, and her American upbringing. Uvaldo had been quoted as saying he would never let his daughter marry across the Rio Grande. Some rich rancher's son would have her hand bestowed upon him; maybe young Glover would be the lucky one. It was madness for Vaughn even to have dreamed of winning her. Yet there still abided that much youth in him.

Sounds of wheels and hoofs interrupted the ranger's reverie. He listened. A buggy had stopped out in front. Vaughn got up and looked round the corner of the house. It was significant that he instinctively stepped out sideways, his right hand low where the heavy gun sheath hung. A ranger never presented his full front to possible bullets; it was a trick of old hands in the service.

Someone was helping a man out of the buggy. Presently Vaughn recognized Colville, a ranger comrade, who came in assisted, limping, and with his arm in a sling.

"How are you, Bill?" asked Vaughn solicitously, as he helped the driver lead Colville into the large whitewashed room.

"All right—fine, in fact, only a—little light-headed," panted the other. "Lost a sight of blood."

"You look it. Reckon you'd have done better to stay at the hospital."

"Medill, there ain't half enough rangers to go—round," replied Colville. "Cap Allerton is hurt bad—but he'll recover. An' he thought so long as I could wag I'd better come back to headquarters."

"Ahuh. What's up, Bill?" asked the ranger quietly. He really did not need to ask.

"Shore I don't know. Somethin' to do with Quinela," replied Colville. "Help me out of my coat. It's hot an' dusty. . . . Fetch me a cold drink."

"Bill, you should have stayed in town if it's ice you want," said Vaughn as he filled a dipper from the water bucket. "Haven't I run this shebang many a time?"

"Medill, you're slated for a run across the Rio—if I don't miss my guess."

"Hell you say! Alone?"

"How else, unless the rest of our outfit rides in from the Brazos. . . . Anyway, don't they call you the 'lone star ranger'? Haw! Haw!"

"Shore you don't have a hunch what's up?" inquired Vaughn again.

"Honest I don't. Allerton had to wait for more information. Then he'll send instructions. But we know Quinela was hangin' round, with some deviltry afoot."

"Bill, that bandit outfit is plumb bold these days," said Vaughn reflectively. "I wonder now."

"We're all guessin'. But Allerton swears Quinela is daid set on revenge. Lopez was some relation, we heah from Mexicans on this side. An' when we busted up Lopez' gang, we riled Quinela. He's laid that to you, Vaughn."

"Nonsense," blurted out Vaughn. "Quinela has another raid on hand, or some other thievery job of his own."

"But didn't you kill Lopez?" asked Colville.

"I shore didn't," declared Vaughn testily. "Reckon I was there when it happened, but Lord! I wasn't the only ranger."

"Wal, you've got the name of it an' that's jist as bad. Not that it makes much difference. You're used to bein' laid for. But I reckon Cap wanted to tip you off."

"Ahuh . . . Say, Bill," continued Vaughn, dropping his head. "I'm shore tired of this ranger game."

"My Gawd, who ain't! But, Vaughn, *you* couldn't lay down on Captain Allerton right now."

"No. But I've a notion to resign when he gets well an' the boys come back from the Brazos."

"An' that'd be all right, Vaughn, although we'd hate to

lose you," returned Colville earnestly. "We all know—in fact everybody who has followed the ranger service knows you should have been a captain long ago. But them pig-headed officials at Houston! Vaughn, your gun record—the very name an' skill that make you a great ranger—have operated against you there."

"Reckon so. But I never wanted particularly to be a captain—leastways of late years," replied Vaughn moodily. "I'm just tired of bein' eternally on my guard. Lookin' to be shot at from every corner or bush! Think what an awful thing it was—when I near killed one of my good friends—all because he came suddenlike out of a door, pullin' at his handkerchief!"

"It's the price we pay. Texas could never have been settled at all but for the buffalo hunters first, an' then us rangers. We don't get much credit, Vaughn. But we know someday our service will be appreciated. . . . In your case everythin' is magnified. Suppose you did quit the service? Wouldn't you still stand most the same risk? Wouldn't you need to be on your guard, sleepin' an' wakin'?"

"Wal, I suppose so, for a time. But somehow I'd be relieved."

"Vaughn, the men who are lookin' for you now will always be lookin', until they're daid."

"Shore. But, Bill, that class of men don't live long on the Texas border."

"Hell! Look at Wes Hardin', Kingfisher, Poggin—gun-men that took a long time to kill. An' look at Cortina, at Quinela—an' Villa. . . . Nope, I reckon it's the obscure relations an' friends of men you've shot that you have most to fear. An' you never know who an' where they are. It's my belief you'd be shore of longer life by stickin' to the rangers."

"Couldn't I get married an' go way off somewhere?" asked Vaughn belligerently.

Colville whistled in surprise, and then laughed. "Ahuh? So that's the lay of the land? A gal!—Wal, if the Texas ranger service is to suffer, let it be for that one cause."

Toward evening a messenger brought a letter from Captain Allerton, with the information that a drove of horses had been driven across the river west of Brownsville, at Rock Ford. They were in charge of Mexicans and presumably had been stolen from some ranch inland. The raid could be laid to Quinela, though there was no proof of it. It bore his brand. Medill's instructions were to take the rangers and recover the horses.

"Reckon Cap thinks the boys have got back from the Brazos or he's had word they're comin'," commented Colville. "Wish I was able to ride. We wouldn't wait."

Vaughn scanned the short letter again and then filed it away among a stack of others.

"Strange business this ranger service," he said ponderingly. "Horses stolen—fetch them back! Cattle raid—recover stock! Drunken cowboy shootin' up the town—arrest him! Bandits looted the San Tone stage—fetch them in! Little Tom, Dick, or Harry lost—find him! Farmer murdered—string up the murderer!"

"Wal, come to think about it, you're right," replied Colville. "But the rangers have been doin' it for thirty or forty years. You cain't help havin' pride in the service, Medill. Half the job's done when these hombres find a ranger's on the trail. That's reputation. But I'm bound to admit the thing is strange an' shore couldn't happen nowhere else but in Texas."

"Reckon I'd better ride up to Rock Ford an' have a look at that trail."

"Wal, I'd wait till mawnin'. Mebbe the boys will come in. An' there's no sense in ridin' it twice."

The following morning after breakfast Vaughn went out to the alfalfa pasture to fetch in his horse. Next to his gun a ranger's horse was his most valuable asset. Indeed a horse often saved a ranger's life when a gun could not. Star was a big-boned chestnut, not handsome except in regard to his size, but for speed and endurance Vaughn had never owned his like. They had been on some hard jaunts together. Vaughn fetched Star into the shed and saddled him.

Presently Vaughn heard Colville shout, and upon hurrying out he saw a horseman ride furiously away from the house. Colville stood in the door waving.

Vaughn soon reached him. "Who was that feller?"

"Glover's man, Uvaldo. You know him."

"Uvaldo!" exclaimed Vaughn, startled. "He shore was in a hurry. What'd he want?"

"Captain Allerton, an' in fact all the rangers in Texas. I told Uvaldo I'd send you down pronto. He wouldn't wait. Shore was mighty excited."

"What's wrong with him?"

"His gal is gone."

"Gone!"

"Shore. He cain't say whether she eloped or was kidnapped. But it's a job for you, old man. Haw! Haw!"

"Yes, it would be—if she eloped," replied Vaughn constrainedly. "An' I reckon not a bit funny, Bill."

"Wal, hop to it," replied Colville, turning to go into the house.

Vaughn mounted his horse and spurred him into the road.

2

VAUGHN'S personal opinion, before he arrived at Glover's ranch, was that Roseta Uvaldo had eloped, and probably with a cowboy or some *vaquero* with whom her father had forbidden her to associate. In some aspects Roseta resembled the vain daughter of a proud don; in the main, she was American bred and educated. But she had that strain of blood which might well have burned secretly to break the bonds of conventionality. Uvaldo, himself, had been a *vaquero* in his youth. Any Texan could have guessed this seeing Uvaldo ride a horse.

There was much excitement in the Uvaldo household. Vaughn could not get any clue out of the weeping kin folks, except that Roseta had slept in her bed, and had risen early to take her morning horseback ride. All Mexicans were of a highly excitable temperament, and Uvaldo was no exception. Vaughn could not get much out of him. Roseta had not been permitted to ride off the ranch, which was something that surprised Vaughn. She was not allowed to go anywhere unaccompanied. This certainly was a departure from the freedom accorded Texan girls; nevertheless any girl of good sense would give the river a wide berth.

"Did she ride out alone?" asked Vaughn, in his slow Spanish, thinking he could get at Uvaldo better in his own tongue.

"Yes, señor. Pedro saddled her horse. No one else saw her."

"What time this morning?"

"Before sunrise."

Vaughn questioned the lean, dark *vaquero* about what clothes the girl was wearing and how she had looked and acted. The answer was that Roseta had dressed in *vaquero* garb, looked very pretty and full of the devil. Vaughn reflected that this was quite easy to believe. Next he questioned the stable boys and other *vaqueros* about the place. Then he rode out to the Glover ranch house and got hold of some of the cowboys, and lastly young Glover himself. Nothing further was elicited from them, except that this same thing had happened before. Vaughn hurried back to Uvaldo's house.

He had been a ranger for fifteen years and that meant a vast experience in Texas border life. It had become a part of his business to look through people. Not often was Vaughn deceived when he put a query and bent his gaze upon a man. Women, of course, were different. Uvaldo himself was the only one here who roused a doubt in Vaughn's mind. This Americanized Mexican had a terrible fear which he did not realize that he was betraying. Vaughn conceived the impression that Uvaldo had an enemy and he had only to ask him if he knew Quinela to get on the track of something. Uvaldo was probably lying when he professed fear that Roseta had eloped.

"You think she ran off with a cowboy or some young feller from town?" inquired Vaughn.

"No, señor. With a *vaquero* or a peon," came the amazing reply.

Vaughn gave up here, seeing he was losing time.

"Pedro, show me Roseta's horse tracks," he requested.

"Señor, I will give you ten thousand dollars if you bring my daughter back—alive," said Uvaldo.

"Rangers don't accept money for their services," replied Vaughn briefly, further mystified by the Mexican's intimation that Roseta might be in danger of foul play. "I'll fetch her back—one way or another—unless she has eloped. If she's gotten married I can do nothin'."

Pedro showed the ranger the small hoof tracks made by Roseta's horse. He studied them a few moments, and then, motioning those following him to stay back, he led his own horse and walked out of the courtyard, down the lane, through the open gate, and into the field.

Every boy born on the open range of vast Texas had been a horse tracker from the time he could walk. Vaughn was a past master at this cowboy art, long before he joined the rangers, and years of man-hunting had perfected it. He could read a fugitive's mind by the tracks he left in dust or sand.

He rode across Glover's broad acres, through the pecans, to where the ranch bordered on the desert. Roseta had not been bent on an aimless morning ride.

Under a clump of trees someone had waited for her. Here Vaughn dismounted to study tracks. A mettlesome horse had been tethered to one tree. In the dust were imprints of a riding boot, not the kind left by cowboy or *vaquero*. Heel and toe were broad. He found the butt of a cigarette smoked that morning. Roseta's clandestine friend was not a Mexican, much less a peon or *vaquero*. There were signs that he probably had waited there on other mornings.

Vaughn got back on his horse, strengthened in the elopement theory, though not yet wholly convinced. Maybe Roseta was just having a lark. Maybe she had a lover Uvaldo would have none of. This idea grew as Vaughn saw where the horses had walked close together, so their riders could hold hands. Perhaps more! Vaughn's silly hope oozed out and died. And he swore at his own ridiculous, vain dreams. It was all right for him to be young enough to have an infatuation for Roseta Uvaldo, but to have entertained a dream of winning her was laughable. He laughed, though mirthlessly. And jealous pangs consumed him. What an adorable, fiery creature she was! Some lucky dog from Brownsville had won her. Mingled with Vaughn's romantic feelings was one of relief.

"Reckon I'd better get back to rangerin' instead of moonin'," he thought grimly.

The tracks led in a roundabout way through the mesquite to the river trail. This was two miles or more from the line of the Glover ranch. The trail was broad and lined by trees. It was a lonely and unfrequented place for lovers to ride. Roseta and her companion still were walking their horses. On this beautiful trail, which invited a gallop or at least a canter, only lovemaking could account for the leisurely gait. Also the risk! Whoever Roseta's lover might be, he was either a fool or plain fearless. Vaughn swore lustily as the tracks led on and on, deeper into the timber that bordered the Rio Grande.

Suddenly Vaughn drew up sharply, with an exclamation. Then he slid out of his saddle, to bend over a marked change in the tracks he was trailing. Both horses had reared, to come down hard on forehoofs, and then jump sideways.

"By God! A holdup!" grunted Vaughn in sudden concern.

Sandal tracks in the dust! A native bandit had been hiding behind a thicket in ambush. Vaughn swiftly tracked the horses off the trail, to an open glade on the bank, where hoof tracks of other horses joined them and likewise boot tracks. Vaughn did not need to see that these new marks had been made by Mexican boots.

Roseta had either been led into a trap by the man she had met or they had both been ambushed by three Mexicans. It was a common thing along the border for Mexican marauders to kidnap Mexican girls. The instances of abduction of American girls had been few and far between, though Vaughn remembered several over the years whom he had helped to rescue. They had been pretty sorry creatures, and one was even demented. Roseta being the daughter of the rich Uvaldo, would be held for ransom and therefore she might escape the usual horrible treatment. Vaughn's sincere and honest love for Roseta made him at once annoyed with her heedless act, jealous of the unknown who had kept tryst with her, and fearful of her possible fate.

"Three hours start on me," he muttered, consulting his watch. "Reckon I can come up on them before dark."

The ranger followed the broad, fresh trail that wound down through timber and brush to the river bottom. A border of arrow weed stretched out across a sand bar. All at once he halted stockstill, then moved as if to dismount. But it was not necessary. He could read from the saddle another story in the sand and this one was one of tragedy. A round depression in the sand and one spot of reddish color, obviously blood, on the slender white stalk of arrow weed, a heavy furrow, and then a path as though made by a dragged body through the green to the river—these easily-read signs added a sinister note to the abduction of Roseta Uvaldo. In Vaughn's estimation it cleared Roseta's comrade of all complicity, except that of heedless risk. And the affair began to savor somewhat of Quinela's work. The ranger wondered whether Quinela, the mere mention of whose name had brought a look of terror into Uvaldo's eyes when Vaughn had spoken to him, might not be a greater menace than the Americans believed. If so, then God help Roseta!

Vaughn took time enough to dismount and trail the path through the weeds where the murderers had dragged the body. They had been bold and careless. Vaughn picked up a cigarette case, a glove, and a watch, and he made sure that by the latter he could identify Roseta's companion on this fatal ride. A point of gravel led out to a deep current in the river, to which the body had been consigned. It might be several days and many miles below where the Rio Grande would give up its dead.

The exigencies of the case prevented Vaughn from going back after food and canteen. Many a time had he been caught in the same predicament. He had only his horse, a gun, and a belt full of cartridges. But they were sufficient for the job that lay ahead to him.

Hurrying back to Star he led him along the trail to the point where the Mexicans had gone into the river. The Rio was treacherous, with quicksand, but it was always safe to follow Mexicans, provided one could imitate them. Vaughn spurred his horse across the oozy sand, and made deep water just in the nick of time. The swift current, however, was nothing for the powerful Star to breast. Vaughn emerged at precisely the point where the Mexicans had climbed out, but to help Star he threw himself forward, and catching some arrow weeds, hauled himself up the steep bank. Star floundered out and plunged up to solid ground.

The ranger mounted again and took the trail without any concern of being ambushed. Three Mexicans bent on a desperate deal of this sort would not hang back on the trail to wait for pursuers. Once up on the level mesquite land it was plain that they had traveled at a brisk trot. Vaughn loped Star along the well-defined tracks of five horses. At this gait he felt sure that he was covering two miles while they were traveling one. He calculated that they should be about fifteen miles ahead of him, unless rough country had slowed them, and that by early afternoon he ought to be close on their heels. If their trail had worked down the river toward Rock Ford he might have connected these three riders with the marauders mentioned in Captain Allerton's letter. But it led straight south of the Rio Grande and showed that the kidnappers had a definite destination in mind.

Vaughn rode for two hours before he began to climb out of the level river valley. Then he struck rocky hills covered with cactus and separated by dry gorges. There was no difficulty in following the trail, but he had to proceed more slowly. He did not intend that Roseta Uvaldo should be forced to spend a night in the clutches of these desperadoes. Toward noon the sun grew hot and Vaughn began to suffer from thirst. Star was soaked with sweat, but showed no sign of distress.

He came presently to a shady spot where it was evident that the abductors had halted, probably to eat and rest. The remains of a small fire showed in a circle of stones. Vaughn got off to put his hand on the mesquite ashes. They were still hot. This meant something, though not a great deal. Mesquite wood burned slowly and the ashes retained heat for a long while. Vaughn also examined horse tracks so fresh that no particle of dust had yet blown into them. Two hours behind, perhaps a little more or less!

He resumed the pursuit, making good time everywhere, at a swift lope on all possible stretches.

There was a sameness to the brushy growth and barren hills and rocky dry ravines, though the country was growing rougher. He had not been through this section before. He crossed no trails. And he noted that the tracks of the Mexicans gradually were heading from south to west. Sooner or later they were bound to join the well-known Rock Ford trail. Vaughn was concerned about this. Should he push Star to the limit until he knew he was close behind the abductors? It would not do to let them see or hear him. If he could surprise them the thing would be easy. While he revolved these details of the problem in his mind he kept traveling full speed along the trail.

He passed an Indian corn field, and then a hut of adobe and brush. The tracks he was hounding kept straight on, and led off the desert into a road, not, however, the Rock Ford road. Vaughn here urged Star to his best speed, and a half hour later he was turning into a well-defined trail. He did not need to get off to see that no horses but the five he was tracking had passed this point since morning. Moreover, it was plain that they were not many miles ahead.

Vaughn rode on awhile at a full gallop, then turning off the trail, he kept Star to that same ground-eating gait in a long detour. Once he crossed a stream bed, up which there would be water somewhere. Then he met the trail again, finding to his disappointment and chagrin that the tracks indicated that the riders had passed. He had hoped to head off the desperadoes and lie in wait for them here.

Mid-afternoon was on him. He decided not to force the issue at once. There was no ranch or village within half a night's ride of this spot. About sunset the Mexicans would halt to rest and eat. They would build a fire.

Vaughn rode down into a rock defile where he found a much-needed drink for himself and Star. He did not relish the winding trail ahead. It kept to the gorge. It was shady and cool, but afforded too many places where he might be ambushed. Still, there was no choice; he had to go on. He had no concern for himself that the three hombres would ambush him. But if they fell in with another band of cut-throats! It was Roseta of whom he was thinking.

Vaughn approached a rocky wall. He was inured to danger. And his ranger luck was proverbial. As he turned the corner of the rock wall he found himself facing a line of men with leveled rifles.

"Hands up, gringo ranger!"

3

VAUGHN was as much surprised by the command given in English as by this totally unexpected encounter with a dozen or more Mexicans. He knew the type all too well. These were Quinela's bandits.

Vaughn raised his hands. Why this gang leader was holding him up instead of shooting on sight was beyond Vaughn's ken. The Mexicans began to jabber like a lot of angry monkeys. If ever Vaughn expected death it was at that moment. He had about decided to pull his gun and shoot it out with them, and finish as many a ranger had before him. But a shrill authoritative voice deterred him. Then a swarthy little man, lean-faced, and beady-eyed, stepped out between the threatening rifles and Vaughn. He silenced the shrill chatter of his men.

"It's the gringo ranger, Texas Medill," he shouted in Spanish. "It's the man who killed Lopez. Don't shoot. Quinela will pay much gold for him alive. Quinela will strip off the soles of his feet and drive him with hot irons to walk on the choya."

"But it's the dreaded gun ranger, señor," protested a one-eyed bandit. "The only safe way is to shoot his cursed heart out here."

"We had our orders to draw this ranger across the river," returned the leader harshly. "Quinela knew his man and the hour. The Uvaldo girl brought him. And here we have him—alive! . . . Garcia, it'd cost your life to shoot this ranger."

"But I warn you, Juan, he is not alone," returned Garcia. "He is but a leader of many rangers. Best kill him quick and hurry on. I have told you already that plenty gringo *vaqueros* are on the trail. We have many horses. We cannot travel fast. Night is coming. Best kill Texas Medill."

"No, Garcia. We obey orders," returned Juan harshly. "We take him alive to Quinela."

Vaughn surveyed the motley group with speculative eyes. He could kill six of them at least, and with Star charging and the poor marksmanship of native bandits, he might break through. Coldly Vaughn weighed the chances. They were a hundred to one that he would not escape. Yet he had taken such chances before. But these men had Roseta, and while there was life there was always some hope. With a tremendous effort of will he forced aside the deadly impulse and applied his wits to the situation.

The swarthy Juan turned to cover Vaughn with a cocked gun. Vaughn read doubt and fear in the beady eyes. He knew Mexicans. If they did not kill him at once there was hope. At a significant motion Vaughn carefully shifted a long leg and stepped face front, hands high, out of the saddle.

Juan addressed him in Spanish.

"No savvy, señor," replied the ranger.

"You speak Spanish?" repeated the questioner in English.

"Very little. I understand some of your Mexican lingo."

"You trailed Manuel alone?"

"Who's Manuel?"

"My *vaquero*. He brought Señorita Uvaldo across the river."

"After murdering her companion. Yes, I trailed him and

two other men, I reckon. Five horses. The Uvaldo girl rode one. The fifth horse belonged to her companion."

"Ha! Did Manuel kill?" exclaimed the Mexican, and it was quite certain that this was news to him.

"Yes. You have murder as well as kidnapping to answer for."

The Mexican cursed under his breath.

"Where are your rangers?" he went on.

"They got back from the Brazos last night with news of your raid," said Vaughn glibly. "And this morning they joined the cowboys who were trailing the horses you stole."

Vaughn realized then that somewhere there had been a mix-up in Quinela's plans. The one concerning the kidnapping of Roseta Uvaldo and Vaughn's taking the trail had worked out well. But Juan's dark, corded face, his volley of unintelligible maledictions directed at his men betrayed a hitch somewhere. Again Vaughn felt the urge to draw and fight it out. What crazy fiery-headed fools these tattered marauders were! Juan had lowered his gun to heap abuse on Garcia. That luckless individual turned green of face. Some of the others still held leveled rifles on Vaughn, but they were looking at their leader and his lieutenant. Vaughn saw a fair chance to get away, and his gun hand itched. A heavy-booming Colt—Juan and Garcia dead—a couple of shots at those other outlaws—that would have stampeded them. But Vaughn as yet had caught no glimpse of Roseta. He put the grim, cold impulse behind him.

The harangue went on, ending only when Garcia had been cursed into sullen agreement.

"I'll take them to Quinela," cried Juan shrilly, and began shouting orders.

Vaughn's gun belt was removed. His hands were tied behind his back. He was forced upon one of the Mexican's horses and his feet were roped to the stirrups. Juan appropriated his gun belt, which he put on with the Mexican's love of vainglory, and then mounted Star. The horse did not like the exchange of riders, and there followed immediate evidence of the cruel iron hand of the outlaw. Vaughn's blood leaped, and he veiled his eyes lest someone see his savage urge to kill. When he raised his head, two of the squat, motley-garbed, and wide-sombreroed Mexicans were riding by, and the second led a horse upon which sat Roseta Uvaldo.

She was bound to the saddle, but her hands were free. She turned her face to Vaughn. With what concern and longing did he gaze at it! Vaughn needed only to see it flash white toward him, to meet the look of gratitude in her dark eyes, to realize that Roseta was still unharmed. She held her small proud head high. Her spirit was unbroken. For the rest, what mattered the dusty disheveled hair, the mud-spattered and dust-covered *vaquero* riding garb she wore? Vaughn flashed her a look that brought the blood to her pale cheeks.

Juan prodded Vaughn in the back. "Ride, gringo." Then he gave Garcia a last harsh command. As Vaughn's horse followed that of Roseta and her two guards into the brook, there rose a clattering, jabbering melee among the Mexicans left behind. It ended in a receding roar of pounding hoofs.

The brook was shallow and ran swiftly over gravel and rocks. Vaughn saw at once that Juan meant to hide his trail. An hour after the cavalcade would have passed a given point here, no obvious trace would show. The swift water would have cleared as well as have filled the hoof tracks with sand.

"Juan, you were wise to desert your gang of horse thieves," said Vaughn coolly. "There's a hard-ridin' outfit on their trail. And some, if not all of them, will be dead before sundown."

"*Quien sabe?* But it's sure Texas Medill will be walking choya on bare-skinned feet *mañana*," replied the Mexican bandit chief.

Vaughn pondered. Quinela's rendezvous, then, was not many hours distant. Travel such as this, up a rocky gorge, was necessarily slow. Probably this brook would not afford more than a few miles of going. Then Juan would head out on to the desert and try in other ways to hide his tracks. As far as Vaughn was concerned, whether he hid them or not made no difference. The cowboys and rangers in pursuit were but fabrications of Vaughn's to deceive the

Mexicans. He knew how to work on their primitive feelings. But Vaughn poignantly realized the peril of the situation and the brevity of the time left him.

"Juan, you've got my gun," said Vaughn, his keen mind working. "You say I'll be dead in less than twenty-four hours. What's it worth to untie my hands so I can ride in comfort?"

"Señor, if you have money on you it will be mine anyway," replied the Mexican.

"I haven't any money with me. But I've got my checkbook that shows a balance of some thousands of dollars in an El Paso bank," replied Vaughn, and he turned round.

The bandit showed his gleaming white teeth in derision. "What's that to me?"

"Some thousands in gold, Juan. You can get it easily. News of my death will not get across the border very soon. I'll give you a check and a letter, which you can take to El Paso, or send by messenger."

"How much gold, Señor?" Juan asked.

"Over three thousand."

"Señor, you would bribe me into a trap. No. Juan loves the glitter and clink of your American gold, but he is no fool."

"Nothing of the sort. I'm trying to buy a little comfort in my last hours. And possibly a little kindness to the señorita there. It's worth a chance. You can send a messenger. What do you care if he shouldn't come back? You don't lose anythin'."

"No gringo can be trusted, much less Texas Medill of the rangers," replied the Mexican.

"Sure. But take a look at my checkbook. You know figures when you see them."

Juan rode abreast of Vaughn, impelled by curiosity. His beady eyes glittered.

"Inside vest pocket," directed Vaughn. "Don't drop the pencil."

The Mexican procured the checkbook and opened it. "Señor, I know your bank," he said, vain of his ability to read, which to judge by his laborious task was limited.

"Ahuh. Well, how much balance have I left?" asked Vaughn.

"Three thousand, four hundred."

"Good. Now, Juan, you may as well get that money. I've nobody to leave it to. I'll buy a little comfort for myself—and kindness to the señorita."

"How much kindness, señor?" asked the Mexican craftily.

"That you keep your men from handlin' her rough—and soon as the ransom is paid send her back safe."

"Señor, the first I have seen to. The second is not mine to grant. Quinela will demand ransom—yes—but never will he send the señorita back."

"But I—thought—"

"Quinela was wronged by Uvaldo."

Vaughn whistled at this astounding revelation. He had divined correctly the fear Uvaldo had revealed. The situation then for Roseta was vastly more critical. Death would be merciful compared to the fate the half-breed peon Quinela would deal her. Vaughn cudgeled his brains in desperation. Why had he not shot it out with these yellow desperadoes? But rage could not further Roseta's cause.

Meanwhile the horses splashed and clattered over the rocks in single file up the narrowing gorge. The steep walls were giving way to brushy slopes that let the hot sun down. Roseta looked back at Vaughn with appeal and trust—and something more in her dark eyes that tortured him.

Vaughn did not have the courage to meet her gaze, except for the fleeting moment. It was only natural that his spirits should be at a low ebb. Never in his long ranger service had he encountered such a desperate situation. More than once he had faced what seemed inevitable death, where there had seemed to be not the slightest chance to escape. Vaughn was not of a temper to give up completely. He would watch for a break till the very last second. For Roseta, however, he endured agonies. He had looked at the mutilated bodies of more than one girl victim of these bandits.

When at length the gully narrowed to a mere crack in the hill, and the water failed, Juan ordered his guards to climb a steep brush slope. There was no sign of any trail. If this brook, which they had waded to its source, led away from the road to Rock Ford, it would take days before rangers or cowboys could possibly run across it. Juan was a fox.

The slope was not easy to climb. Both Mexicans got off their horses to lead Roseta's. If Vaughn had not been tied on his saddle he would have fallen off. Eventually they reached the top, to enter a thick growth of mesquite and cactus. And before long they broke out into a trail, running, as near as Vaughn could make out, at right angles to the road and river trail. Probably it did not cross either one. Certainly the Mexicans trotted east along it as if they had little to fear from anyone traveling it.

Presently a peon came in sight astride a mustang, and leading a burro. He got by the two guards, though they crowded him into the brush. But Juan halted him, and got off Star to see what was in the pack on the burro. With an exclamation of great satisfaction he pulled out what appeared to Vaughn to be a jug or demijohn covered with wickerwork. Juan pulled out the stopper and smelled the contents.

"*Canyu!*" he said, and his white teeth gleamed. He took a drink, then smacked his lips. When the guards, who had stopped to watch, made a move to dismount he cursed them vociferously. Sullenly they slid back into their saddles. Juan stuffed the demijohn into the right saddlebag of Vaughn's saddle. Here the peon protested in a mixed dialect that Vaughn could not translate. But the meaning was obvious. Juan kicked the ragged peon's sandaled foot, and ordered him on, with a significant touch of Vaughn's big gun, which he wore so pompously. The peon lost no time riding off. Juan remounted, and directed the cavalcade to move forward.

Vaughn turned as his horse started, and again he encountered Roseta's dark intent eyes. They seemed telepathic this time, as well as filled with unutterable promise. She had read Vaughn's thought. If there were anything that had dominance in the Mexican's nature it was the cactus liquor, *canyu*. Ordinarily he was volatile, unstable as water, flint one moment and wax the next. But with the burn of *canyu* in his throat he had the substance of mist.

Vaughn felt the lift and pound of his heavy heart. He had prayed for the luck of the ranger, and lo! a peon had ridden up, packing *canyu*.

4

CANYU was a distillation made from the maguey cactus, a plant similar to the century plant. The peon brewed it. But in lieu of the brew, natives often cut into the heart of a plant and sucked the juice. Vaughn had once seen a Mexican sprawled in the middle of a huge maguey, his head buried deep in the heart of it and his legs hanging limp. Upon examination he appeared to be drunk, but it developed that he was dead.

This liquor was potential fire. The lack of it made the peons surly: the possession of it made them gay. One drink changed their mental and physical world. Juan whistled after the first drink: after the second he began to sing "La Paloma." His two guards cast greedy, mean looks backward.

Almost at once the fairly brisk pace of travel that had been maintained slowed perceptibly. Vaughn began to feel more sanguine. He believed that he might be able to break the thongs that bound his wrists. As he had prayed for his ranger luck so he now prayed for anything to delay these Mexicans on the trail.

The leader Juan either wanted the *canyu* for himself or was too crafty to share it with his two men; probably both. With all three of them, the center of attention had ceased to be in Uvaldo's girl and the hated gringo ranger. It lay in that demijohn in Star's saddlebag. If a devil lurked in this white liquor for them, there was likewise for the prisoners a watching angel.

The afternoon was not far enough advanced for the sun to begin losing its heat. Shade along the trail was most inviting and welcome, but it was scarce. Huge pipelike masses of organ cactus began to vary the monotonous scenery. Vaughn saw deer, rabbits, road runners, and butcherbirds. The country was uninhabited and this trail an unfrequented one which certainly must branch into one of the several main traveled trails. Vaughn hoped the end of it still lay many miles off.

The way led into a shady rocky glen. As of one accord the horses halted, without, so far as Vaughn could see, any move or word from their riders. This was proof that the two guards in the lead had ceased to ride with the sole idea in mind of keeping to a steady gait. Vaughn drew a deep breath, as if to control his nervous feeling of suspense. No man could foretell the variety of effects of *canyu* on another, but certain it must be that something would happen soon.

Juan had mellowed considerably. A subtle change had occurred in his disposition, though he was still the watchful leader. Vaughn felt that he was now in even more peril from this Mexican than before the advent of the *canyu*. This, however, would not last long. He could only bide his time, watch and think. His luck had begun to take over. He divined it, trusted it with mounting hope.

The two guards turned their horses across the trail, blocking Roseta's horse, while Vaughn's came up alongside. If he could have stretched out his hand he could have touched Roseta. Many a time he had been thrilled and bewildered in her presence, not to say stricken speechless, but he had never felt as he did now. Roseta contrived to touch his bound foot with her stirrup, and the deliberate move made Vaughn tremble. Still he did not yet look directly down at her.

The actions of the three Mexicans were as clear to Vaughn as crystal. If he had seen one fight among Mexicans over *canyu*, he had seen a hundred. First the older of the two guards leisurely got off his horse. His wide straw sombrero hid his face, except for a peaked, yellow chin, scantily covered with black whiskers. His clothes hung in rags, and a cartridge belt was slung loosely over his left shoulder. He had left his rifle in its saddle sheath, and his only weapon was a bone-handled machete stuck in a scabbard attached to his belt.

"Juan, we are thirsty and have no water," he said. And his comrade, sitting sideways in his saddle, nodded in agreement.

"Gonzalez, one drink and no more," returned Juan, and lifted out the demijohn.

With eager cry the man tipped it to his lips. And he gulped steadily until Juan jerked it away. Then the other Mexican tumbled off his horse and eagerly besought Juan for a drink, if only one precious drop. Juan complied, but this time he did not let go of the demijohn.

Vaughn felt a touch—a gentle pressure on his knee. Roseta had laid her gloved hand there. Then he had to avert his gaze from the Mexicans.

"Oh, Vaughn, I *knew* you would come to save me," she whispered. "But they have caught you. . . . For God's sake, do something."

"Roseta, I reckon I can't do much, at this sitting," replied Vaughn, smiling down at her. "Are you—all right?"

"Yes, except I'm tired and my legs ache. I was frightened badly before you happened along. But now—it's terrible . . . Vaughn, they are taking us to Quinela. He is a monster. My father told me so. . . . If you can't save me you must kill me."

"I shall save you, Roseta," he whispered low, committing himself on the altar of the luck that had never failed him. The glance she gave him then made his blood run throbbing through his veins. And he thanked the fates, since he loved her and had been given this incredible opportunity, that it had fallen to his lot to become a ranger.

Her eyes held his and there was no doubt about the warm pressure of her hand on his knee. But even during this sweet stolen moment, Vaughn had tried to attend to the argument between the three Mexicans. He heard their mingled voices, all high-pitched and angry. In another moment they would be leaping at each others' throats like dogs. Vaughn was endeavoring to think of some encouraging word for Roseta, but the ranger was replaced for the moment by the man who was revealing his heart in a long look into the small pale face, with its red, quivering lips and great dark eyes uplifted, filled with blind faith.

The sound of struggling, the trample of hoofs, a shrill cry of "Santa Maria!" and a sudden blow preceded the startling crash of a gun.

As Vaughn's horse plunged he saw Roseta's mount rear into the brush with its rider screaming, and Star lunged out of a cloud of blue smoke. A moment later Vaughn found himself tearing down the trail. He was helpless, but he squeezed the scared horse with his knees and kept calling, "Whoa there—whoa boy!"

Not for a hundred rods or more did the animal slow up. It relieved Vaughn to hear a clatter of hoofs behind him, and he turned to see Juan tearing after him in pursuit. Presently he turned out into the brush, and getting ahead of Vaughn, turned into the trail again to stop the ranger's horse. Juan proceeded to beat the horse over the head until it almost unseated Vaughn.

"Hold on, man," shouted Vaughn. "It wasn't his fault or mine. Why don't you untie my hands—if you want your nag held in?"

Juan jerked the heaving horse out of the brush and onto the trail, finally leading him back toward the scene of the shooting. But before they reached it Vaughn saw one of the guards coming with Roseta and a riderless horse. Juan grunted his satisfaction, and let them pass without a word.

Roseta seemed less disturbed and shaken than Vaughn had feared she would be. Her dilated eyes, as she passed, said as plainly as any words could have done that they now had one less enemy to contend with.

The journey was resumed. Vaughn drew a deep breath and endeavored to arrange his thoughts. The sun was still only halfway down toward the western horizon. There were hours of daylight yet! And he had an ally more deadly than bullets, more subtle than any man's wit, sharper than the tooth of a serpent.

Perhaps a quarter of an hour later, Vaughn, turning his head ever so slightly, saw, out of the corner of his eye, Juan take another drink of *canyu*. And it was a good stiff one.

Vaughn thrilled as he contained himself. Presently Juan's latest act would be as if it had never been. *Canyu* was an annihilation of the past.

"Juan, I'll fall off this horse pronto," began Vaughn.

"Very good, señor. Fall off," replied Juan amiably.

"But my feet are tied to the stirrups. This horse of yours is skittish. He'll bolt and drag my brains out. If you want to take me alive to Quinela, so that he may have a fiesta while I walk choya, you'd better not let me fall off."

"S. Ranger, if you fall you fall. How can I prevent it?"

"I am so damned uncomfortable with my hands tied back this way. I cain't sit straight. I'm cramped. Be a good fellow, Juan, and untie my hands."

'S. Texas Medill, if you are uncomfortable now, what will you be when you tread the fiery cactus on your naked feet?"

"But that will be short. No man lives such torture long, does he, Juan?"

"The choya kills quickly, señor."

"Juan, have you thought about the gold lying in the El Paso bank? Gold that can be yours for the ride. It will be long before my death is reported across the river. You have plenty of time to get to El Paso with my check and a letter. I can write it on a sheet of paper out of my notebook. Surely you have a friend or acquaintance in El Paso or Juarez who can identify you at the bank as Juan—whatever your name is."

"Yes, señor, I have. And my name is Juan Mendoz."

"Have you thought about what you could do with three thousand dollars? Not Mexican pesos, but real gringo gold!"

"I have not thought, señor, because I do not like to give in to dreams."

"Juan, listen. You are a fool. I know I am as good as daid. What have I been a ranger all these years for? And it's worth this gold to me to be free of this miserable cramp—and to feel that I have tried to buy some little kindness for the señorita there. She is part Mexican, Juan. She has Mexican blood in her. Don't forget that. . . . Well, you are not betraying Quinela. And you will be rich. You will have my horse and saddle, if you are wise enough to keep Quinela from seeing them. You will buy silver spurs—with the long Spanish rowels. You will have jingling gold in your pocket. You will buy a *vaquero*'s sombrero. And then think of your *chata*—your sweetheart, Juan. . . . Ah, I knew it. You have a *chata*. Think of what you can buy her. A Spanish mantilla, and a golden cross, and silver-buckled shoes for her little feet. Think how she will love you for that! . . . Then, Juan, best of all, you can go far south of the border—buy a hacienda, horses, and cattle, and live there happily with your *chata*. You will only get killed in Quinela's service—for a few dirty pesos. . . . You will raise mescal on your hacienda, and brew your own *canyu*. . . . All for so little, Juan!"

"Señor not only has gold in a bank but gold on his tongue. . . . It is indeed little you ask and little I risk."

Juan rode abreast of Vaughn and felt in his pockets for the checkbook and pencil, which he had neglected to return. Vaughn made of his face a grateful mask. This Mexican had become approachable, as Vaughn had known *canyu* would make him, but he was not yet under its influence to an extent which justified undue risk. Still, Vaughn decided, if the bandit freed his hands and gave him the slightest chance, he would jerk Juan out of that saddle. Vaughn did not lose sight of the fact that his feet would still be tied. He calculated exactly what he would do in case Juan's craftiness no longer possessed him. As the Mexican stopped his horse and reined in Vaughn's, the girl happened to turn round, as she often did, and she saw them. Vaughn caught a flash of big eyes and a white little face as Roseta vanished round a turn in the trail. Vaughn was glad for two things, that she had seen him stop and that she and her guard would be unable to see what was taking place.

All through these anxious moments of suspense Juan appeared to be studying the checkbook. If he could read English, it surely was only a few familiar words. The thought leaped to Vaughn's mind to write a note to the banker quite different from what he had intended. Most assuredly, if the El Paso banker ever saw that note Vaughn would be dead;

and it was quite within the realm of possibility that it might fall into his hands.

"Señor, you may sign me the gold in your El Paso bank," said Juan, at length.

"Fine. You're a sensible man, Juan. But I cain't hold a pencil with my teeth."

The Mexican laughed. He was more amiable. Another hour and another few drinks of *canyu* would make him maudlin, devoid of quick wit or keen sight. A more favorable chance might befall Vaughn, and it might be wiser to wait. Surely on the ride ahead there would come a moment when he could act with lightning and deadly swiftness. But it would take iron will to hold his burning intent within bounds.

Juan kicked the horse Vaughn bestrode and moved him across the trail so that Vaughn's back was turned.

"There, señor," said the Mexican, and his lean dark hand slipped book and pencil into Vaughn's vest pocket.

The cunning beggar, thought Vaughn, in sickening disappointment. He had hoped Juan would free his bonds and then hand over the book. But Vaughn's ranger luck had not caught up with him yet.

He felt the Mexican tugging at the thongs around his wrists. They were tight—a fact to which Vaughn surely could attest. He heard him mutter a curse. Also he heard the short expulsion of breath—almost a pant—that betrayed the influence of the *canyu*.

"Juan, do you blame me for wanting those rawhides off my wrists?" asked Vaughn.

"Señor Medill is strong. It is nothing," returned the Mexican.

Suddenly the painful tension on Vaughn's wrists relaxed. He felt the thongs fall.

"*Muchas gracias*, señor!" he exclaimed. "Ahhh! . . . That feels good."

Vaughn brought his hands round in front to rub each swollen and discolored wrist. But all the time he was gathering his forces, like a tiger about to leap. Had the critical moment arrived?

"Juan, that was a little job to make a man rich—now wasn't it?" went on Vaughn pleasantly. And leisurely, but with every muscle taut, he turned to face the Mexican.

5

THE bandit was out of reach of Vaughn's eager hands. He sat back in the saddle with an expression of interest on his swarthy face. The ranger could not be sure, but he would have gambled that Juan did not suspect his deadly intentions. Star was a mettlesome animal, but Vaughn did not like the Mexican's horse, to which he sat bound, and there were several feet between them. If Vaughn had been free to leap he might have, probably would have, done so.

He swallowed his eagerness and began to rub his wrists again. Presently he removed the pencil and book from his pocket. It was not mere pretense that made it something of an effort to write out a check for Juan Mendoz for the three thousand and odd dollars that represented his balance in the El Paso bank.

"There, Juan. May some gringo treat your *chata* someday as you treat Señorita Uvaldo," said Vaughn, handing the check over to the Mexican.

"*Gracias*, señor," replied Juan, his black eyes upon the bit of colored paper. "Uvaldo's daughter then is your *chata*?"

"Yes. And I'll leave a curse upon you if she is mistreated."

"Ranger, I had my orders from Quinela. You would not have asked more."

"What has Quinela against Uvaldo?" asked Vaughn.

"They were *vaqueros* together years ago. But I don't know the reason for Quinela's hate. It is great and just. . . . Now, señor, the letter to your banker."

Vaughn tore a leaf out of his bankbook. On second thought he decided to write the letter in the bankbook, which would serve in itself to identify him. In case this letter ever was presented at the bank in El Paso he wanted it to mean something. Then it occurred to Vaughn to try out the Mexican. So he wrote a few lines.

"Read that, Juan," he said, handing over the book.

The man scanned the lines, which might as well have been written in Greek.

"Texas Medill does not write as well as he shoots," said Juan.

"Let me have the book. I can do better. I forgot something."

Receiving it back Vaughn tore out the page and wrote another.

Dear Mr Jarvis:

If you ever see these lines you will know that I have been murdered by Quinela. Have the bearer arrested and wire to Captain Allerton, of the Rangers, at Brownsville.

At this moment I am a prisoner of Juan Mendoz, lieutenant of Quinela. Miss Roseta Uvaldo is also a prisoner. She will be held for ransom and revenge. The place is in the hills somewhere east and south of Rock Ford trail.

MEDILL

Vaughn reading aloud to the Mexican improvised a letter which identified him, and cunningly made mention of the gold.

"Juan, isn't that better?" he said, as he handed the book back. "You'll do well not to show this to Quinela or anyone else. Go yourself *at once* to El Paso."

As Vaughn had expected, the Mexican did not scan the letter. Placing the check in the bankbook, he deposited it in an inside pocket of his tattered coat. Then without a word he drove Vaughn's horse forward on the trail, and following close behind soon came up with Roseta and her guard.

The girl looked back. Vaughn contrived, without making it obvious, to show her that his hands were free. A look of radiance crossed her wan face. The exertion and suspense had begun to tell markedly. Her form sagged in the saddle.

Juan appeared bent on making up for lost time, as he drove the horses forward at a trot. But this did not last long. Vaughn, looking at the ground, saw the black shadow of the Mexican as he raised the demijohn to his mouth to drink. What a sinister shadow! It forced Vaughn to think of what now should be his method of procedure. Sooner or later he was going to get his hand on his gun, which stuck out back of Juan's hip and hung down in its holster. That moment, when it came, would see the end of his captor. But Vaughn remembered how the horse he bestrode had bolted at the previous gunshot. He would risk more, shooting from the back of this horse than at the hands of the other Mexican. Vaughn's feet were tied in the stirrups with the rope passing underneath the horse. If he were thrown sideways out of the saddle it would be a perilous and very probably a fatal accident. He decided that at the critical time he would grip the horse with his legs so tightly that he could not be dislodged, and at that moment decide what to do about the other Mexican.

After Juan had a second drink, Vaughn slowly slackened the gait of his horse until Juan's mount came up to his horse's flank. Vaughn was careful to keep to the right of the trail. One glance at the Mexican's eyes sent a gush of hot blood over Vaughn. The effect of the *canyu* had been slow on this tough little man, but at last it was working.

"Juan, I'm powerful thirsty," said Vaughn.

"Señor, we come to water hole bime-by," replied the Mexican thickly.

"But won't you spare me a nip of *canyu*?"

"Our mescal drink is bad for gringos."

"I'll risk it, Juan. Just a nip. You're a good fellow and I like you. I'll tell Quinela how you had to fight your men back there, when they wanted to kill me. I'll tell him Garcia provoked you. . . . Juan, you can see I may do you a turn."

Juan came up alongside Vaughn and halted. Vaughn reined his horse head and head with Juan's. The Mexican was sweating; his under lip hung a little; he sat loosely in his saddle. His eyes had lost their beady light and appeared to have filmed over.

Juan waited till the man ahead had turned another twist in the trail with Roseta. Then he lifted the obviously lightened demijohn from the saddlebag and extended it to Vaughn.

"A drop—señor," he said.

Vaughn pretended to drink. The hot stuff was like vitriol on his lips. He returned the jug, making a great show of the effect of the *canyu*, when as a matter of cold fact he was calculating distances. Almost he yielded to the temptation to lean and sweep a long arm forward. But a ranger could not afford to make mistakes. If Juan's horse had been a little closer! Vaughn expelled deeply his bated breath.

"Ah-h! Great stuff, Juan!" he exclaimed, and relaxed again.

They rode on, and Juan either forgot to drop behind or did not think it needful. The trail was wide enough for two horses. Soon Roseta's bright red scarf burned against the gray-green brush again. She was looking back. So was her Mexican escort. And their horses were walking. Juan did not appear to take note of their slower progress. He long had passed the faculty for making minute observations. Presently he would take another swallow of *canyu*.

Vaughn began to talk, to express more gratitude to Juan, to dwell with flowery language on the effect of good drink—of which *canyu* was the sweetest and most potent in the world—of its power to make fatigue as if it were not, to alleviate pain and grief, to render the dreary desert of mesquite and stone a region of color and beauty and melody—even to resign a doomed ranger to his fate.

"Aye, señor—*canyu* is the blessed Virgin's gift to the peon," said Juan, and emphasized this tribute by having another generous drink.

They rode on. Vaughn asked only for another mile or two of lonely trail, free of interruption.

"How far, Juan?" asked Vaughn. "I cannot ride much farther with my feet tied under this horse."

"Till sunset—señor—which will be your last," replied the Mexican.

The sun was still high above the pipes of organ cactus. Two hours and more above the horizon! Juan could still speak intelligibly. It was in his lax figure and his sweating face, especially in the protruding eyeballs, that he betrayed the effect of the contents of the demijohn. After the physical let-down would come the mental slackening. That had already begun, for Juan was no longer alert.

They rode on, and Vaughn made a motion to Roseta that she must not turn to look back. Perhaps she interpreted it to mean more than it did, for she immediately began to engage her guard in conversation—something Vaughn had observed she had not done before. Soon the Mexican dropped back until his horse was walking beside Roseta's. He was a peon, and a heavy drink of *canyu* had addled the craft in his wits. Vaughn saw him bend down and loosen the rope that bound Roseta's left foot to the stirrup. Juan did not see this significant action. His gaze was fixed to the trail. He was singing:

"*Ay, mia querida chata.*"

Roseta's guard took a long look back. Evidently Juan's posture struck him apprehensively, yet did not wholly overcome the interest that Roseta had suddenly taken in him. When he gave her a playful pat she returned it. He caught her hand. Roseta did not pull very hard to release it, and she gave him another saucy little slap. He was reaching for her when they passed out of Vaughn's sight round a turn in the green-bordered trail.

Vaughn gradually and almost imperceptibly guided his horse closer to Juan. At that moment a dog could be heard barking in the distance. It did not make any difference to Vaughn, except to accentuate what had always been true—he had no time to lose.

"Juan, the curse of *canyu* is that once you taste it you must have more—or die," said Vaughn.

"It is—so—señor," replied the Mexican.

"You have plenty left. Will you let me have one more little drink. . . . My last drink of *canyu*, Juan! . . . I didn't tell you, but it has been my ruin. My father was a rich rancher. He disowned me because of my evil habits. That's how I became a ranger."

"Take it, señor. Your last drink," said Juan.

Vaughn braced every nerve and fiber of his being. He leaned a little. His left hand went out—leisurely. But his eyes flashed like cold steel over the unsuspecting Mexican.

Then, with the speed of a striking snake, his hand snatched the bone-handled gun from its sheath. Vaughn pulled the trigger. The hammer fell upon an empty chamber.

Juan turned. The gun crashed. "*Dios!*" he screamed in a strangled death cry.

The leaps of the horses were not quicker than Vaughn. He lunged to catch the Mexican—to keep him upright in the saddle. "Hold, Star!" he called sternly. "Hold!"

Star came down. But the other horse plunged and dragged him up the trail. Vaughn had his gun hand fast on the cantle and his other holding Juan upright. But for this grasp the frantic horse would have unseated him.

It was the ranger's job to manage both horses and look out for the other Mexican. He appeared on the trail riding fast, his carbine held high.

Vaughn let go of Juan and got the gun in his right hand. With the other then he grasped the Mexican's coat and held him straight on the saddle. He drooped himself over his pommel, to make it appear he had been the one shot. Meanwhile, he increased his iron leg grip on the horse he straddled. Star had halted and was being dragged.

The other Mexican came at a gallop, yelling. When he got within twenty paces. Vaughn straightened up and shot him through the heart. He threw the carbine from him and pitching out of his saddle, went thudding to the ground. His horse bumped hard into the one Vaughn rode, and that was fortunate, for it checked the animal's first mad leap. In the melee that followed Juan fell off Star to be trampled under frantic hoofs. Vaughn hauled with all his might on the bridle. But he could not hold the horse and he feared that he would break the bridle. Bursting through the brush the horse ran wildly. What with his erratic flight and the low branches of mesquite, Vaughn had a hard job sticking on his back. Presently he got the horse under control and back onto the trail.

Some few rods down he saw Roseta, safe in her saddle, her head bowed with her hands covering her face. At sight of her

Vaughn snapped out of the cold horror that had enveloped him.

"Roseta, it's all right. We're safe," he called eagerly as he reached her side.

"Oh, Vaughn!" she cried, lifting her convulsed and blanched face. "I knew you'd—kill them. . . . But, my God—how awful!"

"Brace up," he said sharply.

Then he got out his clasp knife and in a few slashes freed his feet from the stirrups. He leaped off the horse. His feet felt numb, as they had felt once when frozen.

Then he cut the ropes which bound Roseta's right foot to her stirrup. She swayed out of the saddle into his arms. Her eyes closed.

"It's no time to faint," he said sternly, carrying her off the trail, to set her on her feet.

"I—I won't," she whispered, her eyes opening, strained and dilated. "But hold me—just a moment."

Vaughn folded her in his arms, and the moment she asked was so sweet and precious that it almost overcame the will of a ranger in a desperate plight.

"Roseta—we're free, but not yet safe," he replied. "We're close to a hacienda—perhaps where Quinela is waiting. . . . Come now. We must get out of here."

Half carrying her, Vaughn hurried through the brush along the trail. The moment she could stand alone he whispered, "Wait here." And he ran onto the trail. He still held his gun. Star stood waiting, his head up. Both other horses had disappeared. Vaughn looked up and down the trail. Star whinnied. Vaughn hurried to bend over Juan. The Mexican lay on his face. Vaughn unbuckled the gun belt Juan had appropriated from him, and put it on. Next he secured his bankbook. Then he sheathed his gun. He grasped the bridle of Star and led him off the trail into the mesquite, back to where Roseta stood. She seemed all right now, only pale. But Vaughn avoided her eyes. The thing to do was to get away and not let sentiment deter him one instant. He mounted Star.

"Come, Roseta," he said. "Up behind me."

He swung her up and settled her in the saddle.

"There. Put your arms around me. Hold tight, for we're going to ride."

When she had complied, he grasped her left arm. At the same moment he heard voices up the trail and the rapid clipclop of hoofs. Roseta heard them, too. Vaughn felt her tremble.

"Don't fear, Roseta. Just you hang on. Here's where Star shines," whispered Vaughn, and guiding the nervous horse into the trail, he let him have a loose rein. Star did not need the shrill cries of the peons to spur him into action.

6

AS the fleeing ranger sighted the peons, a babel of shrill voices arose. But no shots! In half a dozen jumps Star was going swift as the wind and in a moment a bend of the trail hid him from any possible marksman. Vaughn's concern for the girl behind him gradually eased.

At the end of a long straight stretch he looked back again. If *vaqueros* were riding in pursuit the situation would be serious. Not even Star could run away from a well-mounted cowboy of the Mexican haciendas. To his intense relief there was not one in sight. Nevertheless, he did not check Star.

"False alarm, Roseta," he said, craning his neck so he could see her face, pressed cheek against his shoulder. He was most marvelously aware of her close presence, but the realization did not impede him or Star in the least. She could ride. She had no stirrups, yet she kept her seat in the saddle.

"Let 'em come," she said, smiling up at him. Her face was pale, but it was not fear that he read in her eyes. It was fight.

Vaughn laughed in sheer surprise. He had not expected that, and it gave him such a thrill as he had never felt in his life before. He let go of Roseta's arm and took her hand where it clung to his coat. And he squeezed it with far more than reassurance. The answering pressure was unmistakable. A singular elation mounted in Vaughn's heart.

It did not, however, quite render him heedless. As Star turned a corner in the trail, Vaughn's keen glance saw that it was completely blocked by the same motley crew of big-sombreroed Mexicans and horses from which he had been separated not so long before that day.

"Hold tight!" he cried warningly to Roseta, as he swerved Star to the left. He drew his gun and fired two quick shots. He did not need to see that they took effect, for a wild cry rose, followed by angry yells.

Star beat the answering rifle shots into the brush. Vaughn heard the sing and twang of the bullets. Crashings through the mesquites behind, added to the gunshots and lent wings to Star. This was a familiar situation to the great horse. Then for Vaughn it became a strenuous job to ride him, and a doubly fearful one, owing to Roseta. She clung like a broom to the speeding horse. Vaughn, after sheathing his gun, had to let go of her, for he needed one hand for the bridle and the other to ward off the whipping brush. Star made no allowance for that precious part of his burden at Vaughn's back, and he crashed through every opening between mesquites that presented itself. Vaughn dodged and ducked, but he never bent low enough for a branch to strike Roseta.

At every open spot in the mesquite, or long aisle between the cacti, Vaughn looked back to see if any of his pursuers were in sight. There was none, but he heard a horse pounding not far behind and to the right. And again he heard another on the other side. Holding the reins in his teeth Vaughn reloaded the gun. To be ready for snap shots he took advantage of every opportunity to peer on each side and behind him. But Star appeared gradually to be outdistancing his pursuers. The desert grew more open with a level gravel floor. Here Vaughn urged Star to his limit.

It became a dead run then, with the horse choosing the way. Vaughn risked less now from the stinging mesquite branches. The green wall flashed by on each side. He did not look back. While Star was at his best Vaughn wanted to get far enough ahead to slow down and save the horse.

In an hour it would be dusk—too late for even a *vaquero* to track him until daylight had come again.

Roseta stuck like a leech, and the ranger had to add admiration to his other feelings toward her. Vaughn put his hand back to grasp and steady her. It did not take much time for the powerful strides of the horse to cover the miles. Finally Vaughn pulled him into a gallop and then into a lope.

"*Chata*, are you all right?" he asked, afraid to look back, after using that romantic epithet.

"Yes. But I can't—hold on—much longer," she panted. "If they catch us—shoot me first."

"Roseta, they will never catch us now," he promised.

"But—if they do—promise me," she entreated.

"I promise they'll never take us alive. But, child, keep up your nerve. It'll be sunset soon—and then dark. We'll get away sure."

"Vaughn, I'm not frightened. Only—I hate those people—and I mustn't fall—into their hands again. It means worse—than death."

"Hush! Save your breath," he replied, and wrapping a long arm backward round her slender waist he held her tight. "Come, Star, cut loose," he called, and dug the horse's flank with a heel.

Again they raced across the desert, this time in less of a straight line, though still to the north. The dry wind made tears dim Vaughn's eyes. He kept to open lanes and patches to avoid being struck by branches. And he spared Star only when he heard the animal's heaves of distress. Star was not easy to break from that headlong flight, but at length Vaughn got him down to a nervous walk. Then he let Roseta slip back into the saddle. His arm was numb from the long strain.

"We're—far ahead," he panted. "They'll trail—us till dark." He peered back across the yellow and green desert, slowly darkening in the sunset. "But we're safe—thank Gawd."

"Oh, what a glorious ride!" cried Roseta between breaths. "I felt that—even with death so close. . . . Vaughn, I'm such a little—fool. I longed—for excitement. Oh, I'm well punished. . . . But for you—"

"Save your breath, honey. We may need to run again. After dark you can rest and talk."

She said no more. Vaughn walked Star until the horse had regained his wind, and then urged him into a lope, which was his easiest gait.

The sun sank red in the west; twilight stole under the mesquite and the *pale verde*; dusk came upon its heels; the heat tempered and there was a slight breeze. When the stars came out Vaughn took his direction from them, and pushed on for several miles. A crescent moon, silver and slender, came up over the desert.

Young as it was, it helped brighten the open patches and the swales. Vaughn halted the tireless horse in a spot where a patch of grass caught the moonlight.

"We'll rest a bit," he said, sliding off, but still holding on to the girl. "Come."

She just fell off into his arms, and when he let her feet down she leaned against him. "Oh, Vaughn!" He held her a moment, sorely tempted. But he might take her weakness for something else.

"Can you stand? . . . You'd better walk around a little," he said.

"My legs are dead."

"I want to go back a few steps and listen. The night is still. I could hear horses at a long distance."

"Don't go far," she entreated him.

Vaughn went back where he could not hear the heaving, blowing horse, and turned his keen ear to the breeze. It blew gently from the south. Only a very faint rustle of leaves disturbed the desert silence. He held his breath and listened intensely. There was no sound! Even if he were trailed by a hound of a *vaquero* he was still far ahead. All he required now was a little rest for Star. He could carry the girl. On the way back across the open he tried to find the tracks Star had left. A man could trail them, but only on foot. Vaughn's last stern doubt took wing and vanished. He returned to Roseta.

"No sound. It is as I expected. Night has saved us," he said.

"Night and *canyu*. Oh, I watched you, ranger man."

"You helped, Roseta. That Mexican who led your horse was suspicious. But when you looked at him—he forgot. Small wonder . . . Have you stretched your legs?"

"I tried. I walked some, then flopped here. . . . Oh, I want to rest and sleep."

"I don't know about your sleeping, but you can rest riding" he replied, and removing his coat folded it around the pommel of his saddle, making a flat seat there. Star was munching the grass. He was already fit for another race. Vaughn saw to the cinches, and then mounted again, and folded the sleeves of his coat up over the pommel. "Give me your hand. . . . Put your foot in the stirrup. Now." He caught her and lifted her in front of him, and settling her comfortably upon the improvised seat, he put his left arm around her. Many a wounded comrade had he packed this way. "How is—that?" he asked unsteadily.

"It's very nice," she replied, her dark eyes looking inscrutable in the moonlight. And she relaxed against his arm and shoulder.

Vaughn headed Star north at a brisk walk. He could not be more than six hours from the river in a straight line. Canyons and rough going might deter him. But even so he could make the Rio Grande before dawn. Then and then only did he surrender to the astonishing presence of Roseta Uvaldo, to the indubitable fact that he had saved her, and then to thoughts wild and whirling of the future. He gazed down upon the oval face so balanced in the moonlight, into the staring black eyes whose look might mean anything.

"Vaughn, was it that guard or you—who called me *chata*?" she asked, dreamily.

"It was I—who dared," he replied huskily.

"Dared! Then you were not just carried away—for the moment?"

"No, Roseta. . . . I confess I was as—as bold as that poor devil."

"Vaughn, do you know what *chata* means?" she asked gravely.

"It is the name a *vaquero* has for his sweetheart."

"You mean it, señor?" she asked, imperiously.

"Lord help me, Roseta, I did, and I do. . . . I've loved you long."

"But you never told me!" she exclaimed, with wonder and reproach. "Why?"

"What hope had I? A poor ranger. Texas Medill! . . . Didn't you call me 'killer of Mexicans'?"

"I reckon I did. And it is because you *are* that I'm alive to thank God for it. . . . Vaughn, I always liked you, respected you as one of Texas' great rangers—feared you, too. I never knew my real feelings. . . . But I—I love you *now*."

The night wore on, with the moon going down, weird and coldly bright against the dark vaulted sky. Roseta lay asleep in Vaughn's arm. For hours he had gazed, after peering ahead and behind, always vigilant, always the ranger, on that wan face against his shoulder. The silent moonlit night, the lonely ride, the ghostly forms of cactus were real, though Vaughn never trusted his senses there. This was only the dream of the ranger. Yet the sweet fire of Roseta's kisses still lingered on his lips.

At length he changed her again from his right arm back to his left. And she awakened, but not fully. In all the years of his ranger service, so much of which he lived over on this ride, there had been nothing to compare with this. For his reward had been exalting. His longings had received magnificent fulfillment. His duty had not been to selfish and unappreciative officials, but to a great state—to its people—to the native soil upon which he had been born. And that hard duty, so poorly recompensed, so bloody and harrowing at times, had by some enchantment bestowed upon one ranger at least a beautiful girl of the border, frankly and honestly Texan, yet part Spanish, retaining something of the fire and spirit of the Dons who had once called Texas their domain.

In the gray of dawn, Vaughn lifted Roseta down from the weary horse upon the south bank of the Rio Grande.

"We are here, Roseta," he said gladly. "It will soon be light enough to ford the river. Star came out just below Brownsville. There's a horse, Roseta! He shall never be risked again. . . . In an hour you will be home."

"Home? Oh, how good! . . . But what shall I say, Vaughn?" she replied, evidently awakening to the facts of her predicament.

"Dear, who was the feller you ran—rode off with yesterday mawnin'?" he asked.

"Didn't I tell you?" And she laughed. "It happened to be Elmer Wade—*that* morning. . . . Oh, he was the unlucky one. The bandits beat him with quirts, dragged him off his horse. Then they led me away and I didn't see him again."

Vaughn had no desire to acquaint her then with the tragic fate that had overtaken that young man.

'You were not—elopin'?"

"*Vaughn*! It was only fun."

"Uvaldo thinks you eloped. He was wild. He raved."

"The devil he did!" exclaimed Roseta rebelliously. "Vaughn, what did *you* think?"

"Dearest, I—I was only concerned with trackin' you," he replied, and even in the gray gloom of the dawn those big dark eyes made his heart beat faster.

"Vaughn, I have peon blood in me," she said, and she might have been a princess for the pride with which she confessed it. "My father always feared I'd run true to the Indian. Are you afraid of your *chata*?"

"No, darlin'."

"Then I shall punish Uvaldo. . . . I shall elope."

"Roseta!" cried Vaughn.

"Listen." She put her arms around his neck, and that was a long reach for her. "Will you give up the ranger service? I—I couldn't bear it, Vaughn. You have earned release from the service all Texans are so proud of."

"Yes, Roseta. I'll resign," he replied with boyish, eager shyness. "I've some money—enough to buy a ranch."

"Far from the border?" she entreated.

"Yes, far. I know just the valley—way north, under the *Llano Estacado*. . . . But, Roseta, I shall have to pack a gun—till I'm forgotten."

"Very well, I'll not be afraid—way north," she replied. Then her sweet gravity changed to mischief. "We will punish Father. Vaughn, we'll elope right now! We'll cross the river—get married—and drive out home to breakfast. . . . How Dad will rave! But he would have me elope, though he'd never guess I'd choose a ranger."

Vaughn swung her up on Star, and leaned close to peer up at her, to find one more assurance of the joy that had befallen him. He was not conscious of asking, when she bent her head to bestow kisses upon his lips.

MAX BRAND
Wine on the Desert

Frederick Schiller Faust (1892–1944) was born in Seattle, Washington. It was his lifelong ambition to be a poet, but it was as a Western pulp fiction writer under the pseudonym of Max Brand that he became famous. He wrote most often for *Western Story Magazine*, sometimes contributing as many as a million words per year. Brand's Western fiction displays little interest in history or geography (he once said that the West was 'disgusting'), but is often extremely readable nonetheless. His personal dictum for the writing of Western stories was 'action, action, action'. Many of Brand's three hundred novels and countless short stories were turned into films by Hollywood, including his best-known novel, *Destry Rides Again* (1930). Brand himself worked in Hollywood as a scriptwriter for MGM, Columbia and Warners during the late 1930s, before going to Italy as a war correspondent (despite a serious heart condition), where he died from shrapnel wounds.

'Wine on the Desert' is from 1936. It is easy to dismiss Brand as a writer, but the atmosphere and plot of this story are unforgettable.

THERE WAS NO HURRY, EXCEPT for the thirst, like clotted salt, in the back of his throat, and Durante rode on slowly, rather enjoying the last moments of dryness before he reached the cold water in Tony's house. There was really no hurry at all. He had almost twenty-four hours' head start, for they would not find his dead man until this morning. After that, there would be perhaps several hours of delay before the sheriff gathered a sufficient posse and started on his trail. Or perhaps the sheriff would be fool enough to come alone.

Durante had been able to see the wheel and fan of Tony's windmill for more than an hour, but he could not make out the ten acres of the vineyard until he had topped the last rise, for the vines had been planted in a hollow. The lowness of the ground, Tony used to say, accounted for the water that gathered in the well during the wet season. The rains sank through the desert sand, through the gravels beneath, and gathered in a bowl of clay hardpan far below.

In the middle of the rainless season the well ran dry but, long before that, Tony had every drop of the water pumped up into a score of tanks made of cheap corrugated iron. Slender pipe lines carried the water from the tanks to the vines and from time to time let them sip enough life to keep them until the winter darkened overhead suddenly, one November day, and the rain came down, and all the earth made a great hushing sound as it drank. Durante had heard that whisper of drinking when he was here before; but he never had seen the place in the middle of the long drought.

The windmill looked like a sacred emblem to Durante, and the twenty stodgy, tar-painted tanks blessed his eyes; but a heavy sweat broke out at once from his body. For the air of the hollow, unstirred by wind, was hot and still as a bowl of soup. A reddish soup. The vines were powdered with thin red dust, also. They were wretched, dying things to look at, for the grapes had been gathered, the new wine had been made, and now the leaves hung in ragged tatters.

Durante rode up to the squat adobe house and right through the entrance into the patio. A flowering vine clothed three sides of the little court. Durante did not know the name of the plant, but it had large white blossoms with golden hearts that poured sweetness on the air. Durante hated the sweetness. It made him more thirsty.

He threw the reins off his mule and strode into the house. The water cooler stood in the hall outside the kitchen. There were two jars made of a porous stone, very ancient things, and the liquid which distilled through the pores kept the contents cool. The jar on the left held water; that on the right contained wine. There was a big tin dipper hanging on a peg beside each jar. Durante tossed off the cover of the vase on the left and plunged it in until the delicious coolness closed well above his wrist.

"Hey, Tony," he called. Out of his dusty throat the cry was "throw some water into that mule of mine, would you, Tony?"

A voice pealed from the distance.

Durante, pouring down the second dipper of water, smelled the alkali dust which had shaken off his own clothes. It seemed to him that heat was radiating like light from his clothes, from his body, and the cool dimness of the house was soaking it up. He heard the wooden leg of Tony bumping on the ground, and Durante grinned; then Tony came in with that hitch and sideswing with which he accommodated the stiffness of his artificial leg. His brown face shone with sweat as though a special ray of light were focused on it.

"Ah, Dick!" he said. "Good old Dick! . . . How long since you came last! . . . Wouldn't Julia be glad! Wouldn't she be glad!"

"Ain't she here?" asked Durante, jerking his head suddenly away from the dripping dipper.

"She's away at Nogalez," said Tony. "It gets so hot. I said, 'You go up to Nogalez, Julia, where the wind don't forget to blow.' She cried, but I made her go."

"Did she cry?" asked Durante.

"Julia . . . that's a good girl," said Tony.

"Yeah. You bet she's good," said Durante. He put the dipper quickly to his lips but did not swallow for a moment; he was grinning too widely. Afterward he said: "You wouldn't throw some water into that mule of mine, would you, Tony?"

Tony went out with his wooden leg clumping loud on the wooden floor, softly in the patio dust. Durante found the hammock in the corner of the patio. He lay down in it and watched the color of sunset flush the mists of desert dust that rose to the zenith. The water was soaking through his body; hunger began, and then the rattling of pans in the kitchen and the cheerful cry of Tony's voice:

"What you want, Dick? I got some pork. You don't want pork. I'll make you some good Mexican beans. Hot. Ah ha, I know that old Dick. I have plenty of good wine for you, Dick. Tortillas. Even Julia can't make tortillas like me . . . And what about a nice young rabbit?"

"All blowed full of buckshot?" growled Durante.

"No, no. I kill them with the rifle."

"You kill rabbits with a rifle?" repeated Durante, with a quick interest.

"It's the only gun I have," said Tony. "If I catch them in the sights, they are dead . . . A wooden leg cannot walk very far. . . . I must kill them quick. You see? They come close to the house about sunrise and flop their ears. I shoot through the head."

"Yeah? Yeah?" muttered Durante. "Through the head?" He relaxed, scowling. He passed his hand over his face, over his head.

Then Tony began to bring the food out into the patio and lay it on a small wooden table; a lantern hanging against the wall of the house included the table in a dim half circle of light. They sat there and ate. Tony had scrubbed himself for the meal. His hair was soaked in water and sleeked back over his round skull. A man in the desert might be willing to pay five dollars for as much water as went to the soaking of that hair.

Everything was good. Tony knew how to cook, and he knew how to keep the glasses filled with his wine.

"This is old wine. This is my father's wine. Eleven years old," said Tony. "You look at the light through it. You see that brown in the red? That's the soft that time puts in good wine, my father always said."

"What killed your father?" asked Durante.

Tony lifted his hand as though he were listening or as though he were pointing out a thought.

"The desert killed him. I found his mule. It was dead, too. There was a leak in the canteen. My father was only five miles away when the buzzards showed him to me."

"Five miles? Just an hour . . . Good Lord!" said Durante. He stared with big eyes. "Just dropped down and died?" he asked.

"No," said Tony. "When you die of thirst, you always die just one way. . . . First you tear off your shirt, then your undershirt. That's to be cooler. . . . And the sun comes and cooks your bare skin. . . . And then you think . . . there is water everywhere, if you dig down far enough. You begin to dig. The dust comes up your nose. You start screaming. You break your nails in the sand. You wear the flesh off the tips of your fingers, to the bone." He took a quick swallow of wine.

"Without you seen a man die of thirst, how d'you know they start to screaming?" asked Durante.

"They got a screaming look when you find them," said Tony. "Take some more wine. The desert never can get to you here. My father showed me the way to keep the desert away from the hollow. We live pretty good here? No?"

"Yeah," said Durante, loosening his shirt collar. "Yeah, pretty good."

Afterward he slept well in the hammock until the report of a rifle waked him and he saw the color of dawn in the sky. It was such a great, round bowl that for a moment he felt as though he were above, looking down into it.

He got up and saw Tony coming in holding a rabbit by the ears, the rifle in his other hand.

"You see?" said Tony. "Breakfast came and called on us!" He laughed.

Durante examined the rabbit with care. It was nice and fat and it had been shot through the head. Through the middle of the head. Such a shudder went down the back of Durante that he washed gingerly before breakfast; he felt that his blood was cooled for the entire day.

It was a good breakfast, too, with flapjacks and stewed rabbit with green peppers, and a quart of strong coffee. Before they had finished, the sun struck through the east window and started them sweating.

"Gimme a look at that rifle of yours, Tony, will you?" Durante asked.

"You take a look at my rifle, but don't you steal the luck that's in it," laughed Tony. He brought the fifteen-shot Winchester.

"Loaded right to the brim?" asked Durante.

"I always load it full the minute I get back home," said Tony.

"Tony, come outside with me," commanded Durante.

They went out from the house. The sun turned the sweat of Durante to hot water and then dried his skin so that his clothes felt transparent.

"Tony, I gotta be damn mean," said Durante. "Stand right there where I can see you. Don't try to get close. . . . Now listen. . . . The sheriff's gunna be along this trail some time to-day, looking for me. He'll load up himself and all his gang with water out of your tanks. Then he'll follow my sign across the desert. Get me? He'll follow if he finds water on the place. But he's not gunna find water."

"What you done, poor Dick?" said Tony. "Now look. . . . I could hide you in the old wine cellar where nobody . . ."

"The sheriff's not gunna find any water," said Durante. "It's gunna be like this."

He put the rifle to his shoulder, aimed, fired. The shot struck the base of the nearest tank, ranging down through the bottom. A semicircle of darkness began to stain the soil near the edge of the iron wall.

Tony fell on his knees. "No, no, Dick! Good Dick!" he said. "Look! All the vineyard. It will die. It will turn into old, dead wood, Dick . . ."

"Shut your face," said Durante. "Now I've started, I kinda like the job."

Tony fell on his face and put his hands over his ears. Durante drilled a bullet hole through the tanks, one after another. Afterward, he leaned on the rifle.

"Take my canteen and go in and fill it with water out of the cooling jar," he said. "Snap into it, Tony!"

Tony got up. He raised the canteen, and looked around him, not at the tanks from which the water was pouring so that the noise of the earth drinking was audible, but at the rows of his vineyard. Then he went into the house.

Durante mounted his mule. He shifted the rifle to his left hand and drew out the heavy Colt from its holster. Tony came dragging back to him, his head down. Durante watched Tony with a careful revolver but he gave up the canteen without lifting his eyes.

"The trouble with you, Tony," said Durante, "is you're yellow. I'd of fought a tribe of wildcats with my bare hands, before I'd let 'em do what I'm doin' to you. But you sit back and take it."

Tony did not seem to hear. He stretched out his hands to the vines.

"Ah, my God," said Tony. "Will you let them all die?"

Durante shrugged his shoulders. He shook the canteen to make sure that it was full. It was so brimming that there was hardly room for the liquid to make a sloshing sound. Then he turned the mule and kicked it into a dog-trot.

Half a mile from the house of Tony, he threw the empty rifle to the ground. There was no sense packing that useless weight, and Tony with his peg leg would hardly come this far.

Durante looked back, a mile or so later, and saw the little image of Tony picking up the rifle from the dust, then staring earnestly after his guest. Durante remembered the neat little hole clipped through the head of the rabbit. Wherever he went, his trail never could return again to the vineyard in the desert. But then, commencing to picture to himself the arrival of the sweating sheriff and his posse at the house of Tony, Durante laughed heartily.

The sheriff's posse could get plenty of wine, of course, but without water a man could not hope to make the desert voyage, even with a mule or a horse to help him on the way. Durante patted the full, rounding side of his canteen. He might even now begin with the first sip but it was a luxury to postpone pleasure until desire became greater.

He raised his eyes along the trail. Close by, it was merely dotted with occasional bones, but distance joined the dots into an unbroken chalk line which wavered with a strange leisure across the Apache Desert, pointing toward the cool blue promise of the mountains. The next morning he would be among them.

A coyote whisked out of a gully and ran like a gray puff of dust on the wind. His tongue hung out like a little red rag from the side of his mouth; and suddenly Durante was dry to the marrow. He uncorked and lifted his canteen. It had a slightly sour smell; perhaps the sacking which covered it had grown a trifle old. And then he poured a great mouthful of lukewarm liquid. He had swallowed it before his senses could give him warning.

It was wine!

He looked first of all toward the mountains. They were as calmly blue, as distant as when he had started that morning. Twenty-four hours not on water, but on wine!

"I deserve it," said Durante. "I trusted him to fill the canteen. . . . I deserve it. Curse him!" With a mighty resolution, he quieted the panic in his soul. He would not touch the stuff until noon. Then he would take one discreet sip. He would win through.

Hours went by. He looked at his watch and found it was only ten o'clock. And he had thought that it was on the verge of noon! He uncorked the wine and drank freely and, corking the canteen, felt almost as though he needed a drink of water more than before. He sloshed the contents of the canteen. Already it was horribly light.

Once, he turned the mule and considered the return trip; but he could remember the head of the rabbit too clearly, drilled right through the center. The vineyard, the rows of old twisted, gnarled little trunks with the bark peeling off . . . every vine was to Tony like a human life. And Durante had condemned them all to death!

He faced the blue of the mountains again. His heart raced in his breast with terror. Perhaps it was fear and not the suction of that dry and deadly air that made his tongue cleave to the roof of his mouth.

The day grew old. Nausea began to work in his stomach, nausea alternating with sharp pains. When he looked down, he saw that there was blood on his boots. He had been spurring the mule until the red ran down from its flanks. It went with a curious stagger, like a rocking horse with a broken rocker; and Durante grew aware that he had been keeping the mule at a gallop for a long time. He pulled it to a halt. It stood with wide-braced legs. Its head was down. When he leaned from the saddle, he saw that its mouth was open.

"It's gunna die," said Durante. "It's gunna die . . . what a fool I been. . . ."

The mule did not die until after sunset. Durante left everything except his revolver. He packed the weight of that for an hour and discarded it in turn. His knees were growing weak. When he looked up at the stars they shone white and clear for a moment only, and then whirled into little racing circles and scrawls of red.

He lay down. He kept his eyes closed and waited for the shaking to go out of his body, but it would not stop. And every breath of darkness was like an inhalation of black dust.

He got up and went on, staggering. Sometimes he found himself running.

Before you die of thirst, you go mad. He kept remembering that. His tongue had swollen big. Before it choked him, if he lanced it with his knife the blood would help him; he would be able to swallow. Then he remembered that the taste of blood is salty.

Once, in his boyhood, he had ridden through a pass with his father and they had looked down on the sapphire of a mountain lake, a hundred thousand million tons of water as cold as snow. . . .

When he looked up, now, there were no stars; and this frightened him terribly. He never had seen a desert night so dark. His eyes were failing, he was being blinded. When the morning came, he would not be able to see the mountains, and he would walk around and around in a circle until he dropped and died.

No stars, no wind; the air as still as the waters of a stale pool, and he in the dregs at the bottom. . . .

He seized his shirt at the throat and tore it away so that it hung in two rags from his hips.

He could see the earth only well enough to stumble on the rocks. But there were no stars in the heavens. He was blind: he had no more hope than a rat in a well. Ah, but Italian devils know how to put poison in wine that will steal all the senses or any one of them: and Tony had chosen to blind Durante.

He heard a sound like water. It was the swishing of the soft deep sand through which he was treading; sand so soft that a man could dig it away with his bare hands. . . .

Afterward, after many hours, out of the blind face of that sky the rain began to fall. It made first a whispering and then a delicate murmur like voices conversing, but after that, just at the dawn, it roared like the hoofs of ten thousand charging horses. Even through that thundering confusion the big birds with naked heads and red, raw necks found their way down to one place in the Apache Desert.

OWEN WISTER
At the Sign of the Last Chance

Owen Wister (1860–1938) was born in Philadelphia, Pennsylvania, and majored in music at Harvard. After a nervous breakdown in 1885 he went to the West to improve his health. He returned to Harvard to take a law degree, but frequently revisited the West, particularly Wyoming, over the next decade. Following a conversation with Theodore Roosevelt about the literary possibilities of the frontier, Wister wrote his first Western story, 'Hank's Woman', which was published in *Harper's* in 1892. The story and its successor, 'How Lin McClean Went East', were so successful that *Harper's* financed Wister on a grand tour of the frontier, accompanied by the artist Frederic Remington. Wister, like many Easterners, considered the West to be a place of moral regeneration. Accordingly, Wister modified the West to suit this view, portraying the cowboy as a latterday knight-errant. In addition to his classic 1902 novel, *The Virginian*, Wister's other Western fiction includes the novel *Lin McClean* (1897), and four volumes of short stories: *Red Men and White* (1896), *The Jimmyjohn and Other Stories* (1900), *Members of the Family* (1911), and *When West Was West* (1928).

'The Sign of the Last Chance' is from *When West Was West*. As well as being one of the last stories that Wister wrote, it is amongst the most evocative stories ever written about the American West.

MORE FAMILIAR FACES THAN I had hoped to see were there when I came in after leaving my horse at the stable. Would I eat anything? Henry asked. Not until breakfast, I said. I had supped at Lost Soldier. Would I join the game? Not tonight; but would they mind if I sat and watched them till I felt sleepy? It was too early to go to bed. And sitting here again seemed very natural.

"Does it, now?" said Stirling. "You look kind of natural yourself."

"Glad I do. It must be five years since last time."

"Six," said James Work. "But I would have known you anywhere."

"What sort of a meal did he set for you?" Marshal inquired.

"At Lost Soldier? Fried beef, biscuits, coffee and excellent onions."

"Old onions of course?" said Henry. "Cooked?"

"No. Fresh from his garden. Young ones."

"So he's got a garden still!" mused Henry.

"Who's running Lost Soldier these days?" inquired Stirling.

"That oldest half-breed son of Toothpick Kid," said Marshal. "Any folks to supper with you?"

"Why, yes. Six or seven. Bound for the new oil-fields on Red Spider."

"Travel is brisk down in that valley," said Work.

"I didn't know the stage had stopped running through here," said I.

"Didn't you? Why, that's a matter of years now. There's no oil up this way. In fact, there's nothing up this way any more."

They had made room for me, they had included me in their company. Only two others were not in the game. One sat in the back of the room, leaning over something that he was reading, never looking up from it. He was the only one I had not seen before, but he was at home quite evidently. Except when he turned a page, which might have been once every five minutes, he hardly made a movement. He was a rough fellow, wearing the beard of another day; and if reading was a habit with him it was a slow process, and his lips moved in silent pronunciation of each syllable as it came.

Jed Goodland sat off by the kitchen door with his fiddle. Now and then he lightly picked or bowed some fragment of tune, like a man whispering memories to himself.

The others, save one or two that were clean-shaven, also wore the mustaches or the beards of a day that was done.

I had begun to see those beards long before they were gray; when no wire fence mutilated the freedom of the range; when fourteen mess-wagons would be at the spring round-up; when cattle wandered and pastured, dotting the endless wilderness; when roping them brought the college graduate and the boy who had never learned to read into a lusty equality of youth and skill; when songs rose by the camp-fire; and the dim form of the night herder leaned on his saddle horn as under the stars he circled slowly around the recumbent thousands; when two hundred miles stretched between all this and the whistle of the nearest locomotive.

And all this was over. It had begun to end a long while ago. It had ebbed away slowly from these now playing their nightly game as they had once played it at flood-tide. The turn of the tide had come even when the beards were still brown, or red, or golden.

The decline of their day began possibly with the first wire fence; the great ranch life was hastened to its death by the winter snows of 1886; received its mortal stroke in the rustler war of 1892; breathed its last—no, it was still breathing, it had not wholly given up the ghost. Cattlemen and sheepmen, the newcomers, were at deeds of violence with each other. And here in this place, at the poker table, the ghost still clung to the world of the sagebrush, where it had lived its headlong joys.

I watched the graybeards going on with this game that had outlived many a player, had often paused during bloodshed, and resumed as often, no matter who had been carried out. They played without zest, winning or losing little, with now and then a friendly word to me.

They had learned to tolerate me when I had come among them first; not because I ever grew skilled in what they did, either in the saddle or with a gun, but because they knew that I liked them and the life they led, and always had come back to lead it with them, in my tenderfoot way.

Did they often think of their vanished prosperity? Or did they try to forget that, and had they succeeded? Something in them seemed quenched—but they were all in their fifties now; they had been in their twenties when I knew them first.

My first sight of James Work was on a night at the Cheyenne Club. He sat at the head of a dinner-table with some twenty men as his guests. They drank champagne and they sang. Work's cattle in those days earned him twenty per cent. Had he not overstayed his market in the fatal years, he could be giving dinners still. As with him, so with the others in that mild poker game.

Fortune, after romping with them, had romped off somewhere else. What filled their hours, what filled their minds, in these days of emptiness?

So I sat and watched them. How many times had I arrived for the night and done so? They drank very little. They spoke very little. They had been so used to each other for so long! I had seen that pile of newspapers and magazines where the man was reading grow and spread and litter the back of the room since I was twenty.

It was a joke that Henry never could bring himself to throw anything away.

"I suppose," I said to him now, as I pointed to the dusty accumulation, "that would be up to the ceiling if you didn't light your stove every winter with some of it."

Henry nodded and chuckled as he picked up his hand.

The man reading at the back of the room lifted his magazine. "This is October, 1885," he said, holding the shabby cover toward us.

"Find any startling news, Gilbert?"

"Why, there's a pretty good thing," said the man. "Did you know sign-boards have been used hundreds and hundreds of years? Way back of Columbus."

"I don't think I have ever thought about them," said Henry.

"Come to think about it," said James Work, "sign-boards must have started whenever hotels and saloons started, or whatever they called such places at first."

"It goes away back," said the reader. "It's a good piece."

"Come to think about it," said James Work, "men must have traveled before they had houses; and after they had houses travel must have started public houses, and that would start sign-boards."

"That's so," said Henry.

A third player spoke to the reader. "Travel must have started red-light houses. Does he mention them, Gilbert?"

"He wouldn't do that, Marshal, not in a magazine he wouldn't," said James Work.

"He oughtn't," said Henry. "Such things should not be printed."

"Well, I guess it was cities started them, not travel," surmised Marshal. "I wonder whose idea the red light was."

"They had sign-boards in Ancient Rome," answered the man at the back of the room.

"Think of that!" said Henry.

"Might have been one of them emperors started the red light," said Marshal, "same as gladiators."

The game went on, always listless. Habit was strong, and what else was there to do?

"October, 1885," said Marshal. "That was when Toothpick Kid pulled his gun on Doc Barker and persuaded him to be a dentist."

"Not 1885," said James Work. "That was 1886."

"October, 1885," insisted Marshal. "That railroad came to Douglas the next year."

"He's got it correct, Jim," said Henry.

"Where is Toothpick Kid nowadays?" I inquired.

"Pulled his freight for Alaska. Not heard from since 1905. She's taken up with Duke Gardiner's brother, the Kid's woman has," said Henry.

"The Kid wanted Barker to fix his teeth same as Duke Gardiner had his," said Work.

"I don't think I've seen Duke Gardiner since '91," said I.

"When last heard from," said Henry, "Duke was running a joint in El Paso."

"There's a name for you!" exclaimed the man at the back of the room. "'Goat and Compasses"! They had that on a signboard in England. Well, and would you ever guess what it started from! 'God encompasseth us"!'

"Think of that!" said Henry.

"Does it say," asked Work, "if they had any double signs like Henry's here?"

"Not so far, it doesn't. If I strike any, I'll tell you."

That double sign of Henry's, hanging outside now in the dark of the silent town, told its own tale of the old life in its brief way. From Montana to Texas, I had seen them. Does anybody know when the first one was imagined and painted?

A great deal of frontier life it told by the four laconic words. They were to be found at the edges of those towns which rose overnight in the midst of nowhere, sang and danced and shot for a while, and then sank into silence. As the rider from his round-up or his mine rode into town with full pockets, he read "First Chance"; in the morning as he rode out with pockets empty, he read "Last Chance". More of the frontier life could hardly be told in four words. They were quite as revealing of the spirit of an age and people as Goat and Compasses.

That is what I thought as I sat there looking on at my old acquaintances over their listless game. It was still too early to go to bed, and what else was there to do? What a lot of old tunes Jed Goodland remembered!

"Why, where's your clock, Henry?" I asked.

Henry scratched his head. "Why," he meditated—"why, I guess it was last January."

"Did she get shot up again?"

Henry slowly shook his head. "This town is not what it was. I guess you saw the last shootin-up she got. She just quit on me one day. Yes; January. Winding of her up didn't do nothing to her. It was Lee noticed she had quit. So I didn't get a new one. Any more than I have fresh onions. Too much trouble to mend the ditch."

"Where's your Chink tonight?" I inquired. Lee was another old acquaintance; he had cooked many meals and made my bed often, season after season, when I had lodged here for the night.

"I let Lee go—let's see—I guess that must have been last April. Business is not what it used to be."

"Then you do everything yourself, now?"

"Why, yes; when there's anything to do."

"Boys don't seem as lively as they used to be," said Work.

"There are no boys," said Henry. "Just people."

This is what Henry had to say. It was said by the bullet holes in the wall, landmarks patterning the shape of the clock which had hung there till it stopped going last January. It was said by the empty shelves beneath the clock and behind the bar. It was said by the empty bottles which Henry had not yet thrown out. These occupied half one shelf. Two or three full bottles stood in the middle of the lowest shelf, looking lonely. In one of them the cork had been drawn, and could be pulled out by the fingers again, should anyone call for a drink.

"It was Buck Seabrook shot up your clock last time, wasn't it, Henry?" asked Marshal. "You knew Buck?" he said to me; and I nodded.

"Same night as that young puncher got the letter he'd been asking for every mail day," said Work.

"Opened it in the stage office," continued Marshal, "drew his gun and blew out his brains right there. I guess you heard about him?" he said to me again, and I nodded.

"No," Henry corrected. "Not there." He pointed at the ceiling. "Upstairs. He was sleeping in number four. He left no directions."

"I liked that kid," said Stirling, who had been silent. "Nice, quiet, well-behaved kid. A good roper."

"Anybody know what was in the letter?" asked Work.

"It was from a girl," said Henry. "I thought maybe there would be something in it demanding action. There was nothing beyond the action he had taken. I put it inside his shirt with him. Nobody saw it but me."

"What would you call that for a name?" said the reader at the back of the room. "'Goose and Gridiron'."

"I'd call that good," said Work.

"It would sound good to a hungry traveler," said Stirling.

"Any more of them?" asked Henry.

"Rafts of them. I'll tell you the next good one."

"Yes, tell us. And tell us when and where they all started, if it says." In the silence of the cards, a door shut somewhere along the dark street.

"That's Old Man Clarke," said Henry.

"First time I ever heard of him in town," said I.

"We made him come in. Old Man Clarke is getting turrible shaky. He wouldn't accept a room. So he sleeps in the old stage office and cooks for himself. If you put him in New York he'd stay a hermit all the same."

"How old is he?"

"Nobody knows. He looked about as old as he does now when I took this hotel. That was 1887. But we don't want him to live alone up that canyon any more. He rides up to his mine now and then. Won't let anybody go along. Says the secret will die with him. Hello, Jed. Let's have the whole of 'Buffalo Girls'." And Jed Goodland played the old quadrille music through.

"You used to hear that pretty often, I guess," said Henry to me; and I nodded.

Scraping steps shambled slowly by in the sand. We listened.

"He doesn't seem to be coming in," I said.

"He may. He will if he feels like it, and he won't if he feels like not."

"He had to let me help him onto his horse the other day," said Marshal. "But he's more limber some days than others."

Presently the scraping steps came again, passed the door and grew distant.

"Yes," said Work. "Old Man Clarke is sure getting feeble."

"Did you say it was Buck Seabrook shot your clock the last time?"

"Yes. Buck."

"If I remember correct," pursued Stirling, "it wasn't Buck did it, it was that joker his horse bucked off that same afternoon down by the corral."

"That Hat Six wrangler?"

"Yes. Horse bucked him off. He went up so high the fashions had changed when he came down."

"So it was, George." And he chuckled over the memory.

"Where does Old Man Clarke walk to?" I asked; for the steps came scraping along again.

"Just around and around," said Henry. "He always would do things his own way. You can't change him. He has taken to talking to himself this year."

The door opened, and he looked in. "Hello, boys," said he.

"Hello yourself, Uncle Jerry," said Work. "Have a chair. Have a drink."

"Well, maybe I'll think it over." He shut the door, and the steps went shambling away.

"His voice sounds awful old," said Marshal. "Does he know the way his hair and beard look?"

"Buck Seabrook," mused Stirling. "I've not seen him for quite a while. Is he in the country now?"

Henry shook his head. "Buck is in no country any more."

"Well, now, I hadn't heard of it. Well, well."

"Any of you remember Chet Sharston?" asked Marshal.

"Sure," said Stirling. "Did him and Buck have any trouble?"

"No, they never had any trouble," said Henry. "Not they."

"What was that Hat Six wrangler's name?" asked Work.

"He said it was Johnson," replied Henry.

Again the shambling steps approached. This time Old Man Clarke came in, and Henry invited him to join the game.

"No, boys," he said. "Thank you just the same. I'll sit over here for a while." He took a chair. "You boys just go on. Don't mind me." His pale, ancient eyes seemed to notice us less than they did the shifting pictures in his brain.

"Why don't you see the barber, Uncle Jerry?" asked Marshal.

"Nearest barber is in Casper. Maybe I'll think it over."

"'Swan and Harp'," said the man at the back of the room. "That's another."

"Not equal to Goat and Compasses," said Work.

"It don't make you expect a good meal like Goose and Gridiron," said Henry. "I'll trim your hair tomorrow, Uncle Jerry, if you say so."

"Boys, none that tasted her flapjacks ever wanted another cook," said Old Man Clarke.

"Well, what do you think of 'Hoop and Grapes'?"

"Nothing at all," said Henry. "Hoop and Grapes makes no appeal to me."

"You boys never knowed my wife," said Old Man Clarke in his corner. "Flapjacks. Biscuits. She was a buck-skinned son-of-a-bitch." His vague eyes swam, but the next moment his inconsequent cheerfulness returned. "Dance night, and all the girls late," he said.

"A sign-board outside a hotel or saloon," said Marshal, "should have something to do with what's done inside."

"That's so," said Henry.

"Take Last Chance and First Chance," Marshal continued. "Has England anything to beat that, I'd like to know? Did you see any to beat it?" he asked me.

"No, I never did."

"You come for fishing?" asked Old Man Clarke.

"I've brought my rod," I answered.

"No trout in this country any more," said he.

"My creek is fished out. And the elk are gone. I've not jumped a blacktail deer these three years. Where are the antelope?" He frowned; his eyes seemed to be asking questions. "But I'll get ye some meat tomorro', boys," he declared in his threadbare, cheerful voice; and then it trailed off. "All at the bottom of Lake Champlain," he said.

"Have a drink, Uncle Jerry?" said Henry.

"Not now, and thank you just the same. Maybe I'll think it over."

"Buck Seabrook was fine to travel with," said Stirling.

"A fine upstanding cow-puncher," added Work. "Honest clean through. Never knew him to go back on his word or do a crooked action."

"Him and Chet Sharston traveled together pretty much," said Henry.

Stirling chuckled over a memory. "Chet he used to try and beat Buck's flow of conversation. Wanted to converse some himself."

"Well, Chet could."

"Oh, he could some. But never equal to Buck."

"Here's a good one," said the man at the back of the room. "'Bolt-in-Tun'."

"How do they spell a thing like that?" demanded Marshal.

It was spelled for him.

"Well, that may make sense to an Englishman," said Henry.

"Doesn't it say where sign-boards started?" asked Work.

"Not yet." And the reader continued to pore over the syllables, which he followed slowly with moving lips.

"Buck was telling Chet," said Stirling, "of a mistake he made one night at the Southern Hotel in San Antone. Buck was going to his room fair late at night, when a man came around the corner on his floor, and quick as he seen Buck, he put his hand back to his hip pocket. Well, Buck never lost any time. So when the man took a whirl and fell in a heap Buck waited to see what he would do next. But the man didn't do anything more.

"So Buck goes to him and turns him over; and it isn't any stranger, it is a prospector Buck had met up with in Nevada; and the prospector had nothing worse than a flask in his pocket. He'd been aiming to offer Buck a drink. Buck sure felt sorry about making such a mistake, he said. And Chet, he waited, for he knowed very well that Buck hoped he would ask him what he did when he discovered the truth.

"After a while Buck couldn't wait; and so in disappointment he says to Chet very solemn. 'I carried out the wishes of the deceased'."

"'I was lookin' over the transom when you drank his whisky,' says Chet."

"'Where's your memory? You were the man,' says Buck. Well, well, weren't they a nonsensical pair!"

"I remember," said Henry. "They were sitting right there." And he pointed to a table.

"They were playing cooncan," said Marshall. "I remember that night well. Buck was always Buck. Well, well! Why, didn't Buck learn you cooncan?"

"Yes, he did," said I. "It was that same night."

"Boys," said Old Man Clarke over in the corner, "I'll get ye some fresh meat tomorro'."

"That's you, Uncle Jerry!" said Henry heartily. "You get us a nice elk, or a blacktail, and I'll grubstake you for the winter."

"She's coming," said Old Man Clarke. "Winter's coming. I'll shoot any of ye a match with my new .45–90 at a hundred yards. Hit the ace of spades, five out of five."

"Sure you can, Uncle Jerry."

"Flapjacks. Biscuits. And she could look as pretty as a bride," said Old Man Clarke.

"Wasn't it Chet," said Work, "that told Toothpick Kid Doc Barker had fixed up Duke Gardiner's teeth for him?"

"Not Chet. It was Buck told him that."

Henry appealed to me. "What's your remembrance of it?"

"Why, I always thought it was Buck," I answered.

"Buck was always Buck," said Marshal. "Well, well!"

'Who did fix Duke's teeth?"

"It was a traveling dentist. He done a good job, too, on Duke. All gold. Hit Drybone when Duke was in the hospital, but he went North in two or three days on the stage for Buffalo. That's how the play come up."

"Chet could yarn as well as Buck now and then," said Stirling.

"Not often," said Henry. "Not very often."

"Well, but he could. There was the experience Chet claimed he had done in the tornado belt."

"I remember," said Henry. "down in Texas."

"Chet mentioned it was in Kansas."

"San Saba, Texas," said Henry.

"You're right. San Saba. So it was. Chet worked for a gambler there who wanted to be owner of a house that you could go upstairs in."

"I didn't know Chet could deal a deck," said Marshal.

"He couldn't. Never could. He hired as a carpenter to the gambler."

"Chet was handy with tools," said Henry.

"A very neat worker. So the house was to be two stories. So Chet he said he'd help. Said he built the whole thing. Said it took him four months. Said he kep' asking the gambler for some money. The day he could open the front door of his house and walk in and sit down, the gambler told Chet, he'd pay him the total. So they walk out to it the day the job's complete and chairs ready for sitting in, and the gambler he takes hold of the door-knob and whang! a cyclone hits the house.

"The gambler saved the door-knob—didn't let go of it. Chet claimed he had fulfilled his part of the contract, but the gambler said a door-knob was not sufficient evidence that any house had been there. Wouldn't pay Chet a cent."

"They used to be a mean bunch in Texas," said Stirling.

"I was in this country before any of you boys were born," said Old Man Clarke.

"Sure you were, Uncle Jerry," said Henry. "Sure you were."

"I used to be hell and repeat."

"Sure thing, Uncle Jerry."

For a while there was little sound in the Last Chance Saloon save the light notes which Jed Goodland struck on his fiddle from time to time.

"How did that play come up, Henry?" asked Work.

"Which play?"

"Why, Doc Barker and Toothpick Kid."

"Why, wasn't you right there that day?"

"I was, but I don't seem to remember exactly how it started."

"Well," said Henry, "the Kid had to admit that Doc Barker put the kibosh on him after all. You're wrong about

Buck. He didn't come into that." Henry's voice seemed to be waking up, his eyes were waking up.

"Sure he put the kibosh on him," Work agreed energetically.

"Wasn't it the day after they'd corralled that fello' up on the Dry Cheyenne? asked Stirling.

"So it was!" said Marshal. He too was waking up. Life was coming into the talk of all. "That's where the boys corralled him."

"Well," said Stirling, "you couldn't leave a man as slick as he was, foot-loose, to go around and play such a game on the whole country."

"It was at the ranch gate Toothpick Kid saw those new gold teeth of Duke's," said Marshal.

"It wasn't a mile from the gate," said Stirling. "Not a mile. And Toothpick didn't wait to ask Duke the facts, or he'd have saved his money. Duke had happened to trail his rope over the carcasses of some stock. When he was roping a steer after that, his hand was caught between a twist of rope and his saddle horn. So his hand got burned."

"Didn't Buck tell him he'd ought to get Doc Barker to put some stuff on it?"

"Buck did warn him, but Duke wouldn't listen. So Buck had to bring him into the Drybone hospital with an arm that they had to cut his shirt-sleeve for."

"I remember," said Henry. "Duke told me that Buck never said 'I told you so' to him."

"Buck wouldn't. If ever there was a gentleman, it was Buck Seabrook. Doc Barker slashed his arm open from shoulder to elbow. And in twenty-four hours the arm wasn't so big. But it was still pretty big, and it looked like nothing at all, and Duke's brother saw it. They had sent for him. He rode into town, and when he saw the arm and the way it had been cut by Doc Barker he figured he'd lay for Doc and kill him. Doc happened to be out at the C-Y on a case.

"The boys met him as he came back, and warned him to keep out of the way till Duke's brother got sober, so Doc kep' out of the way. No use having trouble with a drunken man. Doc would have had to shoot Duke's brother or take the consequences. Well, next day the brother sobered up, and the boys persuaded him that Doc had saved Duke's life, and he was satisfied and changed his mind and there was no further hard feelings. And he got interested in the traveling dentist who had come into town to pick up business from the boys. He did good work. The brother got a couple of teeth plugged. They kept the dentist quite busy."

"I remember," said Marshal. "Chet and Buck both had work done."

"Do you remember the grass cook-fire Buck and Chet claimed they had to cook their supper with?" asked Work, with animation. Animation was warming each one, more and more. Their faces actually seemed to be growing younger.

"Out beyond Meteetsee you mean?"

"That was it."

"What was it?" asked Marshal.

"Did they never tell you that? Buck went around telling everybody."

"Grass cook-fire?" said Old Man Clarke in his withered voice. "Nobody ever cooked with grass. Grass don't burn half a minute. Rutherford B. Hayes was President when I came into this country. But Samuel J. Tilden was elected. Yes, sir."

"Sure he was, Uncle Jerry," said Henry.

"Well, Buck and Chet had to camp one night where they found a water-hole, but no wood. No sage-brush, no buffalo-chips, nothing except the grass, which was long. So Buck he filled the coffee-pot and lighted the grass. The little flames were hot, but they burned out quick and ran on to the next grass. So Buck he ran after them holding his coffee-pot over the flames as they traveled. So he said Chet lighted some more grass and held his frying-pan over those flames and kep' a-following their trail like he was doing with the coffee-pot. He said that his coffee-pot boiled after a while and Chet's meat was fried after a while, but by that time they were ten miles apart. Walked around hunting for each other till sunrise, and ate their supper for breakfast."

"What's that toon you're playing, Jed?" inquired Stirling.

"That's 'Sandy Land'," replied the fiddler.

"Play it some more, Jed. Sounds plumb natural. Like old times."

"Yes, it does so," said Henry. "Like when the boys used to dance here."

"Dance!" said Old Man Clarke. "None of you never seen me dance here."

"Better have a drink, Uncle Jerry."

"Thank you kindly. Just one. Put some water in. None of you never did, I guess."

"I'll bet you shook a fancy heel, Uncle."

"I always started with the earliest and kept going with the latest. I used to call for 'em too. Salute your partners! Opposite the same! Swing your honey! That's the style I used to be. All at the bottom of Lake Champlain. None of you ever knowed her."

"Have another, Uncle Jerry. The nights are getting cold."

"Thank you kindly. I'll have one more. Winter's coming."

"Any of you see that Wolf Dance where Toothpick wore the buckskin pants?" asked Work. "Wasn't any of you to that?"

"Somebody played it on Toothpick, didn't they?" said Stirling.

"Buck did. Buck wasn't dancing. He was just looking on. Toothpick always said Buck was mad because the Indians adopted him into the tribe and wouldn't take Buck. They gave him a squaw, y'know. He lived with her on the reservation till he left for Alaska. He got her allotment of land with her, y'know. I saw him and her and their kids when I was there. I guess there were twelve kids. Probably twenty by the time he went to Alaska. She'd most always have twins."

"Here's a name for you," said the man at the back of the room. "What have you got to say about 'Whistling Oyster'?"

"Whistling Oyster?" said Henry. "Well, if I had ever the misfortune to think of such a name I'd not have mentioned it to anybody, and I'd have tried to forget it."

"Just like them English," said Marshal.

"Did Toothpick have any novelties in the way of teeth?" asked Stirling.

"If he did, he concealed them," said Work.

"But him and Doc Barker had no hard feelings," said Henry. "They both put the mistake on Doc Gardiner and Duke said, well, they could leave it there if that made them feel happier."

"Doc was happy as he could be already."

"Well, a man would be after what came so near happening to him, and what actually did happen."

"Did you say Buck was dead?" asked Marshal.

"Dead these fifteen years," said Henry. "Didn't you hear about it? Some skunk in Texas caught Buck with his wife. Buck had no time to jump for his gun."

"Well, there are worse ways to die. Poor Buck! D'you remember how he laid right down flat on his back when they told him about Doc and the Kid's teeth? The more the Kid said any man in his place would have acted the same, the flatter Buck laid in the sage-brush."

"I remember," said Stirling. "I was cutting calves by the corral."

"Duke was able to sit up in the hospital and have the dentist work on his cavities. And the dentist edged the spaces with gold, and he cleaned all the teeth till you could notice them whenever Duke laughed. So he got well and rode out to camp and praised Doc Barker for a sure good doctor. He meant his arm of course that Doc had slashed open when they expected he was dying and sent for his brother.

"Duke never thought to speak about the dentist that had come into Drybone and gone on to Buffalo, and the Kid naturally thought it was Doc Barker who had done the job on Duke's teeth. And Buck he said nothing. So Kid drops in to the hospital next time he's in town for a spree at the hog ranch, and invites the Doc to put a gold edging on his teeth for him.

"'Not in my line,' says Doc. 'I'm a surgeon. And I've got no instruments for such a job.'

"'You had 'em for Duke Gardiner,' says the Kid. 'Why not for me?'

"'That was a dentist,' says Doc, 'while I was getting Duke's arm into shape.'

"So Toothpick he goes out. He feels offended at a difference being made between him and Duke, and he sits in the hog ranch thinking it over and comforting himself with some whisky. He doesn't believe in any dentist, and about four o'clock in the afternoon he returns to Doc's office and says he insists on having the job done. And Doc he gets hot and says he's not a dentist and he orders Toothpick out of the office. And Toothpick he goes back to the hog ranch feeling awful sore at the discrimination between him and the Duke.

"Well, about two o'clock a.m. Doc wakes up with a jump, and there's Toothpick. Toothpick thumps a big wad of bills down on the bureau—he'd been saving his time for a big spree, and he had the best part of four or five months' pay in his wad—and Doc saw right away Toothpick was drunk clear through. And Toothpick jams his gun against the Doc's stomach. 'You'll fix my teeth,' he says. 'You'll fix 'em right now. I'm just as good as Duke Gardiner or any other blankety-blank hobo in this country, and my money's just as good as Duke's, and I've just as much of it, and you'll do it now.'"

"I remember, I remember," said Marshal. "That's what the Kid told Doc." He beat his fist on the table and shook with enjoyment.

"Well, of course Doc Barker put on his pants at once. Doc could always make a quick decision. He takes the Kid out where he keeps his instruments and he lights his lamp; and he brings another lamp, and he lights two candles and explains that daylight would be better, but that he'll do the best he can. And he begins rummaging among his knives and scissors which make a jingling, and Toothpick sits watching him with deeper and deeper interest. And Doc Barker he keeps rummaging, and Toothpick keeps sitting and watching, and Doc he brings out a horrible-looking saw and gives it a sort of a swing in the air.

"'Are you going to use that thing on me?' inquires Toothpick.

"'Open your mouth,' says Doc.

"Toothpick opens his mouth but he shuts it again. 'Duke didn't mention it hurt him,' says he.

"'It didn't, not to speak of,' says Doc. 'How can I know how much it will hurt you, if you don't let me see your teeth?' So the Kid's mouth goes open and Doc takes a little microscope and sticks it in and looks right and left and up and down very slow and takes out the microscope. 'My, my, my,' he says, very serious.

"'Is it going to hurt bad?" inquires Toothpick.

"'I can do it,' says Doc, 'I can do it. But I'll have to charge for emergency and operating at night.'

"'Will it take long?' says the Kid.

" 'I must have an hour, or I decline to be responsible,' says the Doc; 'the condition is complicated. Your friend Mr Gardiner's teeth offered no such difficulties.' And Doc collects every instrument he can lay his hands on that comes anywhere near looking like what dentists have. 'My fee is usually two hundred dollars for emergency night operations,' says he, 'but that is for folks in town.'

"Toothpick brings out his wad and shoves it at Doc, and Doc he counts it and hands back twenty dollars. 'I'll accept a hundred and fifty,' he says, 'and I'll do my best for you.'

"By this time Toothpick's eyes are bulging away out of his head, but he had put up too much of a play to back down from it. 'Duke didn't mention a thing about its hurting him,' he repeats.

"'I think I can manage,' says Doc. 'You tell me right off if the pain is too much for you. Where's my sponge?' So he gets the sponge, and he pours some ether on it and starts sponging the Kid's teeth.

"The Kid he's grabbing the chair till his knuckles are all white. Doc lets the sponge come near the candle, and puff! up it flares and Toothpick gives a jump.

"'It's nothing,' says Doc. 'But a little more, and you and I and this room would have been blown up. That's why I am obliged to charge double for these night emergency operations. It's the gold edging that's the risk.'

"'I'd hate to have you take any risk,' says Toothpick. 'Will it be risky to scrape my teeth, just to give them a little scrape, y'know, like you done for Duke?'

" 'Oh, no,' says Doc, 'that will not be risky.' So Doc Barker he takes an ear cleaner and he scrapes, while Toothpick holds his mouth open and grabs the chair. 'There,' says Doc. 'Come again.' And out flies Toothpick like Indians were after him. Forgets the hog ranch and his night of joy waiting for him there, jumps on his horse and makes camp shortly after sunrise. It was that same morning Buck heard about Toothpick and Doc Barker, and laid flat down in the sage-brush."

"Buck sure played it on the Kid at that Wolf Dance," said Work. "Toothpick thought the ladies had stayed after the storm."

Again Marshal beat his fist on the table. We had become a lively company.

"On the Crow reservation, wasn't it?" said Henry.

"Right on that flat between the Agency and Fort Custer, along the river. The ladies were all there."

"She always stayed as pretty as a bride," said Old Man Clarke.

"Have another drink, Uncle Jerry."

"No more, no more, thank you just the same. I'm just a-sittin' here for a while."

"The Kid had on his buckskin and admired himself to death. Admired his own dancing. You remembered how it started to pour. Of course the Kid's buckskin pants started to shrink on him. They got up to his knees. About that same time the ladies started to go home, not having brought umbrellas, and out runs Buck into the ring. He whispers to Kid: 'Your bare legs are scandalous. Look at the ladies. Go hide yourself. I'll let you know when you can come out.'

"Away runs Kid till he finds a big wet sage brush and crawls into it deep. The sun came out pretty soon. But Toothpick sat in his wet sage brush, waiting to be told the ladies had gone. Us boys stayed till the dance was over and away runs Buck to the sage brush.

"'My,' says he, 'I'm sorry, Kid. The ladies went two hours ago. I'll have to get Doc Barker to fix up my memory.'"

"I used to be hell and repeat," said Old Man Clarke from his chair. "Play that again. Play that quadrille," he ordered peremptorily.

The fiddler smiled and humored him. We listened. There was silence for a while.

"'Elephant and Castle'," said the man at the back of the room. "Near London."

"That is senseless, too," said Henry. "We have more sensible signs in this country."

Jed Goodland played the quadrille quietly, like a memory, and as they made their bets, their boots tapped the floor to its rhythm.

"Swing your duckies," said Old Man Clarke. "Cage the queen. All shake your feet. Doe se doe and doe doe doe. Sashay back. Git away, girls, git away fast. Gents in the center and four hands around. There you go to your seats."

"Give us 'Sandy Land' again," said Stirling. And Jed played "Sandy Land".

"Doc Barker became Governor of Wyoming," said Work, "about 1890."

"What year did they abandon the stage route?" I asked.

"Later," said Henry. "We had the mail here till the Burlington road got to Sheridan."

"See here," said the man at the back of the room. "Here's something."

"Well, I hope it beats Elephant and Castle," said Henry.

"It's not a sign-board, it's an old custom," said the man.

"Well, let's have your old custom."

The man referred to his magazine. "It says," he continued, "that many a flourishing inn which had been prosperous for two or three hundred years would go down for one reason or another, till no travelers patronized it any more. It says this happened to the old places where the coaches changed horses or stopped for meals going north and south every day, and along other important routes as well. Those routes were given up after the railroads began to spread.

"The railroad finally killed the coaches. So unless an inn was in some place that continued to be important, like a town where the railroads brought strangers same as the coaches used to, why, the inn's business would dry up. And that's where the custom comes in. When some inn had outlived its time and it was known that trade had left it for good, they would take down the sign of that inn and bury it. It says that right here." He touched the page.

The quiet music of Jed Goodland ceased. He laid his fiddle in his lap. One by one, each player laid down his cards. Henry from habit turned to see the clock. The bullet holes were there, and the empty shelves. Henry looked at his watch.

"Quittin' so early?" asked Old Man Clarke. "What's your hurry?"

"Five minutes of twelve," said Henry. He went to the door and looked up at the sky.

"Cold," said Old Man Clarke. "Stars small and bright. Winter's a'coming, I tell you."

Standing at the open door, Henry looked out at the night for a while and then turned and faced his friends in their chairs round the table.

"What do you say, boys?"

Without a word they rose. The man at the back of the room had risen. Jed Goodland was standing. Still in his chair, remote and busy with his own half-dim thoughts, Old Man Clarke sat watching us almost without interest.

"Gilbert," said Henry to the man at the back of the room, "there's a ladder in the corner by the stairs. Jed, you'll find a spade in the shed outside the kitchen door."

"What's your hurry, boys?" asked Old Man Clarke. "Tomorro' I'll get ye a big elk."

But as they all passed him in silence he rose and joined them without curiosity, and followed without understanding.

The ladder was set up, and Henry mounted it and laid his hands upon the sign-board. Presently it came loose, and he handed it down to James Work who stood ready for it. It was a little large for one man to carry without awkwardness, and Marshal stepped forward and took two corners of it while Work held the others.

"You boys go first with it," said Henry. "Over there by the side of the creek. I'll walk next. Stirling, you take the spade."

Their conjured youth had fled from their faces, vanished from their voices.

"I've got the spade, Henry."

"Give it to Stirling, Jed. I'll want your fiddle along."

Moving very quietly, we followed Henry in silence, Old Man Clarke last of us, Work and Marshal dealing with the sign-board between them. And presently we reached the banks of Willow Creek.

"About here," said Henry.

They laid the sign-board down, and we stood round it, while Stirling struck his spade into the earth. It did not take long.

"Jed," said Henry, "you might play now. Nothing will be said. Give us 'Sound the dead march as ye bear me along'."

In the night, the strains of that somber melody rose and fell, always quietly, as if Jed were whispering memories with his bow.

How they must have thanked the darkness that hid their faces from each other! But the darkness could not hide sound. None of us had been prepared for what the music would instantly do to us.

Somewhere near me I heard a man struggling to keep command of himself; then he walked away with his grief alone. A neighbor followed him, shaken with emotions out of control. And so, within a brief time, before the melody had reached its first cadence, none was left by the grave except Stirling with his spade and Jed with his fiddle, each now and again sweeping a hand over his eyes quickly, in furtive shame at himself. Only one of us withstood it. Old Man Clarke, puzzled, went wandering from one neighbor to the next, saying, "Boys, what's up with ye? Who's dead?"

Although it was to the days of their youth, not mine, that they were bidding this farewell, and I had only looked on when the beards were golden and the betting was high, they counted me as one of them tonight. I felt it—and I knew it when Henry moved nearer to me and touched me lightly with his elbow.

So the sign of the Last Chance was laid in its last place, and Stirling covered it and smoothed the earth while we got hold of ourselves, and Jed Goodland played the melody more and more quietly until it sank to the lightest breath and died away.

"That's all, I guess," said Henry. "Thank you, Jed. Thank you, boys. I guess we can go home now."

Yes, now we could go home. The requiem of the golden beards, their romance, their departed West, too good to live for ever, was finished.

As we returned slowly in the stillness of the cold starlight, the voice of Old Man Clarke, shrill and withered, disembodied as an echo, startled me by its sudden outbreak.

"None of you knowed her, boys. She was a buckskin son-of-a-bitch. All at the bottom of Lake Champlain!"

"Take him, boys," said Henry. "Take Uncle Jerry to bed, please. I guess I'll stroll around for a while out here by myself. Good night, boys."

I found that I could not bid him good night, and the others seemed as little able to speak as I was. Old Man Clarke said nothing more. He followed along with us as he had come, more like some old dog, not aware of our errand nor seeming to care to know, merely contented, his dim understanding remote within himself. He needed no attention when we came to the deserted stage office where he slept. He sat down on the bed and began to pull off his boots cheerfully. As we were shutting his door, he said:

"Boys, tomorro' I'll get ye a fat bull elk."

"Good night, Jed," said Marshal.

"Good night, Gilbert," said Stirling.

"Good night, all." The company dispersed along the silent street.

As we re-entered the saloon—Work and I, who were both sleeping in the hotel—the deserted room seemed to be speaking to us, it halted us on the threshold. The cards lay on the table, the vacant chairs around it. There stood the empty bottles on the shelf. Above them were the bullet holes in the wall where the clock used to be. In the back of the room the magazine lay open on the table with a lamp burning. The other lamp stood on the bar, and one lamp hung over the card-table. Work extinguished this one, the lamp by the magazine he brought to light us to our rooms where we could see to light our bedroom lamps. We left the one on the bar for Henry.

"Jed was always handy with his fiddle," said Work at the top of the stairs. "And his skill stays by him. Well, good night."

A long while afterward I heard a door closing below and knew that Henry had come in from his stroll.

CONRAD RICHTER
Early Americana

Conrad Richter (1890–1968) was born in Pennsylvania. He became a writer at the age of 24, after working as a teamster, farm labourer, bank clerk and journalist. Richter was not exclusively a Western writer, but most of his best fiction is set in the American West, including the novel for which he won the 1951 Pulitzer Prize, *The Town*. (The book is part of a trilogy–with *The Trees*, 1940, and *The Fields*, 1941–set in the Ohio Valley.) Richter's most famous Western novel, however, is probably *The Sea of Grass* (1937), a story about a bitter conflict between homesteaders and a cattle baron. Other Richter books set on the frontier are: *Tracey Cromwell* (1942), *The Lady* (1957), *The Light in the Forest* (1953), and *A Country of Strangers* (1966). Richter's style is highly poetic, and his stories frequently draw on the oral reminiscences of those who lived on the American frontier.

'Early Americana' is from the collection *Early Americana* (1938).

IT HAS SLIPPED ALMOST OUT of reality now, into the golden haze that covers Adobe Walls and the Alamo, so that to-day, behind speeding headlights or in the carpeted Pullman, it seems as if it might never have really been.

But if you are ever on the back of a horse at night far out on the wind-swept loneliness of the Staked Plains, with no light but the ancient horns of the Comanche moon and that milky band of star-dust stirred up by the passing of some celestial herd, a cloud may darken the face of the untamed earth, the wind in your face will suddenly bring you the smell of cattle, and there beyond you for a moment on the dim, unfenced, roadless prairie you can make out a fabulous dark herd rolling, stretching, reaching majestically farther than the eye can see, grazing on the wild, unplanted mats of the buffalo grass.

And now with sudden emotion you know that the faint, twinkling light you see on the horizon is a distant window of that rude, vanished, half-mystical buffalo settlement, Carnuel, as it stood that night sixty-five years ago, the only fixed human habitation on a thousand square miles of unfriendly prairie, with great ricks of buffalo hides looming up like bales of swarthy cotton on a Mississippi levee, and with John Minor standing silently on the gallery of his buffalo post, looking with unreadable eyes on the rude rutted trail running out of sight in the moonlight on its three hundred miles to the railroad, and thinking how many days it had been that no one, east or west, north or south, had come to Carnuel but the rugged old Kansas circuit rider for the settlement's first wedding.

As a rule, there were three hide-buyers in hired buggies rattling in the protection of a wagon train coming back from Dodge; and across the prairie, hunters fresh from the big herds, yelling wildly as they rode up to Seery's saloon, the only place of refreshment in a dozen future counties; and clattering in from every direction, small freighters, their wagons piled high with hides, which lapped over the wheels to the ground so that they looked like huge hayricks bumping over the plain, swaying at every grass clump and threatening to crack the boom pole and spill the wagon. And at night the settlement would be full of bearded men stumbling over wagon tongues, roaring out lusty songs from Seery's bar, and in the smoky light of the post hefting the new rifles and buying cartridges and coffee.

But to-night the only sound from the gallery was the monotonous wind of the Staked Plains blowing soft and treacherous from the south, flapping the loose ends of five thousand buffalo hides, and bringing in from the prairie, now faint, now strong, the yelping of wolves from where cheery camp fires of buffalo chips usually glowed.

In the adobe saloon, its walls marked with notorious names and ribald verses, Dan Seery and a single customer played euchre, the whisky-stained cards rattling on the drum-like hardness of a flint-dry buffalo-hide table.

In his little adobe house the bridegroom, Jack Shelby, took a last look at the room Nellie Hedd had put firmly in place for their wedding to-morrow, from the stove ready to be lighted by the bride's hand to the starched pillow shams on the bed, and then carefully stretched his own bed roll on the kitchen floor.

And in the living-quarters behind John Minor's buffalo post, Chatherine Minor, aged sixteen, tried not to listen to the voices of her father and the circuit rider coming low and grave from the store-room as she brushed her black hair for bed by the light of a square buffalo-tallow candle, and thought of Laban Oldham, who had seldom spoken to her and never even looked at her, and wondered whether he might ask her for a square dance to-morrow night when they celebrated the wedding.

But ten miles out at Oldham Springs, in his father's dug-out high and dry in the *cañada* bank, Laban Oldham wasn't thinking of Chatherine Minor. Straight and untalkative, for all his boyish cheeks, his eyes a deep crockery blue, the long rawhide-coloured hair spilling violently over his linsey collar, he sat with his true love across his knees, polishing the octagon barrel, swabbing out the gleaming bore with bear oil, and rubbing the stock with tallow until it threw back a golden reflection of the candle.

For nearly four years he had done a man's work in the saddle. To-morrow he would really be a man and his own boss at eighteen, and could ride out of Carnuel, a buffalo hunter on the Staked Plains at last, leaving chores and drudgery for ever behind him, his Sharps rifle hard in its scabbard under his leg, and his voice joining Frankie Murphy's in a kind of shouted and unrhymed singing:

I left my old wife in the county of Tyron.
I'll never go back till they take me in irons.
While I live let me ride where the buffalo graze.
When I die, set a bottle to the head of my grave.

His mother, a small, dark woman, bent her face over her needle as if to blot the rifle from her eyes. His father, with a full, tawny moustache and a back like a bull, sat almost invisible in the shadows, silently smoking his pipe. And all evening there was no mention of missing freighters or buffalo hunters, or that it was the boy's last night in the dugout, only that the rotting tow sacks over the ceiling poles were letting the dirt sift through and that what they should do was go away for a night and leave the door open, so a polecat could come in and rid the place of mice.

"The wind's kind of bad from the south to-night," Jesse Oldham once remarked.

The others listened, but you couldn't hear the wind in a dugout.

"I stopped at the Hedds' to-day," Jesse Oldham spoke again. "Nellie sure looks pretty for her weddin'."

Another ten minutes passed while Jesse Oldham used the cotton-wood bootjack and made himself ready for bed.

"You're staying in the settlement till after the wedding, Laban?" his mother begged him.

He nodded, but to himself he said that it was nothing to his liking. With his young eyes hard and pitying on Jack Shelby for giving in so weak to a woman, he would stand with the other men at the kitchen door and never go near the dancing. And at daybreak, when the celebration would be over and Jack Shelby would find himself tied for life to a house and a woman's corset strings, he and

Frankie Murphy would be riding free as air out of Carnuel toward the Little Comanche, where the prairie was alive and moving with a dark tide, and where for ten miles you could hear the endless grunting bellows of fighting bulls, a dull, unceasing mutter that rose to an unforgettable thunder by dawn.

Something came into his blood at the thought, so that he could scarcely sit still. He could see himself and Frankie riding all spring and autumn in the backwash of that shaggy tidal wave as it swept, eddied, and scattered over the far northern plains. They would sell their hides at Dodge and Hays City and perhaps Cheyenne. He would see strange tribes and people, the Arkansas River and the Platte, and the northern mountains that looked like blue clouds floating over the plain. It was a free life, a king's life, with always a new camp and a new country just over the rise. And at night, rolled snug with his companions in their blankets, with the moon sailing high or the snow falling softly, with roast buffalo hump keeping him warm and to-morrow another adventure, he knew he should never come back to sleep again in a house at Carnuel.

Long after the dugout was in darkness, he lay awake in his sagging pole bed, with the familiar scent of earthen walls and rye straw in his nostrils, feeling the warmth of his young brother under the blue quilt beside him and listening to his father and mother breathing in the red-cherry bed that had come in the wagons from Kentucky. His mother's breath was the faster. Rapidly it caught up to his father's deeper breathing, chimed with it, passed it, for all the world like the hoof-beats of Ben and Fanny, his father's and mother's saddle horses, on their way to Nellie Hedd's wedding to-morrow.

On his own speckled pony, Calico, he rode away in the morning, with no more fuss than Cass, his young brother, running admiringly beside him in the other wheel track, as if they were not going to see each other in a few hours at Carnuel. Perched on the bleached skull of a buffalo, the young boy waited until horse and rider were high on the rise against the sky.

"Good-bye, Laban!" he shrilled.

Laban lifted his hand and rode down into his new world. If it hadn't been for Cass he would have liked to turn his head for a last look at the place to carry with him into the country of the Cheyennes and the Sioux—the smoke lifting from his father's dugout, almost invisible within the bank; his mother's great black kettle, for which he had gathered wagon loads of buffalo chips; and swinging their long horns as they came in single file down over the cap rock, his father's red Texas cattle that had grazed the night with antelope and stray buffalo.

Down in the deep prairie crack along the Carnuel River, he passed the Hedd place, busy with preparation for the wedding, the bridegroom's saddled horse already tied to the cotton-wood, the bride drying her dark red hair in the sunshine, and her father's pole buckboard waiting for horses by the door. And when he was up on the cap rock again, he could see rising behind the south ridge a cloud of dust that was surely a crowd of buffalo hunters riding in for Jack Shelby's wedding.

With his long, rawhide-coloured hair leaping at every jump, he turned his pony south-east to meet them, but when he reached the top of the long grassy ridge, the dust had disappeared. And though he stayed there for hours, the wide plain below him remained empty of the crawling ants that would have numbered Frankie Murphy in his deerskin vest and Sam Thompson and Captain Jim Bailey bringing their wives home from their buffalo camps along the Little Comanche.

He had the strangest feeling when at last he turned his pony and rode slowly back to Carnuel. The tiny remote settlement lay in the westering sun like a handful of children's blocks thrown and forgotten on the immensity of the prairie. Still several miles away, he could see a small cluster of persons standing on the gallery of the post, but neither his parents' horses nor the Hedd buckboard had come up from the river.

When he reached the settlement, the spare form of the storekeeper moved out in the rutted trail to meet him.

"Nellie and Jack didn't get them a new day for their weddin'?" he asked in a low voice, but his gaze was sharp and piercing.

"Not when I passed there this mornin'." Out of the corner of one eye the boy glimpsed Chatherine Minor in a new maroon cashmere dress moving quietly to the side of her father. His hand tightened on his bridle rein. "I'll ride down and see what's keepin' them," he said briefly.

John Minor opened his leathery lips as if to say something, and closed them again, but the girl had stiffened.

"Don't go, Laban!" she cried after him.

He made as if he hadn't heard, sitting very straight in the saddle and not looking back, riding away at a steady lope on the familiar trail for the Hedd house and his father's dugout. He would have gone now if a norther had been blowing, white and blinding, across the prairie, but he had never seen the Staked Plains more gentle and mild. The wind had gone down and the late afternoon sunlight slanting across the motionless grass was soft and golden as the candle burning in the little shrine on the wall of Mrs Gonzales's house in Carnuel when her man, Florencio, was somewhere out in this desolate land.

Like a long shadow felled across his path, he reached the edge of the cañon and saw below him that his morning's trail of bright sunshine now lay in twilight and gloom. He pulled up his pony and listened. The rocky depths with their untamed fertile bottoms tangled with shanghai grass and willows, and even the river itself, were utterly silent. For a little he sat there looking back at Carnuel, that had somehow become a distant and golden speck on the sunlit prairie. Then he urged his pony down the trail that the indefatigable pick of Sebastian Hedd had cut wide enough for his buckboard in the sloping cañon wall.

It wasn't so bad, once he was down and accustomed to the heavy shadows, withh Calico splashing cheerfully through the shallow river and the echo of iron shoes thrown back from the rocky walls. A little farther on, the cañon would be home-like, with Sebastian Hedd's fields green in this wild place with winter wheat, and beyond them the peeled logs of the Hedd cabin, with the buckboard drawn up to the door and Jack Shelby's horse tied under the cotton-wood. Even Calico freshened and stepped briskly round the bend in the cañon wall.

It was there, as he expected—the house and the fields Sebastian Hedd had wrested from the wilds, and the old slatted buckboard standing in front of the house. And yet there was something wrong with the familiar scene, something that caused him slowly to stiffen and his pony to halt and snort in the gloomy trail. Jack Shelby's horse was curiously missing and the pole of the buckboard had been propped up on a boulder, and over it had been bent some peculiar and unfamiliar object, pale and glistening in the shadows, and utterly still.

With a fine, inexplicable sweat breaking out of his pores, the boy watched it, little by little edging his pony nearer and leaning over the saddle horn that he could better see. Then, as if struck by a rattlesnake, he stopped. He had made out a feathered shaft like a long, thin, uplifted finger warning him grimly not to come on. And now for the first time he knew the naked and mutilated object on the buckboard tongue for what it was.

A hundred times, night and day, sun and shadow, Laban had travelled this trail, but never had the walls of the cañon pushed in and choked him as they did to-day. He could feel the dark, open door of the wronged little house watching him. And far above him, the layers of cap rock still brilliant in the sun, were the bright walls of the holy city that he could never hope to reach again.

For endless minutes he sat there on Calico, his knees wedged against the pony's shoulders, rigid, waiting, twitching, listening. All he could hear was an unseen horned lark winging its way back to the cap rock from the river, uttering its nameless cry, that never betrayed the direction from which it came or whether it was bird or spirit. And all he could see were the contents of a bride's leather trunk, starched muslin underwear and petticoats, feather-stitched and trimmed with ruffles, and nightgowns, high in the throat and tatted on the wrists, one of them given by his own mother, and all carefully folded away for the bridal journey, now torn and scattered like bits of white rubbish along the trail.

And now, examining again the loaded chamber of his old Sharps with the octagon barrel, he forced his rearing and plunging pony by the tragic little house, his eyes mechanically counting the three pitiable things lying motionless on buckboard tongue and ground.

Everywhere as he rode on rigidly through the cañon dusk, through the clumps of tangled willows that took on the shapes of bows and rifle barrels, and through the tall rank grass that twisted like snaky braids and eagle feathers, he could see his father more clearly than he had ever seen him in the life—splashing his face in the wash-tin before supper, wetting his hair, combing his long, tawny, imperturbable moustache, sitting without expression as he smoked in his chair after supper. And he could see his mother, her black hair combed tightly back from her forehead, tilting the huge coffee-pot, carving a slice from the loaf, or riding sideways on her man's saddle, her right knee hooked over the horn, and behind her his young brother holding on with both hands to the cantle and scratching his itching cheek against the rough homespun back of her basque.

Every fresh turn in the murky trail, boulders lying on the ground twisted the hand on his woolly rawhide reins, and up on the home side of the cap rock in the last searching rays of the sun, distant white specks in the grass flattened his cheeks until he knew them to be forgotten piles of bleaching buffalo bones. And when at last he reached the rise from where he had lifted a hand to Cass that morning, he could see below him in the grassy *cañada* the silent bank that was his father's dugout, and the door standing idly open on its wooden hinges.

Minute by minute he put off the grim duty, and when slowly he pushed his way into the doorway, he found the place as if a shell had struck it—the ticks ripped open, the floor littered with staves of his mother's sour-dough keg, and broken pieces of the beautifully polished red-cherry bed that had come all the way from Kentucky in the wagons, and flour and savage filth over everything. The buffalo robe where Cass used to lie of an evening on the floor before the earthen fireplace was gone without a trace, and so were Cass and his father and mother, the hoofprints of the unshod Ben and Fanny lost among the endless trample of unshod ponies.

Long after darkness had fallen, the boy half ran beside his grunting pony climbing out of the deep silent cañon. Up here on the cap rock he could breathe again. The stars seemed only half as far away. And far across the blackness of the plains he could see that reassuring small spark of yellow light, steady, alive, and more beautiful than all the stars in the sky.

He told himself that his father, who knew the country better than an almanac, might have left his mother in the soft radiance of that light at this moment. And when he rode up in front of the lighted post, the first thing he did was to peer from the saddle toward the dusty panes. But all he could see was the candlelight shining on brand new cinches and cartridge belts and skillets strung along the rafters, and on the full skirts of three women, none of whom was his small mother with her black hair combed tightly back from her forehead.

"That you, Labe?" the voice of the storekeeper came from the dimness.

The boy moved his pony back deeper into the shadows.

"Could you come out here, Mr Minor?" he said in a low tone. "The women, I reckon, better stay where they're at."

At the peculiar quality of his voice, four men, two with rifles, moved with silent stiffness from where they had been standing unseen on the dark side of the gallery—the storekeeper and the saloon-keeper, the gaunt circuit rider, and Seth Falk, a buffalo hunter from Indian territory, thick, bearded, in a buckskin shirt and an old pied brown and white calfskin vest.

"What's the matter, boy?" the circuit rider demanded.

Laban only looked at him, his eyes burning like coals in the darkness.

"I reckon," after a moment he told them, "there won't be a weddin' in the settlement now."

Silence followed except for the short, rapid puffs of Dan Seery's pipe and the circuit rider's hard breathing. Only Seth Falk changed no more than an Indian.

Laban could see him standing there in the dim light, leaning on his rifle, taciturn, inscrutable, his heavy forehead bent characteristically forward. His unreadable black eyes watched the boy from under the edge of his twisted hat-brim.

"They get Jack and the girl both?" he questioned without emotion.

"They got them all," the boy said thickly.

"How about your folks?" John Minor wanted to know.

Laban told him. And when he spoke again, it was very low, so the girl, who, he knew, was standing at the open door of the post, couldn't hear him.

"I got Nellie here on Calico now. She's wrapped up in my sugan." He made every effort to keep his voice from breaking. "You better tell the women not to open it. They did her up mighty bad."

The circuit rider, who was standing nearest the dim shadow of the pony, stiffened as if touched by a grisly hand, and Dan Seery's eyes rolled white. But Seth Falk and John Minor did not move.

For a time the four men stood staring at him and out into the night and at each other and through the open door of the post to the untold women, while a stark awareness grew on the boy that not a wolf or coyote howled on the cap rock this evening.

"We better get Jack and Bass to-night—if we want to bury them," he said bleakly.

"I'll ride down with the boy," Seth Falk spat, and moved off toward the rock corral with his rifle, for all his size as light on his feet as a mountain cat in the darkness.

The Comanche moon hung low in the west as the two horses came slowly and heavily back across the plain from the cañon. In the shadow of the post John Minor and the circuit rider stood waist deep in a wide, sandy trench. There were no boards to waste on a coffin. The three women came slowly out of the post, and the circuit rider put on his long, dark coat to read the burial service. A tall, gaunt, unforgettable figure in rusty black, towering there in front of a pile of shaggy buffalo hides, his voice rang out into the night as if to reach and sear the red infidels where he pictured them lying on the ground like wolves and harlots with their sinful and bloody scalps.

Laban had bared his long, sandy hair at a burial before, but never one that constricted him like this—the late hour, the small handful of people, the rising and falling of a real preacher's voice making the hair on the back of his neck to stir, and all the time the grated tin lantern with its tiny pane of glass and scattered air-holes throwing grotesque shadows on the men with rifles, on the full skirts of the women, still dressed for the wedding, and on the house of Jack Shelby, empty and silent yonder in the darkness.

Even here, when she stood only a few feet from him, the boy did not glance at the tight-lipped face of Chatherine Minor. A blur of maroon dress was all he saw or cared to see. White women didn't belong out here. Their place was back in a gentler land where farmers never heard of turning a furrow with a rifle lashed to the plough handles and where, on a Sunday morning, his mother used to say, she could still remember the peaceful sound of church bells drifting across the blue-grass. And to-night, if they had stayed there, no girl with luxuriant dark-red hair would be lying out here to be buried without it in an old mended sugan for a coffin, and his mother might be surely alive and rocking on a board floor in a Kentucky town with a lighted lamp-post on the corner.

"The Lord giveth," the circuit rider declared, "and the Lord taketh away. And no man knoweth the hour at which the Son of Man cometh."

As if in pagan challenge to the Christian words, a sign appeared slowly out in the darkness, then another. And presently, as they stood there watching, with the lips of Mrs Gonzales moving in Spanish and her hand convulsively crossing the black shawl folded on her breast, three fires far out on the plain burned red holes into the night, a scarlet triangle around the little settlement, fading and flaring in some savage code.

"'And I stood upon the sand of the sea'," the circuit rider said, with abomination in his voice, "'and saw a beast rise up out of the sea, having seven heads and ten horns'."

Sternly, when the rude service was done, John Minor ordered the women into the post, and for a time there was only the whisper of falling sand.

"What are they sayin', Falky?" Dan Seery asked.

"I ain't sartain I savvy," the buffalo hunter muttered. But Laban observed that he gave John Minor a meaning look and then stood with his head thrown forward grimly, watching the fires wax and wane.

For long minutes while they burned to smouldering red sparks on the prairie, John Minor mechanically mounded the wide grave with his shovel, his face bleak and marked, as if what he thought lay too deep in his mind to fetch up without Herculean effort.

"There's something I want to say to you men," he said at last unsparingly.

The boy had been watching his face. He wasn't sure what the storekeeper was about to say, but whatever it was, he was with him. Only the buffalo hunter seemed to know. He swung around slowly. All evening he had said little, and he said nothing now, but his eyes were like burning black fragments as they threw a deep, unutterable look around the little circle, not as if searching their faces, but from some powerful, unspoken feeling.

"I've no notion," John Minor went on harshly, "of letting our women go through what Nellie Hedd went through before those devils scalped her."

Laban felt a sharp, prophetic stab of coldness, as if slivers of blood had congealed in his veins. But John Minor had picked up an old buffalo horn and was bent over his shovel, scraping off the blade with all the deliberation of a man expected to use it for a long time to come.

"What's this you're talking about, man?" the circuit rider demanded sharply.

"The women." John Minor didn't look up at him. "Three of us got to keep extra guns loaded. We'll hold out as long as we can. Then, if it has to be, it's an act of mercy."

He said no more, but Laban felt strangely weak in the knees. Dan Seery's eyes were white and glistening in his beard, and for a moment even the rugged face of the circuit rider lost some of its colour. Only Seth Falk stood there stony and unchanged. And presently he brought out a deck of worn Mexican cards that fetched the quick censure into the circuit rider's cheeks.

"I've throwed out the queen of clubs," he told John Minor.

"I reckon that's good as any other way," the storekeeper said. "Who must we say for the queen of spades? Mrs Gonzales. And Sadie Harrison for the queen of diamonds. And the queen of hearts"—for a moment his face was like leather strained over a drum—"will have to be the other one." He turned and started to pull down a hide that had worked loose from the pile.

"You all savvy?" Seth Falk's gaze swept the men.

With its grotesque legs and clotted ruff, the hide lay on the ground like some dark mis-shapen omen, scarred and blood-stained, its swarthy wool matted with ticks and sandburs, bearing the tin lantern and the pack of cards face downward beside it.

"You draw fust, Dan," the buffalo hunter said briefly.

The saloon-keeper made no movement—just stood there looking down at the deck as if paralysed. John Minor knelt and lifted a card. When Laban saw them glance expectantly at him, he stiffened his back and drew the second. It was the four of spades. The buffalo hunter followed. Relentlessly, now, the drawing went on. With strong disapproval on his face, the circuit rider moved away, and came back again in his long black coat to watch like a gigantic dark moth drawn to the flame.

It seemed to the rigid boy that, except for the slight hiss of the slipping cards, the Staked Plains had never been so hushed. The horned moon had set. The fresh grave slept peacefully. Not a sound came from the post. Their little circle of light lay on the ground like a golden coin in all this illimitable darkness which somewhere held his father and mother and little Cass.

He was dimly aware of turning up a card with a broken corner which suddenly froze in his hands. It was a woman riding a horse, as the queen does in the Mexican deck, her coloured raiment stained and blemished, her face almost obliterated, and above the horse's head the small, curious-shaped Mexican heart. And as soon as he laid it down on the swarthy hide, it turned into the slender body of Chatherine Minor lying silent on the dark adobe floor of the post in the full skirts of the maroon cashmere dress she had made for Nellie Hedd's wedding.

He remembered afterwards John Minor's granite face, and Seth Falk tossing down the queen of yellow diamonds with no more expression than a card in a poker hand, and the latter's little black buffalo eyes watching him as if his face bore some unbecoming colour.

"Come in and John'll give you a drink," he said gruffly.

Laban stood there, rude and unhearing. When the others had gone with the lantern into the post, he kept walking with his rifle between the dark piles of hides.

The strong reek of the skins gave him something that he needed, like a powerful medicine brewed from the Staked Plains themselves. It reached where no whisky could. Kiowas or Comanches were nothing. After what he had seen in the cañon this afternoon, he could mow the painted devils down all day and stay icy cold with hate and clear of regret. But a white person, a woman, and only a girl! For more than an hour he kept walking up and down between the dark piles, and all the while, in the tightened sinews of his arms and legs and in the growing flatness of his cheeks, he seemed to be curing, hardening, drying, almost like one of the buffalo hides itself.

It was very quiet in the post when he came in. Over in a corner, so deep in shadows it seemed impossible to distinguish the faces of the cards, Seth Falk was playing a stolid game of solitaire on a boot-box, a pair of rifles lying beside him on the floor. Sitting under a candle, his Bible open on his knees, was the circuit rider, his rugged face alight as if the sun were shining into some rocky cañon. Dan Seery had just poured himself a stiff drink in a tumbler from a jug beneath the counter. And John Minor, with two guns leaning against the wall, sat writing slowly and methodically at his littered table.

He glanced up as Laban came in and silently indicated an extra rifle lying across a sugar barrel, with several boxes of cartridges on the floor. Something unutterable passed through the boy as he saw it, but he walked over, lifted and sighted it in his cold hands, the newest in buffalo guns, with a coil-spring lever and a long, round barrel. His stiff fingers tried a cartridge in the chamber, then they filled the magazine.

And now he knew that nothing could keep him from looking at the women. They had refused to go to bed, and there they sat in the two high-backed chimney seats. The Mexican woman, Mrs Gonzales, was asleep, her chin forward on her breast, breathing into her tightly drawn *rebozo*. Beside her, the elderly Sadie Harrison's eyes were tightly closed in their bony sockets, her grey hair awry, her long face a picture of aged and bitter resignment.

Only the girl Chatherine was erect and awake, sitting alone on the other bench, her back toward him, hidden behind a post, except for one shoulder and for her full red skirts flowing over the side of the bench to the floor. Once he felt that she was about to turn her head and glance back at him, and he dropped his eyes and began pushing cartridges from the new boxes into the empty loops of his belt.

The clock struck, and the long silence that followed rang louder than the gong. It was this waiting, waiting, Laban told himself, that was going to tell on him. He saw that the circuit rider had closed his Bible and was holding it tightly, like some golden talisman that would warm his cold hands. Seth Falk had shoved up the rows of his unfinished game and was stacking the cards on the box. Leaving one of his rifles against the door jamb, he stepped outside, and Laban could hear his boots clicking no more loudly than a cat's claws up and down the adobe floor of the dark side of the gallery.

John Minor picked up one of his own rifles and started toward the kitchen.

"I'll watch it out there, Mr Minor," Laban said quickly.

He was glad to get out of this place, where, no matter which way he turned his head, he could feel a red woollen dress burning into his eyes. He stepped through the darkened kitchen and out of the kitchen door. Not a star shone in the blackness. No sound rose but the faint stamping of horses around to the front where they had been tied for the night to the gallery posts.

Once he heard the clock strike the half hour and afterwards the rumbling of a moved bench in the post, and then the circuit rider's unmistakable ecclesiastical voice. It seemed to go on and on, and when Laban pushed in the kitchen door, it rang suddenly louder. Curiously he made his way in the dimness to the other door. The candles in the post had burned out and only a pale rosy glow from the dying embers in the fire-place faintly illumined the long, spectral room. In a little circle of shadows, everyone seemed to be standing, the gaunt shadow that was the circuit rider towering above them all, something upheld in one hand, the other dipping into it like the mysterious hand of God. And his voice rang out with powerful solemnity in this unaccustomed place:

"I baptise thee . . . Chatherine Lydia Minor . . . in the name of the Father . . . and the Son . . . and the Holy Ghost."

Slowly the meaning of the baptism to-night came over the boy, and with his fingers biting deeply into his rifle, he slipped back to a kitchen bench. But all the time he grimly sat there he had the feeling that even in that faintest of fantastic light Chatherine Minor had marked his tall form standing and watching at the kitchen door. And when it was all over, he heard her step coming toward him in the kitchen and then her fingers lighting the stub of a candle on the table.

"Can I make some coffee for you, Laban?" she asked.

And now he knew that nothing on earth could keep him from raising his eyes and letting them fall rigidly and for the first time directly on this girl whom, before the sun was an hour high, he might have to turn suddenly and bleakly upon.

There she stood, her dark eyes calmly facing him, taller than he imagined, but already, at sixteen, a woman, her body sturdy as a young cedar in the river brakes. The strong cheek-bones in her face turned abruptly inward, giving a resolute cast to the mouth. But what held his eyes most was her long, black hair, parted in a clear white streak; lustrous hair that he knew a Kiowa or Comanche would sell his life for.

He shook his head. She did not go away abashed; only stood there looking at him.

"You look thin, Laban," she reproved him. "You haven't had anything to eat since morning."

He could see now that her eyes were not black and brazen, as he had thought. They were steady and slaty grey. But what made him steel himself, sitting there with a rifle across his lap, was where her left breast, swelling gently in the folds of her tight red basque, marked the target of her heart.

"I'm not hungry," he said harshly.

She turned quietly away, and he thought she would go, but he could hear her hand on stove and water-bucket and kitchen utensils, and the heel of her firm foot on the adobe floor, and finally there was the fragrance of coffee through the kitchen, almost choking him, and he tried not to look at the picture she made, straight and with a disturbing womanly serenity, handing him a heavy, steaming, white cup and saucer and then bearing one in each hand into the post.

She set a plate of cold roast buffalo hump on the bench beside him and quietly washed the cups and saucers in the wash-tin and put them away on the calico-hung shelves as if she would surely find them there in the morning. Then her competent hands filled the stove, and with a dour mouth he watched her throw her skirts forward to seat herself, sturdy and erect, on the other kitchen bench.

"Papa wants me to stay out here," she said quietly, as if it were the most common thing in the world.

He said nothing. His face, framed in his long, rawhide-coloured hair, was deaf and wintry. He waited grimly for her woman's chitchat, but she sat composed and silent as a man while the stub of a candle flickered out behind them, leaving the scent of burned wicking floating through the dark room.

For a long time they sat in utter silence while the clock struck and a faint grey began to drift like some thin, ghostly semblance of light through the dark window.

"It's starting to get morning, Laban," she whispered. "Are you awake?"

"I'm awake," he told her.

"I think I heard something," she said quietly.

His hands made sure of his rifles. Rising, he felt his way along the cool wall to where an iron bar, fashioned from an old wagon tyre, bolted the door. Minutes passed while he stood there listening, and the black eastern sky grew into a long, lonely stretch of grey, unbroken except for a single well of green that lay like a pool reflecting the evening on a dark lava plain. He had never heard it more preternaturally still. The post at their backs was like the grave. Even the stamping horses were still. He could fancy them in his mind, standing out there in the early light, curving their necks to snuff and listen.

"It isn't anything," he told her. "Just the blood in your ears."

But now that he would deny it, he could hear it for the first time himself, very far away, like the wind in the grass, or the distant Carnuel River rushing down its cañon after a rain, nearer, always faintly nearer, and then evaporating into nothing more than the vast sweep of dark grey sky torn with ragged fissures like the chaos of creation morning.

"It wasn't anything," the girl agreed, whispering. "Just the blood in my ears."

But Laban's fingers were tightening again on the eight-sided barrel of his old Sharps. Something was surely out there, hidden from the post in the mists, like the abandoned hide wagons bleaching their bones on the Staked Plains.

And now, far out on the prairie, he could see them breaking out of the fog rolling in from the river, a thin line of loping riders, the long-awaited crawling ants his eyes had strained for from the ridge that day so long ago that was only yesterday afternoon.

A bench was suddenly overturned in the post. Seth Falk's iron grey nickered. And now they could hear the pleasantest sound in more than a week—the distant hallooing of rough, stentorian voices. And presently the post was filled with bearded men twenty-four hours overdue for Nellie Hedd's wedding, men who had ridden all night in wet chequered linsey shirts and soaked blue flannel shirts and steaming buckskin shirts that smelled of countless hides and buffalo-chip camp fires and black powder and Staked Plains' rain. And all morning the thick tobacco smoke in the post drifted to the grave talk over Jack Shelby and the Hedds and the uprising of the Kiowas, who meant to sweep every white hunter from the buffalo country, and the lost hides, wagons, and hair of the men who had waited too long before raising dust for the big outfits corralled together on the Little Comanche.

For two days and nights Laban Oldham sat cross-legged or lay in his blankets beside the camp fire of Frankie Murphy's men. But all the time while he heard how his mother had ridden into a buffalo camp with her black hair streaming into little Cass's face, and while he listened for the long train of freighters coming with the women and hides, Laban couldn't feel anything half so clearly as Chatherine Minor's snug, warm kitchen, and Chatherine Minor handing him a cup of coffee, with the steam curling over her raven hair, and Chatherine Minor sitting up with him most of the night in the darkened kitchen and whispering to him in the morning if he were awake.

Tall and stiff, the third evening, his long, rawhide-coloured hair gravely swinging, he walked through the post into the now familiar kitchen doorway and beyond, where a girl with her sleeves rolled high stood stirring sour-dough leaven into flour that was not so white as her arms. She did not look around at his step, but her bare upper arms brushed, with quick womanly gestures, stray hairs from his face.

"It's a warm evenin'," he greeted.

"Good evening, Laban." She bent over her work, and her hands made the mixing-pan sing on the table.

"Did you hear the freighters are campin' to-night at Antelope Water?" he went on awkwardly. "Bob Hollister just rode in."

"I reckon you'll be glad to see your folks," she answered, but he thought her deft white hands kneaded more slowly after that.

He sat on the familiar bench and waited unhurriedly for her to be through. The kitchen felt snug and pleasant as the dugout at home—the blur of the red-chequered cloth folded back from the table and the sputter of river cotton-wood in the stove and the homely scent of the sour-dough crock. He could close his eyes and know that either his mother or Chatherine Minor must be here. And when the tins were set to rise on the lid of the red flour-bin, she washed her hands and seated herself on the other bench, throwing her full skirts skilfully forward, as she had that sterner evening a day or two ago, until they rustled into their rightful place.

For a long time they sat there looking at the wall, that held no rifles now, and at the harmless black window, and at each other. And he told himself that he had never thought she would be a woman like this, with her flesh white as snow where it came out of the homespun at her throat, and the soft strength of her young mouth.

"I'm followin' the herd north when it moves, Chatherine," he stammered at length. "But I'm comin' back."

She answered nothing to that.

"I reckoned," he went on rigidly, "maybe you'd wait for me till I got back?"

She looked at him now, and her glance was firm and steady as the prairie itself. "I couldn't promise to wait for a single man, Laban," she said. "Where you're going is a long ways off. And a buffalo hunter can easy forget the way back."

The warm colour stung his cheeks at that, and he stood on his feet very tall, and stepped across the floor and sat down on the bench, and laid his linsey-clad arm rudely around her shoulders.

"The circuit rider isn't gone back to Dodge with the freighters yet," he reminded. "You can make it that he didn't come to Carnuel for nothin', if you want to, Chatherine. Then you won't have to do your waitin' for a single man."

She didn't say anything, but neither did she shake him off, and they sat quiet again while the talk in the post receded to a mere far-away drone and the kitchen candle burned out again, leaving its fragrance and all the room in darkness, except where a dim rectangle of post light fell across the floor. And suddenly he noticed that her breath caught up to his, chimed with it, and passed it, for all the world like the breathing of his father and mother in the beautiful red-cherry bed that had come from Kentucky in the wagons.

And everything, he thought, was well, when of a sudden she buried her face in his shirt and cried, and what she said after that, he thought, was very strange.

"Oh, Laban," her voice came muffled, "she had such beautiful hair!"

Before the week was out, the circuit rider scratched out the names of John McAllister Shelby and Nellie Hedd from an official paper and firmly wrote: "Laban Oldham and Chatherine Lydia Minor." And the settlement had its wedding with four women on the pole-backed chimney seats, and with Mrs Oldham, her dark hair combed back tightly from her forehead, sitting on the chair of honour, and with Jesse Oldham, his back like a bull and his imperturbable moustache, standing with John Minor, and with buffalo hunters along the counter, and the freighters in a reticent knot by the door.

The circuit rider's voice rang in the pans and skillets hanging on the smoke-stained rafters. And when it was over, a huge shaggy hunter rode his horse half-way into the post's open door-way and bellowed for Dan Seery to unlock the saloon. And when he saw the silent couple and the black book of the circuit rider, he stood in his stirrups and roared, shaking his long, grey mane and the blood-stained, weather-beaten fringe of his buck-skins till he looked like an old buffalo bull coming out of the wallow:

"I left my old wife in the county of Tyron.
I'll never go back till they take me in irons.
While I live, let me ride where the buffalo graze.
When I die, set a bottle to the head of my grave."

ERNEST HAYCOX
When You Carry the Star

Ernest Haycox (1899–1950) was born in Portland, Oregon, and spent his boyhood around the mills and lumber camps of the Pacific Northwest. He served with the US Army in France during World War One, and on his return he entered the University of Oregon, graduating in 1923. His initial literary career was unsuccessful—he was reduced to living in a chicken coop, which he decorated with rejection slips—but took off after a period as a reporter for *The Oregonian* and his marriage to Jill Marie Chord. By the 1940s, after a decade of phenomenal output for the pulps, Haycox had become the leading Western writer for the 'slick' magazine, *Saturday Evening Post*. Unlike many popular writers of the period, Haycox did not simply make his characters men of action: he gave them a moral awareness and psychological depth (something which subsequently influenced the entire course of the popular Western). Athough Haycox wrote several fine Western novels—in particular, *Bugles in the Afternoon* (1944) and *The Border Trumpet* (1939)—his real skill always remained the Western short story, at which he was largely unrivalled in the popular tradition. Among the many Haycox stories filmed by Hollywood is 'Stage to Lordsburg', which formed the basis for John Ford's *Stagecoach* (1939).

'When You Carry the Star' is from the Haycox collection *Murder on the Frontier* (1952).

SHERIFF HENRY LINZA WAS TAKING the evening's ease on the porch of his ranch house, ten miles out of Bonita, when he saw the rider come beating across the prairie; and even at that distance he knew. His face settled a little and he tapped the bowl of his pipe against an arm of his chair as if to signal the end of twilight's long peace. "It's Bob Boatwright," said he to his wife. "Funny how he likes to lug bad news to me."

"How can you tell?" asked Miz Linza.

"He's sittin' all over the saddle," chuckled Linza. "Kind of a St Vitus' dance catches him when he gets excited." But when Boatwright, marshal of Bonita, came abreast the porch, Linza was quite grave. Indian summer's cloudy beauty lay over the land and it was hard to think of the crimes of men.

"This is bad, Sheriff," said Boatwright. "Will Denton—he's turned wild."

"Will Denton!" exclaimed Miz Linza. "Why, I don't believe it!"

But Henry Linza shook his head slowly and, leaning forward, prompted Boatwright. "As how, Bob?"

"He walked into Neal Sampson's store an hour ago, pulled the gun and asked for the extra money Neal keeps to accommodate ranch hands after the bank closes. Wouldn't been nothin' but ord'nary robbery but Neal is rattled, makes a move toward the counter and gets a bullet in the heart."

"What then?" grunted Linza.

"It was all over in three minutes," said Boatwright. "Last we saw of Denton he was goin' due west into the heat haze. I couldn't get a posse organized so I come here. The boys are shy of Denton's educated rifle, Sheriff."

"I don't believe it," repeated Miz Linza. "Why, he ate supper with us two weeks ago."

"I hated to come here," said Boatwright, "knowin' he was a friend of yours." And after a lengthening silence he spoke again. "What'll you do, Sheriff?"

Linza's head fell thoughtfully forward. Lines curved down from his lip corners into a squarely definite chin, thus creating an aspect of doggedness, of biting into difficulties and hanging on. Without alleviating humor, that cast of jaw and mouth would have seemed unforgiving and almost brutal; but it was Linza's eyes that gave him away. Candidly blue, they mirrored the shrewdness of a full life and the inevitable compassion arising therefrom.

As an observer and dealer in the misdemeanors of men he had grown great without becoming hard; of that splendid line of southwestern peace officers which had left its impress on an unruly land, there was in him always a puzzlement that certain things had to be.

"Go after him," said he, following a long spell of silence.

"Now?" pressed the marshal.

"Mornin's soon enough," replied Henry Linza. "He's got twelve hundred square miles to roam in and one day makes no difference. Light and rest, Bob."

"Thanks, no, I've got to get back," said Boatwright and cantered away into the deepening dusk.

"He sat here on this porch two weeks ago," murmured Miz Linza. "It don't seem possible."

"He was on the border line then," reflected Linza. "I saw it in him. He wasn't the same. He held a little off from me. He was debatin' the jump whilst he ate my beef."

"But what could make him?" pressed Miz Linza.

Linza shook his head. "If anybody knew the answer to that they'd have the answer to all things. Wild blood, a dark thought, a bad day, a tippin' of the balance in a man's mind, a sudden move—and then it's done and never can be undone. One more rider in the wild bunch."

"Your own friend," said Miz Linza.

"Was," agreed Linza, rising. "But it's himself that took the step across the line, and he'd be the first to realize I've got to go after him. Such," and a deepening regret came to his voice, "is the constituted order of things in a mighty queer world. We better turn in, Henrietta. I'll ride early."

It was, in fact, still short of daylight when Henry Linza pulled out from the ranch, riding one horse and leading another. There was a single gun at his hip, a rifle in its boot, a few necessities within the saddlebags, and some quick grub inside the blanket roll tied to the cantle strings.

In addition he carried a pair of binoculars. "Can't say when I'll return," he told his wife. "My intention is to take Will peaceably. Knowin' his disposition I dunno if he'll agree. But don't worry."

She had been a peace officer's wife too long to show her concern outwardly. All she did was to touch him gently and return to the porch. A hundred yards off he swung in his saddle and raised his hand as a farewell; it was a comfort to know she'd be there waiting for him to come back.

He swung wide of Bonita and thus when day fully arrived and a splendid sun swelled through the sky with a rose-red light, he came to a bridge over a dry river bed, crossed it and stood on the edge of his venture. The leagues rolled away to the distance, southwesterly into a horizon unbroken, northwesterly to a line of hills even now beginning to fade behind an autumn haze. Somewhere yonder Will Denton rode. Halting a moment, Linza was summing up as follows: wherever Denton went the need of food and water and rest would inevitably bring him to certain crossroads.

It became a matter of guessing who, out of Denton's many stanch friends in the country ahead, would shelter the man. As for the first crossroad, the dimmed smudge of Joe Waring's ranch in the distance seemed most likely. Hungry and worn, Will Denton would seek that friendly shelter while debating whether to turn to the southern open or to the northern hills. Waring's was the jump-off.

The day's course outlined, he pushed forward at a gait designed to protect both himself and his horses over a continued trail. It was not one that would have overtaken any hurrying fugitives, but Linza, having twenty years' tracking to his credit, knew wild ones seldom if ever retreated in a straight line after the initial dash. They shifted, they halted, they doubled from point to point. As those more gentle, abiding men whose ranks they forsook, outlaws liked home soil best of all.

For the most part it was a trackless, lonely land and as he plodded on, Linza relapsed into the protection of his thoughts. "Punched cattle with him, ate and slep' with him under the stars. Knew him well, but apparently never knew him at all. He was a laughing man. Now he's got a price on his head. Good wine can stand in the keg too long." Beyond noon he camped under a scrub oak.

Afterwards, riding the second horse, he pressed through heat haze as heavy as fog; and around six o'clock he crossed the Waring front yard to find the owner standing in wait for him—a big, broad man with fat cheeks and a pair of blandly observant eyes.

"Saw you comin', Henry," said he. "Glad to have your feet under my table again. Get down."

"Your conscience is clear, I take it," drawled the sheriff cheerfully and allowed an arriving puncher to take his horses away.

"Why shouldn't it be clear?" retorted Waring; and the both of them grinned.

There were punctilios in this matter that had to be observed, a kind of code grown up from the common mingling of honesty and outlawry. Waring, himself straight as a string, was a friend to both the sheriff and Denton. More than that, there was in him a wide streak of sentiment for the underdog, and many men on the dodge had received casual aid from him. But what he knew he kept strictly behind his smiling eyes. Comprehending this, Linza maintained his peace, ate and returned to sit on the porch with a cigar between his teeth while purple dusk deepened and a faintly stirring breeze brought the fragrance of sage across the yard. The thing went even deeper. Waring's sympathy for the underdog might well lead him into getting word out to Denton of his, Henry Linza's, probable course of hunt. So it became a matter of wits, played on either side with a shrewd courtesy.

"You're in no hurry?" said Waring.

"Plenty of time. The world's a wide place."

"Ahuh," drawled Waring and added gently, "one of the boys came back from town last night. Heard about Will Denton from him."

Linza remained silent, wondering whether this were truth or evasion. Waring leaned forward, concern in his words. "You're both friends of mine of long standing. Hard for me to realize you're the man that's got to take Denton's trail. Henry, one of you is going to get hurt."

"I carry the star," said Linza very quietly.

"And not for a million dollars would you go back on it," muttered Waring. "That damn' fool Denton! He might've known this would happen. You never give up, Henry. I never knew you to give up. And he won't be taken alive. I can tell you that."

"I'll give him every chance to drop his guns," said Linza.

"Why didn't you put a deputy on his trail?"

Linza shook his head slowly. "It would be the same as a lie, Joe. No deputy could catch Will. It takes an old dog full of tricks. It wouldn't even be average honesty for me to send another man out."

"Damn a system that makes this business possible," growled Waring.

Linza sighed a little, remembering Will Denton's recklessly pleasant face as of old. "Maybe—maybe. But bear in mind that Will committed the murder, not the system. I'm turnin' in."

Waring got up, watching the sheriff closely through the shadows. "Listen, you're traveling light. Better let me give you a couple of extra water bags tomorrow."

"Thanks," said Linza casually. "Not a bad idea." And he climbed the stairs to his bedroom. But he didn't immediately roll up for the night; instead, he pulled a chair soundlessly to a window and took station there. A long while afterward he was rewarded by the sight of a rider going off from the barn. In the distance hoofbeats rose and died out. With something like a grim smile on his face, the sheriff abandoned his post and went to bed. "The twelve hundred square miles is cut in half, I think," he mused.

He was away next morning before the mists had risen. Five miles from the ranch he drew in, knowing it was time to make a decision. If he meant to hit for the open land southwesterly it was necessary to swing left at this point; otherwise the hill country beckoned him to turn north. Dwelling on Waring's apparently innocent offer of the water bags and the subsequent rider faring out through the darkness, Linza made up his mind. "Me taking those water bags indicates to Waring I intend to hit the dry trail into the southwest; his messenger would tell Denton that, and Denton would do just the opposite—ride for the hills." Acting on that reasoning, Linza swung somewhat and advanced squarely toward the range of hills shooting tangentially out of the north.

The country began to buckle up and long arroyos led down-grade to a high-bluffed canyon with a silent river idling at the bottom. Linza, roused from his saddle laze, entered the canyon, followed the slanting trail around a bend and found himself in a forlorn, shrunken town hidden from the horizon altogether. This habitation of man appeared to have no purpose and no vitality; and in truth it was but a gateway to the hills and a supply point for the nervous-footed who dodged in and out of sight. Linza, watching all things carefully, knew he had definitely put safe territory behind; the mark of hostility lay on the faces of the few loungers who scanned him with surreptitious, narrow-lidded glances. Pausing to let his horse drink at a stable trough, he considered his surroundings.

"Got to know if Will passed through here. If he didn't, then he's striking into the hills at a point higher up and I've missed his trail somewhere along the line. These folks are his friends, but there is one weak point—"

Turning, he rode farther down the street and dismounted at the general store. Inside the dim, musty place a single occupant's gaunt body stooped over the counter, bald head shining through the half light; when he straightened it was to reveal a face like that of a bloodhound—sad and lined and somehow very honest.

"I'll make out a snack on crackers and cheese, 'Lisha," said the sheriff.

"Love you, Sher'ff," drawled the storekeeper. "What brings you here?"

"Business, 'Lisha."

"Sorry business then," muttered the storekeeper. "It's the only kind we know around these parts."

Linza ate some cheese sandwiches, drank a bottle of warm beer and spoke abruptly: "'Lisha, did Will Denton pass this way?"

The storekeeper met the sheriff's glance steadily. "No. What's he done?"

"You're the only man who would tell me the truth," grunted Linza. "The only one in this town I could ask or believe."

"My fault," said the storekeeper and appeared unusually sad. "Truth is a bad habit up here."

Linza paid for his lunch, went out and rode away to the north, considering the situation.

If his reasoning was correct, Denton's avoidance of the town meant the six hundred square miles was halved to three hundred; in addition there was a constantly accruing advantage on the sheriff's side, for, as the area of pursuit narrowed, the known waterholes, trails and hideouts became fewer. That night, long after dark, he struck a watering place and inspected its edges by match light. Seeing nothing of value, he suddenly changed his tactics, and under cloak of night left the prairie behind him to rise to the bench and its thin sweeps of timber. Some eyes had always been on him while he was in the open. Putting himself into semi-concealment at once switched the nature of the chase. "The hunted animal," he reflected, "never runs when it figures pursuit is lost. It even circles back to find out where the hunter's gone." Dawn found him in a thicket and there he stayed while the fresh hours ran on to noon. Beside him a definite trail ran up in the direction of the range's crest, and it was while he tarried here that a single rider came cantering down, passed him with eyes fixed on the earth and disappeared. Perhaps an hour later this man returned, riding fast and looking troubled.

"Somebody's nervous," reflected Linza. "Will's got stout friends in these parts. Hell to fall back on a plain hunch but I believe I'll go ahead in this direction."

As he went forward, winding in and out of sloping meadows interspersed with yellow-dusted pines, the ever-present attitude of watchfulness continued to deepen. Like some hound in game country, he was keening for a scent he knew ought to be there. Tracks led him onward, passed through bands of cattle and were lost. After the second such happening, Linza left the trail and began to climb in a semicircular manner that around sundown brought him to the edge of a meadow in which a gray cabin sat remote and serene. A brown dog sprawled in the dirt; there was a half-masked lean-to behind the cabin sheltering some implements, and over at the far edge of the meadow an ewe-necked horse grazed. Inside the cabin a woman passed and repassed the door aperture. "Apparently no visitors," said Linza, and went forward.

Instantly the brown dog sprang up snarling and immediately afterward a tall man in a red undershirt strode from the house and took a stand in the yard with a cradled rifle.

Linza rode up.

"Long day behind," said he, amiably. "Could I put up here?"

"You're Linza?" said the man.

"That's right."

"No room fer you in my cabin, sir."

Linza's eyes betrayed a gleam of humor but he said quietly: "Fair answer. I'll roll my blankets up yonder."

"Go beyond my fences afore you do," stated the man.

Linza nodded and rode around the cabin. Two hundred yards on he came to a gate and passed through it. Trees shut off sight of the cabin but he was strongly aroused now and interested in the squatter's subsequent actions. So, a few hundred yards farther ahead, he quartered to the top of a small butte commanding the meadow. The man was not to be seen and Linza, about to retreat, had some oddity tick his mind. Looking more closely, he discovered what he had not observed before and what certainly had been missing at the time he went by the house—a string of white clothes hung on a clothesline.

"It ain't Monday," observed Linza. "And it seems odd the lady would wash near supper time."

Watching for a moment, he finally turned down the butte and continued through the trees. "Will would have glasses and he'd see that washin'," he reflected. "It's a signal to him. Arranged for." It was then dark, a clear cold violet giving way to velvet blackness against which the range made a ragged silhouette. One shot banged from the general direction of the squatter's meadow and its echo sailed over the tree tops and died in small ricocheting fragments. The sound of that gun, primitive and lawless in effect, seemed to defy Henry Linza openly, to taunt and challenge him, and finally to bring him to a decision.

"I'm tradin' on Will's weakness," he muttered. "God knows it's hard enough to have friend set against friend without that. But I'd trade on the weakness of any other and I will not make exceptions. Will, damn you, don't fall into this trap."

Linza moved rapidly toward a depression of the burn, dismounted and picketed his ponies fifty feet apart to keep them from fouling each other. He let the saddle remain on the ridden beast, but he unrolled his blanket beside a protecting deadfall and laid his rifle by it. Going on a distance, he built up a small fire, retreated to the log and ate a pair of cold biscuits.

Not far off, something snapped. A taut, husky voice struck through the shadows.

"Henry—that you?"

Linza swore under his breath. One faint, friendly hope died. "Will, why in hell did you come?"

"You're too old a codger to be buildin' fires for nothin' in country like this. I saw the blaze and I knew you wanted to see me. Well, here I am."

"So I figured," replied Linza, keeping below the log. "Wanted to see you all right, but I had a mite of hope you'd stay away. It's hard business, Will."

Denton's voice was increasingly cold. "Listen—get off my trail. When I heard you was the one after me I knew it had to be a showdown sooner or later. But I'm tellin' you, I'll not be took. Not by you nor anybody else. Get off my trail and keep off it!"

Linza shook his head. This was the inevitable way. Some odd thing happened to a man when he turned killer. Some suppressed fire flamed and would not die. Will Denton was only playing out an old, old story; he had turned wolf. But still the sheriff had his say.

"Give up, Will. Maybe a good lawyer could make out a case for you. Consider a life sentence with the even chance of a pardon some years later. Put down and come forward."

Denton's reply was almost a snarl. "Not me—never!"

"Think of this," urged Linza. "What's left for you now? You'll never sleep sound again. For the rest of your life you'll be ridin' the edges, wishin' to come in and afraid to. Come on, give up."

"You'd make a fine parson," jeered Denton, and the sheriff heard the man's teeth snap, heard the sudden inrush of breath. "I'm on my own hook. I'm not comin' in. Go on back. Get off my trail. I know you and I know myself. If we meet, somebody's goin' to die."

"You know I can't quit," said Henry Linza.

Denton fell silent a moment. Presently he said: "All right, Mister Linza. You've had your warnin'. Expect no consideration from me while we collide. Don't figure friendship will count for anything at all. It won't. If I see you again I won't call out. I'll kill you."

Linza shouted, "You everlastin' fool!"

A single gunshot burst into the night and soared along the slope. Linza's near horse winced, expelled a great gust of air and fell in his tracks. "Keep your head low, Linza!" roared Denton, and there followed a crunching of boot heels across the burn. Linza rose from the log and stared at the blank pall in front of him. Presently he heard Denton's pony struggling up the mountain trail; then the sound of that died.

He crawled to the dead horse, unfastened the gear, and afterward saddled the second animal. Rolling up his blanket roll and tying it, he mounted and waited another long interval with his ear pressed against the night breeze. Far up the side of the range a shot broke out, seeming to be both a challenge and a defiance. When he heard it, Linza went across the burn, entered the trail and began to climb.

"No consideration now," he muttered. "This is a man hunt. And if he thinks he's put me afoot he'll be a mite careless."

The trail wound interminably through the dismal reaches of the night.

Occasionally Linza paused, but never for long, and always the cold, unrelenting thoughts of the hunter plagued him, and the stealth and wariness of the hunter kept him on guard. Sometime after midnight he oriented himself on a dome atop the world, withdrew to a thicket and rolled up for a short sleep. There was the faint smell of wood smoke in the wind.

When he rose the ravines of the range below were brimful of fog that moved like sluggish lake water. Kindling a cautious fire, he boiled coffee and considered it a breakfast.

The strategic importance of his location became more apparent when, after a chill and dismal two hours of waiting, the fog dissipated before sunlight coming across the range in flashing banners that outlined all the rugged angles of the hills boldly. From his station he looked away to lesser ridge tops, to sprawling glens, to the various trails and their intersections; and it was while his patient glance ran from one trail to another that a movement in a corner of his vision caused him to swing slightly and catch sight of a solitary rider slipping from the trees, momentarily pausing in full sight, and disappearing again. He was gone before Linza could get his glasses focused.

Linza lost no time in mounting and running down the slope of the knob he had been posted on—unavoidably exposing himself as he did so. He reached the still dew-damp shelter of the lower pines, struck a runway fresh with the mark of deer tracks and the plantigrade print of bear, and followed it faithfully until he presently arrived at a division point. One fork led descendingly to that crossing where he had seen the man; the other continued along the spine of the ridge.

Wishing to keep his tactical advantage, Linza accepted the latter way and fought through a stiffly resisting accumulation of brush before coming to a fairer path. Traveling faster and all the while sharply watching for the unexpected, he reached, about twenty minutes later, the junction point of his route and another laboring up from the depths of a canyon; and he barely had time to sink into the sheltering brush when the man he was stalking came into sight along the lower trail. Linza cursed silently. It was not Denton.

"Mistake," he muttered. "And could have been damn near fatal to me. Am I bein' towed around the landscape for Will to find?"

The thought stiffened him. He retreated deeper into the brush, scanning one narrow vista and another. Meanwhile the rider came out of the canyon, cut across Linza's vision and disappeared, to reappear momentarily between two great pines at another quarter of the forest.

"Something in that," thought Linza, the hunter's instinct beginning to flow hotter in him. He hauled himself around until he discovered a way of bearing down in the direction of the man. Five minutes later, though hardly more than four hundred feet in distance, the trees ran out upon another meadow. There was a cabin built against a rocky bluff in front of which the rider was then dismounting. Smoke curled from a chimney, but other than that it seemed innocent of trouble. Linza dropped from his horse and crawled to a better vantage point.

The man had left his horse standing beside the cabin, reins down and saddle on. Meanwhile he had slouched forward to a patch of sunshine. Squatting there on his heels, he tapered off a cigarette, lit it and seemed to warm himself leisurely. But at every third or fourth drag of smoke his head made a swift half circle, snapped around and made another.

A moment later, in defiance to his attitude of indolence, the man rose abruptly and strode for an ax standing beside a chopping block. Lifting it, he brought it down, one stroke after another, in rhythmic attacks that sent long ringing waves of sound through the still air. Linza swore to himself, hitched his body a little more forward and turned his glance to that corner of the meadow where the trail entered.

"Something in that," he muttered.

Down the trail was the softly indistinct "clop-clop" of a horse approaching at the canter. The ax strokes ceased and then Will Denton, riding light and alert and casting a continually revolving inspection to all sides, came into view.

Linza stood up behind a tree, the blue eyes assuming a narrower shape. That tolerant face had gone almost dry of emotion. The lips were thin to the point of being bloodless, the lines running down from either corner lay deep as if slashed by a knife. Lifting his gun and holding the snout of it in his free palm a moment, he stared at the nearing fugitive. "I shall give him the chance he would have given me," he whispered, and stepped from the trees directly in front of Denton.

"Throw up your hands, Will!"

Denton's body seemed to spring up from the saddle, every muscle turning and twisting. The sun flashed in his eyes, the jerk of his head loosened his hat and it fell off to let a mane of sorrel hair shake loosely around his temples. Still in motion, his arm dropped, ripped the holstered gun upward and outward. Henry Linza raised his own weapon, took a cool aim at the chest broadly presented to him and fired once. Denton flinched back, sagged and fell from the saddle. There was no farewell; turning from the momentum of his fall, he stared sightlessly at the sky.

The man at the cabin let out a great cry. Linza wheeled to see him running forward in great stumbling strides and the sheriff's metal words sheared through the space. "Drop your gun right there!"

The man halted, cast his gun from him and came on, still cursing. Linza walked forward to the dead Will Denton and stared down. The outlaw's face, streaked with dirt and covered with a stubble beard, looked up with still a measure of that hot passion and that wild lawlessness that had been his at the moment of surprise. Linza's head fell lower and the figure of his one-time friend grew blurred.

"So there's the difference between his kind and mine," said Linza, trying to keep his voice clear. "He's dead—I'm alive."

The other man ran up, halted there. "He mistook the signal! I meant for him to keep away! I wasn't satisfied at all! I had a hunch something was wrong! But he got the signal twisted and come on in! Damn you, Linza!"

"No matter," grunted Linza. "Now or later—this is the end he was bound to meet. It was in the book. But it's hard to see him lyin' there."

"Yeah?" snarled the man. "Still yuh hounded him across the land and got him. It wasn't too hard to do that!"

Henry Linza's jaw came out to make him again seem as if he were biting into something. "You bet not. I will not lie and I won't dodge. Not for him or any other lawbreaker, even down to my own brother. And that goes as long as I carry this star. Go back there and get your horse. I am takin' him to Bonita for a Christian burial—as he would have done with me had he carried the star."

OLIVER LA FARGE
The Young Warrior

Oliver La Farge (1901–1963) was born a member of an elite East Coast family, and was educated at Harvard. His anthropology studies took him to New Mexico, where he became fascinated by Navajo Indian culture. La Farge's 1929 novel set amongst the Navajo, *Laughing Boy*, was an immediate best-seller and won the Pulitzer Prize. As Dee Brown, the author of *Bury My Heart at Wounded Knee*, once remarked, La Farge's Navajos 'stand amongst the first real Indians to appear in fiction'. La Farge's other Western fiction includes *The Enemy Gods* (1937) and the short story collection, *A Pause in the Desert* (1959). In addition to writing fiction (and later working as columnist for *Santa Fe New Mexican*), La Farge continued his career as an anthropologist, leading expeditions to Mexico and Guatemala. For many years he was President of the Association of American Indian Affairs.

'The Young Warrior' was first published in *Esquire* in 1938.

"WE HAD GOOD PROFIT AND good fun," he said. "Truly, we were much amused, and on the way home we laughed a lot. And I tell you that that Nantai, he is a great leader."

He was about eighteen years old, at the age when young men wish to prove themselves and to recite their exploits in the presence of young women. He sprawled beside the fire in the camp of his cousin's band, aware that he had an audience, men who had proved themselves on the warpath, old men, boys his age who had not yet gone fighting, and girls. The fire burnt generously in front of his cousin's wickeyup, he had an audience, and he had something to tell.

He wore the usual knee-high Apache moccasins, a breech-clout, a white man's coat of very fine green material, much too large for him, and a heavy turban of shining, blue silk covered with a design of small, pink and yellow flowers. Across his lap he nursed one of the new, short rifles that load from the back.

Supper was over. He had been quiet, saying nothing about himself, until at last one of the old men asked him about the war party. He lit a corn-husk cigarette. Seeing that they all waited, listening, he went on with his narrative. Now and again a man grunted approval, from time to time a woman would laugh.

We set out on foot for the Mexican settlement at Cottonwood River. There were five of us young men, and Nantai, who had agreed to come as our leader. The raid there was nothing. Most of the people had gone further east for a fiesta, so we simply took what horses we could find, a small amount of goods, and set the houses on fire. The few who were there ran away, and we did not bother hunting for them. There was really very little there, we each got a horse, that was about all. So Nantai took us to the north, to see what we could find.

The next day we came into sight of the road that runs from the far east to the big settlement at Muddy Flat. We rode to the westward, in sight of it. About noon we came up with a train of four wagons, heading west. Nantai took us around them in a circle, and showed us how to watch them.

These were Americans, and we young men were greatly interested in studying them. There were ten American men, several of their women, and two Mexicans. The wagons were drawn by oxen. We spent that day studying the party, while Nantai sent Comes Fighting to scout the back trail, and Crooked Nose ahead, to make sure that they were traveling alone, and no one would interfere with us. Sometimes we rode or walked just out of sight, watching them. Sometimes we hid in the sagebrush and let them travel by us.

They say that Americans are very great fighters. That may be so, but they are easy to scout. If one sits still and makes himself hard to see, the peaceful Indians may none-the-less see one, the Mexicans do sometimes, but the Americans almost never. It is the color of their eyes, I think. By nightfall we knew them pretty well, and after dark we came in close and enjoyed ourselves watching how they did.

Back when we were at peace with the Americans, before they tied up our chief and flogged him that time, Nantai used to go among them. Now he pointed things out to us. For instance, save for one man, they sat staring into the fire, blinding themselves. They built their fire large, here in enemy country, and they slept close to it. The one man who kept his back to the fire, there were things about his way of dressing that Nantai told us to notice. He said that that man was surely one of the Americans from Taos, the ones who go everywhere trapping beaver. Those men are dangerous, he said. It was because of the trapper that their night guard was well kept up, and it would not be easy to run off their stock. They had good saddle horses, and some mules.

When they had gone to sleep, and we had studied their way of placing their guards, we went back to a place where we could camp. There we talked over what we had seen. We were amused about a young man and woman we had watched. The woman seemed to be the daughter of an elderly man, rather fat, who rode mostly in one of the wagons. We thought he was a chief of some kind. The young man wished to court her, but her father did not like it. During the day they dropped back, behind the Mexicans who were herding the spare horses, but then the father mounted a horse, and they separated. In camp at night, they looked towards each other, and yet stayed apart. We joked about the young man's chances, and wondered what the father's objection was. The young man was well dressed, and he rode a good horse.

The next day, some of us wanted to make a quick rush for the spare horses, to see if we could drive some off. Nantai told us to be patient. We were no longer children, he said. It would be many days yet before the train came near to Muddy Flat, let us see what turned up. So we followed them again all that day, amusing ourselves with the courtship and other such matters.

The next night Crooked Nose and I were lying in wait where the young lover stood on guard, when the girl came out to see him. They whispered, hugged each other, and put their mouths together. They pushed their mouths against each other as a form of lovemaking. It seemed to us that here was a chance to take two prisoners. What sort of warrior was this who dealt with a woman while he was on war duty? His power would be destroyed, his eyes dimmed, his medicine would not protect him. It would have been easy to capture them both at those times when their faces were touching. I went off to find Nantai. He called the others, and we all crept back.

Crooked Nose came to meet us. The girl had gone back to the wagons, he said, and the young man was watchful once more. He had been so close to them that he could have touched them with his spear. They had had a long talk, and he thought that they had decided something, he said. We watched awhile longer, then went to our camp. There Crooked Nose and I described what we had seen, and we laughed about the lovemaking.

The next morning the train came to where a road branched off northwards, to the American settlement at the Silver Mine. The settlement was only a few hours' ride away, beyond a range of hills, and we knew that there were soldiers there. We were afraid that the wagons might turn that way, but they went on by.

Very shortly after that I was sitting in a clump of oaks watching the wagons pass. I saw the young man riding a chestnut horse, even better than the one he had had the day before. He dropped back, behind the spare horses, then worked over to the right, the north side of the valley, near the cliffs. He had his gun across his saddle, and acted as if he were hunting.

Pretty soon the girl rode out to the right. She, too, was well mounted, on a buckskin. She idled, looking over the country, and by and by drifted behind the oak clump in which I was hiding. As soon as she was hidden from the wagons, she whipped up her horse and rode fast to the cliffs, meeting the man in the mouth of a little canyon. I signaled to the others, then I went ahead to where I could see these two. They spoke together for a moment, then they went north, up the canyon, riding hard.

We assembled on top of the cliffs, looking down into the canyon. Nantai was pleased.

"They are running away," he said. "This afternoon, they can reach the Silver Mine; there they will marry each other. This is fine. They are bait."

He told Crooked Nose to follow well in the rear. Then he made us ride along the high ground, where the going was difficult. He had us take great care so that if anybody followed the couple, he could see no sign of an enemy on the trail.

We came to the head of the canyon, and climbed up to the flat country on top. Pretty soon we saw them. They were traveling at a steady trot now, well ahead of us. We made a wide circle around them. Then we reached a long valley, leading up to a sort of pass, a notch, where the pinõn and oak brush were thick. We went into that notch, and lay in wait there. Nantai gave us our instructions.

We could watch that couple coming towards us. It made one want to laugh. They were looking at each other much of the time while they rode; they were thinking only of each other and getting married. Then we saw Crooked Nose, slipping along behind them.

Nantai gave the mourning dove call, so Crooked Nose came up on a high place and signaled that no one was following. Then he hid himself. We lay there, thinking of the surprise we were about to cause.

They came along blindly, so close to where we lay that you could see their strange, colorless, American eyes. Then Nantai whooped and we opened fire. We put four arrows and a spear into the man, one arrow into the woman. The man came down dead. We pulled the woman off her horse. First she fought and screamed, then she stood still, then she tried to break away to get to the man, whom Nantai was scalping. Comes Fighting and Short Bow held her, the rest of us stood watching her.

We wanted to keep her until later, but Nantai said there was no time for that. He asked us, "Do you want fun or horses?" Then he put his spear through her, and Walks Slowly took the scalp. Just then Crooked Nose called like a hawk, so we knew others were coming. Nantai had us drive the two horses we had taken, and our own, on to the north through the notch, making a clear trail. Then we hid the animals, and came back to hide near the bodies.

Two men came along riding fast. One was the plump, chief man I mentioned, the woman's father. The other was the trapper. The plump man just watched the tracks and sometimes looked ahead, the trapper kept looking all about him, watching everything. We could see that he was a scout, and that we should have to lie very still when he drew near. It was he who saw the bodies first, when he was about a hundred paces away. They were partly hidden by the brush. He exclaimed, and reined in his horse.

The other man cried out. He did not stop, although the trapper called to him. He galloped right up to them, jumped off his horse, and knelt down by his daughter. We could have killed him easily then, but the trapper had dismounted, too, and was standing with his rifle ready. So we stayed quiet. How well Nantai had foreseen this, how wise he had been to make us ride in the hard going, away to one side, so that there was no sign of us, how wise to kill that girl so that we were not burdened.

When nothing had happened for a long time, the trapper came up slowly. The plump man was still kneeling, saying things in a low voice. The trapper still looked around, until he saw the tracks heading north. Then he said something to the father, and bent over, touching his shoulder.

That way, they both faced to the right, the side on which I was. We on the right lay still. Nantai, Short Bow, and Horse Frightener rose up on the other side and loosed their arrows. That was all there was to it, it was so simple.

Then we went over them for goods of value. While we were doing that, Crooked Nose came up. We were all much interested by the way the woman was dressed. Her skirt was really two skirts, one for each leg, and under it were many layers of clothing, mostly white. We examined them, wondering why anyone should make herself so uncomfortable, and joking about how hard she would be to undress. Then Nantai told us to stop fooling. We took our plunder and the captured horses, and swung back in a wide circle to the road.

We found the wagon train late in the afternoon. It had gone a few miles, and then stopped, to wait for its leader, we supposed. Now its leader and two more of its men were dead. We stayed quiet till after dark. They had fewer men to stand watch, and no one with real experience. A little before dawn two of us started shooting from one side, with the new rifles we had captured. The rest of us came along on the other side and ran off sixteen of their horses.

We met together on the south side of the valley, and rode all that day, making camp in comfort at sunset. Then we divided what we had taken.

On the back of her saddle, that woman had tied a bundle containing a dress of beautiful, smooth material. This new headband of mine—look—is a part of it. She also had more of those clothes for wearing underneath, of fine materials.

Horse Frightener put on some of them, and we joked with him. I received that headband, this coat—it belonged to the father—this new rifle that loads from the back, and four horses. Then we came home at our leisure, talking over all that we had seen, and finding much to laugh at.

JAMES WARNER BELLAH
Command

James Warner Bellah (1899–1976) was born in New York City, and studied at Georgetown, Columbia and Wesleyan Universities. He served with the Royal Air Force during World War One, and with the US Army in the Far East during World War Two, winning the Legion of Merit and the Bronze Star. It was in 1946, on his demobilisation from the army, that Bellah began writing his famous cavalry stories about Fort Starke during the Indian Wars. The director John Ford was a great admirer of Bellah, and based all of his 'cavalry trilogy' of films (*Fort Apache*. *Rio Grande*, and *She Wore a Yellow Ribbon*) on Bellah's Fort Starke stories. Bellah himself, in turn, worked on the screenplay for several of Ford's films, including *Sergeant Rutledge* (1960), which was adapted from his own magazine serial of the same title. Bellah's Western novels are: *Massacre* (1950), *The Apache* (1951), *Ordeal at Blood River* (1959), and *A Thunder of Drums* (1961).

The story 'Command' is from 1946 and was first published, like most of Bellah's Fort Starke stories, in the 'slick' magazine, *Saturday Evening Post*. Together with 'Big Hunt' (1947), the story formed the basis for *She Wore a Yellow Ribbon* (1949), in which John Wayne played the part of Captain Nathan Brittles.

SERGEANT UTTERBACK STIFFENED IN HIS saddle, staring through the yellow sundown haze at a ragged buzzard that circled low in the darkening air ahead of the little column. The only live thing in that prairie wasteland except the three dozen saddle-weary troopers and the two officers who hated each other.

A lone buffalo off there, dead after many migratory years. Dead in some stupid way of his own devising. The thought was John Utterback's. He shifted his weary loins in the saddle and spat into the dust in boredom and apathy. At the head of the halted column, Captain Brittles uncased his glasses and raised them to his eyes in both grimy hands, his gauntlets tucked under his left arm. Mr Cohill, riding back with the point, was about four hundred yards ahead of the captain, coming back toward him. Four lean troopers and the lieutenant outlined against the crimson backwash where the sun had died in agony twenty minutes before. The heads and arched necks of their mounts cut easily upward and easily downward across the sky as they came toward the column outlined sharply in a yellow band of light that touched them like St. Elmo's fire.

"Here's your best body of grass, sir. This slope, with a small run below for water. This slope is your bivouac."

You could smell the column as it stood there, still mounted, waiting. The warm flesh and leather and nitrogen of the horses. The heavy human rancidity of the men, unbathed for nine days. Utterback's mind fingered the roll from force of habit: Atkissons, Blunt, Cartter, Dannecker, Dortmunder, Eskuries, Ershick, Hertwole—and you could smell the green horror above them, thickening as the wind shifted.

"Mr Cohill"—the captain lowered his glasses and looked intently at his second in command—"do you see the rise there to the left behind you across the valley? What are those lumped shapes on the forward slope?"

Nathan Brittles was a gray man that no sun could redden for long. His eyes were agate-gray and his hair was dust-gray, and there was a grayness within him that was his own manner of living, which he discussed with no man and no man questioned. Narrow-hipped and straight-backed. Hard and slender in the leg. Taut, so that when he moved, it was almost as if he would twang. And he did—when he spoke. Not unpleasantly, with a whine, but sharply, like the breech spang of a Spencer.

Flintridge Cohill half circled his horse on the forehand and turned his head, "We started back when we saw them, sir. Sleeping buffalo. A small herd."

"Now that the wind has shifted, take a deep breath, Mr Cohill. Those aren't buffalo, Mr Cohill!" Brittles closed his glasses, cased them and swung the case behind his left hip. He was furious. The red flush of his anger throbbed in his neck muscles. "Take another deep breath, Mr Cohill! Get it in your nostrils and then tell me what's on that other slope!"

And then everyone in the column knew what was on that slope. That they weren't buffalo—either dead or sleeping. They were Mr Gresham and the nine men of the 2nd that they'd come out to find—stripped naked and pincushioned to the ground with arrows, their feet and their right hands hacked off, their bodies purpling and sweet rotten.

Futile anger crawled within Cohill—anger at himself for his inaccuracy; anger at Nathan Brittles for catching it ruthlessly and ripping it wide open—as he always did.

"This is not a schoolroom out here, Mr Cohill, in which you can fail and try again. I call it to your attention, Mr Cohill, that accuracy in observation is a military virtue. Cultivate it. . . . Sergeant Utterback, dismount and unsaddle. This is the bivouac. Graze below the actual crest of the slope, off the skyline. Night grazing area between the military crest and the creek bottom. Use the picket rope, not individual pins, after darkness. Lay it on the ground."

The captain turned slowly and looked back the long way they had come across the flat depression of Paradise Valley; looked back toward the Mesa Roja.

The amber haze of the plains, shot now with the lavender of evening, lay across the distances. Flint Cohill, watching Brittles, felt dread loneliness for a second—the emptiness of a thousand frontier miles converging on him in a vast and whirling radius. Galloping toward him on thundering hoofs, lashed by the riata of oncoming night. And he was a boy again. Back again those few brief years that would put him into the irresponsibility of boyhood once more. A boy, masquerading as a man among grown men, steel-legged in fine boots and antelope-faced trousers. Silken kerchief at his neck, gauntleted and gunned and hatted for the part he would play if they'd let him. But alone now on the empty stage, with no applause. Nothing but his aloneness and the long vista of the years ahead of him, and the echoing memory of his own anger at himself that still clung sullenly to his brain—to be justified, because of his youth, if he could justify it.

Why doesn't Brittles go across to the other slope now and make sure, instead of camping here? If it is Gresham and his men, and they are fresh dead, it's the Santee Sioux war party whose trace we crossed this morning that killed them. It pleased Flint Cohill to be able to think Santee Sioux instead of plain Sioux, as everybody usually did back in the States. That was Sergeant Utterback's doing—Sergeant Utterback going along that trace at noon until he found the broken rattle made of the ends of buffalo toes.

"Sioux, sir"—to Brittles—"Santee Sioux I'd say; about forty strong." There was no triumph in the way John Utterback had said it; only the patience of long service and the acceptance of a fact. Utterback had stood there on foot, looking up at the captain, the broken rattle end in his hand. A modest, thin-faced man, John Utterback. Slope-shouldered almost to deformity, but secure in the system that had made him, knowing the things that he knew, beyond all shadow of doubt and all human timidity, moving quietly within the laws of his life and fearing no man to best him or break him.

Brittles had said, "Or Cheyenne, Utterback. They make rattles much the same. Or Comanches. Or Arapaho. Mount up!"

In memory again, Cohill's silent anger lashed out at Nathan Brittles in the gathering dusk. A stickler for detail and accuracy, even probably if it sacrificed the over-all plan.

That Indian trace was fifteen miles back. With the Sioux making approximately the same rate of march that they were, their wickiups would be no more than thirty miles to the northward. Less, Cohill remembered his teaching suddenly. If they were Sioux, they'd camp away from timber—with their mortal dread of ambush—and near water. They'd be along the Paradise's upper reaches—in the dead lands.

Cohill blurted it suddenly, "Two hours' rest and we can be on the upper reaches of the Paradise by dawn, sir."

"Mr Cohill, I have no orders to be on anyone or anything by dawn or at any other time. My orders are to find Mr Gresham's patrol"—Brittles threw a leg off his animal and dismounted—"and finding him, to go back in to Fort Starke and report it. I think I've found him. I'll know, as soon as the moon rises and I go over and look. Take evening stables. Water in a half an hour. Saddle blankets left on until after the mounts are watered. Remember always, Mr Cohill, that because of the liability to deterioration of the horses, cavalry is a very delicate arm of the service."

There was this in Cohill—that, spurred to the bleeding quick, he still would not talk back. But his mind raced in futile anger, *He's an old woman and he can't hold his temper. Little things infuriate him, but with a big chance like this, he's going to cut and run back in. In a stiff action, I'd probably have to kill him and take over the command.*

Brittles turned again and said, "Mr Cohill, reading minds is an uncomfortable habit." Flint stared and moved his arm imperceptibly toward his revolving pistol. "But suppose for a moment they were Cheyennes, which they well might be, instead of Santee Sioux, they wouldn't be in the dead lands, you see. They'd head for the timber along the lower Mesa Roja branch. So would Arapaho. Kiowas or Comanches would bivouac right in the open timber . . . and they all make rattles out of buffalo toes! Pass the word to Sergeant Utterback that dinner call will be at six-thirty, but the trumpeter will still not sound calls. Mr Cohill, there is no short cut to the top of the glory heap. So we'll not run all over the West tonight looking for one."

To some of them for the rest of their lives, the full moon, rising red gold on the horizon, would bring back what they saw that night, and what they heard, for the dead can whisper restlessly when the cool evening air contracts stiffened diaphragms. By the empty cartridge cases, Gresham's men had sold out dearly—sold out until the panther rush flattened and shredded them across the forward slope of the rise in a ferocious effort to rip their white dignity from them by savage mutilation.

"Whoever did it never wants to meet Mr Gresham's patrol again," Sergeant Utterback growled; "that's why they lopped off their hands and feet to handicap them in case they meet in the Hereafter. They respected them as fighting men—every mother's son is left bald-headed, so he can cross the Shadow Waters without trouble."

The burial shovels were chattering in the hillside shale. Captain Brittles said, "Utterback, do you still think Santee Sioux?"

Sergeant Utterback stood quietly looking off toward the southwest. The moonlight was a limitless white wash across the sea of mist.

"No, sir. Not now, sir."

"Why not?" Brittles snapped. "Speak up!"

Flint Cohill turned toward them, listening intently.

"I made the march from Bent's Fort to Santa Fe with Steve Kearny, and I know an Apache arrow when I see one, sir, even a thousand miles from where they're made."

"Your Sioux of this noon could have brushed with an Apache war party"—Brittles nodded toward the southwest—"and come by Apache arrows that way."

"No." Utterback shook his head. "This job is two days old. It wasn't this morning's Sioux. It's an Apache job."

"How do you reason that?"

"Mostly"—Utterback smiled faintly—"because the captain knows it's Apache work, too, not Sioux work."

Brittles looked at his first sergeant, studying his eyes carefully. "I shall want to move the command out by ten tonight. We go back in to Fort Starke with this word as fast as we can get in."

"Yes, sir."

"When the graves are cairned, Sergeant Utterback, fall the burial party in for services."

". . . for Thine is the kingdom and the power and the glory forever and ever, amen."

The moon was high and small and frozen crystal above the column as it moved out for Fort Starke. Thirty miles already that day, with no knowing how many night miles Brittles would pile up on top of them. Plenty. The order was to halt fifteen minutes in the hour, dismount and unbit for grazing. The order was to trot five minutes after every half hour of walking, to avoid animal fatigue from bad carriage in the saddle, and the liability to sore backs. The order was to dismount and lead, ten minutes in every hour. Walk, trot, lead, halt and graze—and at two in the morning Brittles halted on the Paradise for twenty-five full minutes for watering call.

Flintridge Cohill trudged along, leading, alkali white to mid-thigh. His spurs, dust muffled, sounded like silver dollars clinked deep in the pocket of a greatcoat. He could feel the resentment in the men—resentment at the night march. It was a hard and a sullen thing; and it was there in an occasional angry sneeze, in the dust coughing that became general after a while in spite of long intervals, in a deep and throaty curse rolled into the night on dry saliva.

Cohill could feel the swing and thrust of Sergeant Utterback's legs beside him; he could smell Utterback's rank gaminess above his own, cut by the sweet brownness of the sergeant's eating tobacco, all of it washed hot and cleanly sulphurous by a horse ahead. All of it rushing back again, to be breathed again against the cooling curtain of the dying night.

"Pass the word to mount." It came down the column like cards falling from a table edge, and Utterback, swinging up, stood high for a second in his stirrups. "He's heading up north."

"How's that, sergeant?"

"North," Utterback said.

Cohill pulled his hat brim down under the dying moon and looked high to the horizon, toward Mesa Roja. "You're right." He meant to put a question into it, but if he put one in, Utterback ignored it.

Cohill sat with it for a moment, settling himself to the cold saddle, turning, looking back at the dust-white masks of the faces in the moonlight. The lean-jawed faces and the hard faces. The brutal faces and the weak. The hopeful faces and the finished faces—Jordin, Knight, Lusk, Mallory, Mittendorffer, Norton and Opdyke—and as far as he could see the faces back of him, he knew that they knew that the Old Man was heading up north, and that they questioned it. The flat top of Mesa Roja was dead ahead on the line of march. And it didn't make sense. If they were going back in, fast, to Fort Starke to report an Apache war party—going back in a straight line across their own nine-day circle by a forced night march—Mesa Roja should bear on their left shoulders, not between their mounts' ears.

And then Cohill knew, and his mind was cold and taut with the knowledge, and he was ashamed suddenly for the traditions that had made him, but that could so fail other men.

Brittles had an Apache war party up from the southwest and Gresham's death at their hands to report. So he was forcing the march in to Starke, but in the midst of forcing it, he was taking good care that he gave this morning's Santee Sioux a wide berth. He wouldn't fight if it was handed to him! He was afraid to fight—afraid of himself probably. Knew himself for what Cohill was finding him out to be—superannuated, petty, nerve-racked and afraid.

What we all come to understand sooner or later, Mr Cohill, is that we're not out here to fight Indians. We're out here to watch them and report on them for the Indian Bureau. We fight only if they attack us. I refer you to departmental standing orders, which are most explicit.

Gresham fought, damn you. He had no choice but to fight.

Mr Gresham was young. Probably he was extremely rash.

And you are old, and not fit for this job any longer. If they are really Apaches, it's your duty to cut straight in to Starke and report it. But if they turned out to be those same Santee Sioux—as they well might, for all you really know to the contrary—you could force their attack on a technicality and wipe them out in punishment on the way in. This stupid way—we march all day and march all night, and we're still miles from home, with worn and sullen men and tired animals, and nothing to show for it but a sop to your old man's caution. Cavalry is a delicate arm.

Cohill was conscious that his lips were moving contemptuously with his silent monologue. He covered them with his hand as Utterback turned and looked at him.

"Sergeant, how did you know the captain thought they were Apaches that killed Mr Gresham's detail?"

"I've been his first sergeant for a long time. You get to know."

"I see. Do I get to know?"

"Mr Cohill, the captain's been out here a good many years."

"You're not answering me, is that it? If it's all the same to me, you fell up a tree?"

"No use talking. It ain't learned ever. It's lived. It's a feeling, after all's said and done, sir."

"And you're sure yourself it's an Apache party?"

"Reasonably, only I wouldn't hold to it alone. But I'm dead sure when I know Captain Brittles is sure too. He earns the difference in our pay, sir."

Cohill threw up his head in annoyance. Five hours on the way now. A shade less than three left to dawn. They'd make the foot of the mesa and bivouac there probably, hitting the trail again in the afternoon. What a fool procedure, when the whole command could have been freshened by a night's sleep and grazing after the burial detail.

The moon grew colder and slid down the sky behind them. Knees were thick now and sanded with fatigue, and there was the clamminess of dank sweat in their shirts that their bodies no longer warmed. Mist tatters wove above the prairie, girth high, and in the hollows chilled them with the hand of death. Flintridge heard his name passed softly down the column, "Mr Cohill," and he kneed out to the right and cantered forward.

Brittles sat straight in his saddle, cut there like stone, outlined against the night sky, nose and chin and shoulder—an aging man, riding out his destiny. "Mr Cohill, this is officer's call. Listen carefully. I have Sergeant Sutro ahead of me with the point. You will relieve him with eight men, and push forward fast. Do you recall the ford on the Mesa Roja branch?"

"I do, sir."

"There is a knoll on the mesa side—a knoll that the trail crosses from the mesa top."

"I remember."

"Be there prior to dawn. Build a bivouac fire on your arrival."

"Do what, sir?"

"I want to know it, when you get there. And I want everyone else for miles around to know it, too. Build a bivouac fire. A squad fire. No larger."

"But I can send a file back to tell you when I arrive."

"Disabuse yourself of the idea that this is a debating society, Mr Cohill. In the event of an attack on your position, you will hold the knoll top, fighting on foot. Always hold your fire at dawn to the last possible moment. Remember, the dawn light works for you, but it can fool you in the first half hour in this country. Move out, Mr Cohill. You're the bait on my hook. Wriggle . . . and keep alive!"

High overhead under the rim of Mesa Roja there was an eagle scream in the chilled darkness. The whipsaw blade of it grated down Flint Cohill's damp spine. His lips were drawn thin across his dry teeth. "Don't stand still, Skinnor. Move a little all the time. Move always. Slap the mounts. Keep moving them too." Soft. Words lashed whisper-high across the knoll—whisper-high and rowel-sharp.

The little squad fire burned brightly, and the tired animals held the echo of its gold in the moist jewels of their eyes. Skinnor and Blankenship were with the horses, moving them, keeping them circling their picket pins, ready to cut them free and stampede them. Corporal McKenzie and his five men lay just beyond the wash of light, fanned out behind their flung saddles, waiting and watching and listening and breathing softly. Mr Cohill was wriggling beautifully on the hook.

A great feathery exultation pressed its soft hands upward under his lower ribs, catching his breath every time he drew it. Here, then, is the justification—the final heritage of soldiering—to stand steady, ready to deliver, to bleed and to draw blood. Everything else is the parade ground. And he was afraid for his first shots in anger. His fear was livid and gasping behind the drawn curtain at the back of his mind. To fire and to draw fire. To kill and to be killed. And he could hear the panic whimper of his fear behind its curtain. "Mr Cohill, this is not a schoolroom out here."

Some weed, some bitter prairie flower freshening on the dawn winds, feathered his nostrils, and, with association, brought back the green horror in the moonlight that they had put decently below the ground thirty miles back across the plains.

The play went on. The trap was good. Carefully acted. Cohill crossed into the firelight, and out of it again. Always moving. The natural movement of a small bivouac. Carneal put the spider on, crisping and richening the clean air with the smell of frying bacon.

Neither Sioux nor Apache nor any Plains Indian will fight willingly at night, for a warrior killed in darkness wanders up and down the outer world forever, eternally blind in darkness. But in a little while the dawn would creep across from the eastward, and there on the knoll was a small white-soldier war party like two-yesterdays' party that lay bloating where they had overwhelmed it thirty miles down Paradise Valley. Fire alight and bacon cooking. Mounts unsaddled and warriors sleeping from a long night march to bring back the death news of the other party. Soft for the killing.

Down, then, from the mesa rim silently. Down in the last black darkness on shadow feet. With the ponies led carefully, so that not a stone could chip and skip and arch on ahead in chattering cascade to herald the approach. Not a twig must snap.

Suddenly Flint Cohill could see the pewter trace of the Mesa Roja branch below him. He could see tree boles and the shiny black dampness of a stomped hoof in dew-drenched grass and the grime on the back of his own hand. And it was the dawn opening slowly, like the reflexive lid of a dead eyeball. Then a horse screamed in bowel-torn agony, and three animals were down, thrashing. Skinnor crawled out, dragging a splintered shin bone, cursing in high falsetto. And the air was alive with whiplashing, but no lash cracks. Just the intake gasp, unfinished, threatening. Cruel and thin as the bite of a bone saw.

"Hold your fire, Corporal McKenzie!" Cohill was belly-down in the soaking grass. Five of his horses were running free, fear driven and panic blind. Then the air ripped alive with the war shriek and the gray dawn was throbbing with a thundering rush. So close that it was on them. So close that it was over them. So close that Cohill screamed the order to fire, and they fired, and the wave broke like a brown sea wave on an emerald beach, crested before them on the slope of the knoll, curled mightily upward and crashed over and toward them with the weight of its own speed. Rolling in a spume of thrashing pony hoofs and of torn and howling throats and an agony of shattered bone.

"They are Apaches!"

Those behind broke away and to the left, and passed below the knoll, circling to re-form and roar up again toward the knoll top. Brown oiled bodies hard down on the off-side of ponies, galloping into the teeth of the dawn wind. And the men on the knoll saw them now for the Gresham massacre party, for there were yellow stripes on the legs of some, with the seat and the front cut from the trousers; and there were sabers and yellow silken neckerchiefs and the brass buckles of belts and bandoleers.

Round again and up again frantically into the flaming scythe of Cohill's fire. And again, as they took it, breaking and circling, but this time raggedly bunched, with free ponies racing among them. Cut down to half their number. Torn and bleeding, whirling across the whitening dawn. Battered in their strength, broken and hacked into. Shrieking now in anger and the primitive hurt of animals—frustrated tigers of the Plains.

The raucous brass file of the trumpet scratched across the gunmetal of the new day, and Nathan Brittles' main body came up out of the bottoms of the Mesa Roja branch, splashed hoof-deep across the lower ford and charging as foragers, struck them on their shattered flank, parched sabers drawn and drinking. There was a long and racing moment down the bottoms, horse to horse and man to man, below Cohill's knoll. A red moment of fury. Steel and flesh and livid madness with the black lash of the devil in it to whip it to frenzied crescendo.

Cohill stood above, his shirt black with sweat, watching the bitter finish, the last flaming action and the last free pony pistoled off its flashing hoofs. Below him on the knoll there was a writhing Apache hurling himself up off his dead hips and legs, thrashing his upper body in madness to free himself from the icy shackles of his broken spine. Noiselessly thrashing, like a snake dismembered. And to the left, there was Corporal McKenzie, lying blue-faced and quiet, his hands close to the feathered shaft that was sunk deep in his right side below the ribs—hands rising and falling with the last of his breathing. And Skinnor, with the twisted bloat of his leg stretched out naked before him, smoking evenly on his black-stubbed pipe watching the sun wash that reddened the horizon.

"Mr Cohill, you did that well." Nathan Brittles swung down and plunged his face and hands in the wet grass to clean them and freshen himself. He opened his matted shirt to the waist and tugged it over his head. "You may do. In time."

"You knew they were Apaches yesterday at sundown . . . and you knew they were camped on the mesa top, sir?"

"Mr Cohill,"—Brittles swabbed his bare chest with his shirttail—"Apaches fear only man. They camp as high as they can get, no matter how far it is from water. Had you pushed forward to Mr Gresham's slope, you would have found Mr Gresham, not sleeping buffalo. Had your eyes been sharp, you would have seen this between the slope and last evening's bivouac." Brittles dug a hand deep into his pocket and tugged out a blood-hardened shred of Apache headband of red flannel and handed it over. "Commit it to your diary and your brain." Brittles pulled on his shirt again, "And had you been a plainsman and suspected the Apache, you would have looked at once for smoke at sundown on the highest ground—Mesa Roja."

Cohill's quick admiration was in his eyes, in his blurted words, "You came straight here, sir, to hole them out and pay them off for Gresham. You had no intention of anything else, from the start, but to force the fight." He grinned. "You even had Utterback fooled, until you turned north."

The captain stood quite still for a moment, looking Flint Cohill over very carefully, as if he had never seen him before. "The essence of command is timing, Mr Cohill. A successful commander keeps his own counsel until the right moment. At that time he tells his subordinates everything they should know to do their part of the work properly. Nothing more. My intention was to fool no one. Sergeant Utterback is a soldier. He keeps his mouth shut. The facts are these: My point, temporarily bivouacked at dawn today, came under sudden enemy attack. Fortunately, it was able to hold until I arrived with the main body."

Cohill drew himself up and bowed slightly. "I understand that, sir, perfectly. I am familiar with departmental standing orders which allow defensive actions only, and expressly forbid the attack."

"And yet"—Captain Brittles' eyes never wavered from Cohill's—"they are in direct violation of cavalry tactics, for cavalry is very weak on the defensive. It can defend itself well only by attacking. Most young lieutenants will agree with that, whether or not they examine the reasons."

"I am desperately sorry, sir."

"Mr Cohill, never apologize. It's a mark of weakness. There is a captain out here who tried it once to escape a Benzine Board. He escaped it, but he's been ashamed a little bit ever since. He will die a captain, in spite of his apology. The man who did for him could have worked with him and made him a soldier, if his humanity had been large enough. Mr Cohill, I'm going to make a soldier out of you, if you don't break. You may present my respects to General Cohill when next you write your father. Mr Cohill, take morning stables."

FRANK BONHAM
Burn Him Out

Frank Bonham (1914–1988) was born in Los Angeles, California. He wanted to be a writer from his earliest childhood, and sold his first story, a mystery, in 1936. Soon afterwards he became secretary (in fact, ghostwriter) to the pulp writer, Ed Earl Repp. After three years the relationship ended, and Bonham became a prolific contributor to the pulp and digest magazines in his own right, often writing as many as half a million words a year. Bonham, however, was more than prolific. By the 1950s there was no better writer of formulary Westerns to be found. In addition to his hundreds of short stories, Bonham also wrote eighteen Western novels—among them *Lost Stage Valley* (1948) and *Snaketrack* (1952)—and contributed storylines to such classic TV Western shows as *Tales of Wells Fargo*. Bonham was also an accomplished author of teenage fiction (his 1965 novel, *Durango Street*, was awarded the George G. Stone Centre for Children's Books Award), and detective stories.

'Burn Him Out' was first published in the digest magazine *Argosy* in 1949.

WILL STARRETT SQUATTED BEFORE THE campfire in the creek bottom, drinking his coffee and watching the other men over the rim of his tin cup. In the strong light from the fire, the sweat and the dirt and the weariness made harsh masks of their faces. They were tired men. But pushing up through their fatigue was a growing restlessness. Now and then, a man's face was lost in heavy shadow as he turned away to talk with a neighbor. A head nodded vigorously, and the buzz of talk grew louder. To Starrett, listening, it was like the hum a tin of water makes as it comes to a boil. The men were growing impatient now, and drawing confidence from each other. Snatches of talk rose clearly. Without the courtesy of direct address, they were telling Tim Urban what to do.

Starrett swirled his cup to raise the sugar from the bottom and studied Urban coldly. The man leaned against the wheel of a wagon, looking cornered. He held a cup of coffee in his hand and his puffy face was mottled with sweat and dirt. On his hands and forearms was the walnut stain of grasshopper excrement. He was a man for whom Starrett felt only mild contempt. Urban was afraid to make his own decisions, and yet unable to accept outside advice. The land on which he stood, and on which they had worked all day, was Urban's. The decision about the land was his, too. But because he hesitated, so obviously, other voices were growing strong with eagerness to make up his mind for him. Tom Cowper was the most full-throated of the twenty-five who had fought the grasshoppers since dawn.

"If the damned poison had only come!" he said. "We could have been spreading it tonight and maybe had them stopped by noon. Since it ain't come, Tim—" He scowled and shook his head. "We're going to have to concoct some other poison just as strong."

"What would that be?" Starrett struck a match and shaped the orange light with his hands.

Cowper, a huge man with a purplish complexion, badger-gray hair and tufted sideburns, pondered without meeting Starrett's eyes, and answered without opening his mind.

"Well, we've got time to think of something, or they'll eat this country right down to bedrock. We're only three miles from your own land right now. The hoppers didn't pasture on Urban's grass because they liked the taste of it. They just happened to land here. Once they get a start, or a wind comes up, they'll sweep right down the valley. We've got to stop them here."

Will Starrett looked at him and saw a big angry-eyed man worrying about his land as he might have worried about any investment. To him, land was a thing to be handled like a share of railroad stock. You bought it when prices were low, you sold it when prices were high. Beyond this, there was nothing to say about it.

When Starrett did not answer him, Cowper asked, "What is there to do that we haven't already done? If we can't handle them here on Tim's place, how can we handle them on our own?"

They all knew the answer to that, Starrett thought. Yet they waited for someone else to say it. It was Tim Urban's place to speak, but he lacked the guts to do it. Starrett dropped the match and tilted his chin as he drew on the cigarette. The fire's crackling covered the far-off infinite rattling of the grasshoppers, the night covered the sight of them. But they were still there in every man's mind, a hated, crawling plague sifting the earth like gold-seekers.

They were there with their retching green smell and their racket, as of a herd of cattle in a dry cornfield. Across two miles of good bunch-grass land they had squirmed, eating all but a few weeds, stripping leaves and bark from the trees. They had dropped from the sky upon Urban's home place the night before, at the end of a hot July day. They had eaten every scrap of harness in the yard, gnawed fork-handles and corral bars, chewed the paint off his house and left holes where onions and turnips had been in his garden.

By night, four square miles of his land had been destroyed, his only stream was coffee-colored with hopper excrement. And the glistening brown insects called Mormon crickets were moving on toward the valley's heart as voraciously as though wagonloads of them had not been hauled to a coulee all day and cremated in brush fires. And no man knew when a new hatch of them might come across the hills.

Starrett frowned. He was a dark-faced cattleman with a look of seasoned toughness, a lean and sober man, who in his way was himself a creature of the land. "Well, there's one thing," he said.

"What's that?" Cowper asked.

"We could pray."

Cowper's features angered, but it was his foreman, Bill Hamp, who gave the retort. "Pray for seagulls, like the Mormons?"

"The Mormons claim they had pretty good luck."

With an angry flourish, Hamp flung the dregs of his coffee on the ground. He was a drawling, self-confident Missourian, with truculent pale eyes and a brown mustache. The story was that he had marshaled some cowtown a few years ago, or had been a gunman in one of them.

He had been Cowper's ramrod on his other ranches in New Mexico and Colorado, an itinerant foreman who suited Cowper. He did all Cowper asked of him—kept the cows alive until the ranch could be resold at a profit. To Hamp, a ranch was something you worked on, from month to month, for wages. Land, for him, had neither beauty nor dimension.

But he could find appreciation for something tangibly beautiful like Tom Cowper's daughter, Lynn. And because Starrett himself had shown interest in Lynn, Bill Hamp hated him—hated him because Starrett was in a position to meet her on her own level.

Hamp kept his eyes on Starrett. "If Urban ain't got the guts to say it," he declared, "I have. Set fires! Burn the hoppers out!" He made a sweeping gesture with his arm.

Around the fire, men began to nod. Urban's rabbity features quivered. "Bill, with the grass dry as it is I'd be burned out!"

Hamp shrugged. "If the fire don't get it, the hoppers will," he said.

Cowper sat there, slowly nodding his head. "Tim, I don't see any other way. We'll backfire and keep it from getting out of hand."

"I wouldn't count on that," Starrett said.

"It's take the risk or accept catastrophe," Cowper declared. "And as far as its getting out of hand goes, there's the county road where we could stop it in a pinch."

"Best to run off a strip with gangplows as soon as we set the fires," Hamp said. He looked at Starrett with a hint of humor. Downwind from Tim Urban's place at the head of the valley was Starrett's. Beyond that the other ranches sprawled over the prairie. Hamp was saying that there was no reason for anyone to buck this, because only Urban could lose by the fire.

Starrett said nothing and the opinions began to come.

Finally Cowper said, "I think we ought to take a vote. How many of you are in favor of setting fires? Let's see hands on it."

There were twenty men in the creek bottom. Cowper counted fourteen in favor. "The rest of you against?"

All but Starrett raised their hands. Hamp regarded him. "Not voting?"

"No. Maybe you'd like to vote on a proposition of mine."

"What's that?"

"That we set fire to Cowper's ranch house first."

Cowper's face contorted. "Starrett, we've got grief enough without listening to poor jokes!"

"Burning other men's grass is no joke. This is Urban's place, not yours or mine. I'm damned if any man would burn me out by taking a vote."

Bill Hamp sauntered to the wagon and placed his foot against a wheelhub. "Set by and let ourselves be eaten out—is that your idea?"

"Ourselves?" Starrett smiled.

Hamp flushed. "I may not own land, but I make my living from it."

"There's a difference, Hamp. You need to sweat ten years for a down payment before you know what owning an outfit really means. Then you'd know that if a man would rather be eaten out than burned out, it's his own business."

Hamp regarded him stonily and said, "Are you going to stand there and say we can't fire the place to save the rest?"

Starrett saw the the men's eyes in the firelight, some apprehensive, some eager, remembering the stories about Bill Hamp and his cedar-handled .45. "No," he said. "I didn't say that."

Hamp, after a moment, let a smile loosen his mouth. But Starrett was saying, "I've got nothing against firing, but everything against deciding it for somebody else. Nobody is going to make up Urban's mind for him, unless he agrees to it."

Urban asked quickly, "What would you do, Will?"

It was not the answer Starrett wanted. "I don't know," he said. "What are you going to do?"

Urban knew an ally when he saw one. He straightened, spat in the fire, and with his thumbs hooked in the riveted corners of his jeans pockets, stared at Cowper. "I'm going to wait till morning," he said. "If the poison don't come—and if it don't rain or the wind change—I may decide to fire. Or I may not."

Information passed from Cowper to Bill Hamp, traveling on a tilted eyebrow. Hamp straightened like a man stretching slowly and luxuriously. In doing so, his coat was pulled back ana the firelight glinted on his cartridge belt. "Shall we take that vote again, now that Mr Starrett's finished stumping?" he asked.

Starrett smiled. "Come right down to it, I'm even principled against such a vote."

Hamp's dark face was stiff. The ill-tempered eyes held the red catchlights of the fire. But he could not phrase his anger for a moment, and Starrett laughed. "Go ahead," he said. "I've always wondered how much of that talk was wind."

Cowper came in hastily. "All right, Bill! We've done all we can. It's Urban's land. As far as I'm concerned, he can fight the crickets himself." He looked at Starrett. "We'll know where to lay the blame if things go wrong."

He had brought seven men with him. They got up, weary, unshaven cowpunchers wearing jeans tied at the bottoms to keep the grasshoppers from crawling up their legs. Cowper found his horse and came back, mounted.

"You'll be too busy to come visit us for a while." His meaning was clear—he was speaking of his daughter. "As for the rest of it—I consider that a very dangerous principle you've laid down. I hope it never comes to a test when the hoppers have the land next to *mine*."

They slept a few hours. During the night a light rain fell briefly. Starrett lay with his head on his saddle, thinking of the men he had so nearly fought with.

Cowper would sacrifice other men's holdings to protect his own. That was his way. Urban would protest feebly over being ruined with such haste, but he would probably never fight. Hamp was more flexible. His actions were governed for the time by Cowper's. But if it came to a showdown, if the hoppers finished Urban and moved a few miles east onto Starrett's land, this dislike that had grown into a hate might have its airing.

Starrett wished Cowper had been here longer. Then the man might have understood what he was trying to say. That land was not shares of stock, not just dirt with grass growing on it. It was a bank, a feedlot, a reservoir. The money, the feed, the water were there as long as you used them wisely. But spend them prodigally, and they vanished. Your cattle gaunted down, your graze died. You were broke. But after you went back to punching cows or breaking horses, the grass came back, good as ever, for a wiser cowman to manage.

It was a sort of religion, this faith in the land. How could you explain it to a man who gypsied around taking up the slack in failing ranches by eliminating extra hands, dispensing with a useless horse-herd, and finally selling the thing at a profit?

Ranching was a business with Cowper and Hamp, not a way of life.

Just at dawn the wind died. The day cleared. An hour later, as they were riding, armed with shovels, into the blanket of squirming hoppers to shovel tons of them into the wagons and dozers, a strong wind rose. It was coming from the north, a warm, vigorous breeze that seemed to animate the grasshoppers. Little clouds of them rose and flew a few hundred yards and fell again. And slowly the earth began to shed them, the sky absorbed their rattling weight and they moved in a low cloud toward the hills. Soon the land was almost clean. Where they had passed in their crawling advance, the earth was naked, with only a few clumps of brush and skeletal trees left.

Urban leaned on the swell of his saddle by both elbows. He swallowed a few times. Then he said softly, like a man confessing a sin, "I prayed last night, Will. I prayed all night."

"Then figure this as the first installment on an answer. But this is grasshopper weather. They're coming out of the earth by the million. Men are going to be ruined if they come back out of the brush, and if the wind changes, they will. Don't turn down that poison if it comes."

That day Starrett rode into Antelope. From the station master he learned that Tim Urban's poison had not come. A wire had come instead, saying that the poison had proved too dangerous to handle and suggesting that Urban try Epsom salts. Starrett bought all the Epsom salts he could find—a hundred pounds. Then he bought a ton of rock salt and ordered it dumped along the county road at the southwest border of his land.

He had just ridden out of the hot, shallow canyon of the town and turned down toward the river when he saw a flash of color on the bridge, among the elms. He came down the dusty slope to see a girl in green standing at the rail. She stood turning her parasol as she watched him drop the bridle-reins and come toward her.

"Imagine!" Lynn smiled. "Two grown men fighting over grasshoppers!"

Will held her hand, warm and small in the fragile net of her glove. "Well, not exactly. We were really fighting over foremen. Hamp puts some of the dangedest ideas in Tom's head."

"The way I heard it some ideas were needed last night."

"Not that kind. Hamp was going to ram ruination down Urban's throat."

"You have more tact than I thought," she told him. "It's nice of you to keep saying, 'Hamp.' But isn't that the same as saying 'Tom Cowper?'"

He watched the creek dimple in the rain of sunlight through the leaves. "I've been hoping it wouldn't be much longer. I could name a dozen men who'd make less fuss and get more done than Hamp. If Urban had made the same suggestion to your father, Hamp would have whipped him."

She frowned. "But if Urban had had the courage, he'd have suggested firing himself, wouldn't he? Was there any other way to protect the rest of us?"

"I don't think he was as much concerned about the rest of us as about himself. You've never seen wildfire, have you? I've watched it travel forty miles an hour. July grass is pure tinder. If we'd set fires last night, Tim would have been out of business this morning. And of course the hardest thing to replace would have been his last fifteen years."

"I know," she said. But he knew she didn't. She'd have an instinctive sympathy for Urban, he realized. She was that kind of woman. But she hadn't struggled with the land. She couldn't know what the loss of Urban's place would have meant to him.

"They won't come back, will they?" she asked.

He watched a rider slope unhurriedly down the hill toward them. "If they do, and hit me first, I hope to be ready for them. Or maybe they'll pass me up and land on Tom . . . Or both of us. Why try to figure it?"

She collapsed the parasol and put her hands out to him. "Will—try to understand us, won't you? Dad doesn't want to be a rebel, but if he makes more fuss than you like it's only because he's feeling his way. He's never had a ranch resist him the way this one has. Of course, he bought it just at the start of a drought, and it hasn't really broken yet."

"I'll make you a bargain." Will smiled. "I'll try to understand the Cowpers if they'll do the same for me."

She looked up at him earnestly. "I do understand you—in most things. But then something happens like last night and I wonder if I understand you any better than I do some Comanche brave."

"Some Comanches," he said, "like their squaws blonde. That's the only resemblance I know of."

The horseman on the road came past a peninsula of cotton-woods and they saw it was Bill Hamp. Hamp's wide mouth pulled into a stiff line when he saw Starrett. He hauled his horse around, shifting his glance to Lynn. "Your father's looking all over town for you, Miss Lynn."

She smiled. "Isn't he always? Thanks, Bill." She opened the parasol and laid it back over her shoulder. "Think about it, Will. He can be handled, but not with a spade bit."

She started up the hill. Hamp lingered to roll a cigarette. He said, "One place he can't be handled is where she's concerned."

"He hasn't kicked up much fuss so far," said Starrett.

Hamp glanced at him, making an effort, Starrett thought, to hold the reasonless fury out of his eyes. "If you want peace with him as a neighbor, don't try to make a father-in-law out of him."

Starrett said, "Is this him talking, or you, Bill?"

"It's me that's giving the advice, yes," Hamp snapped. "I'd hate to ram it down your throat, but if you keep him riled up with your moonshining around . . ."

Starrett hitched his jeans up slowly, his eyes on the ramrod.

Lynn had stopped on the road to call to Hamp, and Hamp stared wordlessly at Will and turned to ride after her.

As he returned to the ranch, Starrett thought, *If there's any danger in him, it's because of her.*

Starrett spread the salt in a wide belt along the foothills. Every morning he studied the sky, but the low, dark cloud did not reappear. Once he and Cowper met in town and rather sheepishly had a drink. But Bill Hamp drank a little farther down the bar and did not look at Starrett.

Starrett rode home that evening feeling better. Well, you did not live at the standpoint of crisis, and it was not often that something as dramatic as a grasshopper invasion occurred to set neighbors at each other's throats. He felt almost calm, and had so thoroughly deceived himself that when he reached the cutoff and saw the dark smoke of locusts sifting down upon the foothills in the green afterlight he stared a full ten seconds without believing his eyes.

He turned his horse and rode at a lope to his home place. He shouted at the first puncher he saw, "Ride to Urban's for the dozers!" and sent the other three to the nearest ranches for help. Then he threw some food in a sack and, harnessing a team, drove toward the hills.

There was little they could do that night, other than prepare for the next day. The hoppers had landed in a broad and irregular mass like a pear-shaped birthmark on the earth, lapping into the foothills, touching the road, spreading across a curving mile-and-a half front over the corner of Will Starrett's land.

By morning, eighteen men had gathered, a futile breastplate to break the hoppers' spearhead. Over the undulating grassland spread the plague of Mormon crickets. They had already crossed the little area of salt Starrett had spread. If they had eaten it, it had not hurt them. They flowed on, crawling, briefly flying, swarming over trees to devour the leaves in a matter of moments, to break the branches by sheer weight and strip the bark away.

The men tied cords about the bottoms of their jeans, buttoned their shirt collars, and went out to shovel and curse. Fires were started in coulees. The dozers lumbered to them with their brown-bleeding loads of locusts. Wagonloads groaned up to the bank and punchers shoveled the squirming masses into the gully. Tom Cowper was there with Hamp and a few others.

He said tersely, "We'll lick them, Will." He was gray as weathered board.

But they all knew this was just a prelude to something else. That was as far as their knowledge went. They knew an army could not stop the grasshoppers. Only a comprehensive thing like fire could do that. . . .

They fought all day and until darkness slowed the hoppers' advance. Night brought them all to their knees. They slept, stifled by the smoke of grasshoppers sizzling in the coulees. In the morning Starrett kicked the campfire coals and threw on wood. Then he looked around.

They were still there. Only a high wind that was bringing a scud of rain clouds gave him hope. Rain might stop the hoppers until they could be raked and burned. But this rain might hold off for a week, or a wind might tear the clouds to rags.

There was rage in him. He wanted to fight them physically, to hurt these filthy invaders raping his land.

When he turned to harness his team, he saw Bill Hamp bending over the coffee pot, dumping in grounds. Hamp set the pot in the flames and looked up with a taunt in his eyes. Starrett had to discipline his anger to keep it from swerving foolishly against the ramrod.

The wind settled against the earth and the hoppers began to move more rapidly. The fighters lost a half-mile in two hours. They were becoming panicky now, fearing the locusts would fly again and cover the whole valley.

At noon they gathered briefly. Starrett heard Hamp talking to a puncher. He heard the word "gangplows" before the man turned and mounted his horse. He went over to Hamp. "What do we want with gangplows?"

"We might as well be prepared." Hamp spoke flatly.

"For what?" Cowper frowned.

"In case you decide to fire, Mr Starrett," said Hamp, "and it gets out of hand."

"Shall we put it to a vote?" Starrett asked. An irrational fury was mounting through him, shaking his voice.

"Whenever you say." Hamp drew on his cigarette, enjoying both the smoke and the situation.

Starrett suddenly stepped into him, slugging him in the face. Hamp went down and turned over, reaching for his gun. Starrett knelt quickly with a knee in the middle of his back and wrenched the gun away. He moved back, and as the foreman came up he sank a hard blow into his belly. Hamp went down and lay writhing.

"If you've got anything to say, say it plain!" Starrett shouted. "Don't be campaigning against me the way you did Tim Urban! Don't be talking them into quitting before we've started."

He was ashamed then, and stared angrily about him at the faces of the other men. Tim Urban did not meet his eyes. "We've pretty well started, Will," he said. "You've had our patience for thirty-six hours, and it's yours as long as you need it."

Cowper looked puzzled. He stood regarding Hamp with dismay.

After a moment Starrett turned away. "Let's go," he said.

Cowper said, "How long are we going to keep it up? Do you think we're getting anywhere?"

Starrett climbed to the wagon seat. "I'll make up my mind without help, Tom. When I do I'll let you know."

The sky was lighter than it had been in the morning, the floating continents of cloud leveled to an even gray. It was the last hope Starrett had had, and it was gone. But for the rest of the afternoon he worked and saw to it that everyone else worked. There was something miraculous in blind, headlong labor. It had built railroads and republics, had saved them from ruin, and perhaps it might work a miracle once more.

But by night the hoppers had advanced through their lines. The men headed forward to get out of the stinking mass. Driving his wagon, Starrett was the last to go. He drove his squirming load of hoppers to the coulee and dumped it. Then he mounted to the seat of the wagon once more and sat there with the lines slack in his hands, looking across the hills. He was finished. The plague had advanced to the point from which a sudden strong wind could drive the hoppers onto Cowper's land before even fire could stop them.

He turned the wagon and drove to the new campfire blazing in the dusk. As he drove up, he heard an angry voice in staccato harangue. Hamp stood with a blazing juniper branch in his hand, confronting the other men. He had his back to Starrett and did not hear him at first.

"It's your land, but my living is tied to it just as much as yours. This has got to stop somewhere, and right here is as good a piece as any! He can't buck all of you."

Starrett swung down. "We're licked," he said. "I'm obliged to all of you for the help. Go home and get ready for your own fights."

Hamp tilted the torch down so that the flames came up greedily toward his hand. "I'm saying it plain this time," he said slowly. "We start firing here—not tomorrow, but now!"

"Put that torch down," Starrett said.

"Drop it, Bill!" Tom Cowper commanded.

Hamp thrust the branch closer. "Catch hold, Mr Starrett. Maybe you'd like to toss the first torch."

Starrett said, "I'm saying that none of you is going to set fire to my land. None of you! And you've got just ten seconds to throw that into the fire!"

Bill Hamp watched him, smiled, and walked past the wagons into the uncleared field, into the golden bunchgrass. His arm went back and he flung the torch. In the same movement he pivoted and was ready for the man who had come out behind him. The flames came up behind Hamp like an explosion. They made a sound like a sigh. They outlined the foreman's hunched body and poured a liquid spark along the barrel of his gun.

Will Starrett felt a sharp fear as Hamp's gun roared. He heard a loud smack beside him and felt the wheel stir. Then his arm took the recoil of his own gun and he was blinded for an instant by the gun-flash. His vision cleared and he saw Hamp on his hands and knees. The man slumped after a moment and lay on his back.

Starrett walked back to the fire. The men stood exactly where they had a moment before, bearded, dirty, expressionless. Taking a length of limb-wood, he thrust it into the flames and roasted it until it burned strongly. Then he strode back, stopped by Hamp's body, and flung the burning brand out into the deep grass, beyond the area of flame where Hamp's branch had fallen.

He came back. "Load my wagon with the rest of this wood," he said, "and get out. I'll take care of the rest of it. Cowper, another of our customs out here is that employers bury their own dead."

Halfway home, he looked back and saw the flames burst across another ridge. He saw little winking lights in the air that looked like fireflies. The hoppers were ending their feast in a pagan fire-revel. There would not be enough of them in the morning to damage Lynn Cowper's kitchen garden.

He unsaddled. Physically and spiritually exhausted, he leaned his head against a corral bar and closed his eyes. It had been the only thing left to do, for a man who loved the land as he did. But it was the last sacrifice he could make, and no gun-proud bunch-grasser like Hamp could make it look like a punishment and a humiliation.

Standing there, he felt moisture strike his hand and angrily straightened. Tears! Was he that far gone?

Starting toward the house, he felt the drops on his face. Another drop struck, and another. Then the flood let loose and there was no telling where one drop ended and the other began, as the July storm fell from the sky.

Starrett ran back to the corral. A crazy mixture of emotions was in his head—fear that the rain had come too soon; joy that it came at all. He rode out to catch the others and enlist their aid in raking the hoppers into heaps and cremating them with rock-oil before they were able to move again.

He had not gone over a mile when the rain changed to hail. He pulled up under a tree to wait it out. He sat, a hurting in his throat. The hopper hadn't crawled out of the earth that could stand that kind of pelting. In its way, it was as miraculous as seagulls.

Another rider appeared from the darkness and pulled a winded, skittish horse into the shelter of the elm. It was Tom Cowper.

"Will!" he said. "This—this does it, doesn't it?"

"It does," Starrett replied.

Cowper said, "Have you got a dry smoke on you?"

Starrett handed him tobacco and papers. He smoked broodingly.

"Starrett," he said, "I'll be damned if I'll ever understand a man like you. You shot Hamp to keep him from setting fire to your grass—no, he's not dead—and then you turned right around and did it yourself. Now, what was the difference?"

Starrett smiled. "I could explain it, but it would take about twenty years, and by that time you wouldn't need it. But it's something about burying your own dead, I suppose."

Cowper thought about it. "Maybe you have something," he said. "Well, if I were a preacher I'd be shouting at the top of my voice now."

"I'm shouting," Starrett admitted, "but I'll bet you can't hear me."

After a while, Cowper said, "Why don't you come along with me, when the hail stops? Lynn and her mother will be up. There'll be something to eat, and we can have a talk. That wouldn't be violating one of your customs, would it?"

"It would be downright neighborly," Starrett said.

DOROTHY M. JOHNSON
A Man Called Horse

Dorothy Marie Johnson (1905–1984) was born in Iowa, and was educated, like many Western writers after her, at the University of Montana, Missoula. After several years as a journalist and editor, she returned to the University of Montana as Assistant Professor of Journalism. Although Johnson wrote two well-received Western novels, *Buffalo Woman* (1977) and *All the Buffalo Returning* (1979), her reputation as a Western writer rests on two collections of short stories, *Indian Country* (1953) and *The Hanging Tree* (1957). Johnson dispensed with many of the stereotypes of popular Western fiction, and she was notably sympathetic to the American Indian viewpoint. Among the numerous awards Johnson received for her Western fiction was a Western Writers of America Silver Spur in 1957 and a Western Literature Association Distinguished Achievement Award in 1981. She was also made an honorary member of the Blackfeet tribe in Montana.

The captivity story 'A Man Called Horse' is from *Indian Country*, and was made into a classic Western film of the same title, directed by Elliot Silverstein in 1970.

HE WAS A YOUNG MAN of good family, as the phrase went in the New England of a hundred-odd years ago, and the reasons for his bitter discontent were unclear, even to himself. He grew up in the gracious old Boston home under his grandmother's care, for his mother had died in giving him birth; and all his life he had known every comfort and privilege his father's wealth could provide.

But still there was the discontent, which puzzled him because he could not even define it. He wanted to live among his equals—people who were no better than he and no worse either. That was as close as he could come to describing the source of his unhappiness in Boston and his restless desire to go somewhere else.

In the year 1845, he left home and went out West, far beyond the country's creeping frontier, where he hoped to find his equals. He had the idea that in Indian country, where there was danger, all white men were kings, and he wanted to be one of them. But he found, in the West as in Boston, that the men he respected were still his superiors, even if they could not read, and those he did not respect weren't worth talking to.

He did have money, however, and he could hire the men he respected. He hired four of them, to cook and hunt and guide and be his companions, but he found them not friendly.

They were apart from him and he was still alone. He still brooded about his status in the world, longing for his equals.

On a day in June, he learned what it was to have no status at all. He became a captive of a small raiding party of Crow Indians.

He heard gunfire and the brief shouts of his companions around the bend of the creek just before they died, but he never saw their bodies. He had no chance to fight, because he was naked and unarmed, bathing in the creek, when a Crow warrior seized and held him.

His captor let him go at last, let him run. Then the lot of them rode him down for sport, striking him with their coup sticks. They carried the dripping scalps of his companions, and one had skinned off Baptiste's black beard as well, for a trophy.

They took him along in a matter-of-fact way, as they took the captured horses. He was unshod and naked as the horses were, and like them he had a rawhide thong around his neck. So long as he didn't fall down, the Crows ignored him.

On the second day they gave him his breeches. His feet were too swollen for his boots, but one of the Indians threw him a pair of moccasins that had belonged to the halfbreed, Henri, who was dead back at the creek. The captive wore the moccasins gratefully. The third day they let him ride one of the spare horses so the party could move faster, and on that day they came in sight of their camp.

He thought of trying to escape, hoping he might be killed in flight rather than by slow torture in the camp, but he never had a chance to try. They were more familiar with escape than he was and, knowing what to expect, they forestalled it. The only other time he had tried to escape from anyone, he had succeeded. When he had left his home in Boston, his father had raged and his grandmother had cried, but they could not talk him out of his intention.

The men of the Crow raiding party didn't bother with talk.

Before riding into camp they stopped and dressed in their regalia, and in parts of their victims' clothing; they painted their faces black. Then, leading the white man by the rawhide around his neck as though he were a horse, they rode down toward the tepee circle, shouting and singing, brandishing their weapons. He was unconscious when they got there; he fell and was dragged.

He lay dazed and battered near a tepee while the noisy, busy life of the camp swarmed around him and Indians came to stare. Thirst consumed him, and when it rained he lapped rain water from the ground like a dog. A scrawny, shrieking, eternally busy old woman with ragged graying hair threw a chunk of meat on the grass, and he fought the dogs for it.

When his head cleared, he was angry, although anger was an emotion he knew he could not afford.

It was better when I was a horse, he thought—when they led me by the rawhide around my neck. I won't be a dog, no matter what!

The hag gave him stinking, rancid grease and let him figure out what it was for. He applied it gingerly to his bruised and sun-seared body.

Now, he thought, I smell like the rest of them.

While he was healing, he considered coldly the advantages of being a horse. A man would be humiliated, and sooner or later he would strike back and that would be the end of him. But a horse had only to be docile. Very well, he would learn to do without pride.

He understood that he was the property of the screaming old woman, a fine gift from her son, one that she liked to show off. She did more yelling at him than at anyone else, probably to impress the neighbors so they would not forget what a great and generous man her son was. She was bossy and proud, a dreadful bag of skin and bones, and she was a devilish hard worker.

The white man, who now thought of himself as a horse, forgot sometimes to worry about his danger. He kept making mental notes of things to tell his own people in Boston about this hideous adventure. He would go back a hero, and he would say, "Grandmother, let me fetch your shawl. I've been accustomed to doing little errands for another lady about your age."

Two girls lived in the tepee with the old hag and her warrior son. One of them, the white man concluded, was his captor's wife and the other was his little sister. The daughter-in-law was smug and spoiled. Being beloved, she did not have to be useful. The younger girl had bright, wandering eyes. Often enough they wandered to the white man who was pretending to be a horse.

The two girls worked when the old woman put them at it, but they were always running off to do something they enjoyed more. There were games and noisy contests, and there was much laughter. But not for the white man. He was finding out what loneliness could be.

That was a rich summer on the plains, with plenty of buffalo for meat and clothing and the making of tepees. The Crows were wealthy in horses, prosperous and contented. If their men had not been so avid for glory, the white man thought, there would have been a lot more of them. But they went out of their way to court death, and when one of them met it, the whole camp mourned extravagantly and cried to their God for vengeance.

The captive was a horse all summer, a docile bearer of burdens, careful and patient. He kept reminding himself that he had to be better-natured than other horses, because he could not lash out with hoofs or teeth. Helping the old woman load up the horses for travel, he yanked at a pack and said, "Whoa, brother. It goes easier when you don't fight."

The horse gave him a big-eyed stare as if it understood his language—a comforting thought, because nobody else did. But even among the horses he felt unequal. They were able to look out for themselves if they escaped. He would simply starve. He was envious still, even among the horses.

Humbly he fetched and carried. Sometimes he even offered to help, but he had not the skill for the endless work of the women, and he was not trusted to hunt with the men, the providers.

When the camp moved, he carried a pack trudging with the women. Even the dogs worked then, pulling small burdens on travois of sticks.

The Indian who had captured him lived like a lord, as he had a right to do. He hunted with his peers, attended long ceremonial meetings with much chanting and dancing, and lounged in the shade with his smug bride. He had only two responsibilities: to kill buffalo and to gain glory. The white man was so far beneath him in status that the Indian did not even think of envy.

One day several things happened that made the captive think he might sometime become a man again. That was the day when he began to understand their language. For four months he had heard it, day and night, the joy and the mourning, the ritual chanting and sung prayers, the squabbles and the deliberations. None of it meant anything to him at all.

But on that important day in early fall the two young women set out for the river, and one of them called over her shoulder to the old woman. The white man was startled. She had said she was going to bathe. His understanding was so sudden that he felt as if his ears had come unstopped. Listening to the racket of the camp, he heard fragments of meaning instead of gabble.

On that same important day the old woman brought a pair of new moccasins out of the tepee and tossed them on the ground before him. He could not believe she would do anything for him because of kindness, but giving him moccasins was one way of looking after her property.

In thanking her, he dared greatly. He picked a little handful of fading fall flowers and took them to her as she squatted in front of her tepee, scraping a buffalo hide with a tool made from a piece of iron tied to a bone. Her hands were hideous—most of the fingers had the first joint missing. He bowed solemnly and offered the flowers.

She glared at him from beneath the short, ragged tangle of her hair. She stared at the flowers, knocked them out of his hand and went running to the next tepee, squalling the story. He heard her and the other women screaming with laughter.

The white man squared his shoulders and walked boldly over to watch three small boys shooting arrows at a target. He said in English, "Show me how to do that, will you?"

They frowned, but he held out his hand as if there could be no doubt. One of them gave him a bow and one arrow, and they snickered when he missed.

The people were easily amused, except when they were angry. They were amused, at him, playing with the little boys. A few days later he asked the hag, with gestures, for a bow that her son had just discarded, a man-size bow of horn. He scavenged for old arrows. The old woman cackled at his marksmanship and called her neighbors to enjoy the fun.

When he could understand words, he could identify his people by their names. The old woman was Greasy Hand,

and her daughter was Pretty Calf. The other young woman's name was not clear to him, for the words were not in his vocabulary. The man who had captured him was Yellow Robe.

Once he could understand, he could begin to talk a little, and then he was less lonely. Nobody had been able to see any reason for talking to him, since he would not understand anyway. He asked the old woman, "What is my name?" Until he knew it, he was incomplete. She shrugged to let him know he had none.

He told her in the Crow language, "My name is Horse." He repeated it, and she nodded. After that they called him Horse when they called him anything. Nobody cared except the white man himself.

They trusted him enough to let him stray out of camp, so that he might have got away and, by unimaginable good luck, might have reached a trading post or a fort, but winter was too close. He did not dare leave without a horse; he needed clothing and a better hunting weapon than he had, and more certain skill in using it. He did not dare steal, for then they would surely have pursued him, and just as certainly they would have caught him. Remembering the warmth of the home that was waiting in Boston, he settled down for the winter.

On a cold night he crept into the tepee after the others had gone to bed. Even a horse might try to find shelter from the wind. The old woman grumbled, but without conviction. She did not put him out.

They tolerated him, back in the shadows, so long as he did not get in the way.

He began to understand how the family that owned him differed from the others. Fate had been cruel to them. In a short, sharp argument among the old women, one of them derided Greasy Hand by sneering, "You have no relatives!" and Greasy Hand raved for minutes of the deeds of her father and uncles and brothers. And she had had four sons, she reminded her detractor—who answered with scorn, "Where are they?"

Later the white man found her moaning and whimpering to herself, rocking back and forth on her haunches, staring at her mutilated hands. By that time he understood. A mourner often chopped off a finger joint. Old Greasy Hand had mourned often. For the first time he felt a twinge of pity, but he put it aside as another emotion, like anger, that he could not afford. He thought: What tales I will tell when I get home!

He wrinkled his nose in disdain. The camp stank of animals and meat and rancid grease. He looked down at his naked, shivering legs and was startled, remembering that he was still only a horse.

He could not trust the old woman. She fed him only because a starved slave would die and not be worth boasting about. Just how fitful her temper was he saw on the day when she got tired of stumbling over one of the hundred dogs that infested the camp. This was one of her own dogs, a large, strong one that pulled a baggage travois when the tribe moved camp.

Countless times he had seen her kick at the beast as it lay sleeping in front of the tepee, in her way. The dog always moved, with a yelp, but it always got in the way again. One day she gave the dog its usual kick and then stood scolding at it while the animal rolled its eyes sleepily. The old woman suddenly picked up her axe and cut the dog's head off with one blow. Looking well satisfied with herself, she beckoned her slave to remove the body.

It could have been me, he thought, if I were a dog. But I'm a horse.

His hope of life lay with the girl, Pretty Calf. He set about courting her, realizing how desperately poor he was both in property and honor. He owned no horse, no weapon but the old bow and the battered arrows. He had nothing to give away, and he needed gifts, because he did not dare seduce the girl.

One of the customs of courtship involved sending a gift of horses to a girl's older brother and bestowing much buffalo meat upon her mother. The white man could not wait for some far-off time when he might have either horses or meat to give away. And his courtship had to be secret. It was not for him to stroll past the groups of watchful girls, blowing a flute made of an eagle's wing bone, as the flirtatious young bucks did.

He could not ride past Pretty Calf's tepee, painted and bedizened; he had no horse, no finery.

Back home, he remembered, I could marry just about any girl I'd want to. But he wasted little time thinking about that. A future was something to be earned.

The most he dared do was wink at Pretty Calf now and then, or state his admiration while she giggled and hid her face. The least he dared do to win his bride was to elope with her, but he had to give her a horse to put the seal of tribal approval on that. And he had no horse until he killed a man to get one. . . .

His opportunity came in early spring. He was casually accepted by that time. He did not belong, but he was amusing to the Crows, like a strange pet, or they would not have fed him through the winter.

His chance came when he was hunting small game with three young boys who were his guards as well as his scornful companions. Rabbits and birds were of no account in a camp well fed on buffalo meat, but they made good targets.

His party walked far that day. All of them at once saw the two horses in a sheltered coulee. The boys and the man crawled forward on their bellies, and then they saw an Indian who lay on the ground, moaning, a lone traveler. From the way the boys inched forward, Horse knew the man was fair prey—a member of some enemy tribe.

This is the way the captive white man acquired wealth and honor to win a bride and save his life: He shot an arrow into the sick man, a split second ahead of one of his small companions, and dashed forward to strike the still-groaning man with his bow, to count first coup. Then he seized the hobbled horses.

By the time he had the horses secure, and with them his hope for freedom, the boys had followed, counting coup with gestures and shrieks they had practiced since boyhood, and one of them had the scalp. The white man was grimly amused to see the boy double up with sudden nausea when he had the thing in his hand. . . .

There was a hubbub in the camp when they rode in that evening, two of them on each horse. The captive was noticed. Indians who had ignored him as a slave stared at the brave man who had struck first coup and had stolen horses.

The hubbub lasted all night, as fathers boasted loudly of their young sons' exploits. The white man was called upon to settle an argument between two fierce boys as to which of them had struck second coup and which must be satisfied with third. After much talk that went over his head, he solemnly pointed at the nearest boy. He didn't know which boy it was and didn't care, but the boy did.

The white man had watched warriors in their triumph. He knew what to do. Modesty about achievements had no place among the Crow people. When a man did something big, he told about it.

The white man smeared his face with grease and charcoal. He walked inside the tepee circle, chanting and singing. He used his own language.

"You heathens, you savages," he shouted. "I'm going to get out of here someday! I am going to get away!" The Crow people listened respectfully. In the Crow tongue he shouted, "Horse! I am Horse!" and they nodded.

He had a right to boast, and he had two horses. Before dawn, the white man and his bride were sheltered beyond a far hill, and he was telling her, "I love you, little lady. I love you."

She looked at him with her great dark eyes, and he thought she understood his English words—or as much as she needed to understand.

"You are my treasure," he said, "more precious than jewels, better than fine gold. I am going to call you Freedom."

When they returned to camp two days later, he was bold but worried. His ace, he suspected, might not be high enough in the game he was playing without being sure of the rules. But it served.

Old Greasy Hand raged—but not at him. She complained loudly that her daughter had let herself go too cheap. But the marriage was as good as any Crow marriage. He had paid a horse.

He learned the language faster after that, from Pretty Calf, whom he sometimes called Freedom. He learned that his attentive, adoring bride was fourteen years old.

One thing he had not guessed was the difference that being Pretty Calf's husband would make in his relationship to her mother and brother. He had hoped only to make his position a little safer, but he had not expected to be treated with dignity. Greasy Hand no longer spoke to him at all. When the white man spoke to her, his bride murmured in dismay, explaining at great length that he must never do that. There could be no conversation between a man and his mother-in-law. He could not even mention a word that was part of her name.

Having improved his status so magnificently, he felt no need for hurry in getting away. Now that he had a woman, he had as good a chance to be rich as any man. Pretty Calf waited on him; she seldom ran off to play games with other young girls, but took pride in learning from her mother the many women's skills of tanning hides and making clothing and preparing food.

He was no more a horse but a kind of man, a half-Indian, still poor and unskilled but laden with honors, clinging to the buckskin fringes of Crow society.

Escape could wait until he could manage it in comfort, with fit clothing and a good horse, with hunting weapons. Escape could wait until the camp moved near some trading post. He did not plan how he would get home. He dreamed of being there all at once, and of telling stories nobody would believe. There was no hurry.

Pretty Calf delighted in educating him. He began to understand tribal arrangements, customs and why things were as they were. They were that way because they had always been so. His young wife giggled when she told him, in his ignorance, things she had always known. But she did not laugh when her brother's wife was taken by another warrior. She explained that solemnly with words and signs.

Yellow Robe belonged to a society called the Big Dogs. The wife stealer, Cut Neck, belonged to the Foxes. They were fellow tribesmen; they hunted together and fought side by side, but men of one society could take away wives from the other society if they wished, subject to certain limitations.

When Cut Neck rode up to the tepee, laughing and singing, and called to Yellow Robe's wife, "Come out! Come out!" she did as ordered, looking smug as usual, meek and entirely willing. Thereafter she rode beside him in ceremonial processions and carried his coup stick, while his other wife pretended not to care.

"But why?" the white man demanded of his wife, his Freedom. "Why did our brother let his woman go? He sits and smokes and does not speak."

Pretty Calf was shocked at the suggestion. Her brother could not possibly reclaim his woman, she explained. He could not even let her come back if she wanted to—and she probably would want to when Cut Neck tired of her. Yellow Robe could not even admit that his heart was sick. That was the way things were. Deviation meant dishonor.

The woman could have hidden from Cut Neck, she said. She could even have refused to go with him if she had been *ba-wurokee*—a really virtuous woman. But she had been his woman before, for a little while on a berrying expedition, and he had a right to claim her.

There was no sense in it, the white man insisted. He glared at his young wife. "If you go, I will bring you back!" he promised.

She laughed and buried her head against his shoulder. "I will not have to go," she said. "Horse is my first man. There is no hole in my moccasin."

He stroked her hair and said, "*Ba-wurokee.*"

With great daring, she murmured, "*Hayha,*" and when he did not answer, because he did not know what she meant, she drew away, hurt.

"A woman calls her man that if she thinks he will not leave her. Am I wrong?"

The white man held her closer and lied, "Pretty Calf is not wrong. Horse will not leave her. Horse will not take another woman, either." No, he certainly would not. Parting from this one was going to be harder than getting her had been. "*Hayha*," he murmured. "Freedom."

His conscience irked him, but not very much. Pretty Calf could get another man easily enough when he was gone, and a better provider. His hunting skill was improving, but he was still awkward.

There was no hurry about leaving. He was used to most of the Crow ways and could stand the rest. He was becoming prosperous. He owned five horses. His place in the life of the tribe was secure, such as it was. Three or four young women, including the one who had belonged to Yellow Robe, made advances to him. Pretty Calf took pride in the fact that her man was so attractive.

By the time he had what he needed for a secret journey, the grass grew yellow on the plains and the long cold was close. He was enslaved by the girl he called Freedom and, before the winter ended, by the knowledge that she was carrying his child. . . .

The Big Dog society held a long ceremony in the spring. The white man strolled with his woman along the creek bank, thinking: When I get home I will tell them about the chants and the drumming. Sometime. Sometime.

Pretty Calf would not go to bed when they went back to the tepee.

"Wait and find out about my brother," she urged. "Something may happen."

So far as Horse could figure out, the Big Dogs were having some kind of election. He pampered his wife by staying up with her by the fire. Even the old woman, who was a great one for getting sleep when she was not working, prowled around restlessly.

The white man was yawning by the time the noise of the ceremony died down. When Yellow Robe strode in, garish and heathen in his paint and feathers and furs, the women cried out. There was conversation, too fast for Horse to follow, and the old woman wailed once, but her son silenced her with a gruff command.

When the white man went to sleep, he thought his wife was weeping beside him.

The next morning she explained.

"He wears the bearskin belt. Now he can never retreat in battle. He will always be in danger. He will die."

Maybe he wouldn't, the white man tried to convince her. Pretty Calf recalled that some few men had been honored by the bearskin belt, vowed to the highest daring, and had not died. If they lived through the summer, then they were free of it.

"My brother wants to die," she mourned. "His heart is bitter."

Yellow Robe lived through half a dozen clashes with small parties of raiders from hostile tribes. His honors were many. He captured horses in an enemy camp, led two successful raids, counted first coup and snatched a gun from the hand of an enemy tribesman. He wore wolf tails on his moccasins and ermine skins on his shirt, and he fringed his leggings with scalps in token of his glory.

When his mother ventured to suggest, as she did many times, "My son should take a new wife, I need another woman to help me," he ignored her. He spent much time in prayer, alone in the hills or in conference with a medicine man. He fasted and made vows and kept them. And before he could be free of the heavy honor of the bearskin belt, he went on his last raid.

The warriors were returning from the north just as the white man and two other hunters approached from the south, with buffalo and elk meat dripping from the bloody hides tied on their restive ponies. One of the hunters grunted, and they stopped to watch a rider on the hill north of the teepee circle.

The rider dismounted, held up a blanket and dropped it. He repeated the gesture.

The hunters murmured dismay. "Two! Two men dead!" They rode fast into the camp, where there was already wailing.

A messenger came down from the war party on the hill. The rest of the party delayed to paint their faces for mourning and for victory. One of the two dead men was Yellow Robe. They had put his body in a cave and walled it in with rocks. The other man died later, and his body was in a tree.

There was blood on the ground before the tepee to which Yellow Robe would return no more. His mother, with her hair chopped short, sat in the doorway, rocking back and forth on her haunches, wailing her heartbreak. She cradled one mutilated hand in the other. She had cut off another finger joint.

Pretty Calf had cut off chunks of her long hair and was crying as she gashed her arms with a knife. The white man tried to take the knife away, but she protested so piteously that he let her do as she wished. He was sickened with the lot of them.

Savages! he thought. Now I will go back! I'll go hunting alone, and I'll keep on going.

But he did not go just yet, because he was the only hunter in the lodge of the two grieving women, one of them old and the other pregnant with his child.

In their mourning, they made him a pauper again. Everything that meant comfort, wealth and safety they sacrificed to the spirits because of the death of Yellow Robe. The tepee, made of seventeen fine buffalo hides, the furs that should have kept them warm, the white deerskin dress, trimmed with elk teeth, that Pretty Calf loved so well, even their tools and Yellow Robe's weapons—everything but his sacred medicine objects—they left there on the prairie, and the whole camp moved away. Two of his best horses were killed as a sacrifice, and the women gave away the rest.

They had no shelter. They would have no tepee of their own for two months at least of mourning, and then the women would have to tan hides to make it. Meanwhile they could live in temporary huts made of willows, covered with skins given them in pity by their friends. They could have lived with relatives, but Yellow Robe's women had no relatives.

The white man had not realized until then how terrible a thing it was for a Crow to have no kinfolk. No wonder old Greasy Hand had only stumps for fingers. She had mourned, from one year to the next, for everyone she had ever loved. She had no one left but her daughter, Pretty Calf.

Horse was furious at their foolishness. It had been bad enough for him, a captive, to be naked as a horse and poor as a slave, but that was because his captors had stripped him. These women had voluntarily given up everything they needed.

He was too angry at them to sleep in the willow hut. He lay under a sheltering tree. And on the third night of the mourning he made his plans. He had a knife and a bow. He would go after meat, taking two horses. And he would not come back. There were, he realized, many things he was not going to tell when he got back home.

In the willow hut, Pretty Calf cried out. He heard rustling there, and the old woman's querulous voice.

Some twenty hours later his son was born, two months early, in the tepee of a skilled medicine woman. The child was born without breath, and the mother died before the sun went down.

The white man was too shocked to think whether he should mourn, or how he should mourn. The old woman screamed until she was voiceless. Piteously she approached him, bent and trembling, blind with grief. She held out her knife and he took it.

She spread out her hands and shook her head. If she cut off any more finger joints, she could no more work. She could not afford any more lasting signs of grief.

The white man said, "All right! All right!" between his teeth. He hacked his arms with the knife and stood watching the blood run down. It was little enough to do for Pretty Calf, for little Freedom.

Now there is nothing to keep me, he realized. When I get home, I must not let them see the scars.

He looked at Greasy Hand, hideous in her grief-burdened age, and thought: I really am free now! When a wife dies, her husband has no more duty toward her family. Pretty Calf had told him so, long ago, when he wondered why a certain man moved out of one tepee and into another.

The old woman, of course, would be a scavenger. There was one other with the tribe, an ancient crone who had no relatives, toward whom no one felt any responsibility. She lived on food thrown away by the more fortunate. She slept in shelters that she built with her own knotted hands. She plodded wearily at the end of the procession when the camp moved. When she stumbled, nobody cared. When she died, nobody would miss her.

Tomorrow morning, the white man decided, I will go.

His mother-in-law's sunken mouth quivered. She said one word, questioningly. She said, "*Eero-oshay?*" She said, "Son?"

Blinking, he remembered. When a wife died, her husband was free. But her mother, who had ignored him with dignity, might if she wished ask him to stay. She invited him by calling him Son, and he accepted by answering Mother.

Greasy Hand stood before him, bowed with years, withered with unceasing labor, loveless and childless, scarred with grief. But with all her burdens, she still loved life enough to beg it from him, the only person she had any right to ask. She was stripping herself of all she had left, her pride.

He looked eastward across the prairie. Two thousand miles away was home. The old woman would not live forever. He could afford to wait, for he was young. He could afford to be magnanimous, for he knew he was a man. He gave her the answer. "*Eegya*," he said. "Mother."

He went home three years later. He explained no more than to say, "I lived with Crows for a while. It was some time before I could leave. They called me Horse."

He did not find it necessary either to apologize or to boast, because he was the equal of any man on earth.

STEVE FRAZEE
Great Medicine

Charles Stephen Frazee (1909–) was born in Salida, Colorado, and graduated from Western State College in 1937. For a number of years he worked in the construction industry, before serving with the US Navy, 1943–1945. He began writing fiction in 1946, and during the 1950s was one of the leading writers of Western stories for the pulp and digest magazines. Over the course of the same decade, Frazee also wrote twenty one Western novels, among them: *High Cage* (1957), *Desert Guns* (1957), and *Rendezvous* (1958). His career slowed considerably thereafter, due to extended service as a probation officer. Frazee's pulp Western fiction is distinguished, in particular, by its vivid settings and unusual storylines. Several of Frazee's works have been filmed, most notably the contemporary Western story 'My Brother Down There', which formed the basis for *Running Target* (1956), directed by Marvin Weinstein.

The story 'Great Medicine', which is set on the northern plains, was first published in the digest magazine *Gunsmoke* in 1953.

DEEP IN THE COUNTRY OF the Crows, Little Belly squatted in the alders, waiting for his scouts. The Crows were many and angry in the hills this summer, and there was time to think of that; but since Little Belly was a Blackfoot who had counted five coups he could not allow his fear, even to himself.

He waited in the dappled shadows for more important news than word of Indians who did not love the Blackfeet.

Wild and long before him, the ridges whispered a soft, cool song. In shining steps, beaver ponds dropped to the great river flowing east toward the land of those with the mighty medicine. Dark and motionless, Little Belly waited.

He saw at last brief movement on a far hill, a touch of sun on the neck of a pony, the merest flash of a rider who had come too close to the edge of the trees.

That was No Horns and his appaloosa. No Horns, as ever, was riding without care. He was a Piegan and Little Belly was a Blood, both Blackfeet; but Blackfeet loved no one, sometimes not even each other. So Little Belly fingered his English knife and thought how easily small things caused one to die.

He saw no more of No Horns until the scout was quite close, and by then Whirlwind, the other scout, was also on the ridge. They came to Little Belly, not obliged to obey him, still doubtful of his mission.

Little Belly said to No Horns, "From a great distance I saw you."

"Let the Crows see me also." No Horns stretched on the ground with a grunt. Soon his chest was covered with mosquitoes.

Whirlwind looked to the east. Where the river broke the fierce sweep of ridges there was a wide, grassy route that marked the going and coming of Crows to the plains. Whirlwind pointed. "Two days."

"How many come?" Little Belly asked.

Whirlwind signalled fifty. "The Broken Face leads."

No white man in the mountains was greater than the trapper chief, Broken Face, whom the white men knew as

Yancey. He took beaver from the country of the Blackfeet, and he killed Blackfeet. The Crows who put their arms about him in his camps thought long before trying to steal the horses of his company. If there was any weakness in Broken Face it was a weakness of mercy.

So considering, Little Belly formed the last part of his plan.

Half dozing in the deep shade where the mosquitoes whined their hunting songs, No Horns asked, "What is this medicine you will steal from the white trappers?"

It was not muskets. The Blackfeet had killed Crows with English guns long before other white men came from the east to the mountains. It was not ponies. The Blackfeet traded with the Nez Perces for better horses than any white trapper owned. It was not in the pouches of the white men, for Little Belly had ripped into the pouches carried on the belts of dead trappers, finding no great medicine.

But there was a power in white men that the Blackfeet feared. Twice now they had tried to wipe the trappers from the mountains forever, and twice the blood cost had been heavy; and the white men were still here. Little Belly felt a chill, born of the heavy shade and the long waiting, but coming mostly from the thought that what he must steal might be something that could not be carried in pouches.

He stood up. "I do not know what it is, but I will know it when I see it."

"It is their talk to the sky," Whirlwind said. "How can you steal that?"

"I will learn it."

No Horns grunted. "They will not let you hear."

"I will travel with them, and I will hear it."

"It is their Man Above," Whirlwind said. "He will know you are not a white man talking."

"No," Little Belly said. "It is something they carry with them."

"I did not find it," No Horns said, "and I have killed three white men."

"You did not kill them soon enough," Little Belly said. "They hid their power before they died."

"If their medicine had been strong, I could not have killed them at all." No Horns sat up. He left streaks of blood on the heavy muscles of his chest when he brushed mosquitoes away. "Their medicine is in their sky talk."

Whirlwind said, "The Nez Perces sent chiefs to the white man's biggest town on the muddy river. They asked for a white man to teach them of the Man Above, so that they could be strong like the white men. There were promises from the one who went across these mountains long ago. The chiefs died. No white man came to teach the Nez Perces about the sky talk to make them strong."

"The Nez Perces were fools," Little Belly said. "Does one go in peace asking for the ponies of the Crows? It is not the sky talk of the trappers that makes them strong. It is something else. I will find it and steal it."

Whirlwind and No Horns followed him to the horses. Staying in the trees, they rode close to the river, close to a place where the trappers going to their summer meeting place must pass.

Little Belly took a Crow arrow from his quiver. He gave it to Whirlwind, and then Little Belly touched his own shoulder. Whirlwind understood but hesitated.

He said, "There are two days yet."

"If the wound is fresh when the trappers come, they will wonder why no Crows are close," Little Belly said.

No Horns grinned like a buffalo wolf, showing his dislike of Little Belly. He snatched the arrow from Whirlwind, fitted it to his bow and drove it with a solid chop into Little Belly's shoulder.

With his face set to hide his pain, Little Belly turned his pony and rode into the rocks close by the grassy place to wait for the coming of the trappers. The feathered end of the shaft rose and fell to his motion, sawing the head against bone and muscle.

He did not try to pull the arrow free while his companions were close. When he heard them ride away on the long trip back to Blackfoot country he tried to wrench the arrow from his shoulder. The barbs were locked against bone. They ground on it. The pain made Little Belly weak and savage, bringing water to his face and arms.

He sat down in the rocks and hacked the tough shaft off a few inches from his shoulder. He clamped his teeth close to the bleeding flesh, trying with strong movements of his neck to draw the iron head. Like a dog stripping flesh from a bone he tugged. The arrow seemed to loosen, dragging flesh and sinew with it; but the pain was great. All at once the sky turned black.

Little Belly's pony pulled away from the unconscious man and trotted to join the other two.

When Little Belly came back to the land of sky and grass he was willing to let the arrow stay where it was. It was better, too, that the white men would find him thus. But that night he was savage again with pain. He probed and twisted with the dull point of his knife until blood ran down and gathered in his breech clout. He could not get the arrow out. He thought then that he might die, and so he sang a death song, which meant that he was not afraid to die, and therefore, could not.

He dozed. The night was long, but it passed in time and the sun spread brightness on the land of the Crows. Hot and thirsty, Little Belly listened to the river, but he would not go to it in daylight. It was well he did not, for seven long-haired Crows came by when the sun was high. Three of them saw his pony tracks and came toward the rocks. Others, riding higher on the slope, found the tracks of all three horses. They called out excitedly.

A few seconds more and the three Crows coming toward Little Belly would have found him and chopped him up, but now they raced away to join the main hunt.

All day the wounded Blackfoot burned with thirst. The sun was hotter than he had ever remembered; it heaped coals on him and tortured his eyes with mist. When night came he waded into the tugging current of the river, going deep, bathing his wound and drinking. By the time he crept into the rocks again he was as hot as before. Many visions came to him that night but they ran so fast upon each other afterward he could not remember one of them clearly enough to make significance from it.

Old voices talked to him and old ghosts walked before him in the long black night. He was compressed by loneliness. The will to carry out his plan wavered. Sometimes he thought he would rise and run away, but he did not go.

From afar he heard the trappers the next day. He crawled to the edge of the rocks. The Delaware scouts found him, grim, incurious men who were not truly Indians but brothers of the white trappers. Little Belly hated them.

Without dismounting, they watched him, laughing. One of them tipped his rifle down.

Little Belly found strength to rise then, facing the Delawares without fear. The dark, ghost-ridden hours were gone. These were but men. All they could do to Little Belly was to kill him. He looked at them and spat.

Now their rifles pointed at the chest, but when the Delawares saw they could not make him afraid, they dismounted and flung him on the ground. They took his weapons. They grunted over his strong Nez Perce shield, thumping it with their hands. Then they threw it into the river. They broke his arrows and threw away his bow. One of them kept his knife.

When they took his medicine pouch and scattered the contents on the ground, Little Belly would have fought them, and died, but he remembered that he had a mission.

The big white man who came galloping on a powerful horse was not Broken Face. This white man's beard grew only on his upper lip, like a long streak of sunset sky. His eyes were the color of deep ice upon a river. Strong and white his teeth flashed when he spoke to the Delawares. Little Belly saw at once that the Delawares stood in awe of this one, which was much to know.

The white man leaped from his horse. His rifle was strange, two barrels lying one upon the other.

"Blackfoot," one of the Delawares said.

Curiously, the white man looked at Little Belly.

A Delaware took his tomahawk from his belt and leaned over the Blackfoot.

"No," the white man said, without haste. He laughed. From his pocket he took a dark bone. A slender blade grew from it quickly. With this he cut the arrow from Little Belly's shoulder. He lifted Little Belly to his feet, looking deep into the Blackfoot's eyes.

Little Belly tried to hide his pain.

"Tough one," the white man said.

The Delaware with the tomahawk spoke in Blackfoot. "We should kill him now." He looked at the white man's face, and then, reluctantly, put away his tomahawk.

Broken Face came then. Not far behind him were the mules packed with trade goods for the summer meeting. Long ago a Cheyenne lance had struck Broken Face in the corner of his mouth, crashing through below his ear. Now he never spoke directly before him but always to one side, half whispering. His eyes were the color of smoke from a lodge on a rainy day, wise from having seen many things in the mountains. He put tobacco in his mouth. He looked at Little Belly coldly.

"One of old Thunder's Bloods," he said. "Why didn't you let the Delawares have him, Stearns?"

"I intended to, until I saw how tough he was."

"All Blackfeet are tough." Broken Face spat.

Little Belly studied the two men. The Broken Face was wise and strong, and the Blackfeet had not killed him yet; but already there were signs that the weakness of mercy was stirring in his mind. It was said that Broken Face did not kill unless attacked. Looking into Stearns' pale eyes, Little Belly knew that Stearns would kill any time.

"Couldn't you use him?" Stearns asked.

Broken Face shook his head.

Stearns held up the bloody stub of arrow. He smiled. "No gratitude?"

"Hell!" Broken Face said. "He'd pay you by slicing your liver. He's Blackfoot. Leave him to the Delawares."

"What will they do?"

"Throw him on a fire, maybe. Kill him by inches. Cut the meat off his bones and throw the bones in the river. The Bloods did that to one of them last summer." Broken Face walked to his horse.

"Couldn't you use him to get into Blackfoot country peacefully?" Stearns asked. "Sort of a hostage?"

"No. Any way you try to use a Blackfoot he don't shine at all." Broken Face got on his horse, studying the long ridges ahead. "Likely one of the Crows that was with us put the arrow into him. Too bad they didn't do better. He's no good to us. Blackfeet don't make treaties, and if they did, they wouldn't hold to 'em. They just don't shine no way, Stearns. Come on."

Not by the words, but by the darkening of the Delawares' eyes, Little Belly knew it was death. He thought of words to taunt the Delawares while they killed him, and then he remembered he had a mission. To die bravely was easy; but to steal powerful medicine was greatness.

Little Belly looked to Stearns for mercy. The white man had saved him from the Delawares, and had cut the arrow from his shoulder; but those two deeds must have been matters of curiosity only. Now there was no mercy in the white man's eyes. In one quick instant Little Belly and Stearns saw the utter ruthlessness of each other's natures.

Stearns was greater than Broken Face, Little Belly saw, for Stearns made no talk. He merely walked away.

The Delawares freed their knives. "Is the Blackfoot a great runner?" one asked.

In his own tongue Little Belly spoke directly to Broken Face. "I would travel with you to my home."

"The Crows would not thank me." Broken Face began to ride away, with Stearns beside him.

"Is the Blackfoot cold?" A Delaware began to kick apart a rotten log to build a fire.

"I am one," Little Belly said. "Give me back my knife and I will fight all of Broken Face's Indians! Among my people Broken Face would be treated so."

"What did he say?" Stearns asked Broken Face.

Broken Face told him. He let his horse go a few more paces and then he stopped. For an instant an anger of indecision twisted the good side of Broken Face's mouth. "Let him go. Let him travel with us."

The ring of Delawares was angry, but they obeyed.

It had been so close that Little Belly felt his limbs trembling; but it had worked: deep in Broken Face was softness that had grown since his early days in the mountains because he now loved beaver hides more than strength. Now he was a warrior with too many ponies.

Little Belly pushed between the Delawares and began to gather up the items from his medicine pouch. It shamed him, but if he did not do so, he thought they might wonder too much and guess the nature of his cunning.

Jarv Yancey—Broken Face—said to Stearns, "You saved his hide in the first place. Now you can try to watch him while he's with us. It'll teach you something."

Stearns grinned. "I didn't know him from a Crow, until the Delawares told me. You know Blackfeet. Why'd *you* let him go?"

Broken Face's scowl showed that he was searching for an answer to satisfy himself. "Someday the Blackfeet may catch me. If they give me a running chance, that's all I'll want. Maybe this will help me get it."

"They'll break your legs with a club before they give you that running chance." Stearns laughed.

There was startled shrewdness in the look the Mountain Man gave the greenhorn making his first trip to the Rockies. "You learn fast, Stearns."

"The Scots are savages at heart, Yancey. They know another savage when they see him. Our wounded friend back there has a heart blacker than a beaten Macdonald trapped in a marsh. I took several glances to learn it, but I saw it."

The Delawares rode by at the trot, scattering to go on ahead and on the flanks as scouts. Neither Stearns nor Yancey looked back to see what was happening to Little Belly.

Ahead, the whispering blue of the mountains rose above the clear green of the ridges. There were parks and rushing rivers yet to cross, a world to ride forever. Behind, the mules with heavy packs, the *engagées* cursing duty, the wool-clad trappers riding with rifles aslant gave reason for Jarv Yancey's presence. As Stearns looked through the suntangled air to long reaches of freshness, a joyous, challenging expression was his reason for being here.

Just for a while Yancey thought back to a time when he, too, looked with new eyes on a new world every morning; but now the ownership of goods, and the employment of trappers and flunkies, gave caution to his looks ahead. And he had given refuge to a Blackfoot, which would be an insult to the friendly Crows, an error to be mended with gifts.

Stearns spoke lazily. "When he said, 'I am one,' it touched you, didn't it, Yancey? That's why you didn't let the Delawares have him."

Jarv Yancey grunted.

The Blackfoot walked with hunger in his belly and a great weakness in his legs, but he walked. The horses of the trappers kicked dust upon him. The *engagées* cursed him, but he did not understand the words. He could not be humble, but he was patient.

And now he changed his plan. The Broken Face was not as great as the other white man who rode ahead, although the other was a stranger in the mountains. The cruel calmness of the second white man's eyes showed that he was protected by mighty medicine. Little Belly would steal greatness from him, instead of from Broken Face.

There would be time; it was far to the edge of Blackfoot country.

The one called Stearns took interest in Little Belly, learning from him some Blackfoot speech through talking slowly with the signs. Little Belly saw that it was the same interest Stearns took in plants that were strange to him, in birds, in the rocks of the land. It was good, for Little Belly was studying Stearns also.

It was Stearns who saw that Little Belly got a mule to ride. Also, because of Stearns the Delawares quit stepping on Little Belly's healing shoulder and stopped stripping the blanket from him when they walked by his sleeping place at night.

There was much to pay the Delawares, and there was much to pay all the white men, too, but Little Belly buried insults deep and drew within himself, living only to discover the medicine that made Stearns strong.

By long marches the trappers came closer to the mountains. One day the Crows who had ridden near Little Belly when he lay in the rocks came excitedly into the camp at nooning, waving scalps. The scalps were those of No Horns and Whirlwind. Little Belly showed a blank face when the Crows taunted him with the trophies. They rode around him, shouting insults, until they had worked up rage to kill him.

The Broken Face spoke to them sharply, and their pride was wounded. They demanded why this ancient enemy of all their people rode with the friends of the Crows. They were howlers then, like old women, moaning of their hurts, telling of their love for Broken Face and all white trappers.

Broken Face must make the nooning longer then, to sit in council with the Crows. He told how this Blackfoot with him had once let him go in peace. The Crows did not understand, even if they believed. He said that Little Belly would speak to his people about letting Broken Face come into their lands to trap. The Crows did not understand, and it was certain they did not believe.

Then Broken Face gave presents. The Crows understood, demanding more presents.

Dark was the look the white trapper chief gave Little Belly when the Crows at last rode away. But Stearns laughed and struck Broken Face upon the shoulder. Later, the Blackfoot heard the Delawares say that Stearns had said he would pay for the presents.

That was nothing, Little Belly knew; Stearns gave the Delawares small gifts, also, when they brought him plants or flowers he had not seen before, or birds they killed silently with arrows. It might be that Stearns was keeping Little Belly alive to learn about his medicine. The thought startled him.

Now the mountains were losing their blue haze. At night the air was like a keen blade. Soon the last of the buffalo land would lie behind. There was a tightening of spirit. There were more guards at night, for the land of the Blackfeet was not far ahead. With pride, Little Belly saw how the camp closed in upon itself by night because his people were not far away.

And still he did not know about the medicine.

Once he had thought it was hidden in a pouch from which Stearns took every day thin, glittering knives to cut the hair from his face, leaving only the heavy streak across his upper lip. On a broad piece of leather Stearns sharpened the knives, and he was very careful with them.

But he did not care who saw them or who saw how he used them; so it was not the knives, Little Belly decided. All day Stearns' gun was busy. He brought in more game than any of the hunters, and since he never made sky talk before a hunt, the Blackfoot became convinced that his powerful medicine was carried on his body.

At last Little Belly settled on a shining piece of metal which Stearns carried always in his pocket. It was like a ball that had been flattened. There were lids upon it, thin and gleaming, with talking signs marked on them. They opened like the wings of a bird.

On top of it was a small stem. Every night before he slept Stearns took the round metal from his pocket. With his fingers he twisted the small stem, looking solemn. His actions caused the flattened ball to talk with a slow grasshopper song. And then Stearns would look at the stars, and immediately push the lids down on the object and put it back into his pocket, where it was fastened by a tiny yellow rope of metal.

This medicine was never farther from Stearns' body than the shining rope that held it. He was very careful when the object lay in his hand. No man asked him what it was, but often when Stearns looked at his medicine, the trappers glanced at the sky.

Little Belly was almost satisfied; but still, he must be sure.

One of the *engagées* was a Frenchman who had worked for the English fathers west of Blackfoot country. Little Belly began to help him with the horses in the daytime. The Broken Face scowled at this, not caring for any kind of Indians near his horses. But the company was still in Crow country, and Little Belly hated Crows, and it was doubtful that the Blackfoot could steal the horses by himself, so Broken Face, watchful, wondering, allowed Little Belly to help the Frenchman.

After a time Little Belly inquired carefully of the *engagée* about the metal ball that Stearns carried. The Frenchman named it, but the word was strange, so Little Belly soon forgot it. The *engagée* explained that the moon and stars and the sun and the day and night were all carried in the metal.

There were small arrows in the medicine. They moved and the medicine was alive, singing a tiny song. The *engagée* said one glance was all Stearns needed to know when the moon would rise, when the sun would set, when the day would become night and the night would turn to day.

These things Little Belly could tell without looking at a metal ball. Either the Frenchman was a liar or the object Stearns carried was worthless. Little Belly grew angry with himself, and desperate; perhaps Stearns' medicine was not in the silvery object after all.

All through the last of the buffalo lands bands of Crows came to the company, professing love for the Broken Face, asking why a Blackfoot traveled with him. The trapper chief gave them awls and bells and trinkets and small amounts of poor powder.

He complained to Stearns, "That stinking Blood has cost me twenty dollars in goods, St Louis!"

Stearns laughed. "I'll stand it."

"Why?"

"He wants to kill me. I'd like to know why. I've never seen a man who wanted so badly to kill me. It pleases me to have an enemy like that."

Broken Face shook his head.

"Great friends and great enemies, Yancey. They make life worth living; and the enemies make it more interesting by far."

The Mountain Man's gray eyes swept the wild land ahead. "I agree on that last." After a while he said, "Besides wanting to kill you, like he said, which he would like to do to any white man, what does he want? There was three of them back there where the Delawares found him. He didn't have no cause to be left behind, not over one little arrow dabbed into him. He joined us, Stearns."

"I don't know why, but I know what he wants now." Stearns showed his teeth in a great streaking grin. "I love an enemy that can hate all the way, Yancey."

"If that makes you happy, you can have the whole damned Blackfoot nation to love, lock, stock and barrel." After a time Yancey began to laugh at his own remark.

Little Belly was close to Stearns the evening the grizzly bear disrupted the company, at a bad time, when camp was being made. There was a crashing on the hill where the *engagées* were gathering wood. One of them shouted. The other fired his rifle.

The coughing of an enraged bear came loudly from the bushes. The *engagées* leaped down the hill, throwing away their rifles. Little Belly looked at Stearns. The big white man was holding his medicine. He had only time to snap the lids before grabbing his rifle from where it leaned against a pack. The medicine swung on its golden rope against his thigh as he cocked his rifle.

Confusion ran ahead of the enormous silver bear that charged the camp. The mules wheeled away, kicking, dragging loosened packs. The horses screamed and ran. Men fell over the scattered gear, cursing and yelling as they scrambled for their guns. There were shots and some of them struck the bear without effect.

Thundering low, terrible with power, the grizzly came. Now only Stearns and Little Belly stood in its path, and the Blackfoot was without weapons. Little Belly fought with terror but he stayed because Stearns stayed. The white man's lips smiled but his eyes were like the ice upon the winter mountains.

Wide on his feet he stood, with his rifle not all the way to his shoulder. Tall and strong he stood, as if to stop the great bear with his body. Little Belly covered his mouth.

When Stearns fired, the bear was so close Little Belly could see the surging of its muscles on the shoulder hump and the stains of berries on its muzzle. It did not stop at the sound of Stearns' rifle, but it was dead, for its legs fell under it, no longer driving. It slid almost to Stearns's feet, bruising the grass, jarring rocks.

For a moment there was silence. Stearns poured his laugh into the quiet, a huge deep laugh that was happy, wild and savage as the mountains. He looked at his medicine then, solemnly. He held it to his ear, and then he smiled and put it back into his pocket. He stooped to see how his bullet had torn into the bear's brain through the eye.

There was still confusion, for the mules and horses did not like the bear smell, but Stearns paid no attention. He looked at Little Belly standing there with nothing in his hands. Stearns did not say the Blackfoot was brave, but his eyes said so. Once more he laughed, and then he turned to speak to Broken Face, who had been at the far end of camp when the bear came.

One of the *engagées* shot the bear in the neck. Broken Face knocked the man down for wasting powder and causing the animals more fright.

Quickly Little Belly left to help with the horses, hiding all his thoughts. Truly, this medicine of Stearns' was powerful. Little Belly could say that Stearns was brave, that he shot true, standing without fear, and laughing afterward. All this was true, but still there was the element of medicine which protected a brave warrior against all enemies.

Without it, bravery was not enough. Without it, the most courageous warrior might die from a shot not even aimed at him. In the round thing Stearns carried was trapped all movement of the days and nights and a guiding of the owner in war and hunting.

Now Little Belly was sure about the object, but as he pondered deep into the night, his sureness wore to caution. He could not remember whether Stearns listened to the talk of his medicine before the bear made sounds upon the hill or after the shouts and crashing began.

So Little Belly did not push his plan hard yet. He watched Stearns, wondering, waiting for more evidence. Sometimes the white man saw the hard brown eyes upon him as he moved about the camp, and when he did he showed his huge grin.

Three days from the vague boundary of ridges and rivers that marked the beginning of Blackfoot lands, the Delaware scouts reported buffalo ahead. At once the camp was excited. Broken Face looked at the hills around him, and would not let more than a few ride ahead to hunt.

Stearns borrowed a Sioux bow and arrows from one of the Delawares. He signalled to Little Belly. Riding beside Stearns, the Blackfoot went out to hunt. With them were the Delawares, Broken Face, and a few of the trappers. When Broken Face first saw the weapons Little Belly carried he spoke sharply to Stearns, who laughed.

Little Belly's mule was not for hunting buffalo, so the Blackfoot did not go with the others to the head of the valley where the animals were. He went, instead, to the lower end, where he would have a chance to get among the buffalo when the other hunters drove them. The plan was good. When the buffalo came streaming down the valley, the startled mule was caught among them and had to run with them, or be crushed.

In the excitement Little Belly forgot everything but that he was a hunter. He rode and shouted, driving his arrows through the lungs of fat cows. He could not guide his mount, for it was terror-stricken by the dust and noise and shock of huge brown bodies all around it. When there was a chance the mule ran straight up a hill and into the trees in spite of all that Little Belly could do to turn it.

He saw Stearns still riding, on through the valley and to a plain beyond where the buffalo still ran. Little Belly had one arrow left. He tried to ride after Stearns, but the mule did not like the valley and was stubborn about going into it. By the time the Blackfoot got steady movement from his mount, Stearns was coming back to where Broken Face and some of the other hunters were riding around a wounded bull that charged them in short rushes.

Down in the valley, Stearns said to Yancey, "That bull has a dozen bullets in him!"

"He can take three dozen." Yancey looked up the hill toward Little Belly. "Your Blackfoot missed a good chance to light out."

Stearns was more interested in the wounded buffalo at the moment. The hunters were having sport with it, running their horses at it. Occasionally a man put another shot into it. With purple blood streaming from its mouth and nostrils, rolling its woolly head, the bull defied them to kill it. Dust spouted from its sides when bullets struck. The buffalo bellowed, more in anger than in pain.

"How long can it last?" Stearns asked, amazed.

"A long time," Yancey said. "I've seen 'em walk away with a month's supply of good galena."

"I can kill it in one minute."

Yancey shook his head. "Not even that gun of yours."

"One shot."

"Don't get off your horse, you damned fool!"

Stearns was already on the ground. "One minute, Yancey." He looked at his watch. He walked toward the bull.

Red-eyed, with lowered head, the buffalo watched him. It charged. Stearns fired one barrel. It was nothing. The bull came on. Stearns fired again. The buffalo went down, and like the bear, it died almost at Stearns' feet.

"You damned fool!" Yancey said. "You shot it head-on!"

Stearns laughed. "Twice. For a flash, I didn't think that second one would do the work."

Little Belly had seen. There was no doubt now: Stearns had made medicine with the round thing and it had given him power to do the impossible.

The hunters began to butcher cows. Fleet horses stood without riders. Little Belly had one arrow left, and Stearns was now apart from the others, examining the dead bull. But when the Blackfoot reached the valley Broken Face was once more near Stearns, with his rifle slanting toward Little Belly.

"Take that arrow he's got left," Yancey said.

Stearns did so. "I was going to give him his chance."

"You don't give a Blackfoot any chance!" Yancey started away. "There's other arrows sticking in some of the cows he shot. Remember that, Stearns."

Little Belly did not understand the words, but the happy challenge of Stearns' smile was clear enough.

They went together to one of the cows Little Belly had killed. The white man cut the arrow from its lungs. He put the arrow on the ground and then he walked a few paces and laid his rifle on the grass. He looked at Little Belly, waiting.

The white man still had his medicine. It was too strong for Little Belly; but otherwise, he would not have been afraid to take the opportunity offered him. He tossed his bow toward the mule. The white man was disappointed.

They ate of the steaming hot liver of the cow, looking at each other while they chewed.

That night the company of Broken Face feasted well, ripping with their teeth, the great, rich pieces of dripping hump rib as they squatted at the fires. Little Belly ate with the rest, filling his belly, filling his mind with the last details of his plan.

When the stars were cold above, he rose from his blanket and went to the fire. He roasted meat, looking toward the outer rim of darkness where Stearns slept near Broken Face. Then, without stealth, Little Belly went through the night to where the French *engagée* guarded one side of the horse corral.

The Frenchman saw him coming from the fire and was not alarmed. Little Belly held out the meat. The man took it with one hand, still holding to his rifle. After a time the guard squatted down, using both hands to hold the rib while he ate. Little Belly's hand trailed through the dark, touching the stock of the gun that leaned against the man's leg.

The *engagée* smacked his lips. The meat was still against his beard when Little Belly snatched the gun and swung it. Quite happy the Frenchman died, eating good fat cow. Little Belly took his knife at once. He crouched, listening. The rifle barrel had made sound. Moments later, the horses shifting inside their rope enclosure made sound also.

Little Belly started back to the fire, and then he saw that two trappers had risen and were roasting meat. He put the knife at the back of his belt and went forward boldly. He picked up his blanket and threw it around him. He lay down near Stearns and Broken Face.

One of the trappers said, "Was that Blackfoot sleeping there before?"

Grease dripped from the other trapper's chin as he looked across the fire. "Don't recall. I know I don't want him sleeping near me. I been uneasy ever since that Blood took up with us."

After the white men had eaten they went back to their blankets. The camp became quiet. For a long time Little Belly watched the cold star-fires in the sky, and listened to the breathing of Stearns.

Then, silent as the shadows closing on the dying fire, the Blackfoot moved. At last, on his knees beside Stearns, with the knife in one hand, Little Belly's fingers walked beneath the blanket until he touched and gripped the metal rope of Stearns' great medicine. To kill the owner before taking his medicine would mean the power of it would go with his spirit to another place.

Little Belly's fingers clutched the chain. The other hand swung the knife high.

Out of the dark came a great fist. It smashed against Little Belly's forehead. It flung him back upon the ground. The white stars flashed in his brain, and he did not know that he held the medicine in his hand.

Stearns was surging up. Broken Face was out of his blanket in an instant. The hammer of his rifle clicked. Little

Belly rolled away, bumping into packs of trade goods. He leaped up and ran. A rifle gushed. The bullet sought him. He heard it tear a tree. He ran. The medicine bumped his wrist. Great was Little Belly's exultation.

Stearns' rifle boomed twice, the bullets growling close to Little Belly; but now nothing could harm him. The great medicine was in his hand, and his legs were fleet.

The camp roared. Above it all, Little Belly heard Stearns' mighty laugh. The white man had not yet discovered his terrible loss, Little Belly thought. Stearns and maybe others would follow him now, deep into the lands of his own people.

When day came Little Belly saw no signs that Stearns or any of the white men were pursuing him. It occurred to him that they were afraid to do so, now that he had stolen their greatest power.

The medicine was warm. All night he had carried it in his hand, sometimes listening with awe to the tiny talk it made. It frightened him to think of opening the lids, but he knew he must do so; this medicine that lived must look into his face and know who owned it now. He pried one lid open. There was another with a carved picture of a running horse and talking signs that curved like grass in the wind.

Now Little Belly knew why Stearns' horse had been more powerful and fleeter than any owned by other members of Broken Face's company.

Little Belly opened the second lid. His muscles jerked. He grunted. Golden talking signs looked at him from a white face. There were two long pointing arrows, and a tiny one that moved about a small circle. The song of the medicine was strong and steady, talking of the winds that blew across the mountains, telling of the stars that flowed in the summer sky, telling of the coming and going of the moon and sun.

Here was captured the power of strong deeds, held in the mysterious whispering of the medicine. Now Little Belly would be great forever among the Blackfeet, and his people would be great.

The age-old longing of all men to control events that marched against them was satisfied in Little Belly. He pushed the lids together. He held the medicine in both hands, looking at the sky.

In his pouch was his old medicine that sometimes failed, the dried eye of a mountain lion, a blue feather that had fallen in the forest when Little Belly had seen no bird near, a bright green rock shaped like the head of a pony, the claw of an eagle, and other things.

When the sun was straight above, the Crows were on his trail. He saw all three of them when they rode across a park. His first thought was to run hard, staying in the heavy timber where their ponies could not go. He had learned that on his first war party against the Crows long ago.

One of the enemies would stay on Little Belly's trail. The others would circle around to keep him from reaching the next ridge. It was a matter of running fast. Little Belly started. He stopped, remembering that he had powerful medicine.

He took it from his pouch and looked at it, as Stearns had done before he killed the bear, before he killed the great buffalo. The medicine made its steady whisper in the silent forest. It told Little Belly that he was greater than all enemies.

So he did not run. He went back on his own trail and hid behind a log. No jay warned of his presence. No squirrel shouted at him. His medicine kept them silent. And his medicine brought the Crow, leading his pony, straight to Little Belly.

While the Crow was turning, Little Belly was over the log with his knife. Quickly, savagely, he struck. A few minutes later he had a scalp, a heavy musket, another knife, and a pony. He gave fierce thanks to his medicine.

Little Belly rode into the open below one end of the ridge. The Crow circling there saw him and came to the edge of the trees. Little Belly knew him at once, Thunder Coming, a young war chief of the Crows. They taunted each other. Little Belly waved the fresh scalp. Thunder Coming rode into the open to meet his enemy. Out of rifle-shot, they ran their ponies around each other, yelling more insults.

At last they rode toward each other. Both fired their rifles and missed. At once Thunder Coming turned his horse and rode away to reload.

Little Belly would have done the same, except that he knew how strong his medicine was. He raced after Thunder Coming. The Crow was startled by this breach of custom, but when he realized that he was running from one who chased him, he started to swing his pony in a great circle to come back.

The Blackfoot knew what was in Thunder Coming's mind then. The Crow expected them to try to ride close to each other, striking coup, not to kill but to gain glory.

Little Belly allowed it to start that way. Then he swerved his pony, and instead of striking lightly and flashing past, he crashed into Thunder Coming, and swung the musket like a war club.

Thunder Coming died because he believed in the customs of war between Blackfeet and Crows; but Little Belly knew he died because of medicine he could not stand against. There was meat in Thunder Coming's pouch. That, along with his scalp, was welcome.

For a while Little Belly stayed in the open, waiting for the third Crow to appear. The last enemy did not come. Although the Blackfoot's medicine was great this day, he did not care to wait too long in Crow country. He went home with two Crow scalps and two Crow ponies.

The young men called him brave. The old chiefs were pleased. Little Belly boasted of his medicine. With it, he sang, the white men could be swept from the hills. The Blackfeet became excited, ready for battle. The women wailed against the coming bloodshed.

Each night when the first stars came Little Belly talked to his medicine, just as he had seen Stearns do; but the Blackfoot did not let others see him when he twisted the small stalk that protruded from the flattened ball. The medicine made a tiny whirring noise to show that it was pleased.

While the Blackfeet made ready for war, sending scouts to report each day on the progress of Broken Face and his company, Little Belly guarded his medicine jealously. It was living medicine. It was what the white men would not reveal to the Nez Perces who had sent chiefs down the muddy river. Little Belly had not gone begging white men to tell what made them powerful; he had stolen the secret honorably.

Now he had the strength of a bear and the wisdom of a beaver. His fight against the Crows had proved how mighty was his medicine. With it he would be great, and the Blackfeet would be great because he could lead them to victory against all enemies.

It was right that he should begin by leading them against the trappers. Let the old chiefs sit upon a hill. Every day the scouts returned, telling how carefully the white men held their camps. The scouts named men they had seen in the company, strong warriors who had fought the Blackfeet before.

Thunder and the old chiefs were thoughtful. They agreed it was right for Little Belly to lead the fight.

At last the Blackfeet rode to war.

For several days Jarv Yancey had been worried. The Delaware outriders were not holding far from the line of travel now; they had seen too much spying from the hills, and this was Blackfoot country.

"How do they usually come at you?" Stearns asked.

"When you're not looking for 'em," Yancey said.

"Would they hit a company this big?"

"We'll find out."

Stearns laughed. "Maybe I'll get my watch back."

"Be more concerned with holding onto your hair."

The trappers camped that night in a clump of timber with open space all around it. Yancey sent the guards out into the open, and they lay there in the moonlight, peering across the wet grass, watching for movement from the black masses of the hills. The silence of the mountains rested hard upon them that night.

Cramped and wet, those who stood the early morning watch breathed more easily when dawn came sliding from the sky and brought no stealthy rustling of the grass, no shrieks of bullets.

All that day, the Delawares, on the flanks and out ahead and on the backtrail, seemed to be crowding closer and closer to the caravan. They knew; they smelled it. And Yancey and the other trappers could smell it too. Stearns was quieter than usual, but not subdued. His light blue eyes smiled into the fire that night before he went out to take his turn at guard.

The trappers watched him keenly. They knew how joyfully he risked his neck against big game, doing foolish things. The Bloods were something else.

Mandan Ingalls was satisfied. He said to Sam Williams, "He don't scare for nothing. He's plumb anxious to tackle the Bloods. He'd rather fight than anything."

"He come to the right country for it," Williams said.

That night a nervous *engagée* fired his rifle at a shadow. Without shouting or confusion, the camp was up and ready in a moment. Then men cursed and went back to bed, waiting for the next disturbance. The old heads remembered the war cries of the Blackfeet, the ambushes of the past, and friends long dead. Remembering, the veterans slept well while they could.

When the moon was gone Little Belly led four young men in to stampede the white men's horses. They came out of a spit of timber and crawled to a winding stream. Close to the bank, overhung with grass, they floated down the creek as silently as drifting logs.

They rose above the bank and peered fiercely through the darkness. The smell of animals close by told Little Belly how well his medicine had directed him. A guard's rifle crashed before they were among the horses. After that there was no more shooting, for Broken Face himself was at the corral, shouting orders.

In addition to the rope enclosure around the animals, they were tied together, and then picketed to logs buried in the earth. So while there was a great kicking and thumping and snorting, Little Belly and his companions were able to run with only the horses they cut loose.

But still, it was good. The raiders returned to the main war party with ten animals.

Remembering the uproar and stumbling about when the bear charged the trappers as they prepared to rest, Little Belly set the attack for evening, when Broken Face would be making camp. Two hundred warriors were ready to follow the Blackfoot war chief.

The scouts watched the trappers. The Blackfeet moved with them, staying in the trees on the hills. A few young men tried to surprise the Delawares, but the white men's scouts were wary. In the afternoon Little Belly thought he knew where the trappers would stop, in an open place near a small stand of trees. They did not trust the dark forest, now that they knew the Blackfoot were watching.

Little Belly went to make his medicine.

He opened the lids to look upon the white face with the shining talking signs. Upon the mirror of the medicine was a drop of water, left from last night's swimming in the creek. Little Belly blew it away. His face was close to the medicine. The tiny arrow was not moving. Quickly, he put the round thing to his ear.

There was no whispering. The medicine had died.

Little Belly was frightened. He remembered how Stearns had laughed through the darkness when Little Belly was running away with the round thing. There was trickery in the medicine, for it had died as soon as Little Belly sought its strength to use against white men.

The Blackfoot let the medicine fall. It struck the earth with a solid thump. He stared at it, half expecting to see it run away. And then he saw the tiny arrow was moving again.

Little Belly knelt and held the round thing in his hands. It was alive once more. He heard the talking of the power inside, the power of white men who smiled when they fought. Once more that strength was his. Now he was warm again and his courage was sound.

Even as he watched, the arrow died.

In desperation, with all the memories of Blackfoot sorrows running in his mind, Little Belly tried to make the medicine live. He talked to it by twisting the stalk. For a time the medicine was happy. It sang. The tiny arrow moved. But it died soon afterward. Little Belly twisted the stalk until the round thing choked, and the stalk would not turn any more.

He warmed the medicine, cupping it in his hands against his breast. Surely warmth would bring it back to life; but when he looked again there was no life.

He was savage then. This was white man's medicine, full of trickery and deceit. Little Belly hurled it away.

He went back to the Blackfoot warriors, who watched him with sharp eyes. Wind Eater said, "We are ready."

Looking through a haze of hate and fear, Little Belly looked below and saw that Stearns was riding with the lead scouts. "It is not time yet." The spirit of the medicine had fled back to Stearns.

"We are ready," Wind Eater said.

Little Belly went away to make medicine, this time with the items in his pouch. He did many things. He burned a pinch of tobacco. It made a curl of white smoke in the shape of death.

Yesterday, it would have been death for Blackfoot enemies. Now, Little Belly could not read his medicine and be sure. After a while he went back to the others again. They were restless.

"The white men will camp soon."

"Is not Little Belly's medicine strong?"

"The Broken Face will not be caught easily once he is camped."

"Is not Little Belly's medicine good?" Wind Eater asked.

"It is strong." Little Belly boasted, and they believed him. But his words struck from an emptiness inside. It seemed that he had thrown away his strength with the round thing. In desperation he considered going back to look for it. Maybe it had changed and was talking once more.

"We wait," Wind Eater said. "If Little Belly does not wish to lead us—"

"We go," Little Belly said.

He led the warriors down the hill.

The length of Little Belly's waiting on the hill while dark doubts chilled him was the margin by which the Blackfoot charge missed catching the trappers as the bear had caught them. Little Belly saw that it was so. The thought gave fury to his movements, and if he had been followed to where he rode, the Blackfeet could have overrun the camp in one burst.

They knocked the Delawares back upon the main company. Straight at the camp the Blackfeet thundered, shrieking, firing muskets and arrows. The first shock of surprise was their advantage. The *engagées* leaped for the clump of timber, forgetting all else. The trappers fired. While they were reloading Little Belly urged his followers to carry over them.

He himself got into the camp and fired his musket into the bearded face of a trapper standing behind a mule to reload his rifle. But there was no Blackfoot then at Little Belly's back. All the rest had swerved and were screaming past the camp.

Little Belly had to run away, and he carried the picture of Stearns, who had stood and watched him without firing his two-barrelled rifle when he might have.

The Broken Face gave orders. His men ran the mules and horses into the little stand of trees. They piled packs to lie behind. Broken Face rallied the *engagées*.

It was a fort the Blackfeet tried to ride close to the second time. The rifles of the trappers slammed warriors from the backs of racing ponies.

There would never be a rush directly into the trees, and Little Belly knew it. The fight might last for days now, but in the end, the white men, who could look calmly on the faces of their dead and still keep fighting, would win. They would not lose interest. The power of their medicine would keep them as dangerous four days from now as they were at the moment.

The Blackfeet were not unhappy. They had seen two dead white men carried into the trees, and another crawling there with wounds. There were four dead warriors; but the rest could ride around the trees for a long time, shooting, yelling, killing a few more trappers. And when the Indians tired and went away, it would take them some time to remember that they had not won.

All this Little Belly realized, and he was not happy. True, his medicine had saved him from harm even when he was among the mules and packs; but if the white man's medicine had not betrayed him before the fight, then all the other warriors would have followed close upon him and the battle would be over.

He rode out and stopped all the young men who were racing around the trees, just out of rifleshot. He made them return to the main body of warriors.

"I will kill the Broken Face," Little Belly said.

Wind Eater smiled. "By night?"

"Now. When it is done the others will be frightened with no one to lead them. They will be caught among the trees and we will kill them all." His words were not quite true, Little Belly realized. The men who rode with Broken Face would not fall apart over his death, but an individual victory would prove how strong the Blackfeet were; and then they might go all the way in, as Little Belly had fought Thunder Coming, the Crow war chief.

Cold-seated in Little Belly's reason was the knowledge that one determined charge into the trees would end everything; but a voice whispered, *If the medicine is good.*

Signalling peace, Little Belly rode alone toward the trees. The Broken Face came alone to meet him.

"Before the sun dies I will fight Broken Face here." Little Belly made a sweeping motion with his hand. He saw blood on the sleeve of the white man's shirt, but Broken Face held the arm as if it were not wounded. Little Belly knew that fear had never lived behind the maimed features of the man who watched him coldly.

"When you are dead the Blackfeet will go away?" Broken Face asked.

"If the white men go away when you are dead."

Broken Face's mouth was solemn but a smile touched his eyes briefly. "There will be a fight between us." He went back to the trees.

When Stearns knew what had been said, he grinned. "High diplomacy with no truth involved."

"That's right," Yancey said. "But killing Little Belly will take a heap of steam out of the rest."

"If you can do it."

Yancey was surprised. "I intend to."

"Your arm is hurt. Let me fight him," Stearns said.

Yancey bent his arm. The heavy muscles had been torn by a hunting arrow, but that was not enough to stop him. He looked at his packs, at mules and horses that would be fewer when the Bloods swept past again. Something in him dragged at the thought of going out. It was foolish; it was not sound business.

Casually he looked at his trappers. No matter what he did, they would not doubt his guts. Jarv Yancey's courage was a legend in the mountains and needed no proving against a miserable riled-up Blackfoot war chief. The decision balanced delicately in Yancey's mind. A man died with his partner, if the time came; and a man in command fought for those he hired, or he should not hire good men.

Yancey shook his head. "I'll do it."

"I thought so." Stearns put his arm around Yancey's shoulder in friendly fashion, and then he drove his right fist up with a twist of his body. Yancey's head snapped back. He was unconscious as Stearns lowered him to the ground.

"It's my fault that Little Belly is still alive," Stearns said. He looked at Mandan Ingalls. "You might take a look at Yancey's arm while things are quiet."

Ingalls spat. "For a while after he comes to, you're going to be lucky to be somewhere with only a Blood to pester you. If you don't handle that Blackfoot, Stearns, you'd just as well stay out there."

Stearns laughed. He took his horse from the timber with a rush. Once in the open, looking at the solid rank of Blackfoot cavalry across the grass, he leaped down and adjusted his cinch. He waved his rifle at them, beckoning. He vaulted into the saddle and waited.

The song of the dead medicine was in Little Belly's ears. It mocked him. Once more he had been tricked. Stearns, not Broken Face, was down there waiting. The power of the stolen medicine had gone through the air back to the man who owned it, and that was why the great one who laughed was waiting there, instead of Broken Face.

Silent were the ranks of Blackfeet and silent were the rifles of the trappers. Little Belly hesitated. The fierce eyes of his people turned toward him. In that instant Little Belly wondered how great he might have been without the drag of mystic thinking to temper his actions, for solid in him was a furious courage that could carry him at times without the blessing of strong medicine.

He sent his pony rushing across the grass. He knew Stearns would wait until he was very close, as he had waited for the bear, as he had faced the wounded buffalo. Riding until he estimated that moment at hand, Little Belly fired his musket.

He saw Stearns' head jerk back. He saw the streak of blood that became a running mass on the side of the white man's face. But Stearns did not tumble from his horse. He shook his head like a cornered buffalo. He raised the rifle.

Stearns shot the pony under Little Belly. The Blackfoot felt it going down in full stride. He leaped, rolling over and over in the grass, coming to his feet unharmed. The empty musket was gone then. Little Belly had only his knife.

There was a second voice to the white man's rifle. The silent mouth of it looked down at Little Belly, but the rifle did not speak. Stearns thrust it into the saddle scabbard. He leaped from his horse and walked forward, drawing his own knife. The shining mass of blood ran down his cheek and to his neck. His lips made their thin smile and his eyes were like the ice upon the mountains.

It was then that Little Belly knew that nothing could kill the white man. It was then that Little Belly remembered that his own medicine had not been sure and strong. But still the Blackfoot tried. The two men came together with a shock, striking with the knives, trying with their free hands to seize the other's wrist.

Great was Stearns' strength. When he dropped his knife and grabbed Little Belly's arm with both hands, the Blackfeet could do nothing but twist and strain. The white man bent the arm. He shifted his weight suddenly, throwing his body against Little Belly, who went spinning on the ground with the knife gone from his hand and his shoulder nearly wrenched from its socket.

A roar came from the trees. The Blackfeet were silent. Stearns picked up Little Belly's knife.

Then, like the passing of a cloud, the cold deadliness was gone from Stearns. He held the knife, and Little Belly was sitting on the ground with one arm useless; but the white man did not know what to do with the knife. He threw it away suddenly. He reached out his hand, as if to draw Little Belly to his feet.

The trappers roared angrily. Stearns drew his hand back. Little Belly was no wounded buffalo, no charging bear; there was no danger in him now. Stearns did not know what to do with him. Seeing this, the Blackfoot knew that the greatest of white men were weak with mercy; but their medicine was so strong that their weakness was also strength.

Stearns went back to his horse.

"Shoot the stinking Blood!" a trapper yelled.

Stearns did nothing at all for a moment after he got on his horse. He had forgotten Little Belly. Then a joyful light came to the white man's eyes. He laughed. The white teeth gleamed under the streak of red beard. He drew his rifle and held it high. Straight at the Blackfeet ranks he charged.

For an instant the Bloods were astounded; and then they shouted savagely. Their ponies came sweeping across the trampled grass.

Stearns shot the foremost rider. Then the white man spun his horse and went flying back toward the trees, laughing all the way.

Wild with anger, the Blackfeet followed too far.

They raced past Little Belly and on against the rifle fire coming from the island of trees. They would crush into the camp, fling themselves from their ponies, and smash the white men down! But too many Blackfeet rolled from their ponies. The charge broke at the very instant it should have been pressed all the way.

Little Belly saw this clearly. He knew that if he had been leading there would have been no difference.

His people were brave. They took their dead and wounded with them when they rode away from the steady fire of the trappers' rifles. They were brave, but they had wavered, and they had lost just when they should have won.

For one deep, clear moment Little Belly knew that medicine was nothing; but when he was running away with the rest of the warriors old heritage asserted itself; medicine was all. If the power of Stearns' round object, which could not be stolen for use against white men, had not turned Little Belly's bullet just enough to cause it to strike Stearns' cheek instead of his brain, the fight would have been much different.

Little Belly knew a great deal about white men now. They laughed because their medicine was so strong, so powerful they could spare a fallen enemy. But he would never be able to make his people understand, because they would remember Little Belly was the one who had been spared.

As he ran from the field he knew it would have been better for him if Stearns had not been strong with mercy, which was medicine too.

ELMORE LEONARD
The Tall T

Elmore Leonard (1925–) was born in New Orleans. He served in the US Navy during World War II, and on his return studied English Literature at the University of Detroit. He then worked in advertising and copyrighting before becoming a full-time author. Although Leonard is now primarily famous for his crime thrillers, he began his writing career with Westerns in the early 1950s, publishing his first Western novel, *The Bounty Hunters*, in 1953. His six other Western novels include: *The Law at Randado* (1955), *Hombre* (1961), *Valdez Is Coming* (1970) and *Gunsights* (1979). As with his fiction, Leonard's frontier stories often concern the good man pushed too far.

The following novelette was originally published (under the title 'The Captives') in the digest magazine *Argosy* in 1955. It was filmed by Budd Boetticher as *The Tall T*—one of Boetticher's most memorable Western movies— in 1957, with Randolph Scott and Maureen O'Sullivan in the lead roles. The other Leonard Western stories which have been filmed are *Hombre* /1966, *Valdez Is Coming* /1970 and '3.10 to Yuma'/1957.

HE COULD HEAR THE STAGECOACH, the faraway creaking and the muffled rumble of it, and he was thinking: It's almost an hour early. Why should it be if it left Contention on schedule?

His name was Pat Brennan. He was lean and almost tall, with a deeply tanned, pleasant face beneath the straight hatbrim low over his eyes, and he stood next to his saddle, which was on the ground, with the easy, hip-shot slouch of a rider. A Henry rifle was in his right hand and he was squinting into the sun glare, looking up the grade to the rutted road that came curving down through the spidery Joshua trees.

He lowered the Henry rifle, stock down, and let it fall across the saddle, and kept his hand away from the Colt holstered on his right leg. A man could get shot standing next to a stage road out in the middle of nowhere with a rifle in his hand.

Then, seeing the coach suddenly against the sky, billowing dust hanging over it, he felt relief and smiled to himself and raised his arm to wave as the coach passed through the Joshuas.

As the pounding wood, iron and three-team racket of it came swaying toward him, he raised both arms and felt a sudden helplessness as he saw that the driver was making no effort to stop the teams. Brennan stepped back quickly, and the coach rushed past him, the driver, alone on the boot, bending forward and down to look at him.

Brennan cupped his hands and called, "*Rintoooon!*"

The driver leaned back with the reins high and through his fingers, his boot pushing against the brake lever, and his body half-turned to look back over the top of the Concord. Brennan swung the saddle up over his shoulder and started after the coach as it ground to a stop.

He saw the company name: HATCH & HODGES, and just below it, Number 42 stenciled on the varnished door; then from a side window, he saw a man staring at him irritably as he approached. Behind the man he caught a glimpse of a woman with soft features and a small, plumed hat and eyes that looked away quickly as

Brennan's gaze passed them going up to Ed Rintoon, the driver.

"Ed, for a minute I didn't think you were going to stop."

Rintoon, a leathery, beard-stubbled man in his mid-forties, stood with one knee on the seat and looked down at Brennan with only faint surprise.

"I took you for being up to no good, standing there waving your arms."

"I'm only looking for a lift a ways."

"What happened to you?"

Brennan grinned and his thumb pointed back vaguely over his shoulder. "I was visiting Tenvoorde to see about buying some yearling stock and I lost my horse to him on a bet."

"Driver!"

Brennan turned. The man who had been at the window was now leaning halfway out of the door and looking up at Rintoon.

"I'm not paying you to pass the time of day with"—he glanced at Brennan—"with everybody we meet."

Rintoon leaned over to look down at him. "Willard, you ain't even part right, since you ain't the man that pays me."

"I chartered this coach, and you along with it!" He was a young man, hatless, his long hair mussed from the wind. Strands of it hung over his ears, and his face was flushed as he glared at Rintoon. "When I pay for a coach I expect the service that goes with it."

Rintoon said, "Willard, you calm down now."

"Mr Mims!"

Rintoon smiled faintly, glancing at Brennan. "Pat, I'd like you to meet Mr Mims." He paused, adding, "He's a bookkeeper."

Brennan touched the brim of his hat toward the coach, seeing the woman again. She looked to be in her late twenties and her eyes now were wide and frightened and not looking at him.

His glance went to Willard Mims. Mims came out of the doorway and stood pointing a finger up at Rintoon.

"Driver, you're through! I swear to God this is your last run on any line in the Territory!"

Rintoon eased himself down until he was half-sitting on the seat. "You wouldn't kid me."

"You'll see if I'm kidding!"

Rintoon shook his head. "After ten years of faithful service the boss will be sorry to see me go."

Willard Mims stared at him in silence. Then he said, his voice calmer, "You won't be so sure of yourself after we get to Bisbee."

Ignoring him, Rintoon turned to Brennan. "Swing that saddle up here."

"You hear what I said?" Willard Mims flared.

Reaching down for the saddle horn as Brennan lifted it, Rintoon answered, "You said I'd be sorry when we got to Bisbee."

"You remember that!"

"I sure will. Now you get back inside, Willard." He glanced at Brennan. "You get in there too, Pat."

Willard Mims stiffened. "I'll remind you again—this is *not* the passenger coach."

Brennan was momentarily angry, but he saw the way Rintoon was taking this and he said calmly, "You want me to walk? It's only fifteen miles to Sasabe."

"I didn't say that," Mims answered, moving to the coach door. "If you want to come, get up on the boot." He turned to look at Brennan as he pulled himself up on the foot rung. "If we'd wanted company we'd have taken the scheduled run. That clear enough for you?"

Glancing at Rintoon, Brennan swung the Henry rifle up to him and said, "Yes, sir," not looking at Mims; and he winked at Rintoon as he climbed the wheel to the driver's seat.

A moment later they were moving, slowly at first, bumping and swaying; then the road seemed to become smoother as the teams pulled faster.

Brennan leaned toward Rintoon and said, in the noise, close to the driver's grizzled face, "I wondered why the regular stage would be almost an hour early. Ed, I'm obliged to you."

Rintoon glanced at him. "Thank Mr Mims."

"Who is he anyway?"

"Old man Gateway's son-in-law. Married the boss' daughter. Married into the biggest copper claim in the country."

"The girl with him his wife?"

"Doretta," Rintoon answered. "That's Gateway's daughter. She was scheduled to be an old maid till Willard come along and saved her from spinsterhood. She's plain as a 'dobe wall."

Brennan said, "But not too plain for Willard, eh?"

Rintoon gave him a side glance. "Patrick, there ain't nothing plain about old man Gateway's holdings. That's the thing. Four years ago he bought a half interest in the Montezuma Copper Mine for two hundred and fifty thousand dollars, and he's got it back triple since then. Can you imagine anyone having that much money?"

Brennan shook his head. "Where'd he get it, to start?"

"They say he come from money and made more by using the brains God gave him, investing it."

Brennan shook his head again. "That's too much money, Ed. Too much to have to worry about."

"Not for Willard, it ain't," Rintoon said. "He started out as a bookkeeper with the company. Now he's general manager—since the wedding. The old man picked Willard because he was the only one around he thought had any polish, and he knew if he waited much longer he'd have an old maid on his hands. And, Pat,"—Rintoon leaned closer—"Willard don't talk to the old man like he does to other people."

"She didn't look so bad to me," Brennan said.

"You been down on Sasabe Creek too long," Rintoon glanced at him again. "What were you saying about losing your horse to Tenvoorde?"

"Oh, I went to see him about buying some yearlings—"

"On credit," Rintoon said.

Brennan nodded. "Though I was going to pay him some of it cash. I told him to name a fair interest rate and he'd have it in two years. But he said no. Cash on the line. No cash, no yearlings. I needed three hundred to make the deal, but I only had fifty. Then when I was going he said, 'Patrick'—you know how he talks—'I'll give you a chance to get your yearlings free,' and all the time he's eyeing this claybank mare I had along. He said, 'You bet your mare and your fifty dollars cash, I'll put up what yearlings you need and we'll race your mare against one of my string for the winner.'"

Ed Rintoon said, "And you lost."

"By a country mile."

"Pat, that don't sound like you. Why didn't you take what your fifty would buy and get on home?"

"Because I needed these yearlings plus a good seed bull. I could've bought the bull, but I wouldn't have had the yearlings to build on. That's what I told Mr Tenvoorde. I said, 'This deal's as good as the stock you're selling me. If you're taking that kind of money for a seed bull and yearlings, then you know they can produce. You're sure of getting your money.'"

"You got stock down on your Sasabe place," Rintoon said.

"Not like you think. They wintered poorly and I got a lot of building to do."

"Who's tending your herd now?"

"I still got those two Mexican boys."

"You should've known better than to go to Tenvoorde."

"I didn't have a chance. He's the only man close enough with the stock I want."

"But a bet like that—how could you fall into it? You know he'd have a pony to outstrip yours."

"Well, that was the chance I had to take."

They rode along in silence for a few minutes before Brennan asked, "Where they coming from?"

Rintoon grinned at him. "Their honeymoon. Willard made the agent put on a special run just for the two of them. Made a big fuss while Doretta tried to hide her head."

"Then"—Brennan grinned—"I'm obliged to Mr Mims, else I'd still be waiting back there with my saddle and my Henry."

Later on, topping a rise that was thick with jack pine, they were suddenly in view of the Sasabe station and the creek beyond it, as they came out of the trees and started down the mesquite-dotted sweep of the hillside.

Rintoon checked his timepiece. The regular run was due here at five o'clock. From habit, he inspected his watch, and he was surprised to see that it was only ten minutes after four. He remembered then, his mind picturing Willard Mims as he chartered the special coach.

Brennan said, "I'm getting off here at Sasabe."

"How'll you get over to your place?"

"Hank'll lend me a horse."

As they drew nearer, Rintoon was squinting, studying the three adobe houses and the corral in back. "I don't see anybody," he said. "Hank's usually out in the yard. Him or his boy."

Brennan said, "They don't expect you for an hour. That's it."

"Man, we make enough noise for somebody to come out."

Rintoon swung the teams toward the adobes, slowing them as Brennan pushed his boot against the brake lever, and they came to a stop exactly even with the front of the main adobe.

"Hank!"

Rintoon looked from the door of the adobe out over the yard. He called the name again, but there was no answer. He frowned. "The damn place sounds deserted," he said.

Brennan saw the driver's eyes drop to the sawed-off shotgun and Brennan's Henry on the floor of the boot, and then he was looking over the yard again.

"Where in hell would Hank've gone to?"

A sound came from the adobe. A boot scraping—that or something like it—and the next moment a man was standing in the open doorway. He was bearded, a dark beard faintly streaked with gray and in need of a trim. He was watching them calmly, almost indifferently, and leveling a Colt at them at the same time.

He moved out into the yard and now another man, armed with a shotgun, came out of the adobe. The bearded one held his gun on the door of the coach. The shotgun was leveled at Brennan and Rintoon.

"You-all drop your guns and come on down." He wore range clothes, soiled and sun-bleached, and he held the shotgun calmly as if doing this was not something new. He was younger than the bearded one by at least ten years.

Brennan raised his revolver from its holster and the one with the shotgun said, "Gently now," and grinned as Brennan dropped it over the wheel.

Rintoon, not wearing a handgun, had not moved.

"If you got something down in that boot," the one with the shotgun said to him, "haul it out."

Rintoon muttered something under his breath. He reached down and took hold of Brennan's Henry rifle lying next to the sawed-off shotgun, his finger slipping through the trigger guard. He came up with it hesitantly, and Brennan whispered, barely moving his lips, "Don't be crazy."

Standing up, turning, Rintoon hesitated again, then let the rifle fall.

"That all you got?"

Rintoon nodded. "That's all."

"Then come on down."

Rintoon turned his back. He bent over to climb down, his foot reaching for the wheel below, and his hand closed on the sawed-off shotgun. Brennan whispered, "Don't do it!"

Rintoon mumbled something that came out as a growl. Brennan leaned toward him as if to give him a hand down. "You got two shots. What if there're more than two of them?"

Rintoon grunted, "Look out, Pat!" His hand gripped the shotgun firmly.

Then he was turning, jumping from the wheel, the stubby scattergun flashing head-high—and at the same moment, a single revolver shot blasted the stillness. Brennan saw Rintoon crumple to the ground, the shotgun falling next to him, and he was suddenly aware of powder smoke and a man framed in the window of the adobe.

The one with the shotgun said, "Well, that just saves some time," and he glanced around as the third man came out of the adobe. "Chink, I swear you hit him in mid-air."

"I was waiting for that old man to pull something," said the one called Chink. He wore two low-slung, crossed cartridge belts and his second Colt was still in its holster.

Brennan jumped down and rolled Rintoon over gently, holding his head off the ground. He looked at the motionless form and then at Chink. "He's dead."

Chink stood with his legs apart and looked down at Brennan indifferently. "Sure he is."

"You didn't have to kill him."

Chink shrugged. "I would've, sooner or later."

"Why?"

"That's the way it is."

The man with the beard had not moved. He said now, quietly, "Chink, you shut your mouth." Then he glanced at the man with the shotgun and said, in the same tone, "Billy-Jack, get them out of there," and nodded toward the coach.

Chapter Two

Kneeling next to Rintoon, Brennan studied them. He watched Billy-Jack open the coach door, saw his mouth soften to a grin as Doretta Mims came out first. Her eyes went to Rintoon, but shifted away quickly. Willard Mims hesitated, then stepped down, stumbling in his haste as Billy-Jack pointed the shotgun at him. He stood next to his wife and stared unblinkingly at Rintoon's body.

That one, Brennan was thinking, looking at the man with the beard—that's the one to watch. He's calling it, and he doesn't look as though he gets excited. . . . And the one called Chink. . . .

Brennan's eyes went to him. He was standing hip-cocked, his hat on the back of his head and the drawstring from it pulled tight beneath his lower lip, his free hand fingering the string idly, the other hand holding the long-barreled .44 Colt, pointed down but cocked.

He wants somebody to try something, Brennan thought. He's itching for it. He wears two guns and he thinks he's good. Well, maybe he is. But he's young, the youngest of the three, and he's anxious. His gaze stayed on Chink and it went through his mind: Don't even reach for a cigarette when he's around.

The one with the beard said, "Billy-Jack, get up on top of the coach."

Brennan's eyes raised, watching the man step from the wheel hub to the boot and then kneel on the driver's seat. He's number-three man, Brennan thought. He keeps looking at the woman. But don't bet him short. He carries a big-gauge gun.

"Frank, there ain't nothing up here but an old saddle."

The one with the beard—Frank Usher—raised his eyes. "Look under it."

"Ain't nothing there, either."

Usher's eyes went to Willard Mims, then swung slowly to Brennan. "Where's the mail?"

"I wouldn't know," Brennan said.

Frank Usher looked at Willard Mims again. "You tell me."

"This isn't the stage," Willard Mims said hesitantly. His face relaxed then, almost to the point of smiling. "You made a mistake. The regular stage isn't due for almost an hour." He went on, excitement rising in his voice. "That's what you want, the stage that's due here at five. This is one I chartered." He smiled now. "See, me and my wife are just coming back from a honeymoon and, you know—"

Frank Usher looked at Brennan. "Is that right?"

"Of course it is!" Mims' voice rose. "Go in and check the schedule."

"I'm asking this man."

Brennan shrugged. "I wouldn't know."

"He don't know anything," Chink said.

Billy-Jack came down off the coach and Usher said to him, "Go in and look for a schedule." He nodded toward Doretta Mims. "Take that woman with you. Have her put some coffee on, and something to eat."

Brennan said, "What did you do with Hank?"

Frank Usher's dull eyes moved to Brennan. "Who's he?"

"The station man here."

Chink grinned and waved his revolver, pointing it off beyond the main adobe. "He's over yonder in the well."

Usher said, "Does that answer it?"

"What about his boy?"

"He's with him," Usher said. "Anything else?"

Brennan shook his head slowly. "That's enough." He knew they were both dead and suddenly he was very much afraid of this dull-eyed, soft-voiced man with the beard; it took an effort to keep himself calm. He watched Billy-Jack take Doretta by the arm. She looked imploringly at her husband, holding back, but he made no move to help her. Billy-Jack jerked her arm roughly and she went with him.

Willard Mims said, "He'll find the schedule. Like I said, it's due at five o'clock. I can see how you made the mistake"—Willard was smiling—"thinking we were the regular stage. Hell, we were just going home . . . down to Bisbee. You'll see, five o'clock sharp that regular passenger-mail run'll pull in."

"He's a talker," Chink said.

Billy-Jack appeared in the doorway of the adobe. "Frank, five o'clock, sure as hell!" He waved a sheet of yellow paper.

"See!" Willard Mims was grinning excitedly. "Listen, you let us go and we'll be on our way"—his voice rose—"and I swear to God we'll never breathe we saw a thing."

Chink shook his head. "He's somethin'."

"Listen, I swear to God we won't tell *anything*!"

"I know you won't," Frank Usher said. He looked at Brennan and nodded toward Mims. "Where'd you find him?"

"We just met."

"Do you go along with what he's saying?"

"If I said yes," Brennan answered, "you wouldn't believe me. And you'd be right."

A smile almost touched Frank Usher's mouth. "Dumb even talking about it, isn't it?"

"I guess it is," Brennan said.

"You know what's going to happen to you?" Usher asked him tonelessly.

Brennan nodded, without answering.

Frank Usher studied him in silence. Then, "Are you scared?"

Brennan nodded again. "Sure I am."

"You're honest about it. I'll say that for you."

"I don't know of a better time to be honest," Brennan said.

Chink said, "That damn well's going to be chock full."

Willard Mims had listened with disbelief, his eyes wide. Now he said hurriedly, "Wait a minute! What're you listening to him for? I told you, I swear to God I won't say one word about this. If you don't trust him, then keep him here! I don't know this man. I'm not speaking for him, anyway."

"I'd be inclined to trust him before I would you," Frank Usher said.

"He's got nothing to do with it! We picked him up out on the desert!"

Chink raised his .44 waist-high, looking at Willard Mims, and said, "Start running for that well and see if you can make it."

"Man, be reasonable!"

Frank Usher shook his head. "You aren't leaving, and you're not going to be standing here when the stage pulls in. You can scream and carry on, but that's the way it is."

"What about my wife?"

"I can't help her being a woman."

Willard Mims was about to say something, but stopped. His eyes went to the adobe, then back to Usher. He lowered his voice and all the excitement was gone from it. "You know who she is?" He moved closer to Usher. "She's the daughter of old man Gateway, who happens to own part of the third richest copper mine in Arizona. You know what that amounts to? To date, three-quarters of a million dollars." He said this slowly, looking straight at Frank Usher.

"Make a point out of it," Usher said.

"Man, it's staring you right in the face! You got the daughter of a man who's practically a millionaire. His only daughter! What do you think he'd pay to get her back?"

Frank Usher said, "I don't know. What?"

"Whatever you ask! You sit here waiting for a two-bit holdup and you got a gold mine right in your hands!"

"How do I know she's his daughter?"

Willard Mims looked at Brennan. "You were talking to that driver. Didn't he tell you?"

Brennan hesitated. If the man wanted to bargain with his wife, that was his business. It would give them time; that was the main thing. Brennan nodded. "That's right. His wife is Doretta Gateway."

"Where do you come in?" Usher asked Willard Mims.

"I'm Mr Gateway's general manager on the Montezuma operation."

Frank Usher was silent now, staring at Mims. Finally he said, "I suppose you'd be willing to ride in with a note."

"Certainly," Mims quickly replied.

"And we'd never see you again."

"Would I save my own skin and leave my wife here?"

Usher nodded. "I believe you would."

"Then there's no use talking about it." Mims shrugged and, watching him, Brennan knew he was acting, taking a long chance.

"We can talk about it," Frank Usher said, "because if we do it, we do it my way." He glanced at the house. "Billy-Jack!" Then to Brennan, "You and him go sit over against the wall."

Billy-Jack came out, and from the wall of the adobe, Brennan and Willard watched the three outlaws. They stood in close, and Frank Usher was doing the talking. After a few minutes Billy-Jack went into the adobe again and came out with the yellow stage schedule and an envelope. Usher took them, and against the door of the Concord, wrote something on the back of the schedule.

He came toward them folding the paper into the envelope. He sealed the envelope and handed it with the pencil to Willard Mims. "You put Gateway's name on it and where to find him. Mark it personal and urgent."

Willard Mims said, "I can see him myself and tell him."

"You will," Frank Usher said, "but not how you think. You're going to stop on the main road one mile before you get to Bisbee and give that envelope to somebody passing in. The note tells Gateway you have something to tell him about his daughter and to come alone. When he goes out, you'll tell him the story. If he says no, then he never sees his daughter again. If he says yes, he's to bring fifty thousand in U.S. script divided in three saddle bags, to a place up back of the Sasabe. And he brings it alone."

Mims said, "What if there isn't that much cash on hand?"

"That's his problem."

"Well, why can't I go right to his house and tell him?"

"Because Billy-Jack's going to be along to bring you back after you tell him. And I don't want him some place he can get cornered."

"Oh . . ."

"That's whether he says yes or no," Frank Usher added.

Mims was silent for a moment. "But how'll Mr Gateway know where to come?"

"If he agrees, Billy-Jack'll give him directions."

Mims said, "Then when he comes out you'll let us go? Is that it?"

"That's it."

"When do we leave?"

"Right this minute."

"Can I say good-bye to my wife?"

"We'll do it for you."

Brennan watched Billy-Jack come around from the corral, leading two horses. Willard Mims moved toward one of them and they both mounted. Billy-Jack reined his horse suddenly, crowding Mims to turn with him, then slapped Mims' horse on the rump and spurred after it as the horse broke to a run.

Watching them, his eyes half closed, Frank Usher said, "That boy puts his wife up on the stake and then he wants to kiss her good-bye." He glanced at Brennan. "You figure that one for me."

Brennan shook his head. "What I'd like to know is why you only asked for fifty thousand."

Frank Usher shrugged, "I'm not greedy."

Chapter Three

Chink turned as the two horses splashed over the creek and grew gradually smaller down the road. He looked at Brennan and then his eyes went to Frank Usher. "We don't have a need for this one, Frank."

Usher's dull eyes flicked toward him. "You bring around the horses and I'll worry about him."

"We might as well do it now as later," Chink said.

"We're taking him with us."

"What for?"

"Because I say so. That reason enough?"

"Frank, we could run him for the well and both take a crack at him."

"Get the horses," Frank Usher said flatly and stared at Chink until the gunman turned and walked away.

Brennan said, "I'd like to bury this man before we go."

Usher shook his head. "Put him in the well."

"That's no fit place!"

Usher stared at Brennan for a long moment. "Don't push your luck. He goes in the well, whether you do it or Chink does."

Brennan pulled Rintoon's limp body up over his shoulder and carried him across the yard. When he returned, Chink was coming around the adobe with three horses already saddled. Frank Usher stood near the house and now Doretta Mims appeared in the doorway.

Usher looked at her. "You'll have to fork one of these like the rest of us. There ain't no lady's saddle about."

She came out, neither answering nor looking at him.

Usher called to Brennan, "Cut one out of that team and shoo the rest," nodding to the stagecoach.

Minutes later the Sasabe station was deserted.

They followed the creek west for almost an hour before swinging south toward high country. Leaving the creek,

Brennan had thought: Five more miles and I'm home. And his eyes hung on the long shallow cup of the Sasabe valley until they entered a trough that climbed winding ahead of them through the hills, and the valley was no longer in view.

Frank Usher led them single file—Doretta Mims, followed by Brennan, and Chink bringing up the rear. Chink rode slouched, swaying with the movement of his dun mare, chewing idly on the drawstring of his hat, and watching Brennan.

Brennan kept his eyes on the woman much of the time. For almost a mile, as they rode along the creek, he had watched her body shaking silently and he knew that she was crying. She had very nearly cried mounting the horse—pulling her skirts down almost desperately, then sitting, holding onto the saddle horn with both hands, biting her lower lip and not looking at them. Chink had side-stepped his dun close to her and said something, and she had turned her head quickly as the color rose from her throat over her face.

They dipped down into a barranca thick with willow and cottonwood and followed another stream that finally disappeared into the rocks at the far end. And after that they began to climb again. For some time they rode through the soft gloom of timber, following switchbacks as the slope became steeper, then came out into the open and crossed a bare gravelly slope, the sandstone peaks above them cold pink in the fading sunlight.

They were nearing the other side of the open grade when Frank Usher said, "Here we are."

Brennan looked beyond him and now he could make out, through the pines they were approaching, a weather-scarred stone-and-log hut built snugly against the steep wall of sandstone. Against one side of the hut was a hide-covered lean-to. He heard Frank Usher say, "Chink, you get the man making a fire and I'll get the woman fixing supper."

There had not been time to eat what the woman had prepared at the stage station and now Frank Usher and Chink ate hungrily, hunkered down a dozen yards out from the lean-to where Brennan and the woman stood.

Brennan took a plate of the jerky and day-old pan bread, but Doretta Mims did not touch the food. She stood next to him, half turned from him, and continued to stare through the trees across the bare slope in the direction they had come. Once Brennan said to her, "You better eat something," but she did not answer him.

When they were finished, Frank Usher ordered them into the hut.

"You stay there the night . . . and if either of you comes near the door, we'll let go, no questions asked. That plain?"

The woman went in hurriedly. When Brennan entered he saw her huddled against the back wall near a corner.

The sod-covered hut was windowless, and he could barely make her out in the dimness. He wanted to go and sit next to her, but it went through his mind that most likely she was as afraid of him as she was of Frank Usher and Chink. So he made room for himself against the wall where they had placed the saddles, folding a saddle blanket to rest his elbow on as he eased himself to the dirt floor. Let her try and get hold of herself, he thought; then maybe she will want somebody to talk to.

He made a cigarette and lit it, seeing the mask of her face briefly as the match flared, then he eased himself lower until his head was resting against a saddle, and smoked in the dim silence.

Soon the hut was full dark. Now he could not see the woman though he imagined that he could feel her presence. Outside, Usher and Chink had added wood to the cook fire in front of the lean-to and the warm glow of it illuminated the doorless opening of the hut.

They'll sit by the fire, Brennan thought, and one of them will always be awake. You'd get about one step through that door and *bam*. Maybe Frank would aim low, but Chink would shoot to kill. He became angry thinking of Chink, but there was nothing he could do about it and he drew on the cigarette slowly to make himself relax, thinking: Take it easy; you've got the woman to consider. He thought of her as his responsibility and not even a doubt entered his mind that she was not.

She was a woman, alone. The reason was as simple as that.

He heard her move as he was snubbing out the cigarette. He lay still and he knew that she was coming toward him. She knelt as she reached his side.

"Do you know what they've done with my husband?"

He could picture her drawn face, eyes staring wide-open in the darkness. He raised himself slowly and felt her stiffen as he touched her arm. "Sit down here and you'll be more comfortable." He moved over to let her sit on the saddle blanket. "Your husband's all right," he said.

"Where is he?"

"They didn't tell you?"

"No."

Brennan paused. "One of them took him to Bisbee to see your father."

"My father?"

"To ask him to pay to get you back."

"Then my husband's all right." She was relieved, and it was in the sound of her voice.

Brennan said, after a moment, "Why don't you go to sleep now? You can rest back on one of these saddles."

"I'm not tired."

"Well, you will be if you don't get some sleep."

She said then, "They must have known all the time that we were coming."

Brennan said nothing.

"Didn't they?"

"I don't know, ma'am."

"How else would they know about . . . who my father is?"

"Maybe so."

"One of them must have been in Contention and heard my husband charter the coach. Perhaps he had visited Bisbee and knew that my father . . ." Her voice trailed off because she was speaking more to herself than to Brennan.

After a pause Brennan said, "You sound like you feel a little better."

He heard her exhale slowly and he could imagine she was trying to smile.

"Yes, I believe I do now," she replied.

"Your husband will be back sometime tomorrow morning," Brennan said to her.

She touched his arm lightly. "I *do* feel better, Mr Brennan."

He was surprised that she remembered his name. Rintoon had mentioned it only once, hours before. "I'm glad you do. Now, why don't you try to sleep?"

She eased back gently until she was lying down and for a few minutes there was silence.

"Mr Brennan?"

"Yes, ma'am."

"I'm terribly sorry about your friend:"

"Who?"

"The driver."

"Oh. Thank you."

"I'll remember him in my prayers," she said, and after this she did not speak again.

Brennan smoked another cigarette, then sat unmoving for what he judged to be at least a half hour, until he was sure Doretta Mims was asleep.

Now he crawled across the dirt floor to the opposite wall. He went down on his stomach and edged toward the door, keeping close to the wall. Pressing his face close to the opening, he could see, off to the right side, the fire, dying down now. The shape of a man wrapped in a blanket was lying full-length on the other side of it.

Brennan rose slowly, hugging the wall. He inched his head out to see the side of the fire closest to the lean-to, and as he did he heard the unmistakable click of a revolver being cocked. Abruptly he brought his head in and went back to the saddle next to Doretta Mims.

Chapter Four

In the morning they brought Doretta Mims out to cook; then sent her back to the hut while they ate. When they had finished they let Brennan and Doretta come out to the lean-to.

Frank Usher said, "That wasn't a head I seen pokin' out the door last night, was it?"

"If it was," Brennan answered, "why didn't you shoot at it?"

"I about did. Lucky thing it disappeared," Usher said. "Whatever it was." And he walked away, through the trees to where the horses were picketed.

Chink sat down on a stump and began making a cigarette.

A few steps from Doretta Mims, Brennan leaned against the hut and began eating. He could see her profile as she turned her head to look out through the trees and across the open slope.

Maybe she *is* a little plain, he thought. Her nose doesn't have the kind of a clean-cut shape that stays in your mind. And her hair—if she didn't have it pulled back so tight she'd look a little younger, and happier. She could do something with her hair. She could do something with her clothes, too, to let you know she's a woman.

He felt sorry for her, seeing her biting her lower lip, still staring off through the trees. And for a reason he did not understand, though he knew it had nothing to do with sympathy, he felt very close to her, as if he had known her for a long time, as if he could look into her eyes—not just now, but any time—and know what she was thinking. He realized that it was sympathy, in a sense, but not the feeling-sorry kind. He could picture her as a little girl, and self-consciously growing up, and he could imagine vaguely what her father was like. And now—a sensitive girl, afraid of saying the wrong thing; afraid of speaking out of turn even if it meant wondering about instead of knowing what had happened to her husband. Afraid of sounding silly, while men like her husband talked and talked and said nothing. But even having to listen to him, she would not speak against him, because he was her husband.

That's the kind of woman to have, Brennan thought. One that'll stick by you, no matter what. And, he thought, still looking at her, one that's got some insides to her. Not just all on the surface. Probably you would have to lose a woman like that to really appreciate her.

"Mrs Mims."

She looked at him, her eyes still bearing the anxiety of watching through the trees.

"He'll come, Mrs Mims. Pretty soon now."

Frank Usher returned and motioned them into the hut again. He talked to Chink for a few minutes and now the gunman walked off through the trees.

Looking out from the doorway of the hut, Brennan said over his shoulder, "One of them's going out now to watch for your husband." He glanced around at Doretta Mims and she answered him with a hesitant smile.

Frank Usher was standing by the lean-to when Chink came back through the trees some time later. He walked out to meet him.

"They coming?"

Chink nodded. "Starting across the slope."

Minutes later, two horses came into view crossing the grade. As they came through the trees, Frank Usher called, "Tie up in the shade there!" He and Chink watched the two men dismount, then came across the clearing toward them.

"It's all set!" Willard Mims called.

Frank Usher waited until they reached him. "What'd he say?"

"He said he'd bring the money."

"That right, Billy-Jack?"

Billy-Jack nodded. "That's what he said." He was carrying Rintoon's sawed-off shotgun.

"You didn't suspect any funny business?"

Billy-Jack shook his head.

Usher fingered his beard gently, holding Mims with his gaze. "He can scare up that much money?"

"He said he could, though it will take most of today to do it."

"That means he'll come out tomorrow," Usher said.

Willard Mims nodded. "That's right."

Usher's eyes went to Billy-Jack. "You gave him directions?"

"Like you said, right to the mouth of that barranca, chock full of willow. Then one of us brings him in from there."

"You're sure he can find it?"

"I made him say it twice," Billy-Jack said. "Every turn."

Usher looked at Willard Mims again. "How'd he take it?"

"How do you think he took it?"

Usher was silent, staring at Mims. Then he began to stroke his beard again. "I'm asking you," he said.

Mims shrugged. "Of course, he was mad, but there wasn't anything he could do about it. He's a reasonable man."

Billy-Jack was grinning. "Frank, this time tomorrow we're sitting on top of the world."

Willard Mims nodded. "I think you made yourself a pretty good deal."

Frank Usher's eyes had not left Mims. "You want to stay here or go on back?"

"What?"

"You heard what I said."

"You mean you'd let me go . . . now?"

"We don't need you any more."

Willard Mims' eyes flicked to the hut, then back to Frank Usher. He said, almost too eagerly, "I could go back now and lead old man Gateway out here in the morning."

"Sure you could," Usher said.

"Listen, I'd rather stay with my wife, but if it means getting the old man out here faster, then I think I better go back."

Usher nodded. "I know what you mean."

"You played square with me. By God, I'll play square with you."

Mims started to turn away.

Usher said, "Don't you want to see your wife first?"

Mims hesitated. "Well, the quicker I start traveling, the better. She'll understand."

"We'll see you tomorrow then, huh?"

Mims smiled. "About the same time." He hesitated. "All right to get going now?"

"Sure."

Mims backed away a few steps, still smiling, then turned and started to walk toward the trees. He looked back once and waved.

Frank Usher watched him, his eyes half-closed in the sunlight. When Mims was almost to the trees, Usher said, quietly, "Chink, bust him."

Chink fired, the .44 held halfway between waist and shoulders, the long barrel raising slightly as he fired again and again until Mims went down, lying still as the heavy reports faded into dead silence.

Chapter Five

Frank Usher waited as Billy-Jack stooped next to Mims. He saw Billy-Jack look up, nodding his head.

"Get rid of him," Usher said, watching now as Billy-Jack dragged Mims' body through the trees to the slope and there let go of it. The lifeless body slid down the grade, raising dust, until it disappeared into the brush far below.

Frank Usher turned and walked back to the hut.

Brennan stepped aside as he reached the low doorway. Usher saw the woman on the floor, her face buried in the crook of her arm resting on one of the saddles, her shoulders moving convulsively as she sobbed.

"What's the matter with her?" he asked.

Brennan said nothing.

"I thought we were doing her a favor," Usher said. He walked over to her, his hands covering the butt of his revolver, and touched her arm with his booted toe. "Woman, don't you realize what you just got out of?"

"She didn't know he did it," Brennan said quietly.

Usher looked at him, momentarily surprised. "No, I don't guess she would, come to think of it." He looked down at Doretta Mims and nudged her again with his boot. "Didn't you know that boy was selling you? This whole idea was his, to save his own skin." Usher paused. "He was ready to leave you again just now . . . when I got awful sick of him way down deep inside."

Doretta Mims was not sobbing now, but still she did not raise her head.

Usher stared down at her. "That was some boy you were married to, would do a thing like that."

Looking from the woman to Frank Usher, Brennan said, almost angrily, "What he did was wrong, but going along with it and then shooting him was all right!"

Usher glanced sharply at Brennan. "If you can't see a difference, I'm not going to explain it to you." He turned and walked out.

Brennan stood looking down at the woman for a few moments, then went over to the door and sat down on the floor just inside it. After a while he could hear Doretta Mims crying again. And for a long time he sat listening to her muffled sobs as he looked out at the sunlit clearing now and again seeing one of the three outlaws.

He judged it to be about noon when Frank Usher and Billy-Jack rode out, walking their horses across the clearing, then into the trees, with Chink standing looking after them.

They're getting restless, Brennan thought. If they're going to stay here until tomorrow, they've got to be sure nobody's followed their sign. But it would take the best San Carlos tracker to pick up what little sign we made from Sasabe.

He saw Chink walking leisurely back to the lean-to. Chink looked toward the hut and stopped. He stood hip-cocked, with his thumbs in his crossed gun belts.

"How many did that make?" Brennan asked.

"What?" Chink straightened slightly.

Brennan nodded to where Mims had been shot. "This morning."

"That was the seventh," Chink said.

"Were they all like that?" he asked.

"How do you mean?"

"In the back."

"I'll tell you this: yours will be from the front."

"When?"

"Tomorrow before we leave. You can count on it."

"If your boss gives you the word."

"Don't worry about that," Chink said. Then, "You could make a run for it right now. It wouldn't be like just standing up gettin' it."

"I'll wait till tomorrow," Brennan said.

After a few minutes Brennan realized that the hut was quiet. He turned to look at Doretta Mims. She was sitting up, staring at the opposite wall with a dazed expression.

Brennan moved to her side and sat down again. "Mrs Mims, I'm sorry—"

"Why didn't you tell me it was his plan?"

"It wouldn't have helped anything."

She looked at Brennan now pleadingly. "He could have been doing it for all of us."

Brennan nodded. "Sure he could."

"But you don't believe that, do you?"

Brennan looked at her closely, at her eyes puffed from crying. "Mrs Mims, you knew your husband better than I did."

Her eyes lowered and she said quietly, "I feel very foolish sitting here. Terrible things have happened in these two days, yet all I can think of is myself. All I can do is look at myself and feel very foolish." Her eyes raised to his. "Do you know why, Mr Brennan? Because I know now that my husband never cared for me; because I know that he married me for his own interest." She paused. "I saw an innocent man killed yesterday and I can't even find the decency within me to pray for him."

"Mrs Mims, try and rest now."

She shook her head wearily. "I don't care what happens to me."

There was a silence before Brennan said, "When you get done feeling sorry for yourself I'll tell you something."

Her eyes came open and she looked at him, more surprised than hurt.

"Look," Brennan said. "You know it and I know it—your husband married you for your money; but you're alive and he's dead and that makes the difference. You can moon about being a fool till they shoot you tomorrow, or you can start thinking about saving your skin right now. But

I'll tell you this—it will take both of us working together to stay alive."

"But he said he'd let us—"

"You think they're going to let us go after your dad brings the money? They've killed four people in less than twenty-four hours!"

"I don't care what happens to me!"

He took her shoulders and turned her toward him. "Well, I care about me, and I'm not going to get shot in the belly tomorrow because you feel sorry for yourself!"

"But I can't help!" Doretta pleaded.

"You don't know if you can or not. We've got to keep our eyes open and we've got to think, and when the chance comes we've got to take it quick or else forget about it." His face was close to hers and he was still gripping her shoulders. "These men will kill. They've done it before and they have nothing to lose. They're going to kill us. That means we've got nothing to lose. Now you think about that a while."

He left her and went back to the door.

Brennan was called out of the hut later in the afternoon, as Usher and Billy-Jack rode in. They had shot a mule deer and Billy-Jack carried a hindquarter dangling from his saddle horn. Brennan was told to dress it down, enough for supper and the rest to be stripped and hung up to dry.

"But you take care of the supper first," Frank Usher said, adding that the woman wasn't in fit condition for cooking. "I don't want burned meat just 'cause she's in a state over her husband."

After they had eaten, Brennan took meat and coffee in to Doretta Mims.

She looked up as he offered it to her. "I don't care for anything."

He was momentarily angry, but it passed off and he said, "Suit yourself." He placed the cup and plate on the floor and went outside to finish preparing the jerky.

By the time he finished, dusk had settled over the clearing and the inside of the hut was dark as he stepped inside.

He moved to her side and his foot kicked over the tin cup. He stooped quickly, picking up the cup and plate, and even in the dimness he could see that she had eaten most of the food.

"Mr Brennan, I'm sorry for the way I've acted." She hesitated. "I thought you would understand, else I'd never have told you about—about how I felt."

"It's not a question of my understanding," Brennan said.

"I'm sorry I told you," Doretta Mims said.

He moved closer to her and knelt down, sitting back on his heels. "Look. Maybe I know how you feel, better than you think. But that's not important. Right now you don't need sympathy as much as you need a way to stay alive."

"I can't help the way I feel," she said obstinately.

Brennan was momentarily silent. He said then, "Did you love him?"

"I was married to him!"

"That's not what I asked you. While everybody's being honest, just tell me if you loved him."

She hesitated, looking down at her hands. "I'm not sure."

"But you wanted to be in love with him, more than anything."

Her head nodded slowly. "Yes."

"Did you ever think for a minute that he loved you?"

"That's not a fair question!"

"Answer it anyway!"

She hesitated again. "No, I didn't."

He said, almost brutally, "Then what have you lost outside of a little pride?"

"You don't understand," she said.

"You're afraid you can't get another man—is that what it is? Even if he married you for money, at least he married you. He was the first and last chance as far as you were concerned, so you grabbed him."

"What are you trying to do, strip me of what little self-respect I have left?"

"I'm trying to strip you of this foolishness! You think you're too plain to get a man?"

She bit her lower lip and looked away from him.

"You think nobody'll have you because you bite your lip and can't say more than two words at a time?"

"Mr Brennan—"

"Listen, you're as much woman as any of them. A hell of a lot more than some, but you've got to realize it! You've got to do something about it!"

"I can't help it if—"

"Shut up with that I-can't-help-it talk! If you can't help it, nobody can. All your life you've been sitting around waiting for something to happen to you. Sometimes you have to walk up and take what you want."

Suddenly he brought her to him, his arms circling her shoulders, and he kissed her, holding his lips to hers until he felt her body relax slowly and at the same time he knew that she was kissing him.

His lips brushed her cheek and he said, close to her, "We're going to stay alive. You're going to do exactly what I say when the time comes, and we're going to get out of here." Her hair brushed his cheek softly and he knew that she was nodding yes.

Chapter Six

During the night he opened his eyes and crawled to the lighter silhouette of the doorway. Keeping close to the front wall, he looked out and across to the low-burning fire. One of them, a shadowy form that he could not recognize, sat facing the hut. He did not move, but by the way he was sitting Brennan knew he was awake. You're running out of time, Brennan thought. But there was nothing he could do.

The sun was not yet above the trees when Frank Usher appeared in the doorway. He saw that Brennan was awake and he said, "Bring the woman out," turning away as he said it.

Her eyes were closed, but they opened as Brennan touched her shoulder, and he knew that she had not been asleep. She looked up at him calmly, her features softly shadowed.

"Stay close to me," he said. "Whatever we do, stay close to me."

They went out to the lean-to and Brennan built the fire as Doretta got the coffee and venison ready to put on.

Brennan moved slowly, as if he were tired, as if he had given up hope; but his eyes were alive and most of the time his gaze stayed with the three men—watching them eat, watching them make cigarettes as they squatted in a half-circle, talking, but too far away for their voices to be heard. Finally, Chink rose and went off into the trees. He came back with his horse, mounted, and rode off into the trees again but in the other direction, toward the open grade.

It went through Brennan's mind: He's going off like he did yesterday morning, but this time to wait for Gateway. Yesterday on foot, but today on his horse, which means he's going farther down to wait for him. And Frank went somewhere yesterday morning. Frank went over to where the horses are. He suddenly felt an excitement inside of him, deep within his stomach, and he kept his eyes on Frank Usher.

A moment later Usher stood up and started off toward the trees, calling back something to Billy-Jack about the horses—and Brennan could hardly believe his eyes.

Now. It's now. You know that, don't you? It's now or never. God help me. God help me think of something! And suddenly it was in his mind. It was less than half a chance, but it was something, and it came to him because it was the only thing about Billy-Jack that stood out in his mind, besides the shotgun: *He was always looking at Doretta!*

She was in front of the lean-to, and he moved toward her, turning his back to Billy-Jack sitting with Rintoon's shotgun across his lap.

"Go in the hut and start unbuttoning your dress." He half whispered it and saw her eyes widen as he said it. "Go On! Billy-jack will come in. Act surprised. Embarrassed. Then smile at him." She hesitated, starting to bit her lip. "Damn it, go on!"

He poured himself a cup of coffee, not looking at her as she walked away. Putting the coffee down, he saw Billy-Jack's eyes following her.

"Want a cup?" Brennan called to him. "There's about one left."

Billy-Jack shook his head and turned the sawed-off shotgun on Brennan as he saw him approaching.

Brennan took a sip of the coffee. "Aren't you going to look in on that?" He nodded toward the hut.

"What do you mean?"

"The woman," Brennan said matter-of-factly. He took another sip of the coffee.

"What about her?" Billy-Jack asked.

Brennan shrugged. "I thought you were taking turns."

"What?"

"Now, look, you can't be so young. I got to draw you a map—" Brennan smiled. "Oh, I see . . . Frank didn't say anything to you. Or Chink . . . Keeping her for themselves . . ."

Billy-Jack's eyes flicked to the hut, then back to Brennan. "They were with her?"

"Well, all I know is Frank went in there yesterday morning and Chink yesterday afternoon while you were gone." He took another sip of the coffee and threw out what was left in the cup. Turning, he said, "No skin off my nose," and walked slowly back to the lean-to.

He began scraping the tin plates, his head down, but watching Billy-Jack. Let it sink through that thick skull of yours. But do it quick! Come on, move, you animal!

There! He watched Billy-Jack walk slowly toward the hut. God, make him move faster! Billy-Jack was out of view then beyond the corner of the hut.

All right. Brennan put down the tin plate he was holding and moved quickly, noiselessly, to the side of the hut and edged along the rough logs until he reached the corner. He listened first before he looked around. Billy-Jack had gone inside.

He wanted to make sure, some way, that Billy-Jack would be looking at Doretta, but there was not time. And then he was moving again—along the front, and suddenly he was inside the hut, seeing the back of Billy-Jack's head, seeing him turning, and a glimpse of Doretta's face, and the sawed-off shotgun coming around. One of his hands shot out to grip the stubby barrel, pushing it, turning it up and back violently, and the other hand closed over the trigger guard before it jerked down on Billy-Jack's wrist.

Deafeningly, a shot exploded, with the twin barrels jammed under the outlaw's jaw. Smoke and a crimson smear, and Brennan was on top of him wrenching the shotgun from squeezed fingers, clutching Billy-Jack's revolver as he came to his feet.

He heard Doretta gasp, still with the ringing in his ears, and he said, "Don't look at him!" already turning to the doorway as he jammed the Colt into his empty holster.

Frank Usher was running across the clearing, his gun in his hand.

Brennan stepped into the doorway leveling the shotgun. "Frank, hold it there!"

Usher stopped dead, but in the next second he was aiming, his revolver coming up even with his face, and Brennan's hand squeezed the second trigger of the shotgun.

Usher screamed and went down, grabbing his knees, and he rolled to his side as he hit the ground. His right hand came up, still holding the Colt.

"Don't do it, Frank!" Brennan had dropped the scattergun and now Billy-Jack's revolver was in his hand. He saw Usher's gun coming in line, and he fired, aiming dead center at the half-reclined figure, hearing the sharp, heavy report, and seeing Usher's gun hand raise straight up into the air as he slumped over on his back.

Brennan hesitated. Get him out of there, quick. Chink's not deaf!

He ran out to Frank Usher and dragged him back to the hut, laying him next to Billy-Jack. He jammed Usher's pistol into his belt. Then, "Come on!" he told Doretta, and took her hand and ran out of the hut and across the clearing toward the side where the horses were.

They moved into the denser pines, where he stopped and pulled her down next to him in the warm sand. Then he rolled over on his stomach and parted the branches to look back out across the clearing.

The hut was to the right. Straight across were more pines, but they were scattered thinly, and through them he could see the sand-colored expanse of the open grade. Chink would come that way, Brennan knew. There was no other way he could.

Chapter Seven

Close to him, Doretta said, "We could leave before he comes." She was afraid, and it was in the sound of her voice.

"No," Brennan said. "We'll finish this. When Chink comes we'll finish it once and for all."

"But you don't know! How can you be sure you'll—"

"Listen, I'm not sure of anything, but I know what I have to do." She was silent and he said quietly, "Move back and stay close to the ground."

And as he looked across the clearing his eyes caught the dark speck of movement beyond the trees, out on the open slope. There he was. It had to be him. Brennan could feel the sharp knot in his stomach again as he watched, as the figure grew larger.

Now he was sure. Chink was on foot leading his horse, not coming straight across, but angling higher up on the slope. He'll come in where the trees are thicker, Brennan thought. He'll come out beyond the lean-to and you won't see him until he turns the corner of the hut. That's it. He can't climb the slope back of the hut, so he'll have to come around the front way.

He estimated the distance from where he was lying to the front of the hut—seventy or eighty feet—and his thumb eased back the hammer of the revolver in front of him.

There was a dead silence for perhaps ten minutes before he heard, coming from beyond the hut, "Frank?" Silence again. Then, "Where the hell are you?"

Brennan waited, feeling the smooth, heavy, hickory grip of the Colt in his hand, his finger lightly caressing the trigger. It was in his mind to fire as soon as Chink turned the corner. He was ready. But it came and it went.

It went as he saw Chink suddenly, unexpectedly, slip around the corner of the hut and flatten himself against the wall, his gun pointed toward the door. Brennan's front sight was dead on Chink's belt, but he couldn't pull the trigger. Not like this. He watched Chink edge slowly toward the door.

"Throw it down, boy!"

Chink moved and Brennan squeezed the trigger a split second late. He fired again, hearing the bullet thump solidly into the door frame, but it was too late. Chink was inside.

Brennan let his breath out slowly, relaxing somewhat. Well, that's what you get. You wait, and all you do is make it harder for yourself. He could picture Chink now looking at Usher and Billy-Jack. That'll give him something to think about. Look at them good. Then look at the door you've got to come out of sooner or later.

I'm glad he's seeing them like that. And he thought then: How long could you stand something like that? He can cover up Billy-Jack and stand it a little longer. But when dark comes . . . If he holds out till dark he's got a chance. And now he was sorry he had not pulled the trigger before. You got to make him come out, that's all.

"Chink!"

There was no answer.

"Chink, come on out!"

Suddenly gunfire came from the doorway and Brennan, hugging the ground, could hear the swishing of the bullets through the foliage above him.

Don't throw it away, he thought, looking up again. He backed up and moved over a few yards to take up a new position. He'd be on the left side of the doorway as you look at it, Brennan thought, to shoot on an angle like that.

He sighted on the inside edge of the door frame and called, "Chink, come out and get it!" He saw the powder flash, and he fired on top of it, cocked and fired again. Then silence.

Now you don't know, Brennan thought. He reloaded and called out, "Chink!" but there was no answer, and he thought: You just keep digging your hole deeper.

Maybe you did hit him. No, that's what he wants you to think. Walk in the door and you'll find out. He'll wait now. He'll take it slow and start adding up his chances. Wait till night? That's his best bet—but he can't count on his horse being there then. I could have worked around and run it off. And he knows he wouldn't be worth a damn on foot, even if he did get away. So the longer he waits, the less he can count on his horse.

All right, what would you do? Immediately he thought: I'd count shots. So you hear five shots go off in a row and you make a break out the door, and while you're doing it the one shooting picks up another gun. But even picking up another gun takes time.

He studied the distance from the doorway to the corner of the hut. Three long strides. Out of sight in less than three seconds. That's if he's thinking of it. And if he tried it, you'd have only that long to aim and fire. Unless . . .

Unless Doretta pulls off the five shots. He thought about this for some time before he was sure it could be done without endangering her. But first you have to give him the idea.

He rolled to his side to pull Usher's gun from his belt. Then, holding it in his left hand, he emptied it at the doorway. Silence followed.

I'm reloading now, Chink. Get it through your cat-eyed head. I'm reloading and you've got time to do something.

He explained it to Doretta unhurriedly—how she would wait about ten minutes before firing the first time; she would count to five and fire again, and so on until the gun was empty. She was behind the thick bole of a pine and only the gun would be exposed as she fired.

She said, "And if he doesn't come out?"

"Then we'll think of something else."

Their faces were close. She leaned toward him, closing her eyes, and kissed him softly. "I'll be waiting," she said.

Brennan moved off through the trees, circling wide, well back from the edge of the clearing. He came to the thin section directly across from Doretta's position and went quickly from tree to tree, keeping to the shadows until he was into thicker pines again. He saw Chink's horse off to the left of him. Only a few minutes remained as he came out of the trees to the off side of the lean-to, and there he went down to his knees, keeping his eyes on the corner of the hut.

The first shot rang out and he heard it *whump* into the front of the hut. One . . . then the second . . . two . . . he was counting them, not moving his eyes from the front edge of the hut . . . three . . . four . . . be ready. . . . Five! Now, Chink!

He heard him—hurried steps on the packed sand—and almost immediately he saw him cutting sharply around the edge of the hut, stopping, leaning against the wall, breathing heavily but thinking he was safe. Then Brennan stood up.

"Here's one facing you, Chink."

He saw the look of surprise, the momentary expression of shock, a full second before Chink's revolver flashed up from his side and Brennan's finger tightened on the trigger. With the report, Chink lurched back against the wall, a look of bewilderment still on his face, although he was dead even as he slumped to the ground.

Brennan holstered the revolver and did not look at Chink as he walked past him around to the front of the hut. He suddenly felt tired, but it was the kind of tired feeling you enjoyed, like the bone weariness and sense of accomplishment you felt seeing your last cow punched through the market chute.

He thought of old man Tenvoorde, and only two days ago trying to buy the yearlings from him. He still didn't have any yearlings.

What the hell do you feel so good about?

Still, he couldn't help smiling. Not having money to buy stock seemed like such a little trouble. He saw Doretta come out of the trees and he walked on across the clearing.

JACK SCHAEFER
Emmet Dutrow

Jack Schaefer (1907–) was born in Cleveland, Ohio, and educated at the Oberlin College, Ohio, and Columbia University, New York. He worked as a reporter, publisher and editor before *Shane*, published in 1947, launched him to fame as one of the best post-war writers of Westerns. (His career was undoubtedly helped by George Steven's remarkable film of the novel, starring Alan Ladd, Van Heflin, and Jean Arthur). Like *Shane*, Schaefer's subsequent frontier fiction has been written in a highly economical style, and rooted in the real history of the American West. In particular, Schaefer was influenced by Frederick Jackson Turner's *The Significance of the Frontier in American History*, which explored the different phases of the evolution of the West. Schaefer's Western novels, in addition to Shane, are: *First Blood* (1953), *The Canyon* (1953), *Monte Walsh* (1963), *Company of Cowards* (1957) and *Mavericks* (1967). He has also written three volumes of short stories: *The Big Range* (1953), *The Pioneers* (1954), and *The Kean Land and other stories* (1959).

'Emmet Dutrow' is from the *The Big Range*.

THREE DAYS HE WAS THERE on the rock ledge. I don't think he left it once. I couldn't be sure. I had things to do. But I could see him from my place and each time I looked he was there, a small dark-clad figure, immeasurably small against the cliff wall rising behind him.

Sometimes he was standing, head back and face up. Sometimes he was kneeling, head down and sunk into his shoulders. Sometimes he was sitting on one of the smaller stones.

Three days it was. And maybe the nights too. He was there when I went in at dusk and he was there when I came out in early morning. Once or twice I thought of going to him. But that would have accomplished nothing. I doubt whether he would even have noticed me. He was lost in an aloneness no one could penetrate. He was waiting for his God to get around to considering his case.

I guess this is another you'll have to let me tell in my own way. And the only way I know to tell it is in pieces, the way I saw it.

Emmet Dutrow was his name. He was of Dutch blood, at least predominantly so; the hard-shell deep-burning kind. He came from Pennsylvania, all the way to our new State of Wyoming with his heavy wide-bed wagon and slow, swinging yoke of oxen. He must have been months on the road, making his twelve to twenty miles a day when the weather was good and little or none when it was bad. The wagon carried food and farm tools and a few sparse pieces of stiff furniture beneath an old canvas. He walked and must have walked the whole way close by the heads of his oxen, guiding them with a leather thong fastened to the yoke. And behind about ten paces and to the side came his woman and his son Jess.

They camped that first night across the creek from my place. I saw him picketing the oxen for grazing and the son building a fire and the woman getting her pans from where they hung under the wagon's rear axle, and when my own chores were done and I was ready to go in for supper, I went to the creek and across on the stones in the shallows and towards their fire. He stepped out from it to confront me, blocking my way forward. He was a big man, big and broad and bulky, made more so by the queer clothes he wore. They were plain black of some rough thick material, plain black loose-fitting pants and plain black jacket like a frock-coat without any tails, and a plain black hat, shallow-crowned and stiff-brimmed. He had a square trimmed beard that covered most of his face, hiding the features, and eyes sunk far back so that you felt like peering close to see what might be in them.

Behind him the other two kept by the fire, the woman shapeless in a dark linsey-woolsey dress and pulled-forward shielding bonnet, the son dressed like his father except that he wore no hat.

I stopped. I couldn't have gone farther without walking right into him.

"'Evening, stranger," I said.

"Good evening," he said. His voice was deep and rumbled in his throat with the self-conscious roll some preachers have in the pulpit. "Have you business with me?"

"There's a quarter of beef hanging in my springhouse," I said. "I thought maybe you'd appreciate some fresh meat."

"And the price?" he said.

"No price," I said. "I'm offering you some."

He stared at me. At least the shadow-holes where his eyes hid were aimed at me. "I'll be bounden to no man," he said.

The son had edged out from the fire to look at me. He waved an arm at my place across the creek. "Say mister," he said. "Are those cattle of yours—"

"Jess!" The father's voice rolled at him like a whip uncoiling. The son flinched at the sound and stepped back by the fire. The father turned his head again to me. "Have you any further business?"

"No," I said. I swung about and went back across the creek on the stones and up the easy slope to my little frame ranchhouse.

The next day he pegged his claim, about a third of a mile farther up the valley where it narrowed and the spring floods of centuries ago had swept around the curve above and washed the rock formation bare, leaving a high cliff to mark where they had turned. His quarter section spanned the space from the cliff to the present-day creek. It was a fair choice on first appearances; good bottom land, well-watered with a tributary stream wandering through, and there was a stand of cottonwoods back by the cliff. I had passed it up because I knew how the drifts would pile in below the cliff in winter. I was snug in the bend in the valley and the hills behind protecting me. It was plain he didn't know this kind of country. He was right where the winds down the valley would hit him when the cold came dropping out of the mountains.

He was a hard worker and his son too. They were started on a cabin before the first morning was over, cutting and trimming logs and hauling them with the oxen. In two days they had the framework up and the walls shoulder high, and then the rain started and the wind, one of our late spring storms that carried a lingering chill and drenched everything open with a steady lashing beat. I thought of them there, up and across the creek, with no roof yet and unable to keep a fire going in such weather, and I pulled on boots and a slicker and an old hat and went out and waded across and went up to their place. It was nearly dark, but he and the son were still at work setting another log in place. They had taken pieces of the old canvas and cut holes for their heads and pulled the pieces down over their shoulders with their heads poking through. This made using their arms slow and awkward, but they were still working. He had run the wagon along one wall of the cabin, and with this covering one side and the rest of the old canvas fastened to hang down the other, it formed a low cavelike shelter. The woman was in there, sitting on branches for a floor, her head nearly bumping the bed of the wagon above. I could hear the inside drippings, different from the outside pattern, as the rain beat through the cracks of the wagon planks and the chinks of the log wall.

He stepped forward again to confront me and stop me, a big bulgy shape in his piece of canvas topped by the beard and hat with the shadow-holes in the eyes between.

"It's a little wet," I said. "I thought maybe you'd like to come over to my place where it's warm and dry till this storm wears itself out. I can rig enough bunks."

"No," he said, rolling his tone with the organ stops out. "We shall do with what is ours."

I started to turn away and I saw the woman peering out at me from her pathetic shelter, her face pinched and damp under the bonnet, and I turned back.

"Man alive," I said, "forget your pride or whatever's eating you and think of your wife and the boy."

"I am thinking of them," he said. "And I am the shield that shall protect them."

I swung about and started away, and when I had taken a few steps his voice rolled after me. "Perhaps you should be thanked, neighbour. Perhaps you mean well."

"Yes," I said, "I did."

I kept on going and I did not look back and I waded across the creek and went up to my house and in and turned the lamp up bright and tossed a couple more logs into the fireplace.

I tried once more, about two weeks later. He had his cabin finished then, roofed with bark slabs over close-set poles and the walls chinked tight with mud from the creek bottom. He had begun breaking ground. His oxen were handy for that. They could do what no team of horses could do, could lean to the yoke and dig their split hooves into the sod and pull a heavy ploughshare ripping through the roots of our tough buffalo grass.

That seemed to me foolish, tearing up sod that was perfect for good cattle, getting ready for dirt farming way out there far from any markets. But he was doing it right. With the ground ploughed deep and the sod turned over, the roots would be exposed and would rot all through the summer and fall and by the next spring the ground would be ready to be worked and planted. And meanwhile he could string his fences and build whatever sheds he would need and get his whole place in shape.

We ought to be getting really acquainted, I thought, being the only neighbours there in the valley and more than that, for the nearest other place was two miles away towards town. It was up to me to make the moves. I was the first in the valley. He was the second, the newcomer.

As I said, I tried once more. It was a Saturday afternoon and I was getting ready to ride to town and see if there was any mail and pick up a few things and rub elbows with other folks a bit and I thought of them there across the creek, always working and penned close with only a yoke of oxen that couldn't make the eight miles in less than half a day each way. I harnessed the team to the buckboard and drove bouncing across the creek and to their place. The woman appeared in the cabin doorway, shading her eyes and staring at me. The son stopped ploughing off to the right and let go of the plough handles and started towards me. The father came around the side of the cabin and waved him back and came close to my wagon and stopped and planted his feet firmly and looked at me.

"I'm heading towards town," I said. "I thought maybe you'd like a ride in the back. You can look the place over and meet some of the folks around here."

"No, neighbour," he said. He looked at me and then let his voice out a notch. "Sin and temptation abide in towns. When we came past I saw the two saloons and a painted woman."

"Hell, man," I said, "you find those things everywhere. They don't bite if you let them alone."

"Ah, yes," he said. "Everywhere. All along the long way I saw them. They are everywhere. That is why I stopped moving at last. There is no escaping them in towns. Wherever people congregate, there is sin. I shall keep myself and mine apart."

"All right," I said. "So you don't like people. But how about your wife and the boy? Maybe they'd like a change once in a while."

His voice rolled out another notch. "They are in my keeping." He looked at me and the light was right and for the first time I saw his eyes, bright and hot in their shadow-holes. "Neighbour," he said, all stops out, "have I trespassed on your property?"

I swung the team in an arc and drove back across the creek. I unharnessed the team and sent them out in the side pasture with slaps on their rumps. I whistled the grey in and saddled him and headed for town at a good clip.

That was the last time. After that I simply watched what was happening up the valley. You could sum up most of it with the one word—work. And the rest of it centred on the rock ledge at the base of the cliff where a hard layer jutted out about ten feet above the valley floor, flat on top like a big table. I saw him working there, swinging some tool, and after several days I saw what he was doing. He was cutting steps in the stone, chipping out steps to the ledge top. Then he took his son away from the ploughing for a day to help him heave and pry the fallen rocks off the ledge, all except three, a big squarish one and two smaller ones. Up against the big one he raised a cross made of two lengths of small log. Every day after that, if I was out early enough in the morning and late enough when the dusk was creeping in, I could see him and his woman and the son, all three of them on the ledge, kneeling, and I could imagine his voice rolling around them and echoing from the cliff behind them. And on Sundays, when there would be nothing else doing about their place at all, not even cooking-smoke rising from the cabin chimney, they would be there hours on end, the woman and the son sometimes sitting on the two smaller stones, and the father, from his position leaning over the big stone, apparently reading from a book spread open before him.

It was on a Sunday, in the afternoon, that the son trespassed on my place. He came towards the house slow and hesitating like he was afraid something might jump and snap at him. I was sitting on the porch, the Winchester across my knees, enjoying the sunshine and waiting to see if the gopher that had been making holes in my side pasture would show its head. I watched him come, a healthy young figure in his dark pants and homespun shirt. When he was close, I raised my voice.

"Whoa, Jess," I said. "Aren't you afraid some evil might scrape off me and maybe get on you?"

He grinned kind of foolish and scrubbed one shoe-toe in the dirt. "Don't make fun of me," he said. "I don't hold with that stuff the way father does. He said I could come over anyway. He's decided perhaps you're all right."

"Thanks," I said. "Since I've passed the test, why not step up here and sit a spell?"

He did, and he looked all around very curious and after a while he said: "Father thought perhaps you could tell him what to do to complete the claim and get the papers on it."

I told him, and we sat awhile, and then he said: "What kind of a gun is that?"

"It's a Winchester," I said. "A repeater. A right handy weapon."

"Could I hold it once?" he said.

I slipped on the safety and passed it to him. He set it to his shoulder and squinted along the barrel, awkward and self-conscious.

"Ever had a gun of your own?" I said.

"No," he said. He handed the gun back quickly and stared at the porch floor. "I never had anything of my own. Everything belongs to father. He hasn't a gun anyway. Only an old shotgun and he won't let me touch it." And after a minute: "I never had even a nickel of my own to buy a thing with." And after a couple of minutes more: "Why does he have to be praying all the time, can you tell me that? That's all he ever does, working and praying. Asking forgiveness for sins. For my sins and Ma's sins too. What kind of sins have we ever had a chance to do? Can you tell me that?"

"No," I said. "No, I can't."

We sat awhile longer, and he was looking out at the pasture. "Say, are those cattle—"

"Yes," I said. "They're Herefords. Purebreds. Some of the first in these parts. That's why they're fenced tight."

"How'd you ever get them?" he said. "I mean them and everything you've got here."

"Well," I said, "I was a fool youngster blowing my money fast as I found it. Then one day I decided I didn't like riding herd on another man's cattle and bony longhorns at that when I knew there were better breeds. So I started saving my pay."

"How long did it take?" he said.

"It was eleven years last month," I said, "that I started a bank account."

"That's a long time," he said. "That's an awful long time."

"How old are you, Jess?" I said.

"Nineteen," he said. "Nineteen four months back."

"When you're older," I said, "it won't seem like such a long time. When you're getting along some, time goes mighty fast."

"But I'm not older," he said.

"No." I said. "No. I guess you're not."

We sat awhile longer and then I got foolish. "Jess," I said, "the ploughing's done. That was the big job. The pressure ought to be letting up a bit now. Why don't you drop over here an afternoon or two and help me with my haying. I'll pay fair wages. Twenty-five cents an hour."

His face lit like a match striking. "Hey, mister!" Then: "But Father—"

"Jess," I said, "I never yet heard of work being sinful."

I wondered whether he would make it and Wednesday he did, coming early in the afternoon and sticking right with me till quitting hour. He was a good worker. He had to be to make up for the time he wasted asking me questions about the country and people roundabout, and my place and my stock and the years I'd spent in the saddle. He was back again on Friday. When I called quits and we went across the pasture to the house, the father was standing by the porch waiting.

"Good evening, neighbour," he said. "According to my son you mentioned several afternoons. They are done. I have come for the money."

"Dutrow," I said, "Jess did the work. Jess gets the money."

"You do not understand," he said, the tone beginning to roll. "My son is not yet of man's estate. Until he is I am responsible for him and the fruit of his labour is mine. I am sworn to guard him against evil. Money in an untried boy's pocket is a sore temptation to sin."

I went into the house and took three dollars from the purse in my jacket pocket and went out to Jess and put them in his hand. He stood there with the hand in front of him, staring down at it.

"Jess! Come here!"

He came, flinching and unwilling, the hand still stiff in front of him, and the father took the money from it.

"I'm sorry Jess," I said. "Looks like there's no point in your working here again."

He swung his eyes at me the way a whipped colt does and turned and went away, trying to hold to a steady walk and yet stumbling forward in his hurry.

"Dutrow," I said, "I hope that money burns your hand. You have already sinned with it."

"Neighbour," he said, "you take too much on yourself. My God alone shall judge my actions."

I went into the house and closed the door.

It was about a month later, in the middle of the week, that the father himself came to see me, alone in the mid-morning and wearing his black coat and strange black hat under the hot sun as he came to find me.

"Neighbour," he said, "have you see my son this morning?"

"No," I said.

"Strange," he said. "He was not on his pallet when I rose. He missed morning prayers completely. He has not appeared at all."

He stood silent a moment. Then he raised an arm and pointed a thick forefinger at me. His voice rolled at its deepest. "Neighbour," he said, "if you have contrived with my son to go forth into the world, I shall call down the wrath of my God upon you."

"Neighbour Dutrow," I said, "I don't know what your son's doing. But I know what you're going to do. You're going to shut your yap and get the hell off my place."

I don't think he heard me. He wiped a hand across his face and down over his beard. "You must pardon me," he said, "I am sore overwrought with worry."

He strode away, down to the creek and left along it out of the valley towards town. The coat flapped over his hips as he walked and he grew smaller in the distance till he rounded the first hill and disappeared.

He returned in late afternoon, still alone and dusty and tired, walking slowly and staring at the ground ahead of him. He went past on the other side of the creek and to his place and stopped at the door of the cabin and the woman emerged and they went to the rock ledge and they were still kneeling there when the dark shut them out of my sight.

The next day, well into the afternoon, I heard a horse coming along the trace that was the beginning of the road into the valley and Marshal Eakins rode up to me by the barn and swung down awkward and stiff. He was tired and worn and his left shoulder was bandaged with some of the cloth showing through the open shirt collar.

"Afternoon, John," he said. "Any coffee in the pot you could warm over?"

In the house I stirred the stove and put the pot on to heat. I pointed at his shoulder.

"One of our tough friends?" I said.

"Hell, no," he said. "I can handle them. This was an amateur. A crazy youngster."

When he had his cup, he took a first sip and leaned back in his chair.

"That the Dutrow place up the creek?" he said.

"Yes," I said.

"Must be nice neighbours," he said. "It was their boy drilled me." He tried the cup again and finished it in four gulps and reached for the pot. "His father was in town yesterday. Claimed the boy had run away. Right he was. The kid must have hid out during the day. Had himself a time at night. Pried a window at Walton's store. Packed himself a bag of food. Took a rifle and box of shells. Slipped over to the livery stable. Saddled a horse and lit out."

"He couldn't ride," I said.

"Reckon not," Eakins said. "Made a mess of the gear finding a bridle and getting it on. Left an easy track too. Didn't know how to make time on a horse. I took Patton and went after him. Must have had hours' start, but we were tailing him before ten. Got off or fell off, don't know which, and scrambled into some rocks. I told him we had the horse and if he'd throw out the gun and come out himself there wouldn't be too much fuss about it. But he went crazy wild. Shouted something about sin catching up with him and started blazing away."

"He couldn't shoot," I said.

"Maybe not," Eakins said. "But he was pumping the gun as fast as he could and he got Patton dead centre. We hadn't fired a shot."

Eakins started on the second cup.

"Well?" I said.

"So I went in and yanked him out," Eakins said. "Reckon I was a little rough. Patton was a good man."

He finished the second cup and set it down. "Got to tell his folks. Thought maybe you'd go along. Women give me the fidgets." He pushed at the cup with a finger. "Not much time. The town's a little hot. Trial will be tomorrow."

We walked down to the creek and across and up to their place. The woman appeared in the cabin doorway and stared at us. The father came from somewhere around the side of the cabin. He planted his feet firmly and confronted us. His head tilted high and his eyes were bright and hot in their shadow-holes. His voice rolled at us.

"You have found my son."

"Yes," Eakins said, "we've found him." He looked at me and back at the father and stiffened a little, and he told them, straight, factual. "The trial will be at ten tomorrow," he said. "They'll have a lawyer for him. It's out of my hands. It's up to the judge now."

And while he was talking, the father shrank right there before us. His head dropped and he seemed to dwindle inside his rough black clothes. His voice was scarcely more than a whisper.

"The sins of the fathers," he said, and was silent.

It was the woman who was speaking, out from the doorway and stretching up tall and pointing at him, the first and only words I ever heard her speak.

"You did it," she said. "You put the thoughts of sin in his head, always praying about it. And keeping him cooped in with never a thing he could call his own. On your head it is in the eyes of God. You drove him to it."

She stopped and stood still, looking at him, and her eyes were bright and hot and accusing in the pinched whiteness of her face, and she stood still, looking at him.

They had forgotten we were there. Eakins started to speak again and thought better of it. He turned to me and I nodded and we went back along the creek and across and to the barn and he climbed stiffly on his horse and started towards town.

In the morning I saddled the grey and rode to the Dutrows' place. I was thinking of offering him the loan of the team and the buck-board. There was no sign of any activity at all. The place looked deserted. The cabin door was open and I poked my head in. The woman was sitting on a straight chair by the dead fireplace. Her hands were folded in her lap and her head was bowed over them. She was sitting still. There's no other way to describe what she was doing. She was just sitting.

"Where is he?" I said.

Her head moved in my direction and she looked vaguely at me and there was no expression on her face.

"Is he anywhere around?" I said.

Her head shook only enough for me to catch the slight movement and swung slowly back to its original position. I stepped back and took one more look around and mounted the grey and rode towards town, looking for him along the way, and did not see him.

I had no reason to hurry and when I reached the converted store building we used for a courthouse, it was fairly well crowded. Judge Cutler was on the bench. We had our own judge now for local cases. Cutler was a tall, spare man, full of experience and firm opinions, honest and independent in all his dealings with other people. That was why he was our judge. Marshal Eakins was acting as our sheriff until we would be better organized and have an office established. That was why he had taken charge the day before.

They brought in Jess Dutrow and put him in a chair at one side of the bench and set another at the other side for a witness stand. There was no jury because the plea was guilty. The lawyer they had assigned for Jess could do nothing except plead the youth of his client and the hard circumstances of his life. It did not take long, the brief series of witnesses to establish the facts. They called me to identify him and tell what I knew about him. They called Walton Eakins and had him repeat his story to put it in the court records. The defence lawyer was finishing his plea for a softening of sentence when there was a stirring in the room and one by one heads turned to stare at the outer doorway.

The father was there, filling the doorframe with his broad bulk in its black clothes. Dirt marks were on them as if he had literally wrestled with something on the ground. His hat was gone and his long hair flowed back unkempt. His beard was ragged and tangled and the cheeks above it were drawn as if he had not slept. But his voice rolled magnificently, searching into every corner of the room.

"Stop!" he said. "You are trying the wrong man!"

He came forward and stood in front of the bench, the wooden pedestal we used for a trial bench. He looked up at Judge Cutler on the small raised platform behind it.

"Mine is the guilt," he said. "On my head let the punishment fall. My son has not yet attained his twenty and first birthday. He is still of me and to me and I am responsible for aught that he does. He was put into my keeping by God, to protect him and guard him from temptation and bring him safely to man's estate. My will was not strong enough to control him. The fault therefore is in me, in his father that gave him the sins of the flesh and then failed him. On me the judgement. I am here for it. I call upon you to let him depart and sin no more."

Judge Cutler leaned forward. "Mr Dutrow," he said in his precise, careful manner, "there is not a one of us here today does not feel for you. But the law is the law. We cannot go into the intangibles of human responsibilities you mention. Hereabout we hold that when a man reaches his eighteenth birthday he is a capable person, responsible for his own actions. Legally your son is not a minor. He must stand up to his own judgement."

The father towered in his dirty black coat. He raised an arm and swept it up full length. His voice fairly thundered.

"Beware, agent of man!" he said. "You would usurp the right of God Himself!"

Judge Cutler leaned forward a bit farther. His tone did not change. "Mr Dutrow. You will watch quietly or I will have you removed from this room."

The father stood in the silence and dwindled again within his dark clothes. He turned slowly and looked over the whole room and everyone in it. Someone in the front row moved and left a vacant seat and he went to it and sat down, and his head dropped forward until his beard was spread over his chest.

"Jess Dutrow," Judge Cutler said, "stand up and take this straight. Have you anything to say for yourself?"

He stood up, shaky on his feet, then steadying. The whipped-colt look was a permanent part of him now. His voice cracked and climbed.

"Yes," he said. "I did it and he can't take that away from me! Everything's true and I don't give a damn! Why don't you get this over with?"

"Very well," Judge Cutler said. "There is no dispute as to the pertinent facts. Their logic is plain. You put yourself outside the law when you committed the thefts. While you were still outside the law you shot and killed a peace officer in the performance of his duty and wounded another. You did not do this by accident or in defence of your life. Insofar as the law can recognize, you did this by deliberate intent. By the authority vested in me as a legally sworn judge of the people of this State I sentence you to be hanged tomorrow morning at ten by this courthouse clock."

Most of us were not looking at Jess Dutrow. We were looking at the father. He sat motionless for a few seconds after Judge Cutler finished speaking. Then he roused in the chair and rose to his feet and walked steadily to the doorway and out, his head still low with the beard fanwise on his chest and his eyes lost and unseeable in their deep shadow-holes. I passed near him on the way home about an hour later and he was the same, walking steadily along, not slow, not fast, just steady and stubborn in his face. I called to him and he did not answer, did not even raise or turn his head.

The next morning I woke early. I lay quiet a moment trying to focus on what had wakened me. Then I heard it plain, the creaking of wagon wheels. I went to the door and looked out. In the brightening pinkish light of dawn I saw him going by on the other side of the creek. He had yoked the oxen to the big wagon and was pushing steadily along, leading them with the leather thong. I watched him going into the distance until I shivered in the chill morning air and I went back into the house and closed the door.

It was the middle of the afternoon when he returned, leading the oxen, and behind them on the wagon was the long rectangular box. I did not watch him. I simply looked towards his place every now and then. I had things to do and I was glad I had things to do.

I saw him stop the oxen by the cabin and go inside. Later I saw him standing outside the door, both arms thrust upward. I could not be sure, but I thought his head was moving and he was shouting at the sky. And later I saw him back in the shadow of the rock ledge digging the grave. And still later I saw him there digging the second grave.

That brought me up short. I stared across the distance and there was no mistaking what he was doing. I set the pitchfork against the barn and went down to the creek and across on the stones and straight to him. I had to shout twice, close beside him, before he heard me.

He turned his head towards me and at last he saw me. His face above and beneath the beard was drawn, the flesh collapsed on the bones. He looked like a man riven by some terrible torment. But his voice was low. There was no roll in it. It was low and mild.

"Yes, neighbour?" he said.

"Damn it, man," I said, "what are you doing?"

"This is my wife," he said. His voice did not change, mild and matter-of-fact. "She killed herself." He drew a long breath and added gently, very gently: "With my butchering knife."

I stared at him and there was nothing I could say. At last: "I'll do what I can. I'll go into town and report it. You won't have to bother with that."

"If you wish," he said. "But that is all a foolishness. Man's justice is a mockery. But God's will prevail. He will give me time to finish this work. Then He will deal with me in His might."

He withdrew within himself and turned back to his digging. I tried to speak to him again and he did not hear me. I went to the cabin and looked through the doorway and went away quickly to my place and saddled the grey and rode towards town. When I returned, the last shadows were merging into the dusk and the two graves were filled with two small wooden crosses by them and I saw him there on the ledge.

Three days he was there. And late in the night of the third day the rain began and the lightning streaked and the thunder rolled through the valley, and in the last hour before dawn I heard the deeper rolling rumble I had heard once before on a hunting trip when the whole face of a mountain moved and crashed irresistibly into a canyon below.

Standing on the porch in the first light of dawn, I saw the new broken outline of the cliff up and across the valley and the great slant jagged pile of stone and rubble below where the rock ledge had been.

We found him under the stones, lying crumpled and twisted near the big squarish rock with the wooden cross cracked and smashed beside him. What I remember is his face. The deep-sunk, sightless eyes were open and they and the whole face were peaceful. His God had not failed him. Out of the high heaven arching above had come the blast that gave him his judgement and his release.

THOMAS THOMPSON
Blood on the Sun

Thomas Thompson (1913–) was born in Dixan, California, and graduated from Heald Business College, San Francisco, in 1933. In 1940 he turned to writing as a career, after a variety of jobs as diverse as nightclub entertainer and furniture salesman. Although Thompson published fourteen highly regarded Western novels (most of them published in Doubleday's Double D series), his primary skill was as a short story writer and he won Spur Awards from the Western Writers of America for short stories in 1954 and 1955. His short story collections are: *They Brought Their Guns* (1954), and *Moment of Glory* (1961). In 1971, Thompson received a Levi Strauss Golden Saddleman Award. Thompson—whose Western fiction was strongly influenced by American hardboiled crime fiction—also wrote TV scripts for *Wagon Train*, *Cimarron City* and *Gunsmoke*. For ten years he was associate producer and writer for the *Bonanza* TV Western series.

The short story 'Blood on the Sun' was first published in *America* magazine in 1954 and won a short story Spur Award from the Western Writers of America in 1955.

WE HADN'T EXPECTED HIM. He stood there in the doorway of Doc Isham's store, his lips thin and tight. He looked more like the trouble man I had first figured him to be than like The Preacher we had come to know. He was built like a cowboy, tall and lean-hipped. He was about thirty-five years old, I'd judge. It was hard to tell, and he wasn't a man to say. With all his gentleness, he had never quite lost the cold steadiness that had been in his eyes the night he first came to our valley with a bullet in his chest and more blood on his saddle than there was in his body. He had been a dead man that night, but Grace Beaumont had refused to let him die.

That coldness was in his eyes now as he looked at us, and it bothered me. It was those eyes and his hands, long and tapered and almost soft, that had made me pick him as a gun fighter. "Howdy, neighbors," he said. "I hear you've decided to fight Corby Lane." His voice was soft, but everybody heard it and they all stopped talking.

We were all there. Jim Peterson, tall and blond and nervous, thinking of the bride he had left at home. Fedor Marios, with his great mat of kinky white hair; Mel Martin, the oldest man in the valley. Ted Beaumont was down at the end of the counter with the two farmers from Rincon Valley. They were the ones who had come across the ridge to tell us there was no use trying to deal with Corby Lane. They had tried it, and Corby Lane had moved his sheep through their valley and wiped out their crops completely.

Frank Medlin, the young cowboy who worked for the Walking R over at Seventeen Mile, was also there. It was Frank Medlin who had gotten Ted Beaumont into his latest trouble. The two of them had served six months in jail on a cattle-rustling charge just a few months back.

Ted moved away from the counter, walking a little unsteady. "So help me," he said, "it's The Preacher come to pray!"

I keep calling him The Preacher. He wasn't one, really. His name was Johnny Calaveras, but us folks here in the valley had nearly forgotten that. To us he was The Preacher. It wasn't that he actually held church. It was just in the way he looked at things, calm and peaceful, always expecting the best. That's all right when you're fighting something like weather or grasshoppers, but it wouldn't work against Corby Lane and his hired gunmen, and nobody knew it any better than I did. I had been a sheriff in a boom town before I married and settled down. I knew about men like Corby Lane.

The Preacher looked at Ted, remembering that this boy was Grace Beaumont's brother, and then he looked around the room, measuring every man, and there wasn't a man there who didn't grow restless under that gaze.

"Here's The Preacher," Mel Martin said needlessly. "I reckon that makes all of us." His lie was there in his voice. We hadn't asked The Preacher to join us. We didn't figure he'd want to.

The two farmers from Rincon Valley were standing between Mel Martin and Ted Beaumont. Ted pushed one of them away roughly and stood there peering at The Preacher. "Let's get things out in the open, Preacher," Ted said. "You're always mighty full of high-flown advice, especially for me. I just want you to know that I'm running this show."

The Preacher didn't show any signs of how he had taken that. "Which end of the show you running, Ted?" he said. "The fighting end?"

There was a lot of nervousness and tension in that room. The Preacher's remark struck everybody funny, just as a remark will sometimes when men are keyed to the breaking point. We all laughed, and the color came into Ted Beaumont's cheeks. But Ted wasn't a boy who backed down easy. He took a step closer to The Preacher and he let his eyes run over the man. "Where's your gun, Preacher?" Ted said.

The Preacher stood there, and I saw the half smile on his lips; it was the kind of smile I never like to see on a man. There was bad blood between The Preacher and Ted Beaumont. I caught myself wondering if that was the reason Grace Beaumont and The Preacher had never married, and I figured it must be. They had been in love ever since Grace had nursed him back to health from that gunshot wound he had when he came into the valley.

"I don't wear a gun when I'm talking to my friends, Ted," The Preacher said easily.

It made Ted mad. He was a handsome kid, stocky-built. He had wavy blond hair. He was just twenty, but he had done a man's work from the day his dad had been gored to death by a bull four years back, and all of us accepted him as a man. Ted had set himself up as a sort of leader here, and that was all right with most of us. We were going to need his kind of fire before this day was over.

There wasn't a man in the valley wouldn't have been glad to forget the scrapes the kid had been in, even if only for his sister Grace's sake. But Ted wouldn't let you. He always looked as if he was mad at the world. Now he got that nasty twist to his lip and said, "What you gonna do, Preacher? Sing church songs to them sheep?"

When you're standing there thinking that within a few hours you'll maybe be killing a fellow human being or getting killed yourself, that kind of talk sounds childish. We all felt it. The Preacher said, "Why not? I've heard you and Frank Medlin singin' to cows on night herd. How do you know sheep don't like music?"

The way he said it made Ted look a little foolish. The muscles of his face tightened. Until The Preacher had come in nobody had questioned any of Ted's decisions, and Ted didn't want his decisions questioned now. He said, "Look, Preacher. We've decided on a line. They go one step beyond it and maybe we'll club a few sheep. Maybe we'll hang a few sheepherders." He slapped the gun he had strapped around his middle. "We don't need no sermon from you. This gun will do the talkin'."

The Preacher gave him a long look and then deliberately turned away. He spoke to those two farmers from the other valley. "What happened in Rincon?" he asked.

The two Rincon men started to talk at once, stopped, and then one went ahead. "There's six Mexican herders with the band," the farmer said, "but they won't cause no trouble. It's this Corby Lane and the three men with him.

They're gun fighters, neighbor, and they come on ahead of the sheep."

"We know the setup, Preacher," Ted Beaumont said. His voice was ugly.

The kid was getting under my skin. "The Preacher ain't heard it," I said. "Let him hear it."

"Why?" Ted Beaumont said, turning to me. "So he'll know what verse in the Bible to read? Let's get out of here. I warned you last month a couple of us had to put on guns and fix a boundary if we wanted to keep this valley clear of sheep."

"You mean you and Frank Medlin decided you needed an excuse to wear guns?" The Preacher said.

"If Frank and me are the only two not afraid to wear guns, yes," Ted said bluntly.

The Preacher shook his head. "You're not tough, Ted," he said. "I've told you that before. You're just mixed up."

I saw the wicked anger in Ted's eyes and it wasn't a man's anger. It was the flaring temper of a kid. "I told you I'd handle this without your sermons, Preacher," Ted said.

"You're not going to handle it, Ted," The Preacher said. "Not you or anyone here, the way you got it laid out."

I kept my mouth shut. I liked The Preacher. I wanted to give him his chance. It was old Mel Martin who bristled. "Hold on a minute," Mel said. "There's gettin' to be too much palaver."

"Looks to me like you need some palaver," The Preacher said. "You're gonna expose yourself, let Corby Lane know just how many men you got and what you plan—"

"You got a better idea, Preacher?" Mel said.

"I have," The Preacher said. "Let me go up there and talk to Corby Lane."

It surprised all of us and there was a loud hoot of derision from Ted Beaumont. "You and who else, Preacher?" Ted scoffed. "You and God, maybe?"

I saw the brittle hardness come into The Preacher's eyes, and I could see him fighting to control his temper. "A man could do worse than picking God for a saddle partner, Ted,"

The Preacher said. "But I figured on taking one man with me."

"Who you want to take with you, Preacher?" Ted said, his voice sarcastic. "Old Fedor, maybe?"

The deep red of Fedor Marios' complexion turned to a saddle-tan and I thought he would hit Ted. He didn't have a chance. The Preacher's voice was so soft we barely heard it, but it filled the room like a solid block: "Why don't you come along with me, Ted?"

The color ran out of Ted Beaumont's cheeks. I looked at The Preacher, and I was looking at a man who had fought a losing battle with his temper. He hadn't planned on taking Ted Beaumont up there with him. He had planned on taking me, maybe. I was his best friend. But a man could stand just so much. Even a man like The Preacher. Ever since he had known Grace Beaumont The Preacher had tried to be friendly with her brother. He had taken things from Ted no other man would have taken.

I saw the conflict in Ted Beaumont's face. It was one thing to go up to that sheep camp with ten men back of him. It was another to go it alone with a man like The Preacher. I saw the conflict and I saw Ted make his decision. It was the wrong one. He figured The Preacher was bluffing and he was going to call that bluff.

"Sure, Preacher," Ted said. "I'd like to see you run. What are we waiting for?"

"I got a little business to attend to," The Preacher said. "I'll be back in five minutes and we'll go."

"You sure you'll get back, Preacher?" Ted said.

The Preacher had started toward the door. He stopped and turned. In his eyes was an anger so great that I knew it wasn't aimed at Ted Beaumont alone. It was a bigger thing. An anger toward the thing that made Ted Beaumont the way he was. I couldn't think of the man as The Preacher any more. He was Johnny Calaveras again, a man who had ridden in out of the night with a bullet in his chest. I wouldn't have wanted to cross him right then. He looked at me and said, "You better come with me, Luke, to see I get back all right." He went outside and mounted and I followed him.

He wanted to see Grace and tell her what had happened. That's the way Johnny and Grace were with each other. He headed for the schoolhouse up at the end of the street and I followed.

Grace must have expected him. She had let the kids out for an early recess and I saw her standing by the oak tree out by the pump.

She was one of those women who become really beautiful after you knew them. The trouble Ted had caused her showed in her eyes and in the way she smiled, but the grief she had known was a part of her beauty. Johnny swung down easy and walked over to her, and she put out both her hands and he took them. I loosened my reins and let my horse crop at the grass. I didn't want to listen to what they had to say. It was none of my business.

I glanced at them a couple of times, and they were standing there close together, still holding hands, The Preacher tall and straight and serious.

The kids had spotted them now and they were all standing there, staring like a bunch of calves at a corral fence.

Maybe the wind changed. Maybe Johnny spoke louder. Anyway, I heard him, though I wasn't trying to listen. "Maybe I could have handled it, without a gun, the way we planned," he said. "Maybe I couldn't have. I won't risk it with Ted along."

Suddenly it was as if the two of them had reached the end of a dream and they were all alone in the world, and it wasn't the world as they had wanted it, but the world as it was. I saw Johnny bend his head swiftly and kiss her, and I heard those blasted kids giggle, and it wasn't anything to giggle about.

I saw Grace break away from Johnny's embrace, reluctantly and yet quickly, and then she left the schoolyard and went across the street to the Perkins house, where the schoolteachers always lived. She walked rapidly. When she came back out of the house she had a folded belt and a holstered gun in her hand. She came across the street and handed it to Johnny Calaveras, and I knew it was the same gun he had worn into the valley. No one had seen it since that first night.

"I'll take care of him, Grace," I heard him say. "Maybe it's best this way." He buckled on the gun belt. The dark-brown stains of Johnny's own blood were still on the leather. I felt old and tired and somehow useless, and then I saw Grace Beaumont's eyes and I saw the worry and the end of a dream in them. I didn't have to make any decision. I thought of my own wife and of the love I had seen between Johnny and Grace, a love that was maybe ending here today.

I rode over close to them. "I'm going, too, Johnny," I said.

"I didn't ask you," he said flatly.

"You couldn't stop me."

We rode back to the store, and everyone was out in front. Ted Beaumont was in the street, mounted, a little uncertain. He said, "I see Luke didn't let you get away from him."

Suddenly I felt sorry for Ted Beaumont. He was nothing but a darn'-fool kid itching to get his fingers on a gun. I had seen the signs before. A gun could be a dangerous thing with a kid like Ted. I wondered if Johnny had known what it was like to want a gun more than anything else.

"Get this, kid," Johnny said, and now his eyes were holding Ted. "From here on out I give the orders. Make up your mind to it or drop out now."

I saw Ted bluster, wanting to give a scoffing answer, but that gun, the new look about The Preacher, held him from it. And he couldn't back down now. He said, "What's holding us up?"

"Nothing," Johnny Calaveras said. "Not a thing." . . .

The sheep were an undistinguishable blot against the brown grass, and as Johnny and Ted and I climbed the hill the animals took form and shape and became separate bunches. We could see the herders, men on foot, and their dogs stretched in shady patches, tongues lolling, ears alert. The herders, half asleep under the trees, hadn't noticed us yet. We couldn't be seen from Corby Lane's camp because there was a shoulder of the hill between us and the camp. Ted looked at me. There was an amused, indulgent swagger in his glance, but there were white patches at the corners of his mouth, and I knew he had been watching Johnny Calaveras.

The only thing Johnny had done was to strap on that gun and take off his gloves, but that made the difference. He wasn't The Preacher any more. I could see his right hand just hanging limp at his side almost as if his elbow were broken. Johnny Calaveras was a gun fighter. It was marked on him as clearly as if it had been printed in red letters.

I watched his right hand opening and closing, loosening fingers that had been long unused in their deadly business. I saw Ted Beaumont's lips move, and I knew the fear he was beginning to feel. I had felt it myself.

We had dropped down into a draw, out of sight of the sheep, and Johnny Calaveras reined up sharply. He didn't waste words. "I know Corby Lane," he said. "I can ride into his camp and talk to him without getting shot at. What good it will do, I don't know, but that's the way it has to be." A little of the harshness went out of his voice. "If it should come to a fight," he said, "I want the odds on our side."

He was talking straight to Ted now. There was something cold and deathlike about Johnny's voice. I felt as if I were watching the opening of a grave.

"A gun fighter that stays alive," Johnny said, "never gives a sucker a break. Luke, you ride up this draw and come in behind the camp. Keep your ears open, and don't make a move unless I give the sign, but don't be afraid to shoot if I do."

I think he was trying to make Ted see that there was nothing glamorous about gun fighting. It was brutal stuff with nothing of trust or decency about it. I looked at Ted, wondering if he had seen through this, and I knew he hadn't. He still had that cocky swagger in his eyes, but those white patches at the corners of his mouth were more noticeable. "You want me to ride along with Luke to cover for you?" he said.

"No," Johnny said. "I want you to come along with me. Maybe Luke couldn't hold you if you started to run."

That was like slapping the kid in the face, but it was a smart move. Ted Beaumont would be twice as determined now. He was a little scared, and a little anger right now wouldn't hurt him. I headed on down the draw, riding slow enough not to attract attention, and I saw Johnny and Ted ride up on the ridge to within full sight of the sheep camp.

Luck was with me and my timing was perfect. I came up behind the sheep camp just as Johnny and Ted rode in. The three men standing there by the oak didn't even suspect I was around. They were too busy watching Johnny and Ted, and I was able to dismount and move up into the brush not fifty feet behind them.

One of the men looked more like a sheepherder than he did a gunman, but he kept his hand near his gun as he slouched there against the tree. Another was thick through, a brutal-looking man with shaggy hair and crossed gun belts and blue lips.

The other gunman was slender to the point of being emaciated, and at first I picked this one to be Corby Lane. His clothes seemed to hang on his frame. His shirt moved in the imperceptible breeze, and he gave the impression that if his clothes were removed he would be revealed as a skeleton strung together with spring wire. "You boys just ridin'?" he said. "Or did you want something?"

"I want to talk to Corby Lane," Johnny Calaveras said slowly.

The thin man shifted his position slightly and I felt my finger tightening on the trigger of my rifle. "Corby's taking a siesta," the thin man said. "You can say it to me."

"I'll wait for Corby," Johnny said, smiling. It was a cold, thin smile.

I had watched this kind of thing before. The thin man was measuring Johnny, seeing the things I had seen. He had recognized Johnny for what he was, or for what he had been in the past, and the thin man was smart enough to take it easy. There wouldn't be any fast gunplay. Both men had respect for the damage a .45 slug could do.

"You might have quite a wait," the thin man said. He had glanced across the fire they had burning and beyond to the tent that stood under the oaks.

"I got time," Johnny said.

The other two gunmen were standing back, letting the thin man do all the talking. Johnny and the thin man sparred, making small talk, each one looking for a weak spot in the other. It would have gone on like that until Johnny found the opening he wanted, except for Ted Beaumont.

I had been so busy watching the play between Johnny and the thin man and keeping my rifle ready on the other two gunmen that I had nearly forgotten Ted. He had behaved himself up to this point, and any fool could see what Johnny was doing, stalling, waiting for Corby Lane to show. But I had misjudged The Preacher. Ted said, "We're wasting time, Preacher." Every eye except Johnny's turned toward him.

I saw Johnny tense. "I'll handle this," he snapped.

"You talk too much, Preacher," Ted said. "We come here to run these sheepers out. I do my talking with this!"

Ted's hand slapped down awkwardly and his fingers closed around the butt of his gun. Telling it now, I can see every move. I couldn't then. I threw myself out of the brush, my rifle hip level, and I yelled out for them to throw up their hands. I saw the thin man drop into a half crouch and I saw his gun half clear leather, and then Johnny was sailing out of his saddle and he landed on Ted Beaumont's shoulders. The kid went down hard, the gun spinning out of its holster.

I rammed my rifle barrel against the thin man's back and I heard his grunt of pain. The thin man let his half-drawn gun slip from his fingers, and Johnny had snapped to his feet, his cocked gun in his hand, and he was covering that tent beyond the fire, his eyes sweeping the other two gunmen, warning them.

Johnny didn't even look at Ted. "You're so anxious to get the feel of that gun," Johnny said across his shoulder, "pick it up and see if you can keep them covered." The kid did as he was told.

I knew what had happened to Ted and I felt like taking a club to him. It was as Johnny said. Ted was too blasted anxious to get the feel of his gun, and if he had gotten away with his crazy plan he would have figured himself quite a gunman. I was glad he had failed. I saw him standing there, the wind half knocked out of him, and for a minute I was afraid he was going to be sick. The gunmen had raised their hands and I moved around behind them and took their guns.

The thin man laughed, a high, wild sound. "Where I come from, punk," he said to Ted, "you wouldn't live to be as tall as you think you are."

Ted swallowed hard but he kept his gun trained on the thin man.

Johnny moved over toward the tent. He kept his gun in his hand and he walked toward the door of the tent, walking slowly on the balls of his feet, making no sound. When he was near the tent he moved to one side and he stood there, his hand gripping the butt of the gun. "Come out, Corby," he said softly. "It's Johnny Calaveras."

The flap of the tent moved aside and a man came out. He was round and fat. His eyes were a striking pale blue and his skin looked as if it had never seen the sun. He reminded me of a well-fed snake that had lived too long in the dark. He stood there on his thick legs and stared, his tongue darting in and out. "Is it you, Johnny?" he asked.

"You want to touch me, Corby?" Johnny said. "You want to feel the flesh and bone?"

"Johnny, I figured—"

"You figured I was dead," Johnny said. "Otherwise I would have come after you before this."

Corby Lane looked at his gunmen, lined up there under Ted's and my guns. I saw that Corby Lane was a man who was weak without guns to back him up. "Johnny," he said, "it was all a mistake. It was a mix-up."

"It was that," Johnny Calaveras said. "And you did the mixing. You set a gun trap, and me and Steve walked into it."

This talk didn't make sense, except to tell me that Corby Lane's voice was steadier now. "All right," he said. "So it was planned. But I didn't plan it. It was Steve's idea. He was tired of the way you kept riding him. He was tired of your preaching."

There was a wicked ruthlessness on Johnny's face now, and I thought I was going to see a man killed. For that second Johnny Calaveras was a man without a heart or a soul. His lips were thin, tight against his teeth, and I saw his trigger finger tightening. I saw the sweat on his forehead. I watched him trying to keep from squeezing the trigger. His voice came out on his expelled breath.

"You're a liar," he said. "Steve didn't know anything about it. You told him to raid my camp. He did it because that was what you were paying him for and because he liked to fight. You counted on that. You told him me and my boys were part of the XB outfit. He couldn't tell in the dark that it was my camp he was raiding any more than I could tell it was Steve who was raiding me. You doublecrossed us both, Corby, because you wanted to get rid of me and Steve and you knew there was no other way."

Sometimes a certain dignity comes to a man standing on the edge of eternity. It came to Corby Lane now. His shoulders squared and he faced Johnny Calaveras. "All right," he said flatly. "That's the way it was, and it worked. Steve's dead. He caught a bullet right between the eyes that night." There was perspiration on Corby Lane's moon face, but there was a growing confidence in his voice. "Maybe you fired the bullet that killed him, Johnny," Corby Lane said quietly. "Did you ever think of that?"

Whatever it was, I knew that Corby Lane had hit Johnny Calaveras with everything he had. I saw the old tiredness come into Johnny's eyes, and an old hurt was there in the sag of his shoulders. "Yes," Johnny said. "I've thought of that. And I figured if I hunted you down and killed you it would give me something else to think about."

"I would have been easy to find," Corby Lane said. In some way he had gained the upper hand, and as I watched I realized these two men had known each other not only well but completely. Corby Lane knew of some twist in Johnny's nature that would be a weakness in a gun fighter. I figured I knew what it was. Corby Lane knew that Johnny was a man who would ask himself questions, and that, for a gun fighter, was a dangerous thing. Some day he might ask himself if it was worth while killing again. Corby Lane was gambling that Johnny had already asked himself that question. And

Johnny had, I knew. Otherwise he wouldn't have become the man we called The Preacher.

"Why didn't you come after me, Johnny?" Corby Lane said.

"Because I decided there was only one way to really hurt you, Corby," Johnny said, "and that's the way I'm going to hurt you now. I want that money belt you always carry. Without money to hire guns you're nothing. You're not even worth hunting down."

"If this is a plain holdup why didn't you say so?" Corby Lane said. He tried to put disgust into his voice. "You've sunk pretty low, Johnny."

"That's funny, coming from you," Johnny said. "I want that money belt, and I want more."

"You're forgetting the law, aren't you, Johnny?" Corby Lane said. "They'll excuse a gun fight quicker than they will a robbery."

"Go to the law, Corby," Johnny said. "When you do I'll start talking. The law is still trying to find out what happened to those six soldiers that got killed. The law still wants to know what happened to that payroll the soldiers were packing."

I saw the surprise in Corby Lane's face and then the terror, and I knew Johnny had pulled something out of Corby Lane's past, something that had been long dead. "You can't tie that to me," Corby Lane shouted. "It happened before I even knew you. You don't know anything about it."

"Don't I?" Johnny said. "It didn't happen before you knew Steve. Maybe Steve told me all about it. Maybe it was on Steve's mind so strong he had to talk about it."

I watched Corby Lane. I knew he was trying to decide if Johnny was bluffing or not, and I saw he was afraid to take the chance. He made one last gesture. "If you know so much," he said, "you know Steve was in it. You're admitting that."

"I am," Johnny said. "But Steve is dead. They can't hang a dead man, Corby, but they can sure hang you."

"What do you want, Johnny?" Corby Lane said thickly. He was whipped and scared.

"What money you've got," Johnny said. "We'll call it wages you owed me and Steve. After that, turn those sheep out through the canyon and keep 'em on open graze. I reckon you'll go broke. That's good enough for me, and it would be for Steve. Some day you're going to slip and say the wrong thing, and the Government will know what happened to that payroll pack train. I'll count on it happening. If I ever hear of you making a slip, I'll see that it happens sooner. Give me the money belt, Corby."

The gunmen watched their boss back down. I watched Corby Lane, too, and I watched Johnny Calaveras. I wondered if Johnny really did know enough to hang this man, and Corby Lane was wondering the same thing. I decided I would never know for sure; I knew Corby Lane would never take the chance of finding out. Johnny had him whipped. Lane took off the heavy money belt and handed it to Johnny Calaveras.

The tall, thin gunman spit between his wide-spaced teeth. "So you're Johnny Calaveras," he said. "I've heard of you."

"Move those sheep down into the valley and you'll hear a lot more," Johnny said.

"I reckon I would," the tall gunman said. "But I won't be around." He glanced toward the fire where I had thrown the guns. "If you're finished with me and my boys here," the tall gunman said, "I reckon we'll mosey along." He looked at the money belt Johnny was strapping around his middle. "I don't work for a man that ain't got no money," the gunman said. . . .

As we rode back to town I looked at Ted and his face was serious and ashamed, and I knew he was thinking of the fool he had made of himself. Ted Beaumont had lived a long time in those few minutes back there.

Maybe The Preacher figured he owed us an explanation, but I never thought that was it. Rather, I think he wanted Ted to see everything in the right light. The Preacher stared straight ahead. "I worked for Corby Lane down in New Mexico," he said. "There was a cattle war on and any man who took a job took a gun job." It didn't sound like the rest was really meant for us. "Steve was already working for Corby," he said. "I figured it would be best if I was with Steve."

He was trying to say a lot more, but suddenly it was hard for him to talk. "This Steve," I said. "He was your buddy?"

The tiredness in The Preacher's eyes was something you could feel. "Steve was my brother," he said. "He was a kid who couldn't leave guns alone."

It hit me like a sledge hammer, and I looked at Ted and saw the impact of it numbing him. I thought of Johnny Calaveras, this quiet man we called The Preacher, living with the thought that he might have killed his own brother in a gun trap set by Corby Lane. And suddenly I knew what the fight inside Johnny was as he stood there with a gun held on Corby Lane, and I knew why he had let Corby Lane live. It was his way of proving to himself that he had whipped the past, his way of paying a debt he felt he owed. And I knew now why Johnny Calaveras and Grace Beaumont had never married.

"I used to be pretty proud of my gun speed," The Preacher said quietly. "But spending the rest of your life wondering whether you killed your own brother is quite a price to pay for pride." I glanced at Ted Beaumont; he looked sick. . . .

Everybody was out on the street when we got back to Doc Isham's store. They were standing there looking up toward the south end of the valley. There wasn't any worry in their eyes any more, and I knew that band of sheep had turned east, toward the mouth of the canyon.

Grace was there, and when she looked at Johnny and Ted she knew, without being told, that the two men she loved had reached an understanding. She knew that Johnny had won his right to live his new life. I knew now what it was that had made Grace and Johnny's love for each other so compelling. It was the understanding between them. There wasn't anything about Johnny's past that Grace didn't know, and that knowledge had drawn them together, and at the same time it had held them apart. Johnny would never ask a girl like Grace to marry him until he was sure his past was gone, until he was sure he could settle a fight without killing.

Johnny dismounted, and for a second his shoulder touched Ted Beaumont's shoulder. I saw Ted glance toward the money belt, his eyes questioning. I saw Johnny's quick understanding and I saw his grin, amused, pleased. He unbuckled the belt and tossed it to one of the farmers from Rincon Valley. "Here," he said. "Corby Lane sent this down. Said he hoped it would pay for the damage his sheep did to your crops." He turned then to Ted. I saw Ted stiffen, waiting for the lacing he knew he had coming.

The Preacher said, "If you've a mind to grub out that oak on your place, Ted, I could give you a hand with it tomorrow."

"Thanks, Johnny," Ted said, and he tried to grin.

Johnny took Grace's arm and the two of them walked off together. . . .

I left the valley about ten years back. Johnny and Grace are married now, still in love, still amazed at the goodness of the world. Ted Beaumont married my oldest girl, Lucy. Ted's a good, steady boy now. Outside of that, things haven't changed much. Folks around here still call Johnny Calaveras The Preacher. It's surprising how much respect men can cram into a nickname like that.

THEODORE VICTOR OLSEN
Soldier Blue

Theodore Victor Olsen (1932–) was born in Rhinelander, Wisconsin, and educated at Stevens Point State College. His first Western novel, *Haven of the Hunted* was published in 1956, and some thirty have followed (several written under the pseudonym Joshua Stark) over the ensuing years. Today he is one of the most successful and celebrated authors of popular frontier fiction, frequently mentioned in the same breath as Louis L'Amour. Among his novels are: *The Stalking Moon* (1965), *Arrow in the Sun* (1969), *Lazlo's Strike* (1983), and *Under the Gun* (1989). Olsen has also published a short story collection, *Westward They Rode* (1976).

Two of Olsen's novels have been filmed, *The Stalking Noon* and *Arrow in the Sun*. The former was turned into a movie of the same title by Robert Mulligan in 1968, while the latter, extracted below, became one of the most controversial and famous Western pictures of all time—*Soldier Blue*, directed by Ralph Nelson, 1970. In the film the characters of Honus Gant and Cresta Lee are played by Peter Strauss and Candice Bergen respectively. The extract begins with the Cheyenne attack on the cavalry troop of which Honus Gant is a member.

HONUS' EYES STUNG and watered; his throat was rasped raw by coughing. He tried to catch a decent sight of the enemy through the sullen veils of drifting smoke that had suddenly obscured everything.

At the last moment of their charge, the Cheyennes had divided cleanly and thundered to either side of the troopers like a splitting wave. Using their horsehair support ropes and clinging to their ponies' off flanks, they were almost completely hidden. The troopers shot at the ponies. Several went down in kicking tangles. The rest passed by into the surging smoke and massed brush, and were cut off.

Their intention was clear: to infiltrate to the sides and rear of the trapped soldiers.

Honus' smoke-stung eyes had blurred till he could hardly see at all, but he went on doggedly reloading and firing. His briefly acquired taste for battle had curled up in his guts like a shriveled memory.

Pandemonium on every side. The Indians had abandoned their ponies. They were slithering in among the choking, blinded troopers like deadly shadows.

Honus could make out hardly any of it in the sun-yellowed fog of smoke mingled with dust raised by running ponies. All unreal again: men all along the fringes of the motte locked in weird swaying battle, like actors in a misty chimera. The Cheyennes were everywhere, their cries triumphantly shrill and raking.

Menzies wheeled toward him. "No chance here! Best we run for it, devil take the hindmost—"

A Cheyenne forced his pony in a crashing lunge through the brush to their left. He sprang to the ground almost at Menzies' side. A steel hatchet glittered high in the saffron air, descended. The blade was buried in Menzies' skull before he could even twist to face his opponent, let alone bring up his rifle.

The hand ax stuck fast as the trooper's body toppled sideways. The slippery handle was wrenched from the Indian's fist. He spun on his heel, a hunting knife flashing from its sheath, and leaped at Honus Gant.

Honus was on his feet, a shell chambered, rifle hammer

thumbed back. The Indian was almost on him—a lean coppery breechclouted figure whose charcoaled face was scoured to a feral wildness—when he fired. The side of the Cheyenne's face dissolved in a bloody mask. He fell across Menzies' body.

A violent trembling seized Honus. His breakfast clawed up in his throat like hot bile. Till now he had shot at anonymous figures. Killing a man under your nose was death's reality. Raw and stinking death whose livid freckling was on his shirt and hands.

Devil take the hindmost. O'Hearn's boom was stilled. The remaining troopers were fighting their way into the deeper brush, popping wildly at their enemies or desperately hacking with empty rifles at coup-hungry adversaries. Most of them had pulled to a defensive group. A mistake, for the Cheyennes converged on the lot at once.

Honus—luckily for him—was cut off from the rest. And for the moment found himself totally ignored, the shroud of smoke and dust proving a sudden benison. Escape. There was nothing else now.

He plunged away into the heart of the brush. He had a dim notion of penetrating it as close to the flames as he could bear—reasoning that nobody else would think of braving the intense heat nor expect him to—at an angle that would bring him out well away from the concentration of Cheyennes.

Wild shots riddled the underbrush; several kicked up geysers of dirt close to Honus' legs. He wove his way through the smoky chaos by feel and by instinct, seeking slender breaks between the thickets. His eyes were raw swimming blurs, his bearings gone, but the shooting was falling behind him. He might yet make it. . . .

He was getting close—too close—to the raging wall of flame. The surges of heat washed against his body with a blistering fury now. He found it was impossible to follow along the fire's edge: it was moving too fast, shooting out irregular fiery arms into the unfired brush.

Honus ducked sideways along its path as best he could, his eyes watery wells of pain, retching on the smoke he had swallowed. At one terrifying moment he thought he had charged into the very middle of it. The windy flames roared all around him, flapping like rusty banners in the pitchy billows. The heat nearly made him scream. Running almost totally blind, he slashed frenziedly at the smoking thickets with his rifle and free hand. Sparks flew. Inadvertently he seized a burning switch: it clung and ate into his flesh. Yelling, he smeared the glowing splinters off on his trousers.

Suddenly he pitched out of the fiery thickets. He was through. A gust of good air hit his face. He was past the fire now, past the worst of the brush but not yet out of it.

Caution flagged him to a halt.

He was gagging sickly on the smoke that had clawed his eyes raw; he could feel every throb of his heart in his scorched hand. Just beyond the fiery perimeter where he stood, it was still agonizingly hot, and in a few minutes more the remaining motte would erupt into a vast torch.

But the enemy might be waiting for him out there. He could spare the few seconds needed to clear his eyes and get his rifle loaded. And try to get an idea what he would face next.

He breeched a fresh shell while he blinked his eyes till the landscape took watery form: curving swells of land that fell away to the horizon.

Honus moved cautiously out of the thickets now, but held to the rambling fringe of them as he pushed south at a trot. To be caught in the open would be fatal. Here, if he picked up the approach of riders, he could take instant refuge in the brush and blowing curtain of smoke. He would hold south along the brush to its farthest extent. . . .

Soon the thickets began to dwindle; he followed their curving edge inward, almost to the charred area where the fire had been started. His vision was clearer now. No sign of the enemy. The little shooting that kept up was far to his back.

He was descending a hill into a swale, and he braced his muscles for a quick sprint up the rocky open hill opposite. Then he came to a dead stop, staring.

Somebody hidden among the gaunt sprawl of boulders a short distance upslope had stood up. Miss Cresta Lee, no less. Straight, diminutive, and apparently unhurt, the brown tatters of her skirt feathering in the wind. She waved a hand at him.

Honus felt a quick guilt: he had completely forgotten the girl. He supposed all of them had.

A sound snatched his attention. Hoofs pounding over soft earth as a rider came this way along the motte's edge.

All that Honus could do was melt to the ground and squirm under some low-growing brush. It should conceal him if the man didn't pass too closely. Cresta Lee had already dopped behind her rock again.

A Cheyenne brave came into sight, nudging his mount along in a slow circuit of the thicket, which he was evidently patrolling for escapees. Suddenly he hauled up, his eyes intent on the hillside.

Honus had a good view of the scape even from his cramped vantage. Now he saw what the brave had seen. The brown smudge of Cresta Lee's skirt hem showing at the edge of the boulder that hid her. Enough to seize a plains warrior's eye.

"Hail"

The Cheyenne kicked his pony around, tearing up clods as he sent the animal up the rise in a stretching run.

The girl sprang to her feet and ran like a deer, cutting away at right angles along the slope. The flapping tatters of dress and petticoat hampered her. The brave emitted a laughing yip and swung to cut her off.

Honus scrambled from beneath his bush and came up on one knee, leveling his rifle. He followed the Indian, lined him along the sights, pulled trigger.

The 405 grain bullet slammed into the slight body of the brave like a giant fist and wiped him from his saddle, rolling him over and over like a bundle of rags. His horse bolted away.

Honus went up the hill at a stumbling run. When he reached Cresta Lee, she had relieved the dead Cheyenne of a beaded belt with a hatchet and sheath knife. The Indian's rifle was gone with his horse, secure in a buckskin scabbard.

"Any more of you coming?"

Honus felt that numb shock again, meeting her eyes. They were as untroubled as a child's—and not from the calm that masks hysteria.

"Uh? Er—no, I don't think so. At least I, uh, didn't see any more of our men—"

"All right. Follow me." She spoke over her shoulder; she was already moving away.

"No," Honus said hoarsely. "Not yet. If—"

She halted and looked at him, her brows drawing down. "Listen," she said. "Just listen."

He did.

The shooting had tapered away. There was no sound but the steady snap and crackle of flames, and beyond that an occasional exulting whoop.

It was over for N Troop. For green recruit and seasoned campaigner alike. Over because of Cheyenne strategy. Because everyone knew the reddies would never attack a paymaster. Because chance had thrown together on a single detail two bad officers—an errant coward and an irresponsible fool. . . .

"Come on now," Cresta Lee said sharply. "There's nothing you can do. When they find this one and read the sign they'll be looking for us. Come on . . ."

Nothing you can do. Mechanically Honus fumbled a fresh load into his rifle, and followed her.

She struck into the shallow roll of ridges to the south, moving in a patient, zigzag course. Dully he saw that she moved with an Indian's quick noiseless ease, picking her way over patches along the deep curves of hill where wind or water had torn away sod and soil, exposing gravel and solid shale. A tracker might pick up their spoor with difficulty, but he would be hours following it up.

Had any besides the girl and himself broken out of the trap? It was possible. But not likely. Even if any had, they wouldn't stand a chance without horses. The Cheyennes would run them down quickly on the open plain.

Cresta Lee halted deep in a field of giant splintered boulders.

"We can lay low here," she said quietly. "My guess is that they'll look for us—but not very long or hard. Spotted Wolf won't want to waste the time."

"Spotted Wolf—you're sure this was . . ."

"I saw him."

She settled down on her heels between the gargantuan slabs of rock and folded her arms across her knees. Honus sat down beside her, feeling cold in his guts in spite of the intense reflected heat of the boulders. He stared at the greasy pall of smoke rising above the burning thicket one thousand yards away.

A sharp, involuntary groan left him. What were they doing now? Dispatching the wounded with lance and knife? Looting? He knew that they rarely took prisoners. . . .

Cresta Lee closed her fingers over his arm. "Don't even think about it," she said.

"About what?"

"Going back there now. Nothing you can do, understand? *Nothing*."

Honus stared at her face. Fine beads of sweat pearled her golden skin. Otherwise her face was so cool and opaque, it might have been a mask . . . just a mask. *Does she have any feelings at all?* He shook her hand away.

The boulder field was like a furnace. Sweat puddled in his boots; his clothes were wet dirty rags. His eyes ached from the pounding glitter of sun pouring down on naked rock.

Dead, he thought. All dead. And he was wearing only a few scratches and a burn on his hand. He felt almost traitorous. Yet the fight had turned to a rout at the last, and none had thought of anything but escape.

"They were after you," he said bitterly. "All of this because you—"

"That's a lot of bull," snapped Cresta Lee. "They weren't after me."

"Well, you escaped from them. And no Army paymaster has been attacked by Indians . . . not till today. What else could it be?"

"I don't know. But don't lay this to my account, Mister. In the first place, they wouldn't make up an elaborate trap like this one just to recover a runaway—now would they? In the second—they couldn't have known I was with this detachment to begin with. . . ."

"They must have seen you in the attack!"

"In the wagon from a distance—sure. Dressed as just another white woman. That's what they saw. Only that one you did for saw me up close. Which, as far as I can see, doesn't make a hell of a lot of difference."

"Not to you, apparently," Honus muttered. "Though you'd be safe enough if they did find us, come to that."

"Bull," Cresta Lee said in an unruffled tone. "I don't know what they'd do to me, but it'd be the worst, for sure. Maybe even the burning pole. I not only ran away, I outguessed the trackers who were sent after me. None of which did much for their pride. Least of all Spotted Wolf's. I think . . ." She paused, almost reflectively. "I really think he'd kill me."

"Because of *pride*?"

"Just that." She gave him that wise, cool look. "I was his wife."

It seemed an eternity later that they heard the Cheyennes' last fierce yips of victory trailing in the afternoon distance, as they pounded away toward the south. And a long time after that before the cautious Miss Lee said it was all right to leave the boulder field.

They trudged back to the scene of massacre. . . .

Honus saw total carnage. The vast brush motte had been reduced to ash and char except for a few stripped blackened wands nudging up forlornly here and there. The flames were dying out except at the fringes where orange tongues still licked sporadically at clots of shrubbery. Tatters of smoke curled up in the sunlight, which blazed them to a satiny fog.

Ever practical, Cresta Lee went off by herself to scout the area for anything useful that might be salvaged.

Honus moved across the hot ground like a gaunt plodding zombie. Pallid ash puffed under his boots. He hadn't seen the like of this in his twenty-five years. A scene from a passive inferno. He tramped past the sprawled bodies of men with whom he'd shared barracks and mess table and the light of a hundred campfires. He had been close to only a few. But all had played a part in the sights and sounds of everyday.

He felt the same sad and terrifying jolt of gut-sickness at each different face he looked on, unable to shake the conviction that he, by all rights, should be lying here with the rest. Dead by lance or bullet. Crumpled in a grotesque posture in the smoking shreds of his uniform. He did not want to see and absorb these sights, yet could not keep himself from it. As if the scene had to be forcibly seared into his brain.

He felt a dim surprise that the bodies bore almost no signs of mutilation. He guessed it was true, what his friend the old scout had said—snorting at the atrocity tales created by sensational journalism and spread by scatterbrains. The plains warriors didn't torture. "They takes scalps," the old man had told him, "and they cuts off a dead enemy's left arm, maybe only the left hand. Just that. Gets their name from that. Cheyenne means 'Cut-Arm People' . . ."

A few wanton mutilations showed here and there. Probably inflicted by the handful of sadistic imbeciles that infested any army. The late N Troop had contained a few such men.

He found Lieutenant Rufus Spingam, dashing Indian fighter, slumped on the ground with his back against a boulder, the front of his pretty blue double-breasted miner's shirt soaked with darkly drying blood. His head was sunk on his chest, a breeze stirred his dark curly hair.

Honus remembered hearing that the Indians had not taken Yellow Hair Custer's scalp either—some said out of respect, other because he had died badly, and who in hell could read an Injun's reasons? The Cheyennes might have noticed Spingam's resemblance to his idol. . . .

But there was no way of really telling how the lieutenant or any of them had died. Along with the bodies of their own dead, the Cheyennes had carried off all the troopers' weapons; and the carriage boxes had been torn from their belts. Pieces of uniforms had been scavenged from bodies untouched by the fire.

A little father on, Honus found O'Hearn.

The sergeant had been scalped, left arm taken; the flint head of a snapped-off lance was buried in his chest. Otherwise he looked as if he had lain down to sleep, his face toughly serene. The fighting grin seemed to hover like a contented shadow on his mouth. No need to question how he had died.

In spite of the sick horror gripping him, Honus moved from body to body in a kind of frozen dogged calm. It wasn't till he came on Menzies again, crumpled under the body of the first Cheyenne downed by Honus, that something snapped in him.

Honus felt his eyes start to blur. "I'm sorry," he whispered.

He was. Sorry that he hadn't warmed to a real appreciation of Menzies' friendship, ashamed of the small secret contempt he had felt at the man's crudeness and other lacks. For Menzies had been very much a man in the final and best sense: that was what counted.

It did no good to be sorry. But saying the words aloud let Honus give vent to the anguish that lay behind the madness still chilling his brain.

He prowled aimlessly across the scorched ground, the welling guilty grief changed to anger now. He tramped wildly through the ashes and rubble, kicking at any small burned object.

"What are you doing, for God's sake?"

Cresta Lee's caustic query shocked him back to himself.

He came to a halt, blinking at her. She stood a few yards off, fists on her hips, small and sturdy in the limp tatters of her dress, looking totally out of patience.

"Nothing. I was . . ." He let the words trail.

"Well, just snap to now, will you? We've things to do if we want to get out of this with whole skins. I've been looking around. They didn't leave a lot, but there should be a few articles we can use. So let's . . . are you listening?"

Honus gave her a dull stare. "We have to bury them."

"What! Are you crazy? Only thing we have to do is take what we need and clear out of here!"

Her snappish indignation was a bellows pumping at the live coal of his anger. "Don't you have any decent feelings?"

"Decent is as decent does. Back there"—she gave a small contemptuous nod toward the East and Civilization—"it may mean something. Out in this place, let me tell you, it doesn't mean one damned thing. All that counts is staying alive."

She leaned forward a little from the waist, fists braced on her hips. "And soldier—I mean to stay alive. I slaved and planned two years to get away from them. Now I'm out of it halfway—still free anyhow—and you're not putting me back in it with your damned foolishness! We're way out on the shaggy end of nowhere, and we're going to need each other. Not that you're much, but you have enough nerve, I guess—you can shoot a little. I'm getting out all the way. And you're going to help me."

Honus' jaw had been hardening slowly as she talked, and now a rich crawl of heat was edging up toward his hair, washing out the freckles. Honus Gant was getting madder than he had ever been in his life.

Miss Cresta Lee saw this very plainly. And wisely held her tongue. She watched him warily.

With a great effort, Honus choked down his rage. He had been taught to speak softly to a woman, even if she had a shrewish tongue and an indecent vocabulary, and was, by all odds, the most cold-blooded female he had ever met.

Also his good bedrock of common sense was asserting itself. It was a family trait—one which Honus' great-aunt Maddie, the wonderful old lady who had raised him, had taken pains to cultivate in him.

Cresta Lee was obnoxious, but she was right.

They had escaped the Cheyennes, but their position was still far from cozy. They were miles from any civilized post that either one knew of, and no matter which way they went, they faced a foot journey of many long, possibly dangerous miles. In these circumstances, they had no duty to the dead . . . only themselves.

"All right," Honus said wearily. "We're about halfway between the Pine Hills Agency and Fort Reunion . . . but a little nearer Reunion, I'd say. There are probably a few ranches that are nearer yet, but I couldn't swear to finding them—and if we stick to the road, we can't get lost."

Cresta Lee nodded coolly, "Only we'll follow the road till it splits away from the river. Then we'll follow the river . . ."

"Miss Lee, that's not a wise thought—"

"Look, Janroe River swings way north and then swings back, doesn't it, by Fort Reunion?"

"Of course, but that's my point. The road runs almost straight to Reunion. The river makes that huge loop." The inanity of this bickering—here and now—struck him. But a dull stubborn residue of his anger seemed to push at him. "We'd walk half again as far to reach the same place!"

"Use your head," Cresta Lee snapped. "If Spotted Wolf has taken to making attacks along this road, anybody on it—particularly small parties—will be sitting ducks."

"But when Captain Battles' paywagon fails to arrive on schedule, they'll send out troops to learn what's amiss. They'll meet us—"

"How soon?"

"Well—" A lame pause. "I'd imagine in a few days . . ."

"By which time we could be most of the damned distance to the fort. Look—" She raised her left hand, the fingers outfanned, and ticked them off one by one. "All along the Janroe, there's heavy brush and cover. Get wind of danger and you can find shelter in no time. There's trees here and there, shade when the sun gets fierce. There's food for the picking—bushes loaded with wild plums and berries. A good chance we can scare up a jackrabbit or two. Most important, we're always close to water. So—" She let the hand drop in a flat, unequivocal gesture. "You do what you want, Buster. I'm following the river all the way."

She had already turned in that quick imperative way, tossing the last words across her shoulder as she moved off.

The two of them went carefully over the ashy ground, hunting for anything that might be of use. They didn't find much. Cresta Lee located her wide straw hat that had been blown off when the attack came, hung up in a snag of brush by the creek. She also found one of the blue orange-bordered army blankets trampled in the muddy creekbank. It was badly scorched, partly chopped to ribbons, but after she had done a trimming job with her knife, the remainder made a serviceable skirt, knotted around her waist. Honus found a dented canteen which a bullet had passed through. A couple of wooden plugs would make it usable.

The pack animals that had stampeded might have been rounded up by the raiders, or they might still be running. In either case, they were gone and so were the grub supplies they carried. General Crook, now in charge of the Army's Department of the Platte, had had the troops under his command abandon their heavy baggage and ammunition wagons in favor of pack horses or mules. This ensured the mobility and swiftness essential to pursuing the red foe, but in this case it also emphasized the sobering plight of two survivors. . . .

They searched the Dougherty wagon, which had been over-turned and the wheels smashed. The fire had licked at and blackened its hull, but it was still intact otherwise. However, the Indians had stripped it of the little baggage stored inside.

Even the steel-reinforced payroll chest was gone, Honus was surprised to find. Money in gold or greenbacks was supposed to mean nothing to hostiles—yet they had taken the trouble to unload and probably secure to a travois-drag the heavy locked chest.

The startling fact provoked a startling realization. If this were the first time an Army pay escort had been attacked by Indians, they must have been after nothing more than the money itself.

Spotted Wolf, like most of the great war chiefs, was ordinarily a guerrilla fighter. When you had a small force, poor logistics, limited firepower, you made the hit-and-run tactic the basis of your fight. You harassed the enemy, destroyed or carried off his supplies, in a war of attrition, not of clear-cut victory.

Today's hard-pressed battle and massacre was a total departure for Spotted Wolf. His stratagem had been, as always, immaculate—but no matter how he'd gone about overwhelming a well-armed detachment of U.S. Cavalry, he would have been bound to pay a bloody price. As he had.

He must have been willing to pay it to get his hands on that paychest. But why?

"Come on," Cresta Lee said impatiently.

They moved off from the wagon, continuing their search. But Honus' scanning of the sooty earth was mechanical: his real attention was grappling with a question which he felt was more important than his safety or Cresta Lee's.

His boot kicked something half-buried in the flaky char.

He bent and picked it up. A rifle. The steel barrel had gotten bent so badly, it had been discarded.

It was one of the repeating rifles the Indians had used. A 73 Model Winchester with, he had heard, a lever action so smooth that you could get off all fifteen loads in as many seconds.

Honus turned it thoughtfully in his hands. He said: "Did Spotted Wolf's men have many guns like this—repeaters—before you left?"

Cresta Lee shrugged. "A few."

"But not many?"

"I said a few." She gave him a level stare. "Nothing like as many as they had today, if that's what you mean."

"It is." Honus scowled. "Where did they get so many spanking-new repeaters all at once? Ordinarily they pick up one here, one there, from settlers or pilgrims they've waylaid . . ."

"So?"

"I'm thinking of what it could mean . . . a good-sized band of renegades all armed with rifles like this one. Spotted Wolf might have more in mind than just another little rising to harass settlers and make the Army mad. He might . . ."

Honus paused. The two facts clicked into place like safe tumblers. "That's it," he said softly. "No doubt of it. He's found a source of new weapons. The source has to be . . . white men. The paymaster's chest is for them!"

"I suppose so."

"But didn't you see anything while you were with them? Haven't you any idea . . . ?"

"No. Look, we've found all we're going to here. Let's get going. It's still a couple hours to sunset, and we can cover a good many miles before dark."

Honus looked around him. Men lay dead at this place—unshriven and unburied. The awful fact of it was a silent shout for some word of ceremony . . . man's lonely cry against the inevitable and the unknown. I am more, man had cried since time out of mind, more than an envelope of flesh—

A thick and sluggish ache filled his throat. What should he say? What could he—after living through a day like this one? Humbly thank the Almighty and pray for the souls of the fallen? He could—but the words would taste of ashes.

A few lines of Tennyson came to mind: they seemed right.

"'Was there a man dismayed?

> Not though the soldier knew
> Someone had blundered:
> Theirs not to make reply,
> Theirs not to reason why,
> Theirs but to do and die . . .'"

That would do. It would have to do.

Cresta stood a few paces off, watching him strangely. He said, "All right," and started blindly away.

Two alone on a savage plain. Honus Gant. Quiet, proper and unadventurous Ohio farm lad and erstwhile schoolmaster. Cresta Marybelle Lee. Shrewd, tough and ambitious lass from the New York slums. And more lately, runaway wife of a Cheyenne war chief. Two alone—and on foot. With many hot treacherous miles to go . . .

WAYNE D. OVERHOLSER
Beecher Island

Wayne D. Overholser (1906-) was born in Pomeroy, Washington. He worked as teacher for many years, writing Western fiction when time would allow. He sold his first story to *Popular Western* in 1936, but his career (which has lasted fifty years) really took off when he secured the services of the literary agent, August Lenniger. Overholser's stories subsequently appeared in over seventy pulp magazines. Unlike many of the leading pulp writers of the 1940s and 1950s, Overholser successfully negotiated the decline in the pulp magazine market, and has published over a hundred Western novels. Two of these novels, *The Lawman* (published under the name of Lee Leighton) and *The Violent Land* received Spur Awards from the Western Writers of America as the best novels of 1953 and 1954 respectively.

'Beecher Island' is from 1970, and is a fictional reconstruction of the battle of Beecher Island, September 1868, when a group of Cheyenne led by Woqini (known to the whites as Roman Nose) surrounded a command led by Major George Forsyth.

SAM BURDICK HAD NO NOTION of passing time. All he knew was that the sun was well above the eastern rim of the prairie and the morning was beginning to lose its chill. Only an hour ago, or maybe it had been two, he was camped with the rest of Forsyth's civilian scouts on the bank of the Dry Fork of the Republican when the Indians had tried to stampede the horses and failed. Minutes later the Indians had appeared by the hundreds as suddenly as if they had sprouted out of the ground.

Someone had yelled, "Get to the island," and the scouts had plunged pell-mell across the sandy, nearly dry bed of the stream to an island that was covered by brush and weeds. Sam had heard the command above the frantic commotion, "Dig in! Dig in!" That was exactly what they had done, dug in with butcher knives and tin plates and anything they could use while Indian bullets and arrows swept over their heads.

The scouts' horses were shot down; now and then a man was hit. The Indians had attacked and had been beaten off, but they would come again. No one had told Sam that they would, but he was as sure of it as he was sure of death and taxes.

The old mountain man, Bill Smith, lay behind his dead horse in the pit next to Sam. A bullet had slashed a bloody furrow across Smith's skull, but he had wrapped a bandanna around his head and kept on fighting.

The only firing now was from the Indian sharpshooters who were hiding in the tall grass along the banks, and the answering shots from a few scouts who were equally well hidden in the brush on the low end of the island.

Now that there was this lull in the fighting, Sam had time to draw a deep breath and look at the sky and wonder why he was here. Sure, he was like the others in one way. He felt he was doing something that had to be done.

The Cheyennes had swept across the western end of Kansas, burning and torturing and killing, and they had to be punished. There weren't enough soldiers to do the job in the skeleton army that survived the Civil War, so General Sheridan had told Colonel Forsyth to enlist fifty civilian scouts and see what he could do with the Cheyennes.

They had set out to find Indians and punish them. Well, they had succeeded in finding them, succeeded too well. They'd found hundreds, maybe a thousand, so now it was a question of who was going to punish whom. It was even a question of whether any of the scouts would live to leave the island with odds like this.

"They ain't pushing us right now," Sam said, and then, although he knew better, he asked, "Figure we whipped 'em?"

"Hell, no," the mountain man answered. "They'll hit us again purty soon. We ain't seen hide nor hair o' Roman Nose, and when we do, we'll know it."

Sam closed his eyes, his pulse pounding in his temples. He pressed hard against the body of Sam's dead horse, which lay between him and the edge of the island. You do something like joining the scouts because it's your duty, but there were other reasons, too.

Maybe you're bored by the monotony of farm life or you want to be a hero, or maybe you're in trouble with the law and this is one way you can keep ahead of the sheriff. Or maybe, and Sam guessed this was the most important reason, you see a chance to pick up a few dollars at a time when dollars in central Kansas were about as hard to find as feathers on a fish.

With Sam it had been a proposition of needing the dollars. At the time the farm work wasn't pressing. Still, he hadn't figured on this kind of fight. One scout, William Wilson, had been killed, and several others including Colonel Forsyth were wounded.

Someone holed up in the middle of the island called, "If you men on the outside don't do a little shooting, them red devils will be on top of us again."

"That feller's a fool," Smith said in disgust. "He better git over here and do some o' the shooting he's talkin' about."

Two of the scouts, McCall and Culver, were needled into action by the man who had yelled. They raised up to locate an Indian to shoot at. Smith bellowed, "Git down," but he was too late. One of the sharpshooters shot Culver through the head and caught McCall in the shoulder.

Smith swore bitterly. "Every time we lose a man, we cut down our chances of knocking 'em back on their heels the next time they charge us." He motioned toward the bluffs. "There's the old boy hisself. I knowed Roman Nose would be in it sooner or later. He's got more fight savvy than any other Injun I know."

Quickly Sam rose up to see what was happening and dropped flat again. He'd had time to see hundreds of mounted braves gathered at the foot of the bluffs out of rifle range. One big brave who was wearing a red sash around his waist was haranguing them and making wild gestures as if he was furious over something.

"It was a good thing for us Roman Nose wasn't in on the start of this ruckus," Smith said, "or they'd have grabbed the island afore we got it. The trouble with Injuns is that they want to count coup so bad that even a good fightin' man like Roman Nose don't have no luck gettin' 'em to foller orders."

"How many do you figure are out there?" Sam asked.

"Maybe a thousand," Smith answered, "though it's hard to say for sure, with some of 'em hidin' in the grass and sharpshootin' the way they are. Damn that Forsyth! I tried to tell him yesterday we was follerin' a big party, but you can't never tell an Army man nuthin'."

"Are they all Cheyennes?"

"Mostly, but there's some Oglalas with 'em. Arapahoes, too, chances are, though I ain't spotted any yet."

An arrow flashed over Sam's head, and a moment later a bullet hit the body of his horse with a sudden *thwack*. He dug his nose into the sand, then realized he'd be no good to anyone if he remained in this position.

He raised his head to look and dropped back quickly, puzzled by what he saw. The mounted braves were riding downstream toward a bend in the creek below the island. There didn't seem to be any sense in this maneuver, but the warriors were undoubtedly following Roman Nose's orders. If Smith was right about the great Cheyenne's fighting savvy, there must be very good logic back of what the Indians were doing.

Again there was a momentary lull in the firing. A bugle sounded from somewhere among the Indians, surprising and shocking Sam. He asked, "Where in tunket would a Cheyenne learn to toot a bugle? And where would they find one?"

"They'd find one easy enough," Smith said. "Kill a bunch of soldiers and you get yourself a bugle. Tootin' one's something else. But I don't figger it was an Injun. Chances are one o' William Bent's sons is out yonder with 'em. Some of 'em have turned renegade, and it wouldn't be so hard for one of 'em to have learned a bugle afore he left Fort Bent."

"Looks to me like they're riding downstream," Sam said. "I don't see any reason for that."

"Kind o' funny about Injuns," Smith continued, apparently not hearing what Sam had said. "Now there was Fetterman, who got massacreed by Red Cloud. I'll bet you that right now Roman Nose is thinkin' about what happened to Fetterman and he's tellin' hisself that if he can give us the same treatment, he'll be great like Red Cloud."

Sam had been paying little attention to Smith. He was still puzzling over the reason for the movement downstream, and now a possible explanation came to him. He asked, "You think Roman Nose is taking them downstream to get them lined up for a charge?"

"Downstream?" Smith bellowed, and sat up to get a quick look. He got his head back a second before a bullet whizzed above him. "That'n was a mite close," he said as if he had been annoyed by a passing mosquito.

Sam grinned, thinking he couldn't have been that calm about it. But then the mountain man had been ducking bullets longer than Sam Burdick had been alive.

"Well sir, I'll tell you what you'd better do," Smith said thoughtfully. "The colonel ain't one to listen to me. I ain't his official scout, and Sharp Grover is. One thing's sure. Grover ain't gonna listen to anything I say neither. But

Forsyth oughtta be told what them damn brownskins are doin'."

"Grover's probably told him," Sam said.

"Mebbe so, mebbe not," Smith said. "Just the same, you'd better make a worm out o' yourself and git over there to the colonel and tell him. If we ain't fixed to roll 'em back, they'll roll over us. That's as sartin as there's sin in hell."

"I'll try to get to him," Sam said, and slid out of the shallow trench he had dug behind the body of his horse.

He snaked through the grass, hoping he had time to reach Forsyth. He moved slowly, his body flat against the ground, pushing himself forward with his hands and feet. Once a burst of firing lashed out from the low end of the island. Sam stopped until it was over. Jack Stillwell was hiding there in the tall grass with two older scouts. The three were the best shots in the command.

Sam felt good just remembering they were there. Stillwell was very young, younger even than Sam, but he was not a farm boy. Even though he was still in his teens, he had the reputation of being one of the best scouts on the frontier. Although it had seemed incredible, Sam had heard that Stillwell had once guided a wagon train when he was only twelve. Now that he knew Stillwell, he could believe it.

He went on, still keeping low. He felt as if he were moving at a snail's pace, but he had not been far from Forsyth's trench when he started. Now, not certain where he was, he called, "Colonel."

"Here," Forsyth answered.

Another minute was all it took Sam to reach Forsyth. He saw that the man was suffering. He kept biting his lower lip against the pain that racked his body; sweat made a shiny film across his forehead. Suddenly it occurred to Sam that the colonel was a soldier all the way down to his boot heels, and if they lived through this fight, it would be Forsyth who brought them through.

"Can't the doctor do anything for you?" Sam asked.

"Dr Mooers has suffered a head wound and will not live through the day," Forsyth said. "To make our situation worse, we lost all our medical supplies. We left them in camp when we headed for the island. Of course it's impossible for us to get them now. By the time we have a chance to go after them, the Indians will have carried them off."

Sam considered this, wondering how anyone could have been careless enough to go off and leave the medical supplies. This, plus the loss of the doctor, could be a fatal blow if the battle lasted any length of time. With the possible exception of the officers, Forsyth and Beecher, the scouts could not have lost a man who would be missed as much as Dr Mooers.

"Was there something you wanted to say?" Forsyth asked.

"Yes," Sam said. "I wasn't sure whether you knew or not, but the Indians are drifting downstream toward the bend. Bill Smith and me figure Roman Nose will lead a charge against us as soon as he gets them lined out."

"We're whipped if they run over us," Forsyth said. "They'll trample us to death or shoot us." He hesitated a moment, then called, "Beecher, get ready to repel an attack. It's up to you to see that all the men have their rifles and revolvers loaded. Take the guns of the dead men and the badly wounded and see that the scouts on the low end of the island have them."

Sam crawled back toward his trench, momentarily exposing himself as he left Forsyth's pit. He lay motionless for a few seconds in the tall weeds, thankful he had not been hit, then went on. A minute or so later he was back in his own trench.

"The doc's hard hit and expected to die before night," Sam said. "What's almost as bad is the loss of our medical supplies. They were left in camp this morning."

Smith shrugged at the news. He said, "Well, that whittles down our chances a little more. All we need now is to run out of ammunition, and Roman Nose has got us."

A moment later Sam heard the command, "Load up. Hold your fire till you're given the order."

"Look at 'em come," Smith said, his voice holding a note of admiration. "If I was where I could see this but knowed my hair was gonna stay on my head, I'd say it was a real purty sight."

Sam nodded agreement. In an oblique sort of way he admired the Indians. They were a people fighting for their homes against impossible odds. Now, easing up so he could look over the top of his dead horse, he saw the Indians sweep up the creek. For the time being the sharpshooters' fire had died, so it seemed safe to keep his head up.

Sam's heart began to pound as he watched the great mass of riders gallop up the stream toward the island, sixty wide and eight deep, Roman Nose in the front rank. Then Sam reminded himself it was no time to feel compassion for the Indians. They would kill him as readily as they had killed his saddle horse if they could.

The deadly cold that had nested in the pit of his stomach spread through his belly as his sweaty hands tightened on the Spencer. The Indians were fighting for their homes, but he, Sam Burdick, and his friends Bill Smith and the rest of the scouts, were fighting for their lives.

The Indians swept on up the creek, the painted braves naked except for their moccasins and breechclouts and cartridge belts. They rode bareback, their horse-hair ropes knotted around the middle of their ponies so that it went over their knees. They gripped their horses' manes with their left hand, their rifles held above their heads in their right hands.

Unexpectedly the Indians pulled up just out of rifle range, the sudden silence bringing a tension to Sam's taut nerves that seemed more than he could bear. Again Forsyth shouted, "Hold your fire until I give the order."

Roman Nose had swung out of line to face his men. He talked to them briefly; then he turned back to the scouts and shook his fist at them. He tipped his head and let out a great war cry, hitting his mouth with his hand. Sam, crouched there in his pit, felt a chill travel down his spine. He had never heard such a sound in all his life, a sound he would not forget as long as he lived.

They came on again at a gallop, the long lines as perfect as those of a well-trained drill team. Sam kept his gaze on Roman Nose. *Cruel and brutal*, Sam thought, *but certainly a magnificent physical specimen*. He was big, six feet three or more, and unusually muscular for an Indian. He sat astride his great chestnut horse with perfect balance; his war bonnet was beautiful, the curved buffalo horns just above his forehead, the eagle and heron feathers floating behind him.

Now the sharpshooters opened up from the grass, bullets whistling past Sam's head. Smith said, "They're just figgerin' on keepin' us down, but it won't last long. They'll have to stop shootin' in a minute, or they'll plug their own men."

Smith was right. The firing stopped; the bugle sounded its clear, sharp call as it rang out into the war cries of the charging avalanche of painted warriors.

"Now," Forsyth called.

An instant later Beecher picked up the order, "Now."

The volley made an ear-hammering roar as powder flame lashed out from the Spencers, the bullets tearing great holes in the front rank of the Indians as men and horses fell. They closed ranks and came on. Roman Nose was still in the front, yelling his frightening war cry and holding his rifle above his head.

Another volley and a third and a fourth. Far out on the left flank a medicine man was knocked off his horse. Sam, squeezing off another shot, thought for an instant the charge was broken, but once more they closed ranks and swept on, the prairie grass behind them littered with dead and wounded men and horses.

They were almost to the island now, charging straight into the death-dealing fury of the Spencers. A fifth volley and a sixth, and then Roman Nose was knocked off his horse, the medicine that had brought him through so may savage fights failing him at last.

The big warrior was the key to the charge, the very heart of the attack. When he fell, the charge stopped as if it had rolled up against an impenetrable wall. One more volley, and even in the face of this leaden death the Indians picked Roman Nose up and carried him off the battlefield.

Sam jumped to his feet with the rest of the scouts who could stand, all yelling and emptying their revolvers at the Indians, who were racing away across the prairie. A handful of braves had reached the lower end of the island. If they had come on . . . if Roman Nose had not fallen, they would have overrun the island, and the scouts would have been trampled to death just as Roman Nose had planned.

Sam had been surprised to find himself on his feet, his empty revolver in his hand as he cheered with the rest. This was not like him, but now he felt a great wave of pride engulf him, pride because he was a member of this body of scouts, pride because they had fought hard enough to stay alive, pride in having the courage it took to stay and keep firing in the face of five hundred horsemen who wanted only to kill him and his fellow scouts.

"Get down," Forsyth yelled. "Lie down."

And Beecher, "Get down or you'll have your heads blown off."

Smith reached over and yanked Sam back into his pit just as the sharpshooters opened up once more from the grass, raking the entire island with a vicious, deadly fire. Sam lay in his trench and reloaded his Spencer and revolver, thinking briefly of the insanity of war, of the squaws who loved the Indians who had fallen just as much as some white women loved the scouts who had died since the first dawn attack, just as his own mother loved him.

He lay on his back, the hot morning sun hammering down on him. The powder smoke that had been a drifting cloud above the island was gone now, its acrid smell still lingering in Sam's nostrils. Then it came to him. This was the best the Indians could do. They would never do any better.

He would walk away from this island, he told himself; he would be back on the farm in time to help his father harvest his corn.

ELMER KELTON
Desert Command

Elmer Kelton (1926–) was born in Texas, where he was educated at the University of Texas, Austin. He has worked as a journalist and editor, and served with the US Army in Europe during World War Two. His first Western story appeared in the pulp magazine *Ranch Romances* in 1947, since which date he has established himself as one of the genre's leading authors. Among the many honours he has received for his writing are four Spur Awards from the Western Writers of America, three Western Heritage Awards from the National Cowboy Hall of Fame, and a Life Achievement Award from the Texas Institute of Letters. Kelton has written about the New West as well as the West of the nineteenth century, and his contemporary Western, *The Time It Never Rained* (1972), has been acclaimed as one of the finest American novels of the post-war era. Among the many notable qualities of Kelton's Western fiction are its historical realism and its racial tolerance.

The story 'Desert Command', which features a company of black buffalo soldiers lost in the South-west desert in the 1870s, comes from Kelton's novel, *The Wolf and the Buffalo* (1980). It was first extracted as a short story by Jon Tuska.

THE CAPTAIN WENT THROUGH THE motions of setting up a guard mount, but it was a futile effort. Most of these suffering men could do little to defend themselves should the Indians choose this time to attack. Gideon's vision was so blurred that he could not have drawn a bead. Sergeant Nettles could no longer control his limp. He kept his eyes on the captain and contrived not to move more than necessary when the captain looked in his direction.

Gideon asked, "Sergeant, why don't you take your rest?"

Nettles' eyes flashed in anger. "You tryin' to tell me what to do, *Private* Ledbetter?"

"No, sir. Just come to me that you had a hard day."

"We all had a hard day. Mine ain't been worse than nobody else's."

"You've rode back and forth, walked back and forth, seein' after the men. You gone twice as far as most of us. You rest, why don't you? Tell me what you want done and I'll do it."

"I want you to leave me alone. Ain't nothin' wrong with me that ain't wrong with everybody here."

"The rest of them got no arrow wound that ain't ever healed up."

The anger in Nettles' eyes turned to sharp concern. "It's all right, and I don't want you talkin' about it." He glanced quickly toward the captain and showed relief to find Hollander's attention focused elsewhere.

Gideon said accusingly, "You been hidin' it from him."

He could not remember that he had ever seen Nettles show fear of anything. But the sergeant was fearful now. He gripped Gideon's arm. "Don't you be tellin' him. Don't be tellin' nobody. Without the army, what could I be? Where could I go?"

"Lots of things. Lots of places."

"You know better than that. In the army I'm a sergeant, a *top* sergeant. I'm somebody, and I can *do* somethin'. Anywhere else, I'm just another nigger."

"Captain'll see for hisself sooner or later."

"Not as long as I can move. Now you git to your own business."

Sometime during the early part of the evening Gideon heard horses walking. He pushed up from the ground, listening, hoping it was Jimbo and the canteen carriers coming back. He was momentarily disoriented—dizzy—but he realized the sound was from the wrong direction to be Jimbo. It was coming from along the column's backtrail, to the west. He thought about Indians, but they wouldn't make that much noise. The clinking and clanking meant cavalry horses.

Captain Hollander figured it out ahead of Gideon. He walked to the edge of camp and did his best to shout. "Waters! Sergeant Waters! Up here!" His voice was weak and broke once.

The horses seemed to stop for a moment. The men—one of them, at least—had heard the captain. Hollander shouted again, his voice hoarser now. After a moment, the horses were moving again. The captain grunted in satisfaction. His good feeling was soon spoiled, for the horses kept walking, right on by the knoll.

"Waters!" Hollander tried again. Gideon took up the shout, and so did several others. The riders continued to move, passing the hill and going on eastward. The captain clenched his fists in anger.

Gideon volunteered, "I'll go, sir. I'll fetch them back." Hollander only grunted, but Gideon took that for approval. He started down the hill, his legs heavy. He shouted every so often for Waters, but he heard no reply. When he stopped to listen he could tell that the horses were getting farther from him. He tried to run but could not bring his legs to move that rapidly. He stumbled over the crown of some dried-up bunchgrass and sprawled on his belly. He invested a strong effort into getting on his feet.

Behind him Hollander called, "Come back, Ledbetter. Let them go."

He wavered on the point of insubordination but found he could barely hear the horses anymore. He had no chance to catch them. Wearily he turned and began the struggle back up the hill. It must have taken him an hour to reach the huddled company and fall to the ground.

Hollander stood over him, against the starlight. "You tried."

When he had the breath, Gideon said, "They just never did hear me."

"They heard you. Waters simply did not choose to stop. He's saving himself, or trying to."

A question burned in his mind, and he came near asking it aloud. *Are we going to save ourselves?* His throat was too dry to bring it out.

Nettles came over after a while to see if he was all right.

Gideon demanded, "What was the matter with Sergeant Waters? I *know* he heard me. I never figured *him* to panic out of his head."

"I seen him when the men commenced to groan. It was the groanin' done it. You ever wonder why he drank so much? It was to drive the groanin' sounds out of his mind."

"I don't understand."

"Old days, Waters was a slave catcher. It was him that kept the hounds, and him the white folks give the whip to when he caught a runaway. He didn't have no choice—they'd of took the whip to *him* if he hadn't done it. Now and again they made him keep whippin' a man till the life and the soul was beat out of him. I reckon them dead people been comin' after Waters ever since, in his mind."

The night breeze turned mercifully cool, but it held no hint of moisture. Gideon woodenly stood his guard duty, knowing he would be helpless if anything challenged him. He heard men groaning. The sound made his skin crawl. He could imagine how it had been with Waters. Across the camp someone babbled crazily, hallucinating. Gideon lapsed into sleep of sorts, or unconsciousness. When he awoke, color brightened the east. His head felt as if someone were pounding it with a hammer. His tongue was dry and swollen, his mouth like leather.

Sergeant Nettles lay on his blanket, his eyes open. Gideon crawled to him on hands and knees. He knew what he wanted to say, but his tongue betrayed him. He brought out only a jumble of sounds. He worked at it a long time before he summoned up a little saliva and forced his tongue to more or less his bidding. "You all right, sir?" he asked.

Nettles nodded and pushed himself slowly from the ground. At the edge of camp, Captain Hollander was moving about, the first man on his feet.

Little effort was made toward fixing breakfast. The men could not eat. They could not swallow without water. The captain started trying to pack the mules. The regular packer had fallen behind yesterday with Waters. Gideon began to help. It was almost more than he could do to lift a pack to the level of a mule's back. Had the mules been fidgety, he could not have managed. But they were too miserable to move around.

He could see a little better this morning, for the rest, and his legs moved easier than last night, but the gain was of only minor degree. A stir among the buffalo hunters attracted his attention. He became conscious that many of their horses and pack mules were gone. They had strayed off during the night, or perhaps Indians had stolen into the edge of camp and quietly made away with them. The hunters staggered around uncertainly, accusing one another mostly by gesture, for they were as hard put as the troopers to convert gestures into understandable words. In a little while hunters and soldiers started a ragged march down the gentle slope and left the round hill behind them.

Grasping at hope wherever he could find it, Gideon told himself that perhaps Jimbo and the others had stopped at darkness for fear of losing the trail, and by now they were on the move again, coming to the rescue.

The morning sun was soon punishingly hot. Miles went by slowly and painfully, and Jimbo did not come. Far up into the morning, after a couple of troopers had slumped to the ground, Hollander called for a rest stop. They had moved into a sandy stretch of ground with low-growing stemmy mesquite trees and small oak growth shin- to knee-high. Many of the men draped blankets over these plants and crawled under them as far as they could go for partial protection against the punishing sun.

Gideon turned to look for Sergeant Nettles. He found him shakily trying to dismount from his black horse Napoleon. Gideon reached to help him. He spread a blanket across a bush and pulled the corner of it over Nettles' head.

Young Nash tried to dismount but fell and lay as he had landed. Little Finley sat hunched, crying but not making tears. He tried to talk, but the words were without form.

Hollander was somehow still able to articulate, though he spoke his words slowly and carefully. He said it was his judgment that José had become lost and was not coming back—not today, not ever. The men who had gone on after him with the canteens must be sharing whatever fate had overtaken José.

Thompson argued sternly that somewhere ahead lay Silver Lake, and that it was no doubt José's goal. It couldn't be more than a few more miles—fifteen or twenty at most, he declared.

Hollander shook his head violently, his face flushed. If water were that near, and José had found it, Jimbo and the others would be back by now. The captain pointed southeastward. He still had his compass. Water anywhere else was a guess, and evidently a bad one. But he *knew* there was water in the Double Lakes. It was time to stop gambling and go for the cinch.

Thompson was aghast. "You know how far it is to the Double Lakes? Those darkies of yours—they're almost dead now. They'll never live for another sixty-seventy miles."

"They'll live. They've *got* to live."

Thompson insisted that water lay much closer, to the north-east.

Hollander countered, "You said that yesterday. How far have we come? How many more men can we afford to lose?"

"Go that way," Thompson insisted, pointing his chin across the sandy hills toward Double Lakes, "and you'll lose them all."

"There is water at Double Lakes. There is only death out here in these sands. Will you go with us?"

Thompson turned and studied his hunters. "No, we're trying for Silver Lake. It's there. I know it's there. I beg you, Captain, come on with us."

But Hollander had made up his mind. "I've already gambled and lost. I'll gamble no more on water that may not exist. Best of luck to you, Thompson."

The buffalo hunter saw the futility of further argument. "God go with you, Frank."

Hollander nodded. "May He walk with us all." Anger stood like a wall between the men, but each managed to thrust a hand forward. The two groups parted, the hunters toward the hope of Silver Lake and a short trail, the soldiers toward the certainty of Double Lakes, a long and terrible distance away.

The last time Gideon glimpsed the hunters, fading out of sight far to his left, four were walking, the rest hunched on their horses. Though he had not become personally acquainted and could not have named any except Thompson, he felt an ache of regret, a sense of loss as they disappeared into the shimmering heat.

He had no feeling for time. His legs were deadweights that he dragged along, one step and another and another. His vision blurred again. He trudged with his head down, following the tracks of the men in front of him. He no longer thought ahead, or even thought much at all. He fell into a merciful state of half consciousness, moving his body by reflex and instinct. His tongue had swollen so that it almost filled his mouth, and at times he felt he would choke on it.

He was conscious of hunger but unable to act upon it. He put hardtack into his mouth but could not work up saliva to soften it. It was like dry gravel against his inflexible tongue. He had to dig the pieces out with his finger.

Rarely did the horses or mules urinate, but when they did, someone rushed with a cup. The thought was no longer revolting to Gideon. Captain Hollander passed out brown sugar for the men to stir into the urine and increase its palatability. Some was given back to the horses, which at first refused but later accepted it.

By midafternoon, when the heat was at full fury, a horse staggered and went down. Hollander cut its throat to put it out of its misery. Finley came with his cup and caught the gushing blood and drank it, and others took what they could catch before death overtook the animal and the flow stopped. Some of the men became violently ill; the blood was thick and bitter from the horse's dehydration.

Hollander was compelled to call a halt. Men were strung out for half a mile. Orders meant next to nothing. This was no longer a column of soldiers; it was a loose and straggling collection of half-delirious men struggling for individual survival. Gideon saw Nash fall and wanted to go to help him but for a long time could not move his legs. Only when he saw Sergeant Nettles collapse upon the sun-baked sand did he muster the strength to stagger twenty steps and throw blankets over the men's heads to shield them from the sun. He slumped then, too exhausted to do the same for himself. He lapsed into a dreamlike state and seemed to float away like some bodiless spirit, back to the plantation. He heard the happy voice of Big Ella and the others there, and he splashed barefoot into the cool, flowing river.

The heat abated with sundown, and night brought a coolness which broke Gideon's fever. He roused to the point that he could look about him and see the other men lying in grotesque positions, many groaning, half of them suffering from delirium.

He rallied enough to crawl to Sergeant Nettles. At first he could not tell that the man was breathing. He held his hand just above Nettles' mouth and felt that faint but steady warmth of breath. Probably the sergeant was unconscious. Gideon saw no point in trying to bring him out of it. The Lord was being merciful.

Sometime in the night Captain Hollander started trying to get the men on their feet to use the cooler hours for easier miles. Gideon watched him impassively at first, until the man's strong determination began to reach him. Sergeant Nettles arose and began limping from one man to another. Gideon pushed to his feet and helped.

He heard Hollander say thickly, "Good man, Ledbetter. Get them going."

In the moonlight it was apparent that several horses had wandered away. Judas was gone. Gideon could not bring himself to any emotion over that. Half the men were afoot now, their horses strayed or dead. Many of the pack mules were missing. Nettles asked Gideon to count the men, to be sure they left none behind. He found it difficult to hold the figures in his head. His mind kept drifting to other things, other times, other places far better than this one.

Many blankets and packs were left on the ground as the company moved out. A couple of men dropped their carbines, and Gideon forcibly put them back in their hands. A little later he looked back and saw that one of the men was empty-handed again.

He dreaded sunrise, but it came. He sensed that they had walked or ridden many miles in the cool darkness. The heat was blunted the first couple of hours by a thin cover of dry clouds that held no promise of rain. These burned away, after a time, and the men and horses trudged under the full punishment of an unforgiving July sun.

A transient thought flitted through Gideon's mind. He wondered where the Indians were. It struck him as strange that he had gone so long without the Indians intruding on his consciousness. It occurred to him that it had been most of two days since he had heard them mentioned. Odd, that the mission which had brought the soldiers into this blazing hell had been so completely forgotten in the face of a more elemental challenge, simple survival.

A staggering horse brought the procession to a halt. Without waiting for the captain to give an order, one of the troopers cut the animal's throat, and several fought over the gushing blood. Gideon saw Nettles start toward the men to break up the fight, then go to his knees. Gideon took it upon himself to part the fighters, throwing a couple to the ground with more strength than he had realized he still owned. Little Finley's own horse went down on its rump. Finley stared dumbly, making no effort to join the struggle to capture its blood. He lay down on the short, brittle grass and wept silently, his shoulders shuddering.

Through all of it, Nettles sat helplessly. The spirit was still strong in his black eyes, but the flesh had gone as far as it could. Gideon managed to get the men under some semblance of control, making gruff noises deep in his throat because he could not force his tongue to form clear words. He felt the eyes of Hollander and Nettles upon him. Without being formally bidden to do so, he took command upon himself and motioned and coaxed and bullied most of the men into movement. Lieutenant Judson, weaving a little, got on his droop-headed horse and took the lead.

Soon only five men were left, Gideon and Hollander on their feet, the sunstruck Nash and shattered little Finley lying on the ground, Sergeant Nettles sitting up but unable to keep his legs under him.

By signs more than by words, Nettles conveyed his intention of staying with Nash and Finley until they were able to move. Then he would bring them on, following the company's trail to water. Captain Hollander nodded his assent, though Gideon saw sadness in the man's blue eyes. Hollander took the big black hand in both of his own and squeezed it for a moment, silently saying good-bye to an old friend. Hollander turned away quickly, not looking back. Nettles raised his hand again, and Gideon took it.

The sergeant mumbled, but Gideon made out the words he was trying to say. "Take care of them, soldier."

Gideon tried to assure him he would be back as soon as they found water, but the words would not come. He turned back only once, a hundred yards away, and took a final look at the sergeant, still sitting up, holding the reins of big, black Napoleon. For a moment, in spite of the heat, Gideon felt cold.

The column moved until upwards of midday, when the heat brought more horses to their knees, and more of the men. By this time the company was out of control. Now and then a man in delirium struck out on a tangent of his own, away from the main body. At first Gideon tried to bring them back but soon had to give up, for the effort was a drain on whatever strength he still held in reserve. He stopped thinking ahead but concentrated on bringing one foot in front of the other.

When Lieutenant Judson went down, slipping from the saddle and landing limply in the dry grass, the column stopped. The lieutenant's horse braced its legs and stood trembling. It no longer sweated, though a crust of dried mud clung to its hide. Hollander tried to rouse Judson but could not. Hollander gave a little cry and slumped to the ground, covering his face with his hands. By instinct more than reason, Gideon helped him to a small mesquite and threw a blanket over it to shade him, and to shield the captain's emotions from view of the men. The lieutenant's horse, untethered, began wandering off southward, dragging the reins, drawn by instinct in the direction of Concho. Gideon knew he should make some effort to bring it back, but he lacked the willpower to move. He sat with his legs stretched out before him on the ground and watched the horse stumble away to a slow death somewhere out there on the parched prairie.

After a time, Gideon became aware that the captain was trying to call him. Hollander motioned with his hand. Gideon crawled to the officer on hands and knees.

Hollander extended his silver watch, despair in his sunken eyes. Very slowly, very deliberately, he managed a few clear words. "Wife. Give to my wife and baby."

Gideon reached for the watch until the import of the captain's words penetrated his fevered brain. Hollander was giving up. Gideon looked slowly around him at the men sprawled on the ground, covering their heads with blankets if they still had them, hats if they did not.

If Hollander died, these men would die. Hollander might be no better man than they, but his was the leadership. His was the example they had been conditioned to follow, as they had been conditioned all their lives to follow one white man or another. It came to Gideon that if he accepted the watch, that would release the captain to die in peace.

He felt a flare of deep anger. The captain had no right to die! He had brought these men here; he had to live and take them out. Gideon drew back his hand. Shaking his head, he tried to form words first in his mind, then get them out on his dry, swollen tongue.

"No! You'll live. *You* give it to her."

The captain reached out with both hands, the silver chain dangling. His eyes begged, though his cracked lips formed no discernible words.

Gideon almost gave in to pity, but the anger was still hot in his face. Stubbornly he pulled back. The words came clearly in his mind, though he could not get his tongue to speak them.

You got a baby now, more than likely. You owe that woman, and you owe that baby, and you owe us! You goin' to live if I got to kill you!

Only the anger came out, not the words. But the captain seemed to understand that Gideon refused to release him from his responsibilities. Hollander turned his head away, in the shadow beneath the blanket. He clutched the silver watch against his chest, his shoulders heaving.

In a while he was somehow on his feet again. He motioned for Gideon to help him lift the delirious lieutenant onto the captain's own horse. Gideon tied the young officer in the saddle. Hollander struck out again southeastward, his steps slow and deliberate. He was setting a pace, an example. His shoulders had a determined set. Gideon sensed that the captain would not give up again. He might die, but he would not surrender.

Gideon had trouble distinguishing reality from hallucination. His head roared from fever, and it ached with a steady rhythm like a drumbeat. He imagined he could hear the post band playing a parade-ground march, and he tried in vain to bring his feet into step with it. His vision was distorted, the men stretched out of shape, the prairie rolling in waves. Cajoling, threatening, he got the men to their feet one by one and set them to following the captain. Some moved willingly, some fought him, but by and by he had them all on the move.

Stumbling, bringing up the rear so no one could drop out without his knowledge, Gideon moved in a trance. It occurred to him that a couple of the pack mules had strayed off on their own. Only two were left.

Each time a horse staggered and fell, its throat was cut, and the men caught the blood and gagged it down. The captain's horse gave up after a long time, going to its knees. Gideon struggled to untie the lieutenant but could not bring his unresponsive fingers to the task. He cut the rope and tried to ease the officer to the ground. He lacked the strength to hold him. He and the lieutenant fell together in a heap. Gideon looked up at the horse, afraid it might roll over on them. He dragged himself and the lieutenant away before someone cut the animal's throat.

That was the last of the horses.

He lay struggling for breath; the exertion had been severe. The men were like gaunt scarecrow figures out of a nightmare, their uniforms a dusty gray instead of blue, many hanging in strips and ribbons. The faces were stubbled, the beards matted grotesquely with dust and horses' blood as well as some of their own, for their lips were swollen out of shape and had cracked and bled. They no longer looked like soldiers, they looked like madmen—and Gideon feared he was the maddest of them all.

The packs were untied from the mules, and Lieutenant Judson was lifted aboard one of the last two surviving animals. Again Gideon tried to tie him on, but he could not coordinate his hands and gave up the task. Delirious or not, Judson would have to retain instinct enough to hold himself on the mule.

The ragged column plodded and staggered and crawled until far into the afternoon. Hollander motioned for a rest stop in an open plain that lacked even the low-growing dune mesquites over which a blanket could be stretched for shade. Hardly a blanket was left anyway. The men had dropped them one by one, along with everything else they had carried. Troopers sprawled on the ground, faces down to shield them from the sun. Gideon fell into a state more stupor than sleep. After a time, he felt someone shaking his shoulder. Hollander was motioning for him to get up, and to get the other men up. Gideon went about the task woodenly.

He helped Hollander and one of the other troopers lift the lieutenant back onto the mule.

Gideon saw that Hollander was studying the other mule, which had remained riderless. The wish was plain in the officer's eyes, but Gideon saw there a reluctance, too. They were no longer officers and men; they were simply men, all in a desperate situation together. Hollander was uncertain about using the advantage that might save his life.

Gideon felt a sudden temptation to take the mule himself. He had the strength to do it. At this moment, he was probably the strongest man in the column. Nobody—not even Hollander—could stop him if he made up his mind.

The thought became action to the point that he laid his hands on the reins, and on the mule's roached mane. He leaned against the mule, trying to summon strength to pull himself up. But he could not, and he realized slowly that it was more than simply a matter of strength. It was also a matter of will. Sergeant Esau Nettles forcibly pushed himself into Gideon's mind. In Nettles' eyes, such a thing would be a dishonor upon Gideon and upon the company.

Gideon cried out for Nettles to leave him alone, but in his mind he could see the sergeant's angry eyes burning like fire, and their heat seemed to touch him and force him back from the mule.

Gideon motioned for Hollander to take the mule. Somehow his tongue managed the words. "Ride him. Sir."

He had not been willing to give Hollander release to die, but now he offered him release to live. Hollander stared at him with remorseful eyes. With Gideon's help, he got onto the mule's back. He reached down and took up the reins to lead the mule on which the lieutenant had been placed.

A momentary wildness widened Hollander's eyes. The thought behind it was too clear to miss: with these mules the white men could leave the black soldiers behind and save themselves.

Reading that temptation, Gideon stared helplessly, his mouth hanging open. He knew he could not fairly blame Hollander, for he had almost yielded to the same temptation. One pleading word shaped itself into voice. "Captain . . ."

The wildness passed. Hollander had put aside the thought. He pointed with his chin and motioned for Gideon and the others to follow. They moved off into the dusk, toward a horizon as barren as the one behind them. But the waning of the day's heat brought a rebirth of strength. Gideon kept bringing his legs forward, one short step at a time.

Darkness came. He knew men had dropped out, but he could do nothing any more to help them. He followed the cloudiest notion of time, but somewhere, probably past midnight, he heard a cry from Hollander. Fear clutched at him—fear that Hollander was stricken. Gideon forced his legs to move faster, bringing him up to the mules. He stumbled over an unexpected rut in the prairie, and he went heavily to his hands and knees.

Hollander was making a strange sound—half laugh, half cry. He pointed at the ground. "Trail," he managed. "Trail."

Gideon felt around with his hands in soft sand, trying to find solid ground to help him push back to his feet. Slowly he understood what Hollander was trying to say. He had stumbled into a trail—a rut cut by wagon wheels.

"Shafter," Hollander said plainly. "Shafter's trail."

Shafter. Of course. Colonel Shafter had been all over this country the year before, exploring it in a wetter, more amenable season. These ruts had been cut by his long train of supply wagons.

Lieutenant Judson seemed more dead than alive, responding not at all to Hollander's excitement, or to Gideon's.

Hollander pointed down the trail. "Double Lakes. Come on."

Gideon felt as if he were being stabbed by a thousand sharp needles. Strength pumped into his legs. He struggled to his feet and found voice. "Water, boys. Water, yonderway!"

The men quickened their steps, some laughing madly, some crying without tears. Gideon stood at the trail in the bold moonlight, pointing the troopers after the officers and the mules as they passed him, one by one. When the last had gone—the last one he could see—he turned and followed.

The mules moved out farther and farther ahead of the men afoot, and after a long time Gideon thought he heard them strike a trot. It was probably in his mind, for surely they no longer had that much strength. Unless they had smelled water . . .

That was it, the mules knew water lay ahead. His legs moved faster, easier, because now they were moving toward life, not death.

It might have been one mile or it might have been five. He had walked in a half-world much of the time and had little conception of anything except his revived hope. But suddenly there it was straight in front of him, the broad dust-covered expanse of the dry playa lake, and the moon shining on water that had seeped into the holes the men had dug in another time that seemed as long ago as slavery. The soldiers who had reached there ahead of him lay on their bellies, their heads half buried in the water. Captain Hollander was walking unsteadily around them, using all his strength to pull some men back lest they faint and drown themselves.

"Not too much," he kept saying thickly. "Drink slowly. Drink slowly."

Gideon had no time for reason. He flung himself onto his stomach and dropped his face into the water. The shock was unexpected. He felt his head spinning. He was strangling. Hands grabbed him and dragged him back.

"Easy now. Easy."

He tried to scramble to the water again, even as he choked and gagged, but the hands held him. "Slow, damn it. Slow." The voice was Hollander's.

He lapsed into unconsciousness. It might have lasted a minute, or it could have been much longer. When he came out of it, he was hardly able to raise his head. The terrible thirst returned to him, but this time he realized he had to keep his reason. He pulled himself to the edge of the water and scooped it up in his hands. He realized that if he fell unconscious again it must be on the dry ground, lest he drown before anyone could respond.

The water still had an alkali bite, but that was no longer a detriment. Gideon had never known water so sweet. He rationed himself, drinking a few sips, waiting, then drinking again, always from his cupped hand. He became aware that some men had slid into the water and were splashing around in it with all the joy of unleashed children. That this compromised sanitation never entered his mind; he kept drinking a few swallows at a time. Almost at once, it seemed, his tongue began to shrink. He thought of words, and they began to pass his lips in creditable fashion. "Praise Jesus! Bless the name of Jesus!"

Finally, when he came to a full realization that he would not die, he lay down and wept silently, no tears in his eyes.

There was no guard duty, unless Hollander stood it himself. Occasionally the thirst came upon Gideon with all its furious insistence, and he drank. When finally he came fully awake, the sun was shining warmly in his face. Gradually he heard stirrings, men going to the water or from it. He pushed to his knees, blinking in surprise at a bright sun an hour or more high.

His eyes focused on Captain Hollander, sitting up and staring back. Hollander's face was haggard, his eyes still sunken. But he was an officer again. "Ledbetter, let's see if you can walk."

It took Gideon a minute to get his legs unwound and properly set beneath him. But finally he was standing, swaying. He took a few steps.

"Ledbetter," Hollander said, "I need a noncom. I want you to regard yourself as a corporal."

"And give orders?" Gideon was stunned. "I ain't never led nobody. I been a slave for most of my life."

"So was Sergeant Nettles."

"I sure ain't no Nettles."

"Most of us would still be out there in that hell if it hadn't been for you. Perhaps all of us. Like it or not, you're a corporal." He dismissed further argument. "We left some men behind us. I want you to pick a couple or three of the strongest, fill what canteens we have left and go back. Take a mule." He pointed his chin at Lieutenant Judson. "The lieutenant will ride the other to the base camp and bring up wagons and supplies. I'll send a wagon on after you."

Gideon sought out three men he thought had regained strength enough to walk. Almost everything had been discarded along the way, so they had nothing to eat except a little hardtack. The men drank all the water they could comfortably absorb so they would not have to drain the canteens later. Those would be needed for whatever men they found along the trail. Looping the canteens over the mule, he set out walking, his step improving as he went along. His mind was reasonably clear, and he began mentally upbraiding himself for not counting the men at the lake before he left. He didn't know, really, how many were still out. His memory of yesterday's ordeal was hazy at best. Men had dropped by the wayside—he could remember that—but he could not remember who or how many.

The rescue party came in time to a Mississippian named Kersey, lying in yesterday's blown-out tracks. It took a while to revive him, and then he clutched desperately at the canteen, fighting when anyone tried to pull it away for his own good. Gideon asked if he knew who else might be behind him, but the man could only shake his head. He could not speak.

Gideon left one of his three men with Kersey and set out walking again, northwestward. Before long his legs began to tremble, and he knew he was approaching his limit. He and the other two looked at each other and reached silent agreement. They dropped to rest, the sun hot upon their backs.

By night they had found just one more man. Gideon had managed to shoot a couple of rabbits, and the men shared those, half cooked over a small fire before sundown. They smothered the fire and walked on for a time to get away from the glow, in case it might attract Indians.

All day he had watched the unstable horizon, hoping to see Esau Nettles and Nash and Finley riding toward them. Now and again a distant shape would arise, only to prove itself false as the heat waves shifted and the mirages changed. His hopes ebbed with his strength.

Night gave him time to brood about Jimbo. He could visualize Jimbo and the men who had gone with him, following the trail of the lost guide until one by one they fell. Jimbo would have been the last, Gideon fancied, and he probably had not given up hope until he had made the last step that his legs would take.

More men had dropped out than Gideon had found. The others had probably wandered off in one direction or another. Some might find the lakes for themselves. The others . . . He slept fitfully and dreamed a lot, reliving at times his own agony, seeing at others Jimbo or Esau Nettles, dying alone in that great waste of sand and burned short grass.

They moved again in the coolness of dawn, but the men had less of hope now to buoy them along. Though no one spoke his doubts, they were clear in every man's eyes.

The wagon came as Hollander had promised. The other men stayed behind to leave the load light. Gideon got aboard as guide. The driver and his helper had not been on the dry march. They could only follow the tracks, the trail of abandoned equipment, the swelling bodies of horses that had died one by one along the way. Riding silently on the spring seat as the wagon bounced roughly over dry bunchgrass and shinnery, Gideon drew into a shell, steeling himself for what he had become convinced he would find at the end of the trip.

It was as he had expected, almost. They found little Finley first. To Gideon's amazement, he was still alive. He fought like a wildcat for the canteen Gideon held to his ruined lips. Gideon was unable to keep him from drinking too much at first, and for a while he thought Finley might die from over-filling with the alkali-tainted water.

Like a candle flame flickering before it dies, Gideon's hopes revived briefly. Perhaps finding Finley alive was a good omen.

The hopes were soon crushed. They found black Napoleon, dead. As an act of mercy, Nettles had taken off the saddle and bridle and turned the horse loose on the chance it could save itself. The gesture came too late. Soon Gideon found Esau Nettles and the young trooper Nash lying beneath a blanket spread for shade over a patch of shin oak. Even before he lifted the blanket, Gideon knew with a shuddering certainty. They were dead. He dropped in the sand beside them, drew up his knees and covered his face in his arms.

In the wagon he could hear little Finley whimpering, out of his head. Anger struck at Gideon, sharp, painful and futile. For a moment the anger was against Finley, a liar, a sneak thief, a coward. Why should he live when a man like Esau Nettles had died? For a moment, Gideon's anger turned upon God. Then he realized with dismay that he was railing against the faith drilled into him since boyhood, a faith he had never questioned in his life.

The anger exhausted itself. Only the sorrow remained, deep and wounding.

The trip back to the Double Lakes was slow and silent. Little Finley regained mind enough to be afraid of the two bodies and to move as far from them as possible without climbing out of the wagon. "They're dead," he mumbled once. "Why don't we leave them?"

Gideon chose not to dignify the question by answering it. His contempt for Finley sank deeper into his soul. He made up his mind that he would do whatever he could to force the little man out of this outfit, if not out of the army. He wanted to blame Finley for Nettles' death, though he knew this was not totally valid. Perhaps Nettles had realized he would never make it to the Double Lakes on that bad hip. Perhaps he had stayed behind with Nash and Finley so someone else later would not have to stay behind with him. The more Gideon pondered that possibility, the more he wanted to believe it; it gave reason to Nettles' death, even nobility.

As the wagon went along, it picked up the men who had stayed behind. Most had walked some distance in the direction of the lakes rather than wait to be hauled all the way. All looked in brooding silence at the blanket-covered bodies. Those exhausted climbed into the wagon beside them. Those who could walk continued to do so. Gideon got down and joined them, for he was feeling stronger. The exertion of walking helped the black mood lift itself from him.

Captain Hollander met the wagon as it pulled up to the edge of the lake. Gideon stared, surprised. The captain had shaved and washed out his uniform. It was wrinkled but passably clean, within the limitations of the gyppy water. Army routine had again prevailed over the challenge of the elements.

Hollander counted the men who walked and who climbed out of the wagon. He asked no unnecessary questions. He seemed to read the answers in Gideon's face. He lifted the blanket and looked at the bodies, his face tightening with a sadness he did not try to put into words. "We had better bury them here. This weather . . ."

The digging was left to men who had come up from the supply camp, for they had the strength. Hollander had brought no Bible to read from, an oversight some might regard as indicative of the reasons for the company's travail. The captain improvised a long prayer asking God's blessings upon these men, these devoted servants of their country and their Lord, and upon any others like them who had met death alone on that hostile prairie, unseen except by God's own messengers come to lead them to a better land.

Three more men had wandered into camp during Gideon's absence, men who had lost the trail but somehow retained enough sense of direction to find the lakes. Toward dusk Gideon heard a stir and looked where some of the men were pointing, northward. He saw horsemen coming. His first thought was Indians. But soon he could tell these were soldiers. And the man in the lead was unmistakable.

Jimbo!

Jimbo spurred into a long trot, and Gideon strode forward to meet him. Jimbo jumped to the ground, and the two men hugged each other, laughing and crying at the same time.

In camp, when all the howdies were said and the reunions had lost their initial glow, Jimbo explained that the guide José had missed the Silver Lake he was trying to find and had come instead, somewhat later than he expected, to a set of springs just off Yellow House Canyon. Jimbo and the soldiers who followed had stayed at the springs long enough to recoup their own strength and that of their horses. Some had remained there with the buffalo hunters who straggled in, but Jimbo and three others had filled canteens and set out along their backtrail to carry water to the column they expected to find somewhere behind them. Hollander's decision to strike out for Double Lakes had thwarted them. They marched much farther than they intended and found no one. Fearing that the rest of the company had died, they had returned heavy-hearted to the springs, rested awhile, then set out to find Double Lakes and the base camp below.

Captain Hollander's face twisted in remorse as he listened. The hunters had been right; if he had followed them his troops would have reached water sooner than they did. Perhaps Esau Nettles and Private Nash would not be dead; perhaps others would not still be missing.

Lieutenant Judson tried to reassure him. "You used your best judgment based on the facts at hand, Frank. You knew this water was here. You couldn't know there was water where the hunters wanted to go. They were just guessing. What if they had been wrong? You had the responsibility for all these men. Those hunters could gamble. You could not."

Gideon knew Judson was right, as Hollander had been. But he could see the doubt settling into the captain's eyes. As long as Hollander lived, it would be there, the questions coming upon him suddenly in the darkness of a sleepless night, in the midst of his pondering upon other decisions he would be called upon to make in the future. To the end of his life, Hollander would be haunted by Esau Nettles and the others, and the unanswered question: did it have to be? Gideon looked at him. It was one of the few times in his life he had ever genuinely pitied a white man.

Gideon wrestled awhile with his doubts, then approached the captain hesitantly. "Sir . . ." He took off his hat and abused it fearfully in his nervous hands. "Sir, you done right. Old Sergeant, he'd of said so hisself, if he could. He'd of said you *always* done right."

Hollander stared at the ground a long time before he looked up at Gideon. "Thank you, Ledbetter. There's not a man I'd rather hear that from than you . . . and *him*."

Early on the fifth day, having sent out search parties and having given up hope that any stragglers still out would ever turn up alive, Hollander ordered the company to march southward to the supply camp. Water there was better, and timber along the creek would provide shade. The trip was slow and hot and dry, and Gideon found himself skirting along the edge of fear as terrible memories forced themselves upon him.

Late on the afternoon of the sixth day, a column of mounted men and two army ambulances broke through a veil of dust out of the south. A rider loped ahead of the column, pulling up in the edge of camp. He was the civilian scout Pat Maloney, from the village of Ben Ficklin. He whooped in delight as he saw Captain Hollander and Lieutenant Judson standing beside a wagon.

"Frank Hollander! Dammit, man, we thought you were dead!"

He pumped Hollander's hand excitedly, but that was not enough. The ex-Confederate gripped the Union officer's arms and shook him in a violence of joy. "Tell you the God's truth, Frank, we come to hunt for your body. We thought every man jack of you had died."

His gaze swept the camp. Gideon felt the scout's eyes stop momentarily on him and Jimbo, lighting with pleasure at the sight of them.

Hollander replied gravely, "A few of us *are* dead. The best of us, perhaps."

Maloney looked around a second time, his face going grim as he missed Nettles. "The old sergeant?"

Hollander looked at the ground. "We buried him."

Maloney was silent a moment. "We thought from what we heard that we would have to bury you *all*!" He explained that Sergeant Waters had somehow made it back to Fort Concho, with two others. They had brought a report that Captain Hollander and all his men had been led astray by Indians on that great hostile plain, that they and all those buffalo hunters were dying from heat and thirst. They were certain, Waters reported, that no one except themselves had survived.

Maloney pointed to the approaching column. "You can imagine how that news tore up the post at Concho."

Apprehension struck Hollander. "My wife . . . Adeline. She heard that?"

"Everybody heard it."

"She must be half out of her mind. This, and the baby coming . . . We'll have to send word back right away."

Maloney smiled. "You know I got me a new baby boy, Frank?"

Hollander seemed not quite to hear him. "That's good, Pat. Glad to hear it." But his mind was clearly elsewhere.

Maloney said, "Who knows? He may grow up to marry that little girl *your* wife had. Join the North and South together again, so to speak."

Hollander's eyes widened. He had heard *that*. "A girl, you say? You've seen it?"

"Went by there last thing before I left the post. She looks like her mother. Damn lucky thing, too, because her papa looks like hell."

The trip back to Fort Concho was made slowly and carefully, for more men were afoot than on horseback, and none had completely regained strength. At times even the civilian Maloney would step down from his horse and walk awhile, letting some tired black trooper ride.

Messengers had carried the news of their approach ahead of them, so that most of the people of Saint Angela were lined up to watch the arrival of men who had come back from the dead. An escort and fresh horses were sent out from the post. Hollander and Judson and Maloney rode at the head of the column. Gideon was behind them, urging the men to sit straight and look like soldiers that Esau Nettles would have wanted to claim.

Ordinarily they would not have ridden down the street, but this was an occasion, and the escort wanted to show them off. Lined along Concho Avenue were civilians of all ages, sizes and colors, white to brown to black. Most cheered the soldiers as they passed, though Gideon looked into some eyes and found there the same hostility he had always seen. Nothing, not even the ordeal the soldiers had been through, had changed that. Nothing ever would.

Two-thirds of the way down to Oakes Street, a seedy, bearded man leaned against a post that held up the narrow porch of a new but already-dingy little saloon. As Hollander came abreast of him the man shouted, "Say, Captain, why didn't you do us all a favor and leave the rest of them damned niggers out there?"

Hollander stiffened. He turned in the saddle, rage bursting into his face. He freed his right foot from the stirrup and started to dismount. Maloney caught his arm. "Frank, you ain't got your strength back."

Maloney swung slowly and casually to the ground, handed his reins to Gideon and walked up to the man with a dry and dangerous smile set like concrete. He crouched, and when his fist came up it was like a sledge. The man's head snapped back, then his whole body followed. He slid across the little porch, winding up half in and half out of the open front door.

Maloney looked first to one side, then the other, challenging one and all. Nobody took up his challenge. He reached down for the struggling man.

"Here, friend, let me help you up."

When the man was on his feet, Maloney hit him again, knocking him through the door and into the saloon. With a wink, he took his reins from Gideon's hand, swung back into the saddle and gave the silent Hollander a nod.

"You're welcome," he said.

LOREN D. ESTLEMAN
The Bandit

Loren D. Estleman (1952–) was born at Ann Arbor, Michigan. He matriculated at Eastern Michigan University at Ypsilanti, and then worked as a reporter and journalist. Since 1980 he has been a fulltime writer of Western and crime fiction. Like Elmore Leonard he is better known for his thrillers, particularly his series of prize-winning P.I. novels featuring Detroit-based Amos Walker, but he has also written much stylish Western fiction. Estleman's first Western novel, *The Hider*, was published in 1973p 8, and another eleven have followed, including *Aces and Eights* (1981), for which he received a Spur Award from the Western Writers of America. Estleman's novel, *Bloody Season* (1988), based on the events following the gunfight at the OK Corral, is considered one of the best historical Westerns of recent decades. Estleman has also written a non-fiction work on the Western, *The Wister Trace: Classic Novels of the American frontier* (1987).

The short story 'The Bandit' is from 1986 and was awarded a Spur Award by the Western Writers of America.

THEY CUT HIM LOOSE A day early.

It worried him a little, and when the night captain on his block brought him a suit of clothes and a cardboard suitcase containing a toothbrush and a change of shirts, he considered bringing it up, but in that moment he suddenly couldn't stand it there another hour. So he put on the suit and accompanied the guard to the administration building, where the assistant warden made a speech, grasped his hand, and presented him with a check for $1,508. At the gate he shook hands with the guard, although the man was new to his section and he didn't know him, then stepped out into the gray autumn late afternoon. Not counting incarceration time before and during his trial, he had been behind bars twenty-eight years, eleven months, and twenty-nine days.

While he was standing there, blinking rapidly in diffused sunlight that was surely brighter than that on the other side of the wall, a leather-bonneted assembly of steel and inflated rubber came ticking past on the street with a goggled and dustered operator at the controls. He watched it go by towing a plume of dust and blue smoke and said, "Oldsmobile."

He had always been first in line when magazines donated by the DAR came into the library, and while his fellow inmates were busy snatching up the new catalogs and finding the pages containing pictures of women in corsets and camisoles torn out, he was paging through the proliferating motoring journals, admiring the photographs and studying the technical illustrations of motors and transmissions. Gadgets had enchanted him since he saw his first steam engine aboard a Missouri River launch at age ten, and he had a fair idea of how automobiles worked. However, aside from one heart-thudding glimpse of the warden's new Locomobile parked inside the gates before the prison board decided its presence stirred unhealthy ambitions among the general population, this was his first exposure to the belching, clattering reality. He felt like a wolf whelp looking on the harsh glitter of the big world outside its parents' den for the first time.

After the machine had gone, he put down the suitcase

to collect his bearings. In the gone days he had enjoyed an instinct for directions, but it had been replaced by other, more immediate survival mechanisms inside. Also, an overgrown village that had stood only two stories high on dirt streets as wide as pastures when he first came to it had broken out in brick towers and macadam and climbed the hills across the river, where an electrified trolley raced through a former cornfield clanging its bell like a mad mother cow. He wasn't sure if the train station would be where he left it in 1878.

He considered banging on the gate and asking the guard, but the thought of turning around now made him pick up his suitcase and start across the street at double-quick step, the mess-hall march. "The wrong way beats no way," Micah used to put it.

It was only a fifteen-minute walk, but for an old man who had stopped pacing his cell in 1881 and stretched his legs for only five of the twenty minutes allotted daily in the exercise yard, it was a hike. He had never liked walking anyway, had reached his majority breaking mixed-blood stallions that had run wild from December to March on the old Box W, and had done some of his best thinking and fighting with a horse under him. So when at last he reached the station, dodging more motorcars—the novelty of that wore off the first time—and trying not to look to passersby like a convict in his tight suit swinging a dollar suitcase, he was sweating and blowing like a wind-broke mare.

The station had a water closet—a closet indeed, with a gravity toilet and a mirror in need of resilvering over a white enamel basin, but a distinct improvement over the stinking bucket he had had to carry down three tiers of cells and dump into the cistern every morning for twenty-nine years. He placed the suitcase on the toilet seat, hung up his hat and soaked coat, unhooked his spectacles, turned back his cuffs, ran cold water into the basin, and splashed his face. Mopping himself dry on a comparatively clean section of roller towel, he looked at an old man's unfamiliar reflection, then put on his glasses to study it closer. But for the mirror in the warden's office it was the first one he'd seen since his trial; mirrors were made of glass, and glass was good for cutting wrists and throats. What hair remained on his scalp had gone dirty-gray. The flesh of his face was sagging, pulling away from the bone, and so pale he took a moment locating the bullet-crease on his forehead from Liberty. His beard was yellowed white, like stove grime. (All the men inside wore beards. It was easier than trying to shave without mirrors.) It was his grandfather's face.

Emerging from the water closet, he read the train schedule on the blackboard next to the ticket booth and checked it against his coin-battered old turnip watch, wound and set for the first time in half his lifetime. A train to Huntsford was pulling out in forty minutes.

He was alone at his end of the station with the ticket agent and a lanky young man in a baggy checked suit slouched on one of the varnished benches with his long legs canted out in front of him and his hands in his pockets. Conscious that the young man was watching him, but accustomed to being watched, he walked up to the booth and set down the suitcase. "Train to Huntsford on schedule?"

"Was last wire." Perched on a stool behind the window, the agent looked at him over the top of his *Overland Monthly* without seeing him. He had bright predatory eyes in a narrow face that had foiled an attempt to square it off with thick burnsides.

"How much to Huntsford?"

"Four dollars."

He unfolded the check for $1,508 and smoothed it out on the ledge under the glass.

"I can't cash that," said the agent. "You'll have to go to the bank."

"Where's the bank?"

"Well, there's one on Treelawn and another on Cross. But they're closed till Monday."

"I ain't got cash on me."

"Well, the railroad don't offer credit."

While the agent resumed reading, he unclipped the big watch from its steel chain and placed it on top of the check. "How much you allow me on that?"

The agent glanced at it, then returned to his magazine. "This is a railroad station, not a jeweler's. I got a watch."

He popped open the lid and pointed out the engraving. "See that J.B.H.? That stands for James Butler Hickok. Wild Bill himself gave it to me when he was sheriff in Hays."

"Mister, I got a scar on my behind I can say I got from Calamity Jane, but I'd still need four dollars to ride to Huntsford. Not that I'd want to."

"Problem, Ike?"

The drawled question startled old eardrums thickened to approaching footsteps. The young man in the checked suit was at his side, a head taller and smelling faintly of lilac water.

"Just another convict looking to wrestle himself a free ride off the C. H. & H.," the agent said. "Nothing I don't handle twice a month."

"What's the fare?"

The agent told him. The man in the checked suit produced a bent brown wallet off his right hip and counted four bills onto the window ledge.

"Hold up there. I never took a thing free off nobody that wasn't my idea to start."

"Well, give me the watch."

"This watch is worth sixty dollars."

"You were willing to trade it for a railroad ticket."

"I was not. I asked him what he'd give me on it."

"Sixty dollars for a gunmetal watch that looks like it's been through a thresher?"

"It keeps good time. You see that J.B.H.?"

"Wild Bill. I heard." The man in the checked suit counted the bills remaining in his wallet. "I've got just ten on me."

He closed the watch and held it out. "I'll give you my sister's address in Huntsford. You send me the rest there."

"You're trusting me? How long did you serve?"

"He's got a check drawn on the state bank for fifteen hundred," said the agent, separating a ticket from the perforated sheet.

The man in the checked suit pursed his lips. "Mister, you must've gone in there with some valuables. Last I knew, prison wages still came to a dollar a week."

"They ain't changed since I went in."

Both the ticket agent and the man in the checked suit were staring at him now. "Mister, you keep your watch. You've earned that break."

"It ain't broke, just dented some. Anyway, I said before I don't take charity."

"Let's let the four dollars ride for now. Your train's not due for a half hour. If I'm not satisfied with our talk at the end of that time, you give me it to hold and I'll send it on later, as a deposit against the four dollars."

"Folks paying for talking now?"

"They do when they've met someone who's been in prison since Hayes was President and all they've had to talk to today is a retiring conductor and a miner's daughter on her way to a finishing school in Chicago." The man in the checked suit offered his hand. "Arthur Brundage. I write for the *New Democrat*. It's a newspaper, since your time."

"I saw it inside." He grasped the hand tentatively, plainly surprising its owner with his grip. "I got to tell you, son, I ain't much for talking to the papers. Less people know your name, the less hold they got on you, Micah always said."

"Micah?"

He hesitated. "Hell, he's been dead better than twenty-five years, I don't reckon I can hurt him. Micah Hale. Maybe the name don't mean nothing now."

"These old cons, they'll tell you they knew John Wilkes Booth and Henry the Eighth if you don't shut them up." The ticket agent skidded the ticket across the ledge.

But Brundage was peering into his face now, a man trying to make out the details in a portrait fogged and darkened with years.

"You're Jubal Steadman."

"I was when I went in. I been called Dad so long I don't rightly answer to nothing else."

"Jubal Steadman." It was an incantation. "If I didn't fall in sheep dip and come up dripping double eagles. Let's go find a bench." Brundage seized the suitcase before its owner could get his hands on it and put a palm on his back, steering him toward the seat he himself had just vacated.

"The Hale-Steadman Gang," he said, when they were seated. "Floyd and Micah Hale and the Steadman brothers and Kid Stone. When I was ten, my mother found a copy of the *New York Detective Monthly* under my bed. It had Floyd Hale on the cover, blazing away from horseback with a six-shooter in each hand at a posse chasing him. I had to stay indoors for a week and memorize a different Bible verse every day."

Jubal smiled. His teeth were only a year old and he was just a few months past grinning like an ape all the time. "Then dime writers made out like Floyd ran the match, but that was just because the Pinkertons found out his name first and told the papers. We all called him Doc on account of he was always full of no-good clabber and he claimed to study eye doctoring back East for a year, when everyone knew he was in the Detroit House of Corrections for stealing a mail sack off a railroad hook. He told me I'd never need glasses." He took his off to polish them with a coarse handkerchief.

Brundage had a long notepad open on his knee. He stopped writing. "I guess I should have accepted that watch when you offered it."

"It ain't worth no sixty dollars. I got it off a fireman on the Katy Flyer when we hit it outside Choctaw in '73."

"You mean that was a story about Wild Bill?"

"Never met him. I had them initials put in it and made up the rest. It pulled me through some skinny times. Folks appreciated a good lie then, not like now."

"Readers of the *New Democrat* are interested in the truth."

He put his spectacles back on and peered at the journalist over the rims. But Brundage was writing again and missed it.

"Anyway, if there was someone we all looked to when things went sore, it was Doc's brother Micah. I reckon he was the smartest man I ever knew or ever will. That's why they took him alive and Doc let himself get shot in the back of the head by Kid Stone."

"I always wondered if he really did that just for the reward."

"I reckon. He was always spending his cut on yellow silk vests and gold hatbands. I was in prison two years when it happened so I can't say was that it. That blood money busted up all the good bunches. The Pinks spent years trying to undercut us with the hill folk, but it was the rewards done it in the end."

"The Kid died of pneumonia three or four years ago in New Jersey. He put together his own moving picture outfit after they let him go. He was playing Doc Holliday when he took sick."

"Josh always said Virge was a born actor. Virgil, that was the Kid's right name."

"I forget if Joshua was your older or your younger brother."

"Older. Billy Tom Mulligan stabbed him with a busted toothbrush first year we was inside. They hung him for it. Josh played the Jew's harp. He was playing it when they jumped us after Liberty."

"What really happened in Liberty?"

Jubal pulled a face. "Doc's idea. We was to hit the ten-twelve from Kansas City when it stopped to water and take on passengers, and the bank in town at the same time. We recruited a half dozen more men for the job: Creek Eddie, Charley MacDonald, Bart and Barney Dee, and two fellows named Bob and Bill, I never got their last names and couldn't tell which was which. Me and Josh and my kid brother Judah went with Micah and Charley MacDonald on the bank run and the rest took the train. Bart and Barney was to ride it in from Kansas City and sit on the conductor and porters while Doc and them threw down on the engineer and fireman and blew open the express car with powder. Doc said they wouldn't be expecting us to try it in town. He was dead-right there. No one thought we was that stupid."

"What made Micah go along with it?"

"Fambly bliss. Doc was threatening to take Kid Stone and start his own bunch because no one ever listened to them good plans he was coming up with all the time, like kidnapping the Governor of Missouri and holding him for ransom. Creek Eddie learned his trade in the Nations, so when we heard he was available, Micah figured he'd be a good influence on Doc. Meantime Creek Eddie thought the train thing was a harebrained plan but figured if Micah was saying yes to it, it must be all right." He showed his store teeth. "You see, I had twenty-nine years to work this all out, and if I knew it then—well, I wouldn't of had the twenty-nine years to work it all out.

"Micah and Charley and Josh and Judah and me, we slid through that bank like a grease fire and come out with seven thousand in greenbacks and another four or five thousand in securities. *And* the bank president and his tellers and two customers hollering for help on the wrong side of the vault door on a five-minute time lock. We never made a better or a quieter job. That was when we heard the shooting down at the station."

"A railroad employee fired the first shot, if I remember my reading."

"It don't matter who fired it. Bart and Barney Dee missed the train in Kansas City, and the conductor and a porter or two was armed and free when Doc and the rest walked in thinking the opposite. Creek Eddie got it in the back of the neck and hit the ground dead. Then everybody opened up, and by the time we showed with the horses, the smoke was all mixed up with steam from the boiler. Well, you could see your hand in front of your face, but not to shoot at. That didn't stop us, though.

"Reason was, right about then that time lock let loose of them folks we left in the bank, and when they hit the street yammering like bitch dogs, that whole town turned vigilante in a hot St. Louis minute. They opened up the gun shop and filled their pockets with cartridges and it was like Independence Day. I think as many of them fell in their own cross-fire as what we shot.

"Even so, only six men was killed in that spree. If you was there trying to hold down your mount with one hand and twisting back and forth like a steam governor to fire on both sides of its neck and dodging all that lead clanging off the engine, you'd swear it was a hundred. I seen Charley take a spill and get dragged by his paint for twenty feet before he cleared his boot of the stirrup, and Judah got his jaw took off by a bullet, though he lived another eight or nine hours. Engineer was killed, and one rubbernecker standing around waiting to board the train, and two of them damn-fool townies playing Kit Carson on the street. I don't know how many of them was wounded; likely not as many as are still walking around showing off their old gall-bladder scars as bullet-creases. I still got a ball in my back that tells me when it's fixing to rain, but that didn't give me as much trouble at the time as this here cut that kept dumping blood into my eyes." He pointed out the white mark where his hairline used to be. "Micah took one through the meat on his upper arm, and my brother Josh got it in the hip and lost a finger, and they shot the Kid and took him prisoner and arrested Charley, who broke his ankle getting loose of that stirrup. Doc was the only one of us that come away clean.

"Judah, his jaw was just hanging on by a piece of gristle. I tied it up with his bandanna, and Josh and me got him over one of the horses and we got mounted and took off one way while Doc and Micah and that Bill and Bob went the other. We met up at this empty farmhouse six miles north of town that we lit on before the job in case we got separated, all but that Bill and Bob. Them two just kept riding. We buried Judah that night."

"The posse caught up with you at the farmhouse?" asked Brundage, after a judicious pause.

"No, they surprised Josh and me in camp two nights later. We'd split with the Hales before then. Micah wasn't as bad wounded as Josh and we was slowing them down, Doc said. Josh could play that Jew's harp of his, though. Posse come on afoot, using the sound of it for a mark. They threw down on us. We gave in without a shot."

"That was the end of the Hale-Steadman Gang?"

A hoarse stridency shivered the air. In its echo, Jubal consulted his watch. "Trains still run on time. Nice to know some things stay the same. Yeah, the Pinks picked up Micah posing as a cattle-buyer in Denver a few months later. I heard he died of scarlatina inside. Charley MacDonald got himself shot to pieces escaping with Kid Stone and some others, but the Kid got clear and him and Doc put together a bunch and robbed a train or two and some banks until the Kid shot him. I reckon I'm what's left."

"I guess you can tell readers of the *New Democrat* there's no profit in crime."

"Well, there's profit and profit." He stood up, working the stiffness out of his joints, and lifted the suitcase.

Brundage hesitated in the midst of closing his notebook.

"Twenty-nine years of your life a fair trade for a few months of excitement?"

"I don't reckon there's much in life you'd trade half of it to have. But in them days a man either broke his back and his heart plowing rocks under in some field or shook his brains loose putting some red-eyed horse to leather or rotted behind some counter in some town. I don't reckon I'm any older now than I would of been if I done any of them things to live. And I wouldn't have no youngster like you hanging on my every word neither. Them things become important when you get up around my age."

"I won't get that past my editor. He'll want a moral lesson."

"Put one in, then. It don't . . ." His voice trailed off.

The journalist looked up. The train was sliding to a stop inside the vaulted station, black and oily and leaking steam out of a hundred joints. But the old man was looking at the pair of men coming in the station entrance. One, sandy-haired and approaching middle age in a suit too heavy for Indian summer, his cherry face glistening, was the assistant warden at the prison. His companion was a city police officer in uniform. At sight of Jubal, relief blossomed over the assistant warden's features.

"Steadman, I was afraid you'd left."

Jubal said, "I knew it."

As the officer stepped to the old man's side, the assistant warden said, "I'm very sorry. There's been a clerical error. You'll have to come back with us."

"I was starting to think you was going to let me have that extra day after all."

"Day?" The assistant warden was mopping his face with a lawn handkerchief. "I was getting set to close your file. I don't know how I overlooked that other charge."

Jubal felt a clammy fist clench inside his chest. "Other charge?"

"For the train robbery. In Liberty. The twenty-nine years was for robbing the bank and for your part in the killings afterward. You were convicted also of accessory in the raid on the train. You have seventeen years to serve on that conviction, Steadman. I'm sorry."

He took the suitcase while the officer manacled one of the old man's wrists. Brundage left the bench.

"Jubal—"

He shook his head. "My sister's coming in on the morning train from Huntsford tomorrow. Meet it, will you? Tell her."

"This isn't the end of it. My paper has a circulation of thirty thousand. When our readers learn of this injustice—"

"They'll howl and stomp and write letters to their congressmen, just like in '78."

The journalist turned to the man in uniform. "He's sixty years old. Do you have to chain him like a maniac?"

"Regulations." He clamped the other manacle around his own wrist.

Jubal held out his free hand. "I got to go home now. Thanks for keeping an old man company for an hour."

After a moment Brundage took it. Then the officer touched the old man's arm and he blinked behind his spectacles and turned and left the station with the officer on one side and the assistant warden on the other. The door swung shut behind them.

As the train pulled out without Jubal, Brundage timed it absently against the dented watch in his hand.

The Hundred Best Western Novels

The following is a personal list, based largely on my own reading and preferences. However, since the intention of the list is to give the interested reader suggestions for further reading, I have occasionally included books which have achieved classic status or have had a significant influence on the course of Western fiction, although they are not personal favourites. The dates refer to the year of first publication. The list is arranged in alphabetical order by surname, not in order of preference or importance.

Edward Abbey *The Monkey Wrench Gang*, 1971
Andy Adams *The Log of a Cowboy*, 1903
Clifton Adams *Tragg's Choice*, 1969
Ann Ahlswede *Hunting Wolf*, 1960
Verne Athanas *Maverick*, 1956
Gertrude Atherton *The Californians*, 1898
Todhunter Ballard *Gold in California*, 1965
Thomas Berger *Little Big Man*, 1964
Frank Bonham *Lost Stage Valley*, 1948
Snaketrack, 1952
B.M. Bower *Chip of the Flying U*, 1906
Max Brand *Destry Rides Again*, 1930
Will C. Brown *The Nameless Breed*, 1960
W.R. Burnett *Saint Johnson*, 1930
Benjamin Capps *The Trail to Ogallala*, 1964
Sam Chance, 1965
Forrest Carter *The Vengeance Trail of Josey Wales*, 1976

Willa Cather *O Pioneers!*, 1913
My Antonia, 1918
Walter Van Tilburg Clark *The Ox-Bow Incident*, 1940
James Fenimore Cooper *The Last of the Mohicans*, 1826
Stephen Crane *The Blue Hotel*, 1898
E.L. Doctorow *Welcome to Hard Times*, 1960
Loren D. Estleman *Bloody Season*, 1988
Max Evans *The Hi Lo Country*, 1961
Howard Fast *The Last Frontier*, 1941
Harvey Fergusson *Blood of the Conqueror*, 1921
Home in the West, 1940
Vardis Fisher *Children of God*, 1939
Steve Frazee *Rendezvous*, 1958
Norman A. Fox *Night Passage*, 1956
Bill Gulick *A Drum Calls West*, 1962
The Land Beyond, 1958
Zane Grey *Riders of the Purple Sage*, 1912
The Vanishing America, 1925
A.B. Guthrie *The Big Sky*, 1947
The Way West, 1949
Frank Gruber *Fort Starvation*, 1953
Ernest Haycox *Bugles in the Afternoon*, 1944
Border Trumpet, 1939
Will Henry (pseud. Henry Wilson Allen)
From Where the Sun Now Stands, 1960
Gates of the Mountain, 1963
The Last Warpath, 1966.
Tony Hillerman *A Thief of Time*, 1989
Paul Horgan *A Distant Trumpet*, 1960
Emerson Hough *The Covered Wagon*, 1922
Heart's Desire, 1905
Helen Hunt Jackson *Ramona*, 1884
Elmer Kelton *Buffalo Wagons*, 1956
The Day the Cowboys Quit, 1970
The Time It Never Rained, 1973
The Wolf and the Buffalo, 1980
Ken Kesey *One Flew Over the Cuckoo's Nest*, 1962
Oliver La Farge *The Enemy Gods*, 1937
Laughing Boy, 1929

Louis L'Amour *Hondo*, 1953
Last Stand at Papago Wells, 1957
Tom Lea *The Wonderful Country*, 1952
Lee Leighton (pseud. Wayne D. Overholser)
Lawman, 1953
Alan LeMay *The Searchers*, 1954
Elmore Leonard *Hombre*, 1961
Valdez is Coming, 1969
Bliss Lomax (pseud. Henry Sinclair Drago)
The Leatherburners, 1939
Jack London *The Call of the Wild*, 1903
Noel M. Loomis *Short Cut to Red River*, 1958
Rim of the Caprock, 1959
Milton Lott *The Last Hunt*, 1954
Giles A Lutz *The Honyocker*, 1962
Thomas McGuane *Nobody's Angel*, 1981
Something to be Desired, 1981
Larry McMurtry *Horseman, Pass By*, 1961
Lonesome Dove, 1985
James A. Michener *Centennial*, 1974
N. Scott Momaday *House Made of Dawn*, 1968
Frank Norris *The Octopus*, 1901
Nelson C. Nye *Riders By Night*, 1950
T.V. Olsen *Bitter Grass*, 1967
Arrow in the Sun, 1969
Stephen Overholser *A Hanging in Sweetwater*, 1975
Wayne D. Overholser *The Violent Land*, 1954
Lewis B. Patten *Death of a Gunfighter*, 1968
Bones of the Buffalo, 1967
John Prebble *The Buffalo Soldiers*, 1958
Bill Pronzini *The Hangings*, 1989
Eugene Manlove Rhodes *Pasó Por Aquí*, 1927
Conrad Richter *The Sea of Grass*, 1937
Mari Sandoz *The Tom-Walker*, 1947
Jack Schaefer *Shane*, 1949
Monte Walsh, 1963
Luke Short *Savage Range*, 1939
Sunset Graze, 1942
Leslie Marmon Silko *Storyteller*, 1981

Wallace Stegner *The Big Rock Candy Mountain*, 1943
John Steinbeck *The Grapes of Wrath*, 1939
W.C. Tuttle *Thicker Than Water*, 1927
Mark Twain *Roughing It*, 1872
Frank Waters *The Man who Killed the Deer*, 1942
Stewart Edward White *Folded Hills*, 1934
Harry Whittington *Saddle the Storm*, 1954
Owen Wister *The Virginian*, 1902

The Hundred Best Western Short Stories

The same rules of selection and arrangement are applied here as with the hundred best Western novels. The dates and places of publication are usually, but not always, those of first publication.

Clifton Adams, 'Hell's Command', *A Western Bonanza*, ed. Todhunter Ballard, 1969
Ann Ahlswede, 'The Promise of the Fruit', *The Pick of the Roundup*, ed. Stephen Payne, 1963
Henry Wilson Allen, 'Isley's Stranger', *Legend and Tales of the Old West*, 1962
Todhunter Ballard, 'The Builder of Murderer's Bar', *WWA Silver Anniversary Anthology*, 1977
S. Omar Barker, 'Bad Company,' *Saturday Evening Post*, 1955
'Champs at the Chuckabug', *Great Stories of the West*, ed. N. Collier, 1971
James W. Bellah, 'Command', *Saturday Evening Post*, 1946
'Massacre', *Saturday Evening Post*, 1947
Frank Bonham, 'Burn Him Out', *Argosy*, 1949
'Lovely Little Liar', *Star Western*, 1951
B.M. Bower, 'Bad Penny', *Argosy*, 1933
Max Brand, 'Wine on the Desert', *Max Brand's Best Western Stories*, ed. W. F. Nolan, 1981
Will C. Brown, 'Red Sand', *Spur Western Novels*, 1955
Raymond Carver, 'Sixty Acres', *The Stories of Raymond Carver*, 1985

Willa Cather, 'El Dorado', *New England Magazine*, 1901
'On the Divide', *Overland Monthly*, 1896
Walter Van Tilburg Clark, 'The Wind and Snow of Winter', *The Watchful Gods*, W. Van Tilburg Clark, 1944
Stephen Crane, 'A Man and Some Others', *The Western Writings of Stephen Crane*, ed. F. Bergon, 1979
'The Bride Comes to Yellow Sky', ditto.
'Twelve o'clock', ditto.
William Cunningham, 'The Cloud Puncher', *Out West*, ed. J. Schaefer, 1955
Peggy Simpson Curry, 'The Bride Wore Spurs', *Western Romances*, P.S. Curry, 1973
'The Brushoff', *Saturday Evening Post*, 1957
Robert Easton, 'To Find a Place', *Great Tales of the American West*, ed. H.G. Maule, 1944
Loren D. Estleman, 'The Bandit', *The Best of the West*, 1986
Max Evans, 'Candles in the Bottom of the Pool', *South Dakota Review*, 1973
'One Eyed Sky', *Three Short Novels*, 1963
Howard Fast, 'Spoil the Child', *Out West*, J. Schaefer, 1955.
Clay Fisher, 'The White Man's Road', *The Horse Soldiers*, ed. B. Pronzini and M.H. Greenberg, 1988
Vardis Fisher, 'Joe Burt's Wife', *Love and Death*, 1959
'The Scarecrow', *Out West*, ed. J. Schaefer, 1955
Richard Ford, 'Great Falls', *Granta*, 1987
'Winterkill', *Esquire*, 1983
Norman A. Fox, 'Only the Dead Ride Proudly', *The Valiant Ones*, 1957
Steve Frazee, 'Great Medicine', *Gunsmoke*, 1953
'The Man at Gantt's Place', *Argosy*, 1951
'The Singing Sands', *15 Western Tales*, 1954
Zane Grey, 'Sienna Waits', *Zane Grey's Greatest Western Stories*, ed. L. Grey, 1971
'Yaqui', ditto.
Fred Grove, 'Commanche Woman', *The Pick of the Roundup*, ed. S. Payne, 1963
Bill Gulick, 'The Shaming of Broken Horn', *Saturday Evening Post*, 1960
'Thief In Camp', *Saturday Evening Post*, 1958

A.B. Guthrie, 'The Therefore Hog', *The Big It and other stories*, AB Guthrie, 1952
Bret Harte, 'The Luck of Roaring Camp', *Overland Monthly*, 1868.
'The Outcasts of Poker Flat', ditto.
'Tennessee's Partner', ditto, 1869.
Ernest Haycox, 'McQuestion Rides', *The Best Western Stories of Ernest Haycox*, 1975
'Stage to Lordsburg', *By Rope & Lead*, E. Haycox, 1951.
'When You Carry the Star', *Murder on the Frontier*, E. Haycox, 1952
O. Henry, 'Caballero's Way', *Heart of the West*, O. Henry, 1907
'The Last of Troubadours', ditto.
'The Higher Abdication', ditto.
Will Henry (pseud. H.W. Allen), 'The Tallest Indian in Toltepec', *Great Western Stories*, 1965
Paul Horgan, 'The Peach Stone', *The Peach Stone and Other Stories*, Paul Horgan, 1967
Emerson Hough, "'Curly' Gets Back On the Soil', *Western Story*, 1923
Dorothy M. Johnson, 'Lost Sister', *Collier's*, 1956
'A Man Called Horse', *Indian Country*, Dorothy M. Johnson, 1953
Ryerson Johnson, 'Traitor of the Natchez Trace', *10 Story Western*, 1943
Elmer Kelton, 'The Man on the Wagontongue', *They Won Their Spurs*, ed. Nelson Nye, 1962
Oliver La Farge, 'All the Young Men', *All the Young Men*, Oliver La Farge, 1939
'A Pause in the Desert', *A Pause in the Desert*, Oliver La Farge, 1957
'The Young Warrior', *Esquire*, 1938.
Louis L'Amour, 'The Gift of Cochise', *War Party*, Louis L'Amour, 1961
'War Party', ditto, 1961
Elmore Leonard, '3.10 to Yuma', *The Killers*, ed. P. Dawson, 1955
'The Captives', *Argosy*, 1955

Jack London, 'All Gold Canyon', *Moon Face*, J. London, 1901
'The One Thousand Dozen', *Jack London: Stories of Adventure*, 1980
'Love of Life', ditto.
Noel M. Loomis, 'Grandfather Out of the Past', *Frontier West*, 1959
'When the Children Cry for Meat', *The Texans*, ed. B. Pronzini and M.H. Greenberg, 1988
George Milburn, 'Heel, Toe and 1, 2, 3, 4', *No More Trumpets*, George Milburn, 1933
John G. Neihardt, 'The Alien', *The Lonesome Trail*, J. G. Neihardt, 1907
'The Last Thunder Song', ditto.
T.V. Olsen, 'They Walked Tall', *Pick of the Roundup*, ed. S. Payne, 1963
'The Man We Called Jones', *The Gunfighters*, ed. B. Pronzini and M.H. Greenberg, 1987
Wayne D. Overholser, 'Petticoat Brigade', *Zane Grey's Western Magazine*, 1948
'Beecher Island', *With Guidons Flying*, Western Writers of America, 1970
Lewis B. Patten, 'They Called Him a Killer', *Complete Western Book Magazine*, 1955
John Prebble, 'A Town Called Hate', *Saturday Evening Post*, 1961
Bill Pronzini, 'All the Long Years', *Westeryear*, 1988.
Frederic Remington, 'A Sergeant of the Orphan Troop', *Crooked Trails*, F. Remington, 1898
Eugene Manlove Rhodes, 'The Bird in the Bush', *Redbook*, 1917.
'Beyond the Desert', *The Best Novels and Stories of Eugene Manlove Rhodes*, 1934. **Conrad Richter**, 'Early Americana', *Early Americana & Other Stories*, C. Richter, 1934
'Smoke Over the Prairie', ditto.
Mari Sandoz, 'The Girl in the Humbert', *Out West*, ed. J. Schaefer, 1955
Jack Schaefer, 'Emmett Dutrow', *The Big Range*, J. Schaefer, 1953

'One Man's Honour', *Argosy*, 1962
Luke Short, 'Court Day', *Collier's*, 1939
'Danger Hole', *Western Writers of America Anniversary Anthology*, 1969
Wallace Stegner, 'The Colt', *Southwest Review*, 1943
John Steinbeck, 'The Red Pony', *The Red Pony*, J. Steinbeck, 1937.
Thomas Thompson, 'Blood on the Sun', *America Magazine*, 1954
'Gun Job', *They Brought Their Guns*, T. Thompson, 1954
Mark Twain, 'The Jumping Frog of Calaveras County', *The Portable Mark Twain*, 1983
Wayne Ude, 'Enter Ramona, Laughing', *Buffalo & Other Stories*, W. Ude, 1975
Stewart Edward White, 'The Honk-Honk Breed', *Arizona Nights*, S. E. White, 1907
Owen Wister, 'How Lin McLean Went East', *Harper's*, 1892
'The Sign of the Last Chance', *When West Was West*, O. Wister 1928

[illegible]

[illegible]

[illegible]

[illegible]

[illegible]

[illegible]

[illegible]

[illegible]

[illegible]

[illegible]

[illegible]

[illegible]